Activity-Based Costing and Activity-Based Management for Health Care

Judith J. Baker, PhD, CPA
Executive Director
Resource Group, Ltd.
Dallas, Texas

An Aspen Publication®
Aspen Publishers, Inc.
Gaithersburg, Maryland
1998

Library of Congress Cataloging-in-Publication Data

Baker, Judith J.
Activity-based costing and activity-based management for health care / Judith J. Baker.
p. cm.
Includes bibliographical references and index.
ISBN 0-8342-1115-7 (hardback)
1. Health facilities—Business management. 2. Activity-based costing. 3. Managerial accounting. I. Title.
RA971.3.B35   1998
362.1'068'1—dc21   97-38539
CIP

Orders: (800) 638-8437
Customer Service: (800) 234-1660

About Aspen Publishers • For more than 35 years, Aspen has been a leading professional publisher in a variety of disciplines. Aspen's vast information resources are available in both print and electronic formats. We are committed to providing the highest quality information available in the most appropriate format for our customers. Visit Aspen's Internet site for more information resources, directories, articles, and a searchable version of Aspen's full catalog, including the most recent publications:
http://www.aspenpub.com
Aspen Publishers, Inc. • The hallmark of quality in publishing
Member of the worldwide Wolters Kluwer group.

Editorial Resources: Brian MacDonald
Library of Congress Catalog Card Number: 97-38539
ISBN: 0-8342-1115-7

Printed in the United States of America

1 2 3 4 5

To my parents for the past.
To Bear for the present and future.

Table of Contents

Contributors

Judith J. Baker, PhD, CPA
Executive Director
Resource Group, Ltd.
Dallas, Texas

Victor R. Barr, BS
Executive Director
St. Andrew's At-Home Services
St. Louis, Missouri

Clark B. Bitzer, BSci
Cost Analyst
Lake Hospital System
Painesville, Ohio

Nancy M. Bowllan, RN, MN, CS
Psychiatric Clinical Nurse Specialist
Community Nursing Center, School of Nursing
University of Rochester
Rochester, New York

Georgia F. Boyd, BS
Cost Accountant
Fiscal Department
Valley View Hospital
Glenwood Springs, Colorado

John J. Brocketti, MBA
Vice-President, Finance
Meridia Health System
Cleveland, Ohio

Nancy H. Chevalier, RN, PNP
Clinical Faculty
Community Nursing Center, School of Nursing
University of Rochester
Rochester, New York

Patricia Chiverton, EdD, RN
Associate Dean
Community Nursing Practice
Director of Nursing
Strong Behavioral Services
University of Rochester School of Nursing
University of Rochester Medical Center
Rochester, New York

John F. Congelli, BBA
Vice President of Finance
Chief Financial Officer
Genesee Memorial Hospital
Batavia, New York

Mec B. Cothron, DPh
Pharmacy Director
Columbia Hendersonville Hospital
Hendersonville, Tennessee

Michael A. Fitzpatrick, MD, FAAFP
Chief Financial Officer
Chief Operating Officer
Xavier HealthCare, PLLC
Elizabethtown, Kentucky

Victoria G. Hines, MHA
Associate Dean for Administration and Finance
Instructor, Clinical Nursing
School of Nursing
University of Rochester
Rochester, New York

Charles A. Keil, AAS
Cost Accountant
Genesee Memorial Hospital
Batavia, New York

Beau Keyte, BSE, MBA
President
Branson, Inc.
Newark, Delaware

Lorraine Lawrence, MSN
Pediatric Nurse Practitioner
Community Nursing Center, School of Nursing
University of Rochester
Rochester, New York

Cynthia McClard, DPh, MS
President
Clinical Management Consultants, Inc.
Brentwood, Tennessee

Richard G. Melecki, MA, MPA
Principal
Certified Quality Engineer
Ryerson Management Associates
Akron, Ohio

Cindyleigh Mocilnikar, RN
Manager of Specialty Services
Meridia Home Care Services
Meridia Home Health
Mayfield Village, Ohio

Christine A. Pierce, MSN, RN, CS
Vice President, Home Care Services
Meridia Health System
Cleveland, Ohio

Marta Hudson Ramsey, RN, MS
Special Projects Administration
Columbia Overland Park Regional Medical
  Center
Overland Park, Kansas

Jan Steinel, RN, RRT, BSN
Patient Care Coordinator, Pulmonary Services
Meridia Home Care Services
Meridia Home Health
Mayfield Village, Ohio

Ted J. Stuart, Jr., MD, MBA
Family Physician
Glendale, Arizona

Karen S. Vroman, RN, BSN, MEd, AAHA
Associate Vice President of Health Care and
  Older Adult Services
Program Planning and Evaluation
National Benevolent Association
St. Louis, Missouri

Patricia Hinton Walker, PhD, FAAN
Dean and Professor
University of Colorado Health Sciences Center
School of Nursing
Denver, Colorado

Timothy D. West, PhD, CPA
Assistant Professor of Accounting
Iowa State University
Ames, Iowa

Preface

I want the reader to understand the concept of activity-based costing (ABC) and activity-based management (ABM) and then to understand their application to his or her own organization. The many faces of ABC can be confusing. In this book we have presented a series of examples to illustrate the varied ways in which ABC can be understood and applied.

Experience and educational backgrounds vary. The reader with clinical education and experience is going to look for information that is different from what an accountant will seek. The reader with financial management educa-tion and experience is going to look for infor-mation that is different from what a policy maker will seek. In addition, individual learning styles vary, from visual to text oriented to purely spreadsheet oriented.

My goal is to make ABC and ABM compre-hensible to the reader in the reader's own con-text of experience and training. Our array of examples, case study applications, and explana-tions are designed to trigger recognition for people with a variety of backgrounds and expe-riences.

Acknowledgments

My partner and spouse, R.W. "Bear" Baker, has contributed greatly to the production of this book through his computer and graphics support.

## CHAPTER 1

Introduction to Activity-Based Costing

Judith J. Baker

CHAPTER OUTLINE

Introduction
The Concept of Cost Accounting
The Concept of Activity-Based Costing
ABC versus Traditional Cost Accounting
Two Basic Views
The Framework of ABC
Conclusion

INTRODUCTION

In today's competitive environment, a health care cost accounting system should accomplish cost efficiency without a negative impact on the quality of service delivery, provide information for management to maximize resources, and assist in continuous quality improvement. Activity-based costing (ABC) accomplishes all three of these aims.

In the early 1970s, ABC was considered an alternative method. In the cost accounting texts of that time it was primarily termed "activity accounting." In the early 1980s, ABC gained favor for industrial entities in the United States. The manufacture of products was a natural application for ABC. The cost accountants responsible for the implementation of ABC in the industrial settings began to publish concerning their experiences. In the early 1990s, implementation by service entities began to gather momentum. This trend was influenced by Brim-

son and Antos' book about activity-based management (ABM) for service industries, government entities, and nonprofit organizations.[1] By the mid-1990s, a trend toward the adoption of ABC by health care organizations had become well established.[2] This book is an outgrowth of that trend.

THE CONCEPT OF COST ACCOUNTING

Activity-based costing is a particular type of cost accounting methodology. Cost accounting, in turn, is a subset of management accounting. Management accounting has an internal focus, because it is intended for use by management in decision making. The internal focus of management accounting contrasts with that of financial accounting, whose focus is external. In other words, financial accounting applies generally accepted accounting principles to create statements intended for third parties outside the organization.[3]

Management accounting techniques, in contrast, use information from different disciplines (including accounting) and from multiple sources to assist management with internal problem solving. In this context, then, we can understand that management accounting techniques may well differ from generally accepted accounting principles, and these techniques will also differ from one organization to another. Because they do not adhere to any particular set of rules, a great deal of philosophical flexibility is left to the organization's decision makers.[4] To summarize, management accounting theory emerges from the discipline of accounting theory but also draws on a multidisciplinary array of organizational, behavioral, and decisional sciences.[5]

Cost accounting allows measurement and provides cost information. The more specific the unit of service in question, the more complex is cost measurement. It is far easier to determine the total costs of a department than it is to determine the cost of a specific unit of service, such as a particular lab test. The tracing and measurement of costs is one of the more difficult—and one of the most important—tasks for health care organizations today.[6]

To conclude: It is not a case of measuring the cost to determine the underlying reality; rather, it is a case of taking a philosophical perspective and then measuring the cost from that viewpoint.[7] This leads to Baker's truism about activity-based costing: **There is no one right way.**

THE CONCEPT OF ACTIVITY-BASED COSTING

Activity-based costing has two major elements—cost measures and performance measures. Activity-based costing is a methodology that measures the cost and performance of activities, resources, and cost objects. Resources are assigned to activities, then activities are assigned to cost objects based on their use. Activity-based costing recognizes the causal relationships of cost drivers to activities.

The basic concept of ABC is that activities consume resources to produce an output. (See Figure 1–1.) Expenses should be separated and matched to the level of activity that consumes the resources. Specifically, the expenses that are needed to produce individual units of a particular service or product should be separated from the expenses that are incurred to produce different products or services or to serve different payers. This separation should be independent of how many units are produced or sold.

The ABC approach differs from the traditional approach because of its fundamental concentration on activities. An ABC approach uses both financial and nonfinancial variables as bases for cost allocation. A typical ABC approach utilizes more indirect cost pools than does the traditional approach and uses a greater number of cost drivers as cost allocation bases.

There is a need for ABC in health care because competition in health care is a driving force while productivity and efficiency remain serious concerns. The pressures of managed care have resulted in new cost-finding demands, in particular the relating of costs to performance and outcomes. ABC can deliver the information to maximize resources and to relate costs to performance and outcome measures. Management decision makers can utilize ABC information to accomplish cost efficiency without negatively impacting the quality of service delivery while also assisting in continuous quality improvement.

Two particular circumstances propel health care's present need for resource consumption and service cost information: (1) diversity of service delivery and (2) transition in payer mix. Today's health care system encompasses a wide diversity of services. In order to manage them, it is important to determine the amount of resources that are consumed by each service. The complexity of widely varied service delivery systems can be readily managed with activity-based costing. In years past, health care

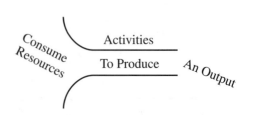

Figure 1–1 Theory of Resource Consumption. *Source:* Copyright © 1997, Resource Group, Ltd., Dallas, Texas.

institutions were not impelled to discover resource consumption and cost of services. The reimbursement methods did not apply such pressure. Today, however, because of transition in the payer mix, managed care and capitation impel the acquisition of such knowledge.

ABC is gaining ascendancy in the health care field because of its flexibility in these two areas. ABC can be applied across all care levels and its methodology is particularly suited to the complexities of health care service delivery. Activity-based costing will meet the needs of any type of health care provider. Acute care, long-term care, home care, physicians' groups, and integrated delivery systems will all find suitable applications.

Performance measures are a particular benefit of activity-based costing. Managed care requirements usually include some requirement to measure outcomes. Outcome measures are, of course, a type of performance measure and can thus be integrated into an ABC system.

ABC VERSUS TRADITIONAL COST ACCOUNTING

The traditional view of cost accounting is that services or products consume resources. The activity-based costing view is that services or products consume activities, then activities consume resources (Figure 1–2).

By contrast, ABC is causal; it is based on cause and effect. The driver is the cause of activity and the activity reveals the effect of the driver (Figure 1–3). These definitions and relationships are matched with the first example of ABC calculations in Chapter 3. Traditional cost accounting systems are often designated as either job costing or process costing systems. In actual fact, most health care systems are a hybrid combination. ABC is not an alternative costing system that replaces job costing or process costing, or a hybrid combination. Instead, ABC is an approach to developing the cost numbers that are used in the job costing or process costing or hybrid combination costing system. The distinctive feature of ABC is its focus

on activities as the fundamental cost objects. The costs of these activities are then assigned to other cost objects such as services, patients, or payers.[8]

Traditional cost systems normally allocate overhead (indirect) costs to individual services or products based on some measure of service or product volume. The major management limitation of the traditional cost system is that it is not strategic; that is, it allows cross-subsidies between services or products. The essential difference between traditional cost accounting methods and activity-based costing methodology is that ABC can eliminate cross-subsidies.

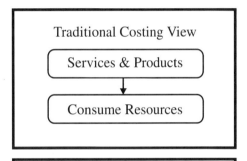

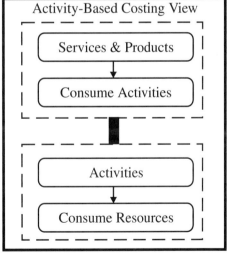

Figure 1–2 Two Views of Costing: Traditional vs. ABC. *Source:* Copyright © 1997, Resource Group, Ltd., Dallas, Texas.

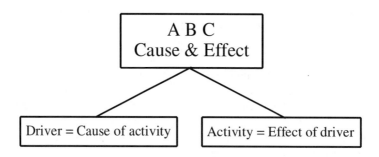

Figure 1–3 Cause and Effect in ABC. *Source:* Copyright © 1997, Resource Group, Ltd., Dallas, Texas.

With ABC it is possible to cost individual services, patients, or contracts, thus isolating the cost of service delivery for specific cost objects.

Most health care costing systems are reimbursement driven. The most common health care costing systems in use today are ratio of cost to charges (RCC) and relative value units (RVUs).[9] This commentary serves as an overview only; a discussion of methodology and examples of RCC and RVU calculations are presented in Chapter 3.

There are contrasts between ABC and traditional health care costing methods. There are also advantages and disadvantages within each. These are highlighted below.

The advantages of RCC are: (1) its easy method; (2) its configuration, the same as Medicare cost reporting ratios; and (3) its familiarity over time (especially with financial managers who have cost reimbursement experience). The disadvantages of RCC are that: (1) the calculation is tied to revenue, thus forcing the assumption that revenue proportions accurately reflect resource consumption; (2) aggressive reimbursement maximizing (such as "grossing up" techniques) increases revenue amounts, thus skewing the ratio; and (3) there is no cost containment emphasis.[10]

The advantages of RVUs are: (1) it recognizes resources consumed in service delivery; (2) its service-level cost is determined from a clinical base instead of a reimbursement base; and (3) it presents a methodology for the cost of acquiring resources. The disadvantage of RVUs is: it assumes that every RVU consumes exactly the same set of resources, in a proportion that always remains exactly proportionate. (This major weakness is not recognized by many managers who rely on RVUs for costing purposes.)[11]

The advantages of ABC are: (1) resources consumed at the treatment level are more precisely defined and reflected; and (2) resources consumed by the particular cost object (or cost objective) are more directly tracked and identified. The disadvantages of ABC are: (1) ABC is the most recent of the three methods, and therefore is not yet as well known; and (2) some members of management may not want more precise costs to become known.[12]

TWO BASIC VIEWS

There are two basic views of ABC. The first is the cost assignment view. The assignment of cost in ABC generally occurs in two stages (Figure 1–4), from resources to activities (first stage) and then from activities to cost objects (second stage). *Resources* are an economic element that is applied or used in the performance of activities. Salaries and supplies, for example, are resources used in the performance of activities. *Activities* are an aggregation of actions performed within an organization that is useful for the purposes of activity-based costing. *Cost objects* are any patient, product, service, con-

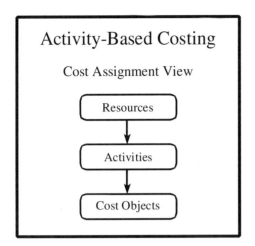

Figure 1–4 Activity-Based Costing: Cost Assignment View. *Source:* Copyright © 1997, Resource Group, Ltd., Dallas, Texas.

tract, project, or other work unit for which a separate cost measurement is desired.

The second basic view of ABC is the process view. The process viewpoint provides a report of either what is happening or what has happened (Figure 1–5). The definition of *activity* remains the same as for the cost assignment view; that is, an aggregation of actions performed within an organization that is useful for purposes of activity-based costing. *Cost drivers* are any factor that causes a change in the cost of an activity. An activity may have multiple cost drivers associated with it. Note that the allocation bases used for applying costs to, say, services are called cost drivers. They include any causal factor that increases the total costs of the activity. To apply costs to services, it is possible to use both volume-related allocation bases or other nonvolume-related allocation bases. Performance measures are indicators of the work performed and the results achieved in an activity, process, or organizational unit. Performance measures may be financial or nonfinancial.

THE FRAMEWORK OF ABC

There are many different ways to accumulate costs in a health care organization. For the most part, however, management seems to focus on three: units of service, programs, and responsibility centers (e.g., departments). There are three basic steps for implementing an ABC system: (1) defining activities that support output; (2) defining links between activities and outputs; and (3) developing the cost of activities (in many cases costs are gathered by an organizational unit and a special allocation methodology has to be used in order to relate costs to the activities).[13] The three basic steps are used to implement the system regardless of whether units of service, programs, or responsibility centers are the focus of management's cost accumulation.

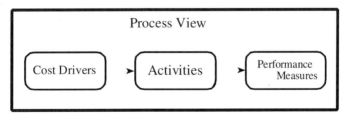

Figure 1–5 Activity-Based Costing: The Process View. *Source:* Copyright © 1997, Resource Group, Ltd., Dallas, Texas.

In cost accounting terminology, the areas where the costs are grouped together are called *cost pools*. If the focus of management's cost accumulation is a unit of service, such as a lab test, then each unit of service becomes a cost pool. If the focus of cost accumulation is a program, then each program becomes a cost pool.[14] Cost pools are often used in a two-stage accumulation process in ABC. For example, Cooper and Kaplan[15] view costing in ABC as a two-stage procedure. In the first stage, costs of support resources are assigned to the appropriate resources, creating cost pools. In the second stage, the cost pools are allocated to products or services. The allocation of cost is determined by each product or service's activity consumption.[16]

Not all proponents of ABC follow the cost pool procedure, however. Turney and Stratton[17] designate the different stages by different types of cost drivers. They describe resource drivers as the mechanisms used to assign the cost of resources to activities (the first stage) and activity drivers as the mechanism to assign the cost of activities to services or products. Whatever the technical manipulation (cost pools or resource and activity drivers), the underlying principle of ABC must always be remembered: Products consume activities and activities consume resources.

CONCLUSION

The flexibility of activity-based costing is its great strength. In this book, we have gathered a variety of ABC applications. We will present ABC case studies across the continuum of care: hospitals, long-term care facilities, home care agencies, physicians' offices, and integrated delivery systems. Through these varied applications we want to show you the variety and possibilities of the new costing power for health care: activity-based costing.

NOTES

1. J. Brimson and J. Antos, *Activity-Based Management for Service Industries, Government Entities, and Nonprofit Organizations* (New York: John Wiley & Sons, 1994).

2. J.J. Baker, Provider Characteristics and Managed Care/ Competition Environmental Factors Associated with Hospital Use of Costing Systems (PhD diss., Fielding Institute, Santa Barbara, CA, 1995), 30.

3. C. Horngren et al., *Cost Accounting: A Managerial Emphasis*, 8th ed. (Englewood Cliffs, NJ: Prentice Hall, 1994), 4.

4. A. Belkaoui, *Conceptual Foundations of Management Accounting* (Reading, MA: Addison-Wesley Publishing, 1980), 7.

5. Baker, Provider Characteristics and Managed Care, 4.

6. M. Ziebell and D. DeCoster, *Management Control Systems in Nonprofit Organizations* (New York: Harcourt Brace Jovanovich, 1991), 805.

7. Ibid., 807.

8. Horngren et al., *Cost Accounting*, 161.

9. Baker, Provider Characteristics and Managed Care, 67.

10. See T.D. West et al., "Contrasting RCC, RVU, and ABC for Managed Care Decisions," *Healthcare Financial Management* (August 1996): 56; and Baker, Provider Characteristics and Managed Care, 13–14.

11. See West et al., "Contrasting RCC, RVU, and ABC," 58; and Baker, Provider Characteristics and Managed Care, 14.

12. See West et al., "Contrasting RCC, RVU, and ABC," 59; and Baker, Provider Characteristics and Managed Care, 14–15.

13. W. Rotch, "Activity-Based Costing in Service Industries," *Cost Management* (summer 1990): 6.

14. Ziebell and DeCoster, *Management Control Systems*, 808.

15. R. Cooper and R.S. Kaplan, *The Design of Cost Management Systems: Text, Cases, and Readings* (Englewood Cliffs, NJ: Prentice Hall, 1991), 101.

16. J.J. Baker, *Activity-Based Costing to Survive Capitation* (Burr Ridge, IL: Richard D. Irwin, 1995), 38.

17. P.B. Turney and A.J. Stratton, "Using ABC to Support Continuous Improvement," *Management Accounting* (September 1992): 47.

## CHAPTER 2

Introduction to Activity-Based Management

Judith J. Baker

CHAPTER OUTLINE

INTRODUCTION

In health care today, activity-based management (ABM), springing from the discipline of cost management, must deal with a multidisciplinary activity-based costing (ABC), and/or activity-based management system. In the past such a system might have been referred to as a service delivery (e.g., production) system or a process system or even a marketing system. But today it is much more accurate to visualize the ABC/ABM model as "an economic model of the organization that integrates data from many information systems, financial and operational."[1] Although the model presents greater complexities to manage, it also offers greater opportunities for integration with strategic planning and continuous improvement programs.

THE CONCEPT OF COST MANAGEMENT

When taken in the context of a continuous improvement philosophy, cost management is defined as a set of actions that managers take to satisfy customers as those managers continuously reduce and control costs.[2] Health care cost management is often predicated on the principles of responsibility accounting, the basic idea of which focuses on identifying managers or organizational units that are accountable for the performance of revenue or expense plans.[3] This approach personalizes the management control system because cost management is now viewed from the personal standpoint of an individual manager rather than from the standpoint of an institution.[4]

Responsibility accounting generally rests within designated responsibility centers. Health care organizations' cost management systems in the past have exhibited widespread utilization of responsibility centers. A responsibility center is a unit formed to perform a set of activities in which a specific individual or manager has the authority and responsibility for accomplishing the unit's objectives. The use of responsibility centers ties the performance measures and other indicators directly to a specific manager.[5] Why has there been widespread past utilization of responsibility centers in health care? Because a responsibility center equates to a department, and departments have been the cost accumulation centers in traditional health care accounting systems. Although responsibility centers are utilized in activity-based management, the method by which they are assigned will center on activities rather than on the traditional departmental designations.

Cost management within a specific organization will reflect that organization's philosophy. As discussed in the previous chapter, cost management systems primarily focus on three types of cost accumulation: units of service (products), programs, and responsibility centers (or departments). If the focus of cost accumulation is a unit of service or a procedure, then that unit of service or procedure becomes a cost pool. If the focus of cost accumulation is a program, then that program becomes a cost pool. If the cost accumulation is by departments, they become the cost pools.[6] Organizational philosophy and strategic planning should guide this focus. The methods by which activity-based costing arrive at more accurate costs will vary from traditional cost accounting systems. Decisions about the activity-based management focus will still be required in order to guide how these more accurate costs will be assembled, and these decisions will be specific to the individual organization.

THE CONCEPT OF ACTIVITY-BASED MANAGEMENT

Activity-based management has two basic elements: (1) It identifies the activities performed in an organization, and (2) it determines their cost and performance in terms of both time and quality.[7] The two basic elements produce three components: activity analysis, the purpose of which is to identify the activities; cost driver analysis, the purpose of which is to determine costs; and performance measurement analysis, the purpose of which is to determine performance and its appropriate measures. (See Figure 2–1.)

Creating a cost management system for ABM begins with a foundation. The foundation of an ABM cost management system is built on information about activities. The benefits of an ABM system include the ability for managers to:

- derive more accurate cost targets and performance targets from strategic planning
- identify and reduce waste in activities and in cost
- improve the quality of pricing and/or estimating decision due to more accurate costing of services[8]

The individuals involved in ABM decision making should form a multidisciplinary team.

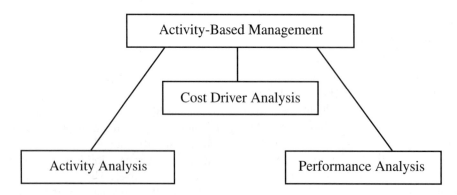

Figure 2–1 The Components of Activity-Based Management. *Source:* Copyright © 1997, Resource Group, Ltd., Dallas, Texas.

The strategic planning of the organization must be an integral part of the system choices. Decisions about the system will be influenced by management's view of responsibility accounting. At this point, management should view responsibility accounting from an activity-based management viewpoint.

Activity-based responsibility accounting provides a database of actions that have been costed out and thus can be used in many different ways. The activity-based responsibility accounting system replaces the rigid structure of the general ledger. An activity-based responsibility accounting system operates in a two-step methodology. It first identifies interrelated activities in an organization, then it approximates the resources that these actions consume. Activity-based costing clearly reflects this linkage between a pool of costs and the activities that drive the pool, because the cost pool is divided by the activity volume that causes it.[9]

Activity-based management works in tandem with continuous improvement initiatives. In the early 1990s, Johnson[10] emphasized that companies need to map and improve customer-focused (patient- or payer-focused) processes and to link the use of activity-based costing with the generation of continuous process improvement. This method of utilizing ABC is especially well suited for the health care industry.

Many health care organizations adopt process improvement methods based on W. E. Deming's philosophy. Deming was a pioneer in process improvement. He refined the PDCA approach to continuous process improvement (P = planning; D = doing; C = checking; A = acting). The PDCA cycle is continuous, thus the "Deming wheel." Critical paths, care plans, and their variance analyses are often tied to the PDCA cycle.[11] The process as defined by the critical path or care path then can be linked to ABC and ABM.

The three components of activity-based management—activity analysis, cost driver analysis, and performance measurement analysis—combine to create a powerful tool for cost management in today's health care organizations.

We will examine each component in succeeding sections of this chapter. We will examine performance measure analysis first because the choice of performance measures to be produced by the system is an initial planning step in the implementation of ABC and ABM systems. We will then address activity analysis, the heart of ABC and ABM, followed by a view of cost driver analysis.

PERFORMANCE MEASUREMENT ANALYSIS

The aim of performance measures in ABM is to monitor the activity process and/or business process. In other words, performance measures provide a picture of the process in terms of output quality, volume flexibility, service mix, and timeliness.[12]

Performance measures can be defined as indicators of the work performed and the results achieved in an activity, process, or organizational unit. Note that performance measures may be financial or nonfinancial. The organizational choices of performance measures should be shaped by the organization's philosophy and strategic planning, not by perceived constraints of existing systems.

Performance measures should be an integral part of the evaluation of activities in ABC and ABM. Performance measures should be defined for every significant activity. (Although performance can include both technical characteristics and system effectiveness, note that ABM performance measure analysis focuses on system effectiveness.)[13]

The determination of performance measures when defining each significant activity should address questions such as:

- What does it cost?
- How much time does it take? (referring to lead time and cycle time)
- How well is the activity performed?
- How flexible is the activity in response to changes in the service operations environment?[14]

Performance measures imply evaluation to employees. Consideration must be given to employee reaction when implementing the performance measure phases of ABC or ABM. A well-designed management control system should motivate employees toward effective and efficient achievement of the organization's goals. This type of motivation requires a viable flow of relevant information about ABC or ABM within the organization. Expectations about the appropriate performance measures must be communicated to all affected employees.[15] A good example of getting the staff behind the ABC effort is described in Braintree Hospital's implementation of ABC in conjunction with a nurse time–patient acuity measurement system. The staff was included throughout the ABC process and open communication about the project was the rule.[16]

To conclude: Performance measures for ABM must be in accordance with the strategic planning and the goals of the organization; they must provide both financial and nonfinancial measures, with a balance between the two types of measures; and they should reflect the continuous improvement initiatives of the organization.[17]

ACTIVITY ANALYSIS

Activity analysis is the heart of ABC and ABM. According to Cooper and Kaplan, activity analysis

> enables managers to slice into the business in many different ways— by product or group of similar products, by individual customer or client group, or by distribution channel— and gives them a close-up view of whatever slice they are considering. ABC analysis also illuminates exactly what activities are associated with that part of the business and how those activities are linked to the generation of revenues and the consumption of resources[18]

For health care purposes, consider the "individual customer or client group" in the quote above to be the individual patient or the payer; consider the "distribution channel" to be a particular service delivery provider within a health system, the rehab hospital within an integrated delivery system (IDS), perhaps.

ABC and ABM center on activities. Thus, the nature and specificity of the activity analysis guides the classification and precision of the resultant ABC/ABM costing system.

An activity represents the work performed within an organization. ABC or ABM focuses on costing at the activity level. An activity is associated with both inputs and outputs. The inputs (staff, supplies, technical equipment) are brought together to produce an output (a service or a product). As one author put it:

> For example, in the hospital setting, surgical procedures performed in the operating room (OR) represent activities. The inputs of medical personnel (e.g., surgeons, anesthesiologists, nurses), OR technology (e.g., patient monitoring equipment, life-support systems), and surgical supplies (e.g., latex gloves, gauze pads, bandages) are combined for the purpose of producing successful patient outcomes[19]

Brimson uses a seven-step approach to activity analysis.[20] We will briefly examine a summary of these seven steps.

1. Determine activity scope. A clear definition limits and specifies the range of activities so that information about the activities can be efficiently collected.
2. Select activity units, approaches, and data collection.
   - Determine activity units. This is a strategic decision that will impact all actions thereafter. The activity unit to be analyzed must be divided into groups that have a single identifiable purpose. Although the activity units may match existing organizational

units, it is more common that they will cross over organizational boundaries. It is essential to redefine the organizational units into appropriate activity units so the analysis will be both comprehensive and cost-effective.

- Select an activity approach. This is another strategic decision that will again impact all actions thereafter. The activity approach categories are generally business process, function, and organization.

- Select an activity data collection technique. The data collection technique can be by observation, by interview, by questionnaire, by diary or log, or by a combination of techniques. A panel of experts is still another technique that is sometimes used. The key criteria are the degree of precision to be attained and the cost of measurement.

3. Define activities. Activities should be defined with a noun and a verb. Generic labels such as "output" are not specific enough.

4. Rationalize activities. The activity analysis data collection should yield activity lists. Activities should be rationalized while structuring and reviewing the activity lists. Striking a balance between too much specificity (thus too expensive to manage) and too little specificity (thus not yielding sufficiently precise answers) is the point of this exercise.

5. Classify activities as primary/secondary. Each activity should be classified. The terms primary and secondary relate to the relationship of the activity types—one to the other.

6. Create an activity map. The activity map illustrates the relationship among functions, business processes, and activities. The map reflects the organization's activities and its cost structure in terms of activity consumption.

7. Finalize and document activities. The final step is to compile a composite list of activities that support all analysis requirements.

In summary: Activity analysis breaks out the individual components of an organization's system. Examining individual components allows an understandable and manageable activity analysis.

COST DRIVER ANALYSIS

A cost driver is any factor that causes a change in the cost of an activity. An activity may have multiple cost drivers associated with it. In the case of health care applications, an activity almost always has multiple cost drivers associated with it. In other words, the cost assignment bases used for applying costs to, say, services are called cost drivers. These drivers will include any causal factor that increases the total costs of the activity. To apply costs to services, it is possible to use both volume-related allocation bases or other nonvolume-related allocation bases. This is an important point to remember.

In Chapter 1, we discussed the framework of ABC. We examined the use of cost pools in that context. In this chapter, we will readdress the use of cost pools, relating the use of cost pools to the specific types of drivers to be used in the ABC or ABM methodology. Remember that we are discussing methodology choices only; either choice is a part of ABC or ABM principles and theory.

As discussed previously, in cost accounting terminology, the areas where the costs are grouped together are called cost pools. If the focus of management's cost accumulation is a unit of service, such as a lab test, then each unit of service becomes a cost pool. If the focus of cost accumulation is a program, then each program becomes a cost pool.[21] Cost pools are often used in a two-stage accumulation process in ABC. For example, Cooper and Kaplan[22] view costing in ABC as a two-stage procedure. In the first stage, costs of support resources are assigned to the appropriate resources, creating cost pools. In the second stage, the cost pools are allocated to products or services. The allocation of cost is determined by each product or service's activity consumption.[23]

Not all proponents of ABC follow the cost pool procedure, however. Turney and Stratton[24] designate the different stages by different types of cost drivers. They describe resource drivers as the mechanisms to assign the cost of resources to activities (the first stage) and activity drivers as the mechanism to assign the cost of activities to services or products. Whatever the technical manipulation (cost pools or resource and activity drivers), the underlying principle of ABC must always be remembered: Products consume activities and activities consume resources.

If costs are accumulated through resource drivers and activity drivers, then we should know that for every resource there is a resource driver. For every resource there are one or more activities (usually many more than one in the case of health care). For every activity there is an activity driver. A resource driver is a measure of the quantity of resources consumed by an activity. An example of a resource driver is the percentage of total square feet occupied by an activity. This factor is used to allocate a portion of the cost of operating the facilities to the activity. An activity driver is a measure of the frequency and intensity of the demands that are placed on activities by cost objects. An activity driver is used to assign costs to cost objects. It represents a line item on the bill of activities for a service or patient. (Note that sometimes an activity driver is used as an indicator of the output of an activity.)

The differential between the two methods just described has created much confusion in comprehending and comparing different applications of ABC or ABM. We only have to remember Baker's truism about activity-based costing: There is no one right way.

There must be cost driver analysis for ABM. The purpose of cost driver analysis is to identify activities that impact subsequent activities. The impact may be an influence on cost or an influence on performance. One way to view cost drivers is as a root cause. Thus, if, for example, you could remove the activity that creates the initial activity in the sequence, you also may be able to remove all subsequent activities. This type of impact would be appropriate when identifying and removing nonvalue-added activities. The removal of the initial activity should also result in the removal of the remaining activities.

There are hundreds of activities occurring in a health care organization, but there may only be a few cost drivers that are critical. These are the drivers that impact the success of the organization. Making the choices to isolate and identify the significant drivers is a difficult proposition. After all, the greater the desired accuracy of costs, the larger the number of drivers required. The decision about cost drivers should take into account three elements: (1) the cost of measurement, (2) the cost of errors, and (3) the cost of the induced behavior. The purpose of the exercise is to make a decision that provides the most benefit for the lowest overall cost[25] while at the same time achieving an ac-ceptable degree of precision appropriate to the objectives of the organization.

CONCLUSION

We perform activity-based costing to have information so that we can perform activity-based management. The ABC experience is not maximized unless appropriate activity-based management is applied to the results. In this book, we have gathered a variety of ABC applications; these applications also show us the manner in which ABM is exercised. Thus, we will present ABC or ABM case studies across the continuum of care: hospitals, long-term care facilities, home care agencies, physicians' offices, and integrated delivery systems. Through these varied applications, we will show you the variety and possibilities of the new costing power for health care: activity-based costing that results in opportunities for activity-based management.

NOTES

1. R.S. Kaplan, "In Defense of Activity-Based Cost Management," *Management Accounting* (November 1992): 58.

2. C. Horngren et al., *Cost Accounting: A Managerial Emphasis*, 8th ed. (Englewood Cliffs, NJ: Prentice Hall, 1994), 29.

3. J.J. Baker, *Activity-Based Costing to Survive Capitation* (Burr Ridge, IL: Richard D. Irwin, 1995), A.4.

4. R. Garrison, *Managerial Accounting*, 6th ed. (Homewood, IL: Richard D. Irwin, 1991), 307.

5. M. Ziebell and D. DeCoster, *Management Control Systems in Nonprofit Organizations* (New York: Harcourt Brace Jovanovich, 1991), 179.

6. Ibid., 807–808.

7. J. Brimson and J. Antos, *Activity-Based Management for Service Industries, Government Entities, and Nonprofit Organizations* (New York: John Wiley & Sons, 1994), 15.

8. J. Brimson, *Activity Accounting: An Activity-Based Costing Approach* (New York: John Wiley & Sons, 1991), 58.

9. C.J. McNair, "Interdependence and Control: Traditional vs. Activity-Based Responsibility Accounting," *Cost Management* (summer 1990): 22.

10. H.T. Johnson, *Relevance Regained: From Top-Down Control to Bottom-Up Empowerment* (New York: Free Press, 1992), 33.

11. J. Cryer and R. Miller, *Statistics for Business: Data Analysis and Modeling* (Boston: PWS-Kent Publishing, 1991), 12.

12. Brimson and Antos, *Activity-Based Management*, 108.

13. M.R. Ostrenga et al., *Guide to Total Cost Management* (New York: John Wiley & Sons, 1992), 81.

14. Brimson and Antos, *Activity-Based Management*, 187.

15. Zeibell and DeCoster, *Management Control Systems*, 808.

16. L.P. Carr, "Unbundling the Cost of Hospitalization," *Management Accounting* (November 1993): 43–48.

17. See Ostrenga, *Guide to Total Cost Management*, 37; and Baker, *Activity-Based Costing*, 98.

18. R. Cooper and R.S. Kaplan, "Profit Priorities from Activity-Based Costing," *Harvard Business Review* (May–June 1991): 131.

19. R.H. Ramsey, "Activity-Based Costing for Hospitals," *Hospital and Health Services Administration* 39, no. 3 (1994): 396.

20. Brimson, *Activity Accounting*, 82–97.

21. Zeibell and DeCoster, *Management Control Systems*, 808.

22. R. Cooper and R.S. Kaplan, *The Design of Cost Management Systems: Text, Cases and Readings* (Englewood Cliffs, NJ: Prentice Hall, 1991), 101.

23. Baker, *Activity-Based Costing*, 38.

24. P.B. Turney and A.J. Stratton, "Using ABC to Support Continuous Improvement," *Management Accounting* (September 1992): 47.

25. R. Cooper, "The Rise of Activity-Based Costing—Part Three: How Many Cost Drivers Do You Need, and How Do You Select Them?" *Cost Management* (winter 1989): 35, 45.

## CHAPTER 3

How Activity-Based Costing Works in Health Care

Judith J. Baker

CHAPTER OUTLINE

Background
Traditional Costing Methods
Activity-Based Costing Systems
Conclusion

BACKGROUND

This chapter examines two traditional health care costing methods: the ratio of cost to charges (RCC) method and the relative value unit (RVU) method. Both the RCC method and the RVU method cost at the procedure level.

Procedure-level costs play a particular role in the costing system framework. It is important to arrive at procedure-level costs. Hospital service delivery, for example, involves two types of cost control because there are two levels of service delivery. (The ultimate service that is delivered is treatment of the patient.) The first level uses hospital resources for clinical procedures. Common examples are X-rays or lab tests. Costs for supplying these resources can generally be controlled by hospital financial managers.

The second level of service delivery involves the particular combination of procedures ordered by the patient's physician. The hospital financial manager cannot directly control what is ordered by the physician. The cost of procedures must be available in order to properly identify usage patterns, costs, and variances that are caused by different physician practice patterns. Isolating costs by procedures can thus yield valuable management accounting information.

TRADITIONAL COSTING METHODS

The RCC costing method and the RVU costing method are the traditional costing methods.

The RCC costing method estimates the cost of procedures through charges. It can be described as an imputed procedure-level method. RCC, however, is a simplistic method of imputing the procedure costs. Costs are collected at the cost center (departmental) level. A ratio is calculated for the proportion of total cost center or departmental costs to that cost center's total charges. To find the imputed cost of an individual procedure, the department-wide ratio (of cost to charges) is multiplied times the actual charge for that procedure. For example:

Step A. Calculate Ratio of Cost to Charges

Step B. Calculate the Cost of a Procedure
  B.1: Assume the charge for Procedure #63 is $100.00.

$$\frac{\text{Total Laboratory Department Costs}}{\text{Total Laboratory Department Charges}} =$$

$$\frac{477227}{660777} = 0.722221 \text{ RCC}$$

B.2: Therefore:

Cost Allocated to Procedure #63
= $100.00 × 0.722221 = $72.22

([charge] × [RCC] = [cost])

This overly simplistic method of estimation often results in misleading procedure-level data because it is highly averaged. The use of RCC costing in the 1980s (subsequent to the implementation of prospective payment systems [PPSs]) was reported to be widespread.[1] In the mid-1990s, the use of RCC is still widespread.[2] One reason that RCC usage remains widespread is because the ratio of cost to charges is part of the Medicare cost reporting forms. Thus, the ratio must be calculated by any provider who is certified to participate in the Medicare program. Ready availability contributes to RCC's common usage.

Examples of RCC calculations on cost reporting forms appear as Exhibits 3–1 and 3–2. Exhibit 3–1 represents the hospital cost report Form HCFA-2552-92 Worksheet C, Part 1. Individual cost centers appear as vertical line items on this form. Total costs (for purposes of Medicare reporting) for each cost center appear in column five. Total charges (for purposes of Medicare reporting) for each cost center appear in column six. The ratio of cost to charges appears in column seven.

Exhibit 3–2 represents the skilled nursing facility cost report Form HCFA-2540-96 Worksheet C. Individual cost centers appear as vertical line items on this form. Total costs (for purposes of Medicare reporting) for each cost center appear in column one. Total charges (for purposes of Medicare reporting) for each cost center appear in column two. The ratio of cost to charges appears in column three.

The RVU costing method traces specific costs at the time of treatment. It is sometimes called "bottom-up" because it begins with the treatment. As its name implies, the RVU method measures the relative value of resources consumed by each procedure. RVU is thus a procedures-based method.

The basic RVU theory is as follows. Costs are first allocated to major cost components that are comprised of direct labor, direct supplies, and departmental overhead. An index of RVUs is then developed to weight each cost component utilized in the procedure. Once the RVUs are developed they are used to determine procedure cost. RVUs are based on an index of 1.0 and provide a useful method of uniform measurement. In general, the more complex a procedure, the higher the RVU.[3] Table 3–1 is an example.

An example of RVUs for an orthopedic practice appears as Exhibit 3–3. In this exhibit, the procedure code appears in the left-hand column, followed by the procedure description. The number of procedures performed for the past year in the practice appears in the next four columns as follows: number of procedures for Medicare, for Blue Cross/Blue Shield, and for all other, plus the grand total. (Thus, on the first line, 45 + 22 +17 = 84 total procedures #20610 performed during the year.)

The second column from the right, headed RVUs, represents the relative value of a single procedure of this type. (Thus, on the first line, the relative value of one procedure #20610 is 1.36.) The final column on the right-hand side represents the weighted RVUs for the practice. (Thus, on the first line, 84 procedures times a relative value of 1.36 apiece equals 114: the total). Annual Relative Value Service Units for the practice for the year totals 40,000. The 40,000 will be used as the denominator in determining an average annual weight (per Annual

Table 3–1 Resource Use Procedure

Code	Level	Description	RVU
99272	Low	2nd Consultation	1.75
27253	Medium	Repair Hip Dislocation	28.70
27487	High	Knee Joint Replacement	68.48

Exhibit 3–1 Example of RCC Computation Using Form HCFA-2552

COMPUTATION OF RATIO OF COSTS TO CHARGES   PROVIDER NO: 00-0000   PERIOD: From 10/1/XX to 9/30/XX   WORKSHEET C PART 1

	COST CENTER DESCRIPTIONS	Total Cost (From Wkst. B, Part I, Col. 27) 1	RT/PT Limit Adjust- ment 2	Total Costs 3	RCE Dis- allowance 4	Total Costs 5	Total Charges 6	Cost or Other Ratio 7	TEFRA Inpatient Ratio 8	PPS Inpatient Ratio 9
	INPATIENT ROUTINE SERVICE COST CENTERS									
25	Adults and Pediatrics (General Routine Care)	12,620,000		12,620,000	7,000	12,613,000	18,520,000			
26	Intensive Care Unit	730,000		730,000	5,000	725,000	989,000			
27	Coronary Care Unit	895,000		895,000	5,000	890,000	788,000			
28	Burn Intensive Care Unit	587,000		587,000		587,000	501,000			
29	Surgical Intensive Care Unit									
30	Other Special Care (Specify)									
31	Subprovider I	810,000		810,000	4,000	806,000	766,000			
31.01	Subprovider II	875,000		875,000	3,000	872,000	992,000			
33	Nursery	390,000		390,000	1,000	389,000	743,000			
34	Skilled Nursing Facility	298,000		298,000		298,000	246,000			
35	Other Nursing Facility	510,000		510,000		510,000	398,000			
36	Other Long-Term Care	197,000		197,000		197,000	354,000			

continues

Exhibit 3–1 continued

COST CENTER DESCRIPTIONS	Total Cost (From Wkst. B, Part I, Col. 27) 1	RT/PT Limit Adjust-ment 2	Total Costs 3	RCE Dis-allowance 4	Total Costs 5	Total Charges 6	Cost or Other Ratio 7	TEFRA Inpatient Ratio 8	PPS Inpatient Ratio 9	
ANCILLARY SERVICE COST CENTERS										
37 Operating Room	2,810,000		2,810,000		2,810,000	3,470,000	0.809798	0.809798	0.809798	37
38 Recovery Room	478,000		478,000		478,000	598,000	0.799333	0.799333	0.799333	38
39 Delivery Room and Labor Room	595,000		595,000		595,000	520,000	1.144230	1.144230	1.144230	39
40 Anesthesiology	752,000		752,000	2,000	750,000	1,020,000	0.737254	0.737254	0.735291	40
41 Radiology—Diagnostic	2,100,000		2,100,000	25,000	2,075,000	2,030,000	1.034481	1.034481	1.022167	41
42 Radiology—Therapeutic	710,000		710,000		710,000	980,000	0.724423	0.724423	0.724423	42
43 Radioisotope	279,000		279,000		279,000	411,000	0.678832	0.678832	0.678832	43
44 Laboratory	1,990,000		1,990,000	9,000	1,981,000	2,710,00 0	0.734313	0.734313	0.730996	44
45 PBP Clinical Lab Srvc—Prgm Only	74,000		74,000		74,000	97,000	0.762887	0.762887	0.762887	45
46 Whole Blood & Packed Red Blood Cells	145,000		145,000		145,000	202,000	0.717821	0.717821	0.717821	46
47 Blood Storing, Processing & Trans.	40,000		40,000		40,000	51,000	0.784314	0.784314	0.784314	47
48 Intravenous Therapy	128,000		128,000		128,000	147,000	0.870748	0.870748	0.870748	48

Note: Form HCFA-2552-92 has been superseded by Form HCFA-2552-96, which has three columns for charges (inpatient, outpatient, and total). Instructions for this worksheet are published in HCFA Pub. 15II, Sections 3620 and 3620.1. This form is for illustrative purposes only.

Source: Reprinted from HCFA-2552-92 (11-92). Instructions for this worksheet are published in HCFA Pub. 15 II. Section 2813.1.

Exhibit 3–2 Example of RCC Computation Using Form HCFA-2540-96

RATIO OF COST TO CHARGES FOR ANCILLARY AND OUTPATIENT COST CENTERS	PROVIDER NO.: 00-0000	PERIOD: FROM 1-1-xx TO 12-31-xx	WORKSHEET C	
Cost Center	TOTAL (From Wkst B, Pt. I, Col. 18)	Total Charges	Ratio (col. 1 divided by col. 2)	
	1	2	3	
ANCILLARY SERVICE COST CENTERS				
21 Radiology	114780	126075	0.910410	21
22 Laboratory	139144	155955	0.892206	22
23 Intravenous Therapy	—	—	—	23
24 Oxygen (Inhalation) Therapy	111669	121805	0.916785	24
25 Physical Therapy	135398	146987	0.921156	25
26 Occupational Therapy	183815	151142	1.216174	26
27 Speech Pathology	40619	44096	0.921149	27
28 Electrocardiology	—	—	—	28
29 Medical Supplies Charged	105812	190077	0.556680	29
30 Drugs Charged to Patients	222210	252474	0.880130	30
31 Dental Care - Title XIX only	—	—	—	31
32 Support Surfaces	89770	95299	0.941983	32
33 Other Ancillary Service Cost	56242	61866	0.909094	33
OUTPATIENT SERVICE COST CENTERS				
34 Clinic	389373	286171	1.360631	34
35 R H C				35
36 Other Outpatient Service Cost				36
75 Total	1588832			75

FORM HCFA-2540-96 (/96) (INSTRUCTIONS FOR THIS WORKSHEET ARE PUBLISHED IN HCFA PUB. 15 II, SECTION 3527)

Source: Reprinted from HCFA-2540-96 (96). Instructions for this worksheet are published in HCFA Pub. 15 II, Section 3527.

Exhibit 3–3 Total Relative Value Units (Orthopedic)

| | | | | Number of Procedures Performed | | | |
Code	Proc Descptn	M'care	BC/BS	Other	Total	RVUs	Total RVUs
20610	Drain/inj. jnt	45	22	17	84	1.36	114
20663	Appl thigh brc	66	30	28	124	10.82	1342
27244	Rpr thigh fx	46	44	17	107	35.17	3763
27253	Rpr hip disloctn	66	25	40	131	28.70	3760
27310	Expl. knee jnt	83	36	13	132	20.41	2694
27427	Knee reconstrtn	70	45	29	144	26.38	3799
27440	Rev. knee jnt	26	25	36	87	24.69	2148
27448	Inc. thigh	72	53	34	159	26.56	4223
27487	Knee jnt replmnt	86	72	63	221	68.48	15134
27580	Fusion of knee	23	19	8	50	32.44	1622
99204	OV, New L-4	100	88	60	248	2.59	642
99212	OV, Estab L-2	90	76	50	216	0.72	156
99214	OV, Estab L-4	75	52	22	149	1.52	226
99241	OV Consult, L-1	66	63	53	182	1.29	235
99272	2nd Opn Consult	22	41	18	81	1.75	142

Total Annual Relative Value Service Units   40,000

Source: Reprinted with permission from *Business Network Manual: Making the Transition to Managed Care,* © 1994, McGraw-Hill Healthcare Education Group.

Relative Value Service Unit) for allocating overhead costs, for example.

The key weakness of the RVU costing system is its assumption that each RVU consumes an identical set of resources in a constant proportion.[4] This issue is not commonly understood by many health care managers who presently utilize an RVU system.

To summarize: In the RCC costing method, *costs are imputed* through cost to charge ratios. This method estimates the cost of procedures through charges. It can be termed an *imputed procedure-level method.* In the RVU costing method, *costs are indexed* by relative value units. This method traces specific costs at the time of treatment. It is sometimes called bottom-up costing because it begins with the treatment. As the name implies, the RVU method measures the relative amount of resources consumed by each procedure. RVU is thus an *indexed procedures-based method.*

ACTIVITY-BASED COSTING SYSTEMS

In ABC systems, *costs are traced by activities*—across departments or cost centers. ABC holds that services and products consume activities, and activities consume resources. (In contrast, traditional cost accounting holds that services and products consume resources.)

The treatment of allocated costs in ABC differs from traditional systems in that overhead is allocated first by tracing actual cost by activity where possible. The balance of overhead is allocated through a cause-and-effect with activities. Cost allocation for overhead (e.g., those items not traced) is accomplished in ABC through a multistage process. The technical manipulation that results in the allocation can be accomplished by alternative methods. Some theorists[5] view costing with ABC as a two-stage procedure. In the first stage, costs of support resources are assigned to the appropriate resources; thus creating cost pools. The second stage will be discussed in Chapter 7.

ABC identifies resource consumption more precisely. ABC works in tandem with continuous improvement initiatives. A significant advantage for managers is that nonvalue-added activities can be readily isolated and identified with the ABC costing method. A laboratory department example shows how ABC works.[6] The calculation of the laboratory test setup costs is illustrated in Table 3–2. The text describes the costing approaches and the laboratory organization rationale. The case study calculations are presented in Table 3–3. Table 3–3 contains the assumptions and statistics to be used in the calculations. It then presents two methods of calculating cost for the individual laboratory tests. The first method is activity-based costing, and the second method is the traditional cost accounting approach.

For instance, activity-based costing can be used in determining the standard full-cost-per-service unit, such as the standard full costs of the various tests conducted in a hospital laboratory, as given in Table 3–3. (A simple application, the costing of laboratory tests, is chosen over other more complicated examples, such as the costing of a surgical operation, to make the illustration of activity-based costing more effective.)

In applying activity-based costing to this hospital setting, the first task is to identify all activities that are required in performing the tests. These activities are simplified for illustration purposes and can be described as follows: This hospital laboratory is responsible for performing four different kinds of tests—P, Q, R, and S. Each test requires a specific setup of tools and equipment, which are maintained by the maintenance department of the hospital. Once the tools and equipment are set up, the laboratory technicians use the materials and supplies that were delivered by the supply processing and distribution department to perform the tests. As the tests are conducted, the clerks must complete the required documents and distribute the test results to the appropriate parties.

After identifying the activities, the amount of hospital resources required to carry out these activities is recorded, and a summary of the laboratory's cost and operating data is given in the

Table 3–2 Calculating Laboratory Test Setup Costs

Determination of the Setup Cost of Lab Tests with the Use of Activity-Based Costing

		Laboratory Tests			
		P	*Q*	*R*	*S*
1	Wage rate per setup labor hour ($)	30.00	30.00	30.00	30.00
2	Setup labor time (# Direct labor hours per setup)	.05	.08	.12	.15
3	# Setups	5,000	6,000	16,000	2,500
4	Total hours all setups (2 × 3)	250	480	1,920	375
5	Total cost (1 × 4) ($)	7,500	14,400	57,600	11,250
6	# Tests	100,000	60,000	80,000	5,000
7	Setup cost per test (5/6) ($)	.0750	.2400	.7200	2.2500

Source: Copyright ©1997, Resource Group, Ltd., Dallas, Texas.

upper panel of Table 3–3. That is, in addition to the costs of labor, materials, and supplies that are directly associated with each test, other expenses such as clerical support, setup, tools, and equipment are required in operating the laboratory. Also, because the laboratory requires services of both the maintenance department and the supply processing and distribution department, the costs of providing such support services are charged to the laboratory by using specific allocation bases. This allocated overhead, even though not directly incurred by the laboratory, is essential to the proper functioning of the laboratory. It must be included in determining the standard full costs for the four laboratory tests.

As the indirect costs of operating the laboratory are identified, they are applied to the four tests on the basis of the activities undertaken in performing each specific test. For instance, for each test performed there is a certain amount of documentation and paperwork that must be completed by the clerks. If the amount of time that is required for these functions is more or less the same for each test, it is appropriate to apply costs of clerical support to the tests on a per-test basis. Setup direct labor hours and machine hours, on the other hand, are more appropriate for applying costs of setup as well as tools and equipment to the laboratory tests respectively because the cause-effect relationships are more transparent here. For the allocated overhead, two other cost drivers are used: machine hours for the maintenance department costs and material dollars for the supply processing and distribution department costs. This is because the longer the tools and equipment are used in laboratory tests, the more maintenance is required. Also, the larger the amount of materials handled, the more service is required of the supply processing and distribution department. Therefore, with the use of activity-based costing, the standard full costs for the

four laboratory tests P, Q, R, and S are $7.4200, $7.1060, $15.6825, and $8.6880, respectively.

As illustrated in the previous example, various cost drivers can be chosen for applying indirect costs to cost objects under activity-based costing as long as a cause-effect relationship is evident. Conventional costing, on the other hand, usually uses one volume-related allocation base in cost application. For instance, if direct labor hour is chosen as the allocation base, the standard full costs for the four laboratory tests P, Q, R, and S are $7.60, $8.40, $14.58, and $7.20, respectively (Table 3–3(b)), which are quite different from the costs computed by using activity-based costing (Table 3–3(a)). The difference is most significant with test Q (an increase of 18.21 percent) and test S (a decrease of 17.13 percent).

In fact, conventional costing has again overcosted the high-volume tests (P and Q) and undercosted the low-volume tests (R and S), as evidenced in the manufacturing sector. Activity-based costing reports a more accurate computation of standard full costs by focusing on the activities of the laboratory and the resources those activities consume, as well as choosing cost drivers that exhibit a cause-effect relationship, with the overhead charged to the laboratory.

Much of the work involved in this case study occurs prior to the cost calculations. The primary task is to gather the necessary information. In the laboratory example, the necessary information is listed in Exhibit 3–4. The total types of lab test classifications and the number of each type of lab test run each year should be available from the system. The cost of material and supplies per test may be available from the hospital's system. If the system cannot provide per-test costs then other measures must be taken in order to obtain the data. The direct labor hours per test by type of test will probably not be available. This information will then have to be obtained through measurement. Methods of

Table 3–3 Standard Full Cost per Laboratory Test with the Use of Activity-Based Costing and Conventional Costing

Laboratory tests	Number of tests per year	Materials and supplies per test	Direct labor hour (DLH) per test	Machine (m/c) hour per test	Number of setups	Direct labor hour per setup
P	100,000	$ 5.00	0.05	0.220	5,000	0.05
Q	60,000	3.20	0.10	0.050	6,000	0.08
R	80,000	12.50	0.04	0.600	16,000	0.12
S	5,000	2.00	0.10	0.828	2,500	0.15
Wage rate			$30.00			$30.00

Department overhead*:
Clerical support	$ 147,000
Setup	90,750
Tools and equipment	30,856
	268,606

Allocated overhead†:
Maintenance	$ 46,284
Supply processing and distribution	8,510
	$ 54,794
Total overhead	$ 323,400

(a) Activity-based costing

Overhead rates:

Clerical support	= $147,000/245,000 tests	= $ 0.600 per test
Setup	= $ 90,750/ 3,025 setup DLH	= $30.000 per setup DLH
Tools and equipment	= $ 30,856/ 77,140 m/c hour	= $ 0.400 per m/c hour
Maintenance	= $ 46,284/ 77,140 m/c hour	= $ 0.600 per m/c hour
Supply processing and distribution	= $ 8,510/$ 1,702,000	= $ 0.005 per material $

Laboratory tests	P	Q	R	S
Materials and supplies	$5.0000	$3.2000	$12.5000	$2.0000
Direct labor	1.5000	3.0000	1.2000	3.0000
Department overhead:				
Clerical support	0.6000	0.6000	0.6000	0.6000
Setup	0.0750	0.2400	0.7200	2.2500
Tools and equipment	0.0880	0.0200	0.2400	0.3312
Allocated overhead:				
Maintenance	0.1320	0.0300	0.3600	0.4968
Supply processing and distribution	0.0250	0.0160	0.0625	0.0100
Standard full cost per test	$7.4200	$7.1060	$15.6825	$8.6880

continues

Table 3–3 continued

(b) Conventional costing
Overhead rate = $323,400/14,700 = $22.00 per DLH

Laboratory tests	P	Q	R	S
Materials and supplies	$5.0000	$3.2000	$12.5000	$2.0000
Direct labor	1.5000	3.0000	1.2000	3.0000
Overhead	1.1000	2.2000	0.8800	2.2000
Standard full cost per test	$7.6000	$8.4000	$14.5800	$7.2000

*The categories of department overhead have been greatly simplified for illustration.

†*Allocated overhead* refers to costs incurred by support departments that are charged to the laboratory for services provided. The categories of allocated overhead have also been greatly simplified for illustration.

Source: Reprinted from Y. Chan, Improving Hospital Cost Accounting with Activity-Based Costing, *Health Care Management Review,* Vol. 18, No. 1, p. 74, © 1993, Aspen Publishers, Inc.

---

measurement are discussed in Chapters 4 and 6. The machine hours per test by type of test will also probably not be available. This information will also have to be obtained through measurement. The number of setups by type of test likewise will probably not be available and will have to be obtained through measurement. The direct labor hours per setup by type of test will almost surely not be available. If such is the case, this information will have to be obtained through measurement.

It is informative to compare the calculation of line items in the activity-based costing example (Table 3–3(a)) with calculation of line items in

---

Exhibit 3–4 Information Gathered for Laboratory Case Study

- Total types of lab test classifications (P, Q, R, and so forth)
- Number of each type of lab tests per year
- Cost of material and supplies per test (by type of test)
- Direct labor hours per test (by type of test)
- Machine hours per test (by type of test)
- Number of setups (by type of test)
- Direct labor hour per setup (by type of test)

Source: Copyright © 1997, Resource Group, Ltd., Dallas, Texas.

---

the conventional costing example (Table 3–3(b)). Notice that the labor cost is the same for both the ABC and the traditional examples. This is because they are each actual. Likewise, notice that the supplies cost is the same for both the ABC and the traditional examples. This is also because they are each actual. Notice that the treatment of overhead makes up the entire differential in the costing between the two methods. The traditional example has used one basis of allocation for the entire overhead amount. It has used direct labor hours to allocate the entire $323,400 laboratory overhead. The ABC method has used a different cost assignment basis for each overhead line item.

Certain decisions had to be made before the activity-based costing calculation could be undertaken. The treatment of each element of overhead had to be chosen. The cost assignment basis for each item is listed in Exhibit 3–5.

The activity-based costing method has seven line items in its calculation.

1. The first item is material and supplies, which is a direct cost.
2. The second item is direct labor, which is a direct cost.
3. The third item is clerical support, which is part of departmental overhead.

Exhibit 3–5 Cost Assignment Basis for Each Line Item

(A) Activity-Based Costing Method	*Basis*
Direct Costs:	
Material and supplies	Actual per test
Direct labor	Actual per test
Department Overhead:	
Clerical support	Equally per test
Setup	Setup direct labor hours (actual)
Tools and equipment	Machine hours
Allocated Overhead:	
Maintenance	Machine hours
Supply processing and distribution	Material dollars
(B) Traditional Costing	*Basis*
Direct Costs:	
Material and supplies	Actual per test
Direct labor	Actual per test
Department Overhead:	
All overhead	Direct labor hours

Source: Copyright ©1997, Resource Group, Ltd., Dallas, Texas.

4. The fourth item is setup, which is part of departmental overhead.
5. The fifth item is tools and equipment, which is part of departmental overhead.
6. The sixth item is maintenance, which is part of allocated overhead from outside the department.
7. The seventh item is supply processing and distribution, which is part of allocated overhead from outside the department.

The traditional costing method has three line items in its calculation.

1. The first item is material and supplies, which is a direct cost.
2. The second item is direct labor, which is a direct cost.
3. The third item is all overhead. (In other words, the five line items in the activity-based costing calculation totaled $323,400. The entire amount of $323,400 is handled as one item to allocate in the traditional costing method.)

This case study has, of necessity, been greatly simplified.

Exhibit 3–6 presents the results of costing each laboratory test by the ABC method contrasted with the results under the traditional method. Two of the tests costed out higher under ABC than traditional. The other two tests costed out higher under traditional than under ABC. Why is this finding important? The cost of actual service delivery for each type of lab test has been set out with ABC. If, for example, the hospital has been offered a capitated contract that involves a significant number of lab tests, this information would be important to

Exhibit 3–6 Over-Under Results of Costing

Test	Conventional	ABC	*Difference per Test*
P	$7.6000	$7.4200	(0.1800)
Q	$8.4000	$7.1060	(1.2940)
R	$14.5800	$15.6825	+1.1025
S	$7.2000	$8.6880	+1.4880

Source: Copyright ©1997, Resource Group, Ltd., Dallas, Texas.

management decision making. On a more global view, the cost-effective service delivery within a department allows basic management to become more precise and thus more effective. A third basic use is to use this information to set and to profile performance measures within the laboratory.

Finally, as a rule of thumb, ABC generally costs out low-volume items at a higher cost than does traditional cost accounting methods. The reason is obvious. There is generally a certain amount of preparation and basic activity involved no matter whether the volume is high or low. The individuality of costing for each service (lab tests in this example) therefore highlights this differential. This finding would be of use to activity-based management, as discussed in a Chapters 8 and 10.

It should be noted that some confusion arises in the area of RVUs and ABC. This confusion arises in language, or terminology, and in the understanding of which costing methodology is actually being used. ABC can and does use RVUs as drivers on occasion, but it should be understood that the RVUs are utilized as a part of the ABC activity-based approach to costing.

To illustrate the questions that should be addressed, refer to Exhibit 3–7. This exhibit is a truncated version of an example appearing in Chapter 7. It illustrates cost allocation by

Exhibit 3–7 An Example of Cost Allocation by RVUs

DEPT.—RADIOLOGY–DIAGNOSTIC   CC #557

Service Code	Procedure	# Proce- dures	RVUs (hrs.)	Weighted RVUs (hrs.) (qty RVU)	Alloc Cost	Cost/Proc
557140	SKULL ROUTINE	5,600	0.33	1,848	38,242	6.83
557170	CHEST PA & LAT.	47,500	0.18	8,550	176,930	3.72
557210	RIBS UNILATERAL	3,600	0.18	648	13,409	3.72
557230	SPINE CERVICAL ROUT	6,000	0.32	1,920	39,732	6.62
557280	PELVIS	1,500	0.32	480	9,933	6.62
557320	LIMB SHOULDER	2,600	0.31	806	16,679	6.41
557330	LIMB UPPER ARM	650	0.31	202	4,170	6.41
557340	LIMB ELBOW	2,300	0.31	713	14,754	6.41
557350	LIMB FOREARM (RADIUS)	2,000	0.31	620	12,830	6.41
557360	LIMB WRIST	3,400	0.31	1,054	21,811	6.41
557370	LIMB HAND	3,800	0.31	1,178	24,377	6.41
557380	LIMB FINGER OR THUMB	5,000	0.31	1,550	32,075	6.41
557390	LIMB FINGER MULTIPLE	350	0.31	109	2,245	6.41
557400	LIMB HIP UNILATERAL	2,200	0.26	572	11,837	5.38
557410	LIMB HIP BILATERAL	650	0.26	169	3,497	5.38
557420	LIMB FEMUR	1,100	0.26	286	5,918	5.38
557430	LIMB KNEE ONLY	3,350	0.26	871	18,024	5.38
557790	SPECIAL PROCEDURES	1,700	2.00	3,400	70,358	41.39
	TOTAL ALL OTHER	6,700	0.33	2,207	45,679	6.82
	TOTAL	100,000		27,182	$562,500	$5.62

Source: Adapted from A. Baptist, A General Approach to Costing Procedures in Ancillary Departments, *Topics in Health Care Financing*, p. 41, © 1987, Aspen Publishers, Inc.

RVUs. However, we need to ask where the RVU hours came from. That is, are they published weights (e.g., coming from an outside authoritative source)? Or were they derived through an internal activity analysis? We cannot tell the answer from the study of the exhibit itself.

CONCLUSION

The potential benefits of using ABC rather than traditional volume-based costing (VBC) include: (1) more accurate costs of services delivered, (2) better discrimination between profitable and unprofitable services and service lines, (3) improved pricing and contracting strategies, (4) improved management decision-making capability, (5) greater ease of determining relevant costs, and (6) reduced nonvalue-added costs.[7] In other words, activity-based costing systems produce data that are potentially more accurate than do the traditional health care costing systems. Thus, these data should produce better managerial decisions.

NOTES

1. T.A. Gilman, "Hospitals Recognize Need to Install or Improve Cost Accounting Systems," *Healthcare Financial Management* (November 1985): 86.

2. J.J. Baker, Provider Characteristics and Managed Care/Competition Environmental Factors Associated with Hospital Use of Costing Systems (PhD diss., Fielding Institute, Santa Barbara, CA, 1995), 22.

3. J.J. Baker, *Activity-Based Costing to Survive Capitation* (Burr Ridge, IL: Richard D. Irwin, 1995), 35.

4. T.D. West et al., "Contrasting RCC, RVU, and ABC for Managed Care Decisions," *Healthcare Financial Management* (August 1996): 58.

5. R. Cooper and R.S. Kaplan, "Profit Priorities from Activity-Based Costing," *Harvard Business Review* (May–June 1991): 133.

6. Y. Chan, "Improving Hospital Cost Accounting with Activity-Based Costing," *Health Care Management Review* 18, no. 1 (1993): 71–77.

7. See Cooper and Kaplan, "Profit Priorities," 135; also see Baker, *Activity-Based Costing to Survive*, 83.

## CHAPTER 4

Activity Analysis

Judith J. Baker

CHAPTER OUTLINE

THE IMPORTANCE OF ACTIVITY ANALYSIS IN ABC

Activity analysis provides the core data that are essential to activity accounting. Activity analysis represents a methodology to analyze an organization's outputs and identify those processes that generate the output. The purpose of activity analysis is to identify the significant activities of an organization so that a specific basis for describing business processes and determining their cost and performance can be established.[1]

Activity analysis provides a great deal of information about an organization, including:

- what work is done
- how much work is done (e.g., workload)
- how the work is done
- cost of doing the work
- quality of the work
- time to perform the work
- output of the work

- patient and/or supplier relationships
- service relationships[2]

In other words, activity analysis quantifies significant activities within the organization.

ELEMENTS OF ACTIVITY ANALYSIS

There are four generally accepted elements to activity analysis:

1. Define activities
2. Classify activities
3. Create an activity map
4. Complete an analysis

First, define activities. In the case of health care, activities can be broadly defined to include all actions that are involved in creating and delivering a service. The first-level definition of activities is the only step in activity analysis that does not take the specific organization into account. In other words, activities are defined in their most elemental sense: What is done in an enterprise?[3] This elemental form becomes a view of basic transactions. In fact, early activity accounting was sometimes called transaction accounting.

Defining activities is a vital planning step that is essential to the success of the ABC project. It should not be truncated, and it should not be rushed. In real life, we find this step is often jeopardized because of unrealistic project time lines and due dates.

Second, classify activities. All activities should be classified. Although defining activities has universal elements, classifying activities is organization specific. Classifying activities has three levels: (1) collect activity data, (2) designate as primary or secondary, and (3) review and validate.

Activity data can be collected by several methods. These include time studies, observation, interviews, and questionnaires. Sometimes combinations of these methods are also used. You can be innovative about obtaining data, because varied approaches are possible. The nature of the organization and its management can sometimes guide you toward the best approach. Sometimes all data is acquired as the result of a specific ABC project. In other cases, activity data exists—or is presently being gathered—due to some other initiative within the organization. We will discuss six different potential activity data sources, beginning with program development data and concluding with critical paths or care paths.

Program development data. If a new program has been implemented and activities are now being defined for it, inquire about the program implementation materials. Exhibit 4–1 presents a good example of implementation design questions for a new program that converted easily to a starting point for certain areas of activity analysis.

Process data. Process is often examined in order to define and designate the activities. The system in place within an organization can often provide a starting point for defining process. Certain activities to be performed in a sequential manner may be documented somewhere within the organization. This source, whatever it may be, can provide a starting point. An example is provided in Figure 4–1. In this case, the flowchart illustrates the information management system of the organization. Specific activities assigned to particular job positions become obvious when one studies this flowchart. It was created for another purpose but can

Exhibit 4–1 Activity Analysis Example: Implementation Design Questions

---

Subspecialty Unit Implementation Design Questions To Be Considered and Answered

1. Who will keep up the logs (Admission, ED, and so forth)?
2. Who will get the referral signed?
3. Who will get the consent/patient Bill of Rights signed?
4. Who will decide selection/exclusion of patients?
5. Who will delegate/assign patients?
6. Who will be responsible to get completed charts to filing area?
7. Who will communicate with ED to let them know who is seeing patients and who those patients are?
8. Who will educate other disciplines on an ongoing basis?
9. Who will inform the physician whether or not his or her patient signs the consent?
10. Who will file the paperwork kept on the unit?

Courtesy of University of Rochester, School of Nursing, Rochester, New York.

---

serve as our starting point as to what activities are required. Likewise, Figure 4–2 presents a flowchart that involves activities for more individuals.

Performance measure data. Activity analysis aids the establishment and/or enhancement of performance measures. This analysis highlights which activities are associated with which part of the operation, and it should be noted that this association does not necessarily follow the general ledger (G/L) grouping of expenses into G/L cost centers. The exposé of this association is a vital part of activity analysis. It allows a view of how these activities are associated with earning revenues and consuming resources,[4] and this view is key to establishing or enhancing the measures of performance for the organi-

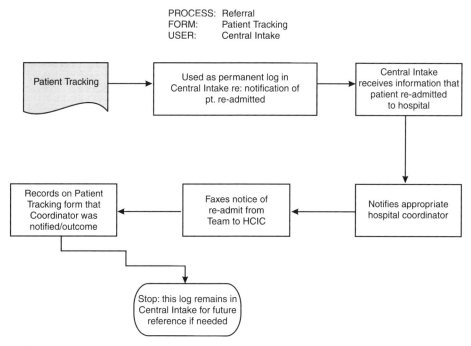

PROCESS: Referral
FORM: Patient Tracking
USER: Central Intake

Figure 4–1 Central Intake Activities: Patient Tracking. Courtesy of Meridia Home Care Services, Mayfield Village, Ohio.

zation. Activity-based costing also includes performance measures. Sometimes these sources provide counts of such performance. For example, refer to Figure 4–3. This figure represents a flowchart from which required activities can be extracted. See also Exhibit 4–2. This exhibit presents the form required as an adjunct to the activities laid out in Figure 4–3.

Another situation is illustrated in Figure 4–4. The required activities are enumerated. Then Exhibit 4–3 presents the required form that will show how much of the activity was actually required (performance and/or quantity of activity).

Remember that the examples presented here are starting points and must be developed further for our purposes.

Reengineering data. Reengineering projects often yield activity analysis data. The reengineering may be initiated for this purpose[5] or

may be the result of a separately conceived project. Whatever the motivation that created the study, cost reduction effort through process improvement may well yield the basic information to create an ABC pilot project. In other words, the linking of process data with ABC is a natural fit.

Case management data. The vice president of nursing at Boston's Braintree Hospital took a case management approach to activity analysis.[6] She worked out a method to analyze the amount and mix of nursing services consumed by different types of patients. The data she gathered was classified using activity analysis methodology. Cost of the nursing services was then assigned using ABC. In other words, the nursing activity data was gathered first as a case management project and the costing methodology was put into place as a second step. A similar sequence of events occurred with University

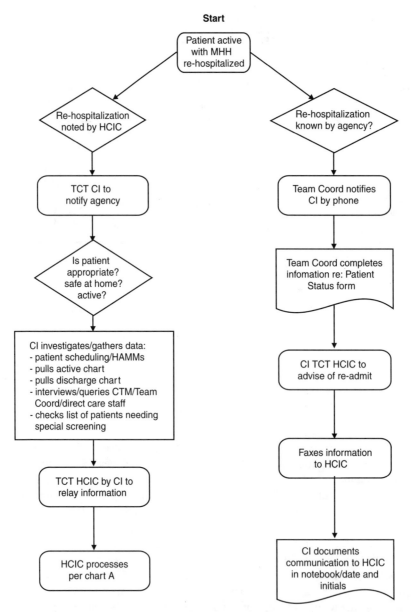

Figure 4–2 Central Intake Activities: Miscellaneous Functions. Courtesy of Meridia Home Care Services. Mayfield Village, Ohio.

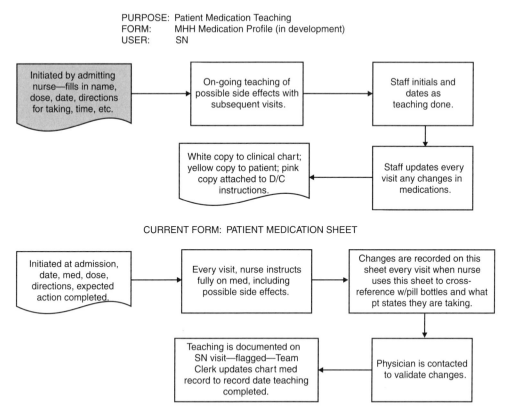

PURPOSE: Patient Medication Teaching
FORM: MHH Medication Profile (in development)
USER: SN

Initiated by admitting nurse—fills in name, dose, date, directions for taking, time, etc. → On-going teaching of possible side effects with subsequent visits. → Staff initials and dates as teaching done.

White copy to clinical chart; yellow copy to patient; pink copy attached to D/C instructions. ← Staff updates every visit any changes in medications.

CURRENT FORM: PATIENT MEDICATION SHEET

Initiated at admission, date, med, dose, directions, expected action completed. → Every visit, nurse instructs fully on med, including possible side effects. → Changes are recorded on this sheet every visit when nurse uses this sheet to cross-reference w/pill bottles and what pt states they are taking.

Teaching is documented on SN visit—flagged—Team Clerk updates chart med record to record date teaching completed. ← Physician is contacted to validate changes.

Figure 4–3 Patient Medication Teaching Activities. Courtesy of Meridia Home Care Services, Mayfield Village, Ohio.

Exhibit 4–2 Patient Medication Required Form

MERIDIA HOME HEALTH

Patient Medication Sheet

Patient:				Pharmacy/Phone #:	
M.D./Phone #:				Allergies:	
Date	Medication	Dose	Directions for Taking Medication	Medication Purpose	Potential Side Effects

Courtesy of Meridia Home Care Services, Mayfield Village, Ohio.

PURPOSE: To Document Notification of HCA of Change to Monday Schedule
FORM: Changes to AIDE Schedule to Monday
USER: Weekend Team Coordinator, Receptionist

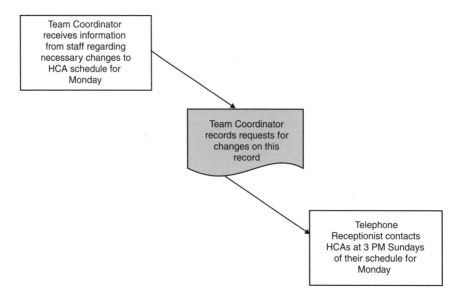

Figure 4–4 Weekend Schedule Change Activities. Courtesy of Meridia Home Care Services, Mayfield Village, Ohio.

Exhibit 4–3 Weekend Schedule Change Required Form

Aide	Added To Schedule			Removed From Schedule		Notification			
	Patient	Phone #	Zip	Patient	Zip	Time	Verbal To Aide	Answering Machine	Message to Call Back
						am/pm			
						am/pm			
						am/pm			
						am/pm			
						am/pm			
						am/pm			
						am/pm			
						am/pm			
						am/pm			
						am/pm			

Changes To Aide Schedule For _____

Courtesy of Meridia Home Care Services, Mayfield Village, Ohio.

of Rochester clinicians. Details about their time study and its conversion to ABC are presented in Chapter 6.

Critical path or care path data. Critical path and care path analysis provides a useful framework to analyze activities. Such analysis allows the collecting of parallel data about the type and amount of resources actually used for care delivery. An excellent opportunity for process improvement and the identification of non-value-added activities is also afforded when this framework is utilized for activity analysis. An example of a hospital critical path is presented as Exhibit 4–4 (Acute Myocardial Infarction Critical Pathway).[7] The case study in Chapter 19 presents a planning model for skilled nursing facility costed clinical pathways. And the case study in Chapter 20 presents an implementation model for a hospital-based skilled nursing facility costed clinical pathway.

After the activity data has been collected through the method (or methods) selected, it must be classified as primary or secondary. A primary activity produces output used outside an organizational unit. In the usual industrial approach to ABC, a secondary activity occurs within the department and supports the primary activity.[8] A secondary activity would never produce an output used outside the organizational unit on its own and would always occur within the department.

In the case of health care organizations, there are a multitude of activities going on outside the actual department. Certain of these activities are also supporting the primary activity, even though they are outside the department. In this case, we need to modify the usual industrial ABC concept of primary and secondary. We will add another term—*support*. For health care purposes, we will define a primary activity as that which is face-to-face with the patient. A secondary activity supports the primary activity to complete a patient encounter or an episode of care. A support activity supports the activities involved in the patient encounter or the episode of care. The designation of inside or outside the department does not pertain. Thus, we will classify health care activities as *primary* and *secondary* to equal a patient encounter or episode of care and *support* to support the patient encounter or episode of care. This modification of terminology is considered a patient-focused approach. It fits well with the critical path or care path process. It works especially well when the cost object centers on procedures.

I recommend visualizing activity classification as a bulls-eye. Figure 4–5 illustrates an archery target. The bulls-eye, or center of the target, is the primary activity. In the case of health care, the primary activity is face-to-face with the patient. The next ring on the target is the secondary activity. The secondary activity is still involved with the patient but does not require the patient's presence. Charting is a good example of a secondary activity. The primary and secondary activities combined represent a patient encounter or an episode of care. The third ring on the target represents these support activities. The support activities can be visualized as having multiple slices of the ring.

Primary and *secondary* are ABC terms created for industrial costing system purposes. The term *primary* has a different connotation in health care. It is used in a clinical sense. As we adapt ABC to our purposes for health care, we may have to adapt primary as used in other industries to some other term. We sometimes use *patient-focused*. Note that the case study about community-based health care applications of ABC (see Chapter 21) uses *client-focused* as a substitute for *primary*.

In the industrial applications of ABC the classification of activities between primary and secondary is necessary to apportion the cost of secondary activities to the primary activities and to manage the ratio of secondary activities to primary activities.[9] The modification to primary-secondary-support merely adds one more level to the ratio.

The data that have been collected should be reviewed for accuracy and completeness and for consistency and uniformity. It should be validated. Validation can include comparisons with annual historic cycles and/or with utilization

Exhibit 4-4 Critical Pathway: Acute Myocardial Infarction

Activities	Day 0 (Preadmission)	Day 1	Day 2	Day 3	Day 4	Day 5	Day 6
Admit patients	Patient reservation Insurance verification Routine admission testing						
Provide nursing care		Complete blood chemistry	Complete blood chemistry	Complete blood chemistry	Complete blood chemistry	Complete blood chemistry	Complete blood chemistry
Perform diagnostics		CBC with differential	CBC	CBC	CBC	CBC	CBC
		Cardiac isoenzymes q 8 hr	PTT (if on heparin)	PTT (if on heparin)	PTT (if on heparin)	12-lead ECG daily and per protocol	12-lead ECG
		PT, PTT, ACT initially and PTT q 6 hr	Cardiac isoenzymes if not at baseline	Cardiac isoenzymes if not at baseline	Cardiac isoenzymes if not at baseline		
		Beta hCG	12-lead ECG daily and per protocol	12-lead ECG daily and per protocol	12-lead ECG daily and per protocol		
		12-lead ECG daily	MUGA scan or echocardiogram, if indicated				
		Chest X-ray					
Provide nursing care		ECG monitoring	ECG monitoring	ECG monitoring	ECG monitoring	ECG monitoring	ECG monitoring
Administer ECG & other tests		HR, RR, BP q 1 hr	HR, RR, BP q 2 hr	HR, RR, BP q 2 hr	HR, RR, BP q 4 hr	HR, RR, BP q 4 hr	HR, RR, BP q 4 hr

Provide nursing care	Rhythm strip q shift and p.r.n. Continuous oximetry Heart sounds, breath sounds q 1–2 hr	Rhythm strip q shift and p.r.n. Continuous oximetry Heart sounds and breath sounds q 2 hr	Rhythm strip q shift and p.r.n. D/C oximetry Assess other body systems as needed	Rhythm strip q shift and p.r.n.	Rhythm strip q shift and p.r.n. Assess other body systems as needed	Rhythm strip q shift and p.r.n. Assess other body systems as needed	Assess other body systems as needed
Cardiac catheterization	Heparin IV NTG continuous IV infusion Beta blocker	Heparin IV Titrate and D/C NTG infusion NTG SL, transdermal Beta blocker	Heparin IV NTG SL, transdermal, or spray Beta blocker	D/C heparin NTG SL, transdermal, or spray Beta blocker	NTG SL, transdermal, or spray Beta blocker	NTG SL, transdermal, or spray Beta blocker
Dispense medications	Calcium channel blocker ACE inhibitor ASA Morphine IV, analegesics Stool softener Sedative Antiemetic	Beta blocker Calcium channel blocker ACE inhibitor ASA Analgesics Stool softener Sedative	Calcium channel blocker ACE inhibitor ASA Analgesics Stool softener Sedative	Calcium channel blocker ACE inhibitor ASA Analgesics Stool softener Sedative	Calcium channel blocker ACE inhibitor ASA Analgesics Stool softener Sedative	Calcium channel blocker ACE inhibitor ASA Analgesics Stool softener
Provide meals	Low-salt, low-fat, low-cholesterol, or ADA diet	Low-salt, low-fat, low-cholesterol, or ADA diet	Low-salt, low-fat, low-cholesterol, or ADA diet	Low-salt, low-fat, low-cholesterol, or ADA diet	Low-salt, low-fat, low-cholesterol, or ADA diet, NPO after 2400 for stress test	Low-salt, low-fat, low-cholesterol, or ADA diet

continues

Exhibit 4–4 continued

Activities	Day 0 (Preadmission)	Day 1	Day 2	Day 3	Day 4	Day 5	Day 6
Provide nursing care		Bed rest (semi-Fowler's) assistance with ADLs	OOB to chair Assistance with ADLs	OOB to chair Assistance with ADLs	Ambulation, ADLs with assistance	Ambulation with supervision	Ambulation with supervision
Provide therapy		IV access / Antiembolism stockings / Intake and output / Oxygen 2 liters/min	IV access / Antiembolism stockings / Intake and output / Oxygen 2 liters/min	IV access / Antiembolism stockings / Intake and output / Possibly D/C O_2	IV access / Transfer to telemetry unit / Antiembolism stockings / D/C intake and output	IV access / Antiembolism stockings	Stress test / D/C IV access after
Provide nursing services—teaching		Orientation to CCU and hospital routines / Review of C.P. / Cardiac teaching begins	Instruction on diet / Cardiac teaching	Orientation to the difference between CCU and telemetry unit / Cardiac teaching	Cardiac teaching	Explanation of stress test / Complete cardiac teaching	Written instructions: medications, what to report, activity limits, and next appointment
Discharge planning		Social services / Discharge teaching begins	Dietary and cardiac rehabilitation / Plan for family teaching	Discharge teaching	Discharge teaching	Discharge teaching / Plan discharge	Discharge to home

Source: Reprinted from S. Udpa, Activity-Based Costing for Hospitals, *Health Care Management Review,* Vol. 21, No. 3, p. 87–89, © 1996, Aspen Publishers, Inc.

data. It is imperative that individuals who are familiar with the organization be involved in review and validation.

Third, create an activity map. The purpose of an activity map is to graphically illustrate the interrelationship between functions and business processes and activities. An activity map will describe the cost structure in terms of the activities that are consumed.

The framework of health care productivity (or lack of it) takes shape as the overall organization is portrayed as an assortment of links between activities.[10] Illustrating activities in their proper sequence—mapping them—exposes relevant relationships. The activity map literally reveals the framework to which the activity-based costs will be attached. It provides a picture of the costing framework.

These flowcharts summarize the findings of activity linkages. They provide a summary of what has been discovered—a view of the process. These maps must be reviewed as project findings because they truly describe the cost structure in terms of the activities that are consumed. The maps also provide a valuable baseline point of reference when monitoring the changes that are implemented as a result of activity analysis and the subsequent activity mapping.

The guidelines for activity mapping are summarized as follows:

1. Break processes down into a network of activities.
2. Record the network in a flowchart format.
3. Create a related sequence of activities.
4. Map activities to business processes and business processes to functions—this is an optional guideline. Not all ABC projects use the process approach. It is therefore labeled optional in this summary.

Two examples of activity mapping are presented here. One is for an internal process—collections—and one is for a clinical process.

The example of an activity map for collections is presented as Exhibit 4–5. Note that some activities are grouped in a particular con-

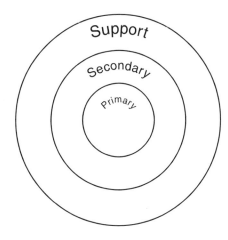

Figure 4–5 Classifying Activities: The Bulls-Eye Method. *Source:* Copyright © 1997, Resource Group, Ltd., Dallas, Texas.

figuration because of internal control requirements.

The underlying processes for a family practice are presented in Exhibit 4–6. These processes are unique to this practice. (This is proper. ABC should be unique and specific to each organization where it is implemented.) Note that laboratory sits separately on this summary of processes. The rationale is this: Laboratory tests are sometimes performed internally and sometimes performed outside the family practice office. Thus, the lab tests are not an inherent or integral part of the internal process. The rationale is very particular to this practice, which is dominated by managed care payers.

An example of one activity map created for the same family practice is presented as Figure 4–6. This activity map is for a 99213 office visit without lab. Note that the arrangement of the map allows for the structural processes to be tracked. A case study of this family practice, including numerous activity maps, can be found in Chapter 13.

Fourth, complete an analysis. Completing the analysis involves creating a list of activities that reflect the organizational activities. Activities should also be documented. The most common method of documentation is through a bill of activities (BOA). The bill of activities is a list (or a series of lists). The BOA consists of activities that are required to produce a process or a service. In addition to listing the activities, it usually lists the volume of such activities that are required to produce the process or service.

Documentation to complete the analysis should clear up loose ends. Completion of the analysis also should include a series of reviews

Exhibit 4–5 Activity Mapping Example for Collection Process

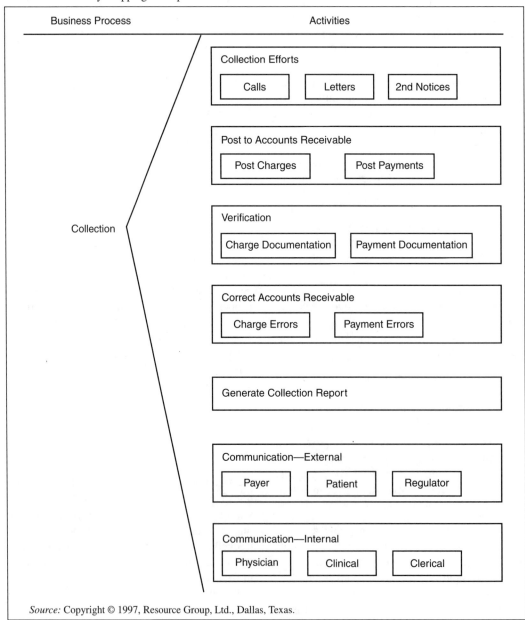

Source: Copyright © 1997, Resource Group, Ltd., Dallas, Texas.

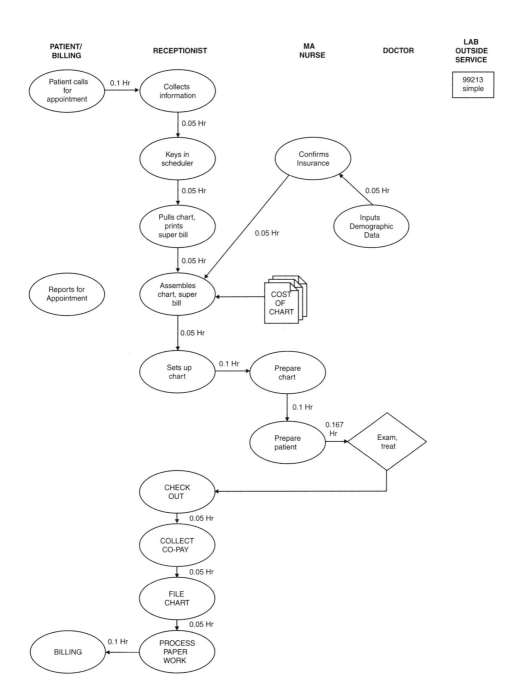

Figure 4–6 Example of Activity Mapping for a Family Practice

Exhibit 4–6 Summary of Processes at Northwest Family Practice

---

MEDICAL PROCESSES

Surgical Procedures
Emergency Medicine Activity
Clinical Testing
Injections
Patient Preparation
Review Outside Data
Medical Administration

NONMEDICAL PROCESSES

Consult
Billing
Document Intake
Phone Intake Plus Message
Filing In and Out

MANAGEMENT ACTIVITY

Finance
Marketing
Strategy
Human Resources
CIS

LABORATORY

Source: Copyright © 1997, Resource Group, Ltd., Dallas, Texas.

---

value-added activities consume resources without adding value to patient services. Helmi and Tanju[11] suggest creating a flow-chart of key activities to identify which activities provide value-added services. The nonvalue-added services should then be eliminated or at least significantly reduced through monitoring.[12] The activity analysis also can be planned as an integral part of creating a business value chain.[13]

Dr. Loop of the Cleveland Clinic Foundation reaffirms that the objective in (activity-based) cost accounting is to determine the pattern of resource consumption in order to define profit and cost drivers. He presents data from a survey of community hospitals where a reimbursement dollar was spent as follows:[14]

16 cents = medical care

7 cents = management and supervision

6 cents = transportation

20 cents = idle time

29 cents = documentation

8 cents = hotel and patient services

14 cents = scheduling and coordinating care

Dr. Loop's point is that activity analysis provides opportunities to identify and manage non-value-added time.

and sign-offs by the appropriate levels of management.

MULTIPLE USES FOR ACTIVITY ANALYSIS

The results of activity analysis can be applied to multiple uses. Good planning is essential in order to receive the maximum benefit from the effort that is expended in activity analysis.

Identification of nonvalue-added activities is a good example of an additional use. Non-

CALCULATING THE COST-BENEFIT OF ACTIVITY ANALYSIS

Good planning also entails putting effort where maximum benefit will be realized. One of the common errors in implementing ABC is to put an equal amount of effort into unequal analyses. Thus, the best use of available project resources is not accomplished. Part of calculating cost-benefit is determining the scope of activity analysis. After all, activity analysis is the process of analysis-time use. A cost-benefit analysis can guide the scope of such analysis.

For example, how many support costs should be analyzed and how many should be allocated on a more arbitrary basis? Ask: "What will be gained from the analysis?" Guidance on the scope of activity analysis can extend the impact of activity analysis enormously. Guidance will strengthen the project by ensuring that project resources are wisely expended.

CONCLUSION

Activity analysis is multifaceted. It supports multiple objectives,[15] including continuous improvement, business process redesign, organizational restructuring through reengineering, time reduction, and patient satisfaction.

NOTES

1. J. Brimson and J. Antos, *Activity-Based Management for Service Industries, Government Entities, and Nonprofit Organizations* (New York: John Wiley & Sons, 1994), 103.

2. Ibid., 103.

3. Ibid., 65.

4. R. Cooper and R.S. Kaplan, "Profit Priorities from Activity-Based Costing," *Harvard Business Review* (May–June 1991): 131.

5. J.H. Evans III et al., "Cost Reduction and Process Reengineering in Hospitals," *Journal of Cost Management* (May–June 1997): 26.

6. L.P. Carr, "Unbundling the Cost of Hospitalization," *Management Accounting* (November 1993): 44, 46.

7. S. Udpa, "Activity-Based Costing for Hospitals," *Health Care Management Review* 21, no. 3 (1996): 87–89.

8. Brimson and Antos, *Activity-Based Management*, 130.

9. J. Brimson, *Activity Accounting: An Activity-Based Costing Approach* (New York: John Wiley & Sons, 1991), 96.

10. J.B. Canby IV, "Applying Activity-Based Costing to Healthcare Settings," *Healthcare Financial Management* (February 1995): 51.

11. M.A. Helmi and M.N. Tanju, "Activity-Based Costing May Reduce Costs, Aid Planning," *Healthcare Financial Management* (November 1991): 95.

12. Ibid., 95.

13. M.R. Ostrenga, "Activities: The Focal Point of Total Cost Management," *Management Accounting* (February 1990): 43.

14. F. Loop, "You Are in Charge of Cost," *Annals of Thoracic Surgery* 60 (1995): 1511.

15. Brimson and Antos, *Activity-Based Management*, 104.

## CHAPTER 5

Activity Costing

Judith J. Baker

CHAPTER OUTLINE

INTRODUCTION

The primary purpose of this chapter is to deconstruct an example of activity costing that employs the ABC methodology. The secondary purpose of this chapter is to compare the activity-based costing calculations with a conventional cost system calculation. The example concerns two diagnosis-related groups (DRGs), along with the services and procedures contained within them. Their cost will be calculated using ABC methodology. The ABC cost calculations will be deconstructed. The cost of the two services and procedures will also be calculated using traditional costing. The results will then be compared. This example uses a two-step cost driver allocation.[1] It is a common ABC methodology, though there are other ABC variations available, some of which have been previously described.

COST OBJECT—MAKING A CHOICE

The choice of cost object, or cost objective, will have an impact on your activity-based costing project. The structure of your project will be determined by the cost object. The cost object for this example is the DRG. St. Joseph Hospital has selected two DRGs (along with the services and procedures contained within them) for this comparative cost calculation. One (DRG 1X1) is high acuity, whereas the other (DRG 1X2) is low acuity. Both require the same length of stay (LOS) of five days. (See Exhibit 5–1.)

The health care delivery system has been profiled. Critical pathways have been created and activity analysis has been performed (see Exhibit 4–4 in the previous chapter). Activities have been aggregated into activity centers. St. Joseph's has identified ten activity centers (Exhibit 5–2). For purposes of ABC cost calculations, each of these activity centers becomes a cost pool.

LINKING COSTS TO ACTIVITIES

The concepts of tracing and of allocating permeate ABC methodology. There are ABC-specific definitions for each term. *Tracing* is the assignment of cost to an activity or a cost object using an observable measure of the consumption of resources by an activity. Tracing is gen-

Exhibit 5–1 Example of Two Services/Procedures for ABC Cost Calculations

St. Joseph Hospital offers 2 services/procedures:

DRG 1X1

LOS = 5 days

Patient Acuity Level = High-Acuity Stay

Step-Down = Transfer to Nursing Home after Hospital Stay

DRG 1X2

LOS = 5 days

Patient Acuity Level = Low-Acuity Stay

Step-Down = Not Applicable

Source: Data from S. Udpa, Activity-Based Costing for Hospitals, *Health Care Management Review,* Vol. 21, No. 3, p. 93, © 1996, Aspen Publishers, Inc.

Exhibit 5–2 Ten Activity Centers for ABC Cost Calculations

St. Joseph Hospital has identified ten activity centers:

Admit Patients
Cardiac Catheterizations
Administer ECG Tests
Provide Meals
Administer Laboratory Tests
Provide Nursing Care
Dispense Medications
Provide Therapy Services
Perform Diagnostic Imaging
Operate Patients

Each of these activity centers becomes a cost pool for purposes of ABC cost calculations.

Source: Data from S. Udpa, Activity-Based Costing for Hospitals, *Health Care Management Review,* Vol. 21, No. 3, p. 92, © 1996, Aspen Publishers, Inc.

erally preferred to allocation if the data exist or can be obtained at a reasonable cost. *Allocating* is the process of assigning cost to an activity or cost object when a direct measure does not exist. In some cases, allocations can be converted to tracings by incurring additional measurement costs.

Cost assignment is the umbrella term designating either tracing or allocation. Its formal ABC definition is the tracing or allocation of resources to activities or cost objects. Direct costs are directly assigned, or traced, to the activity center. Indirect costs are assigned to various activity centers through the use of various first-stage cost drivers. For example, the purpose of the first-stage cost drivers discussed below is to allocate overhead costs to activity centers.

St. Joseph's cost flow has been analyzed using cost drivers. This ABC example uses two stages of cost drivers. The first stage of cost drivers concerns inputs. The cost of inputs are traced into cost pools. The cost pools are created for each activity center. Two types of cost linkage then occur. The direct costs are handled in one way and the indirect costs are handled in another way. For purposes of activity-based costing, direct costs are considered to be traced, whereas indirect costs are considered to be allocated.

Another way to think of first-stage cost drivers is to consider them as a type of allocation base. Exhibit 5–3 presents examples of first-stage cost drivers, or allocation bases, for various types of hospital overhead costs. Note that alternative cost driver choices are presented for some of the line items; for example, either number of meals or number of employees as a driver for cafeteria. Also note that the overhead costs are grouped into four categories: labor-related, equipment-related, space-related, and service-

Exhibit 5–3 First-Stage Cost Drivers

	HOSPITAL OVERHEAD COSTS	FIRST-STAGE COST DRIVERS
Labor-related	Supervision	Number of employees/payroll dollars
	Personnel services	Number of employees
Equipment-related	Insurance on equipment	Value of equipment
	Taxes on equipment	Value of equipment
	Medical equipment depreciation	Value of equipment/equipment hours used
	Medical equipment maintenance	Number of maintenance hours
Space-related	Building rental	Space occupied
	Building insurance	Space occupied
	Power costs	Space occupied, volume occupied
	Building maintenance	Space occupied
Service-related	Central administration*	Number of employees/patient volume
	Central service[†]	Quantity/value of supplies
	Medical records, and billing/accounting	Number of documents generated/patient volume
	Cafeteria	Number of meals/number of employees
	Information system	Value of computer equipment/number of programming hours
	Laundry	Weight of laundry washed
	Marketing	Patient volume

*Central administration costs include salaries of the president, vice president, and other central administrative staff.

[†]Central service costs include supplying, reclaiming, and sterilizing supplies such as gloves, needles, glassware, syringes, linens, surgical packs, and instruments.

Source: Reprinted from S. Udpa, Activity-Based Costing for Hospitals, *Health Care Management Review*, Vol. 21, No. 3, p. 91, © 1996, Aspen Publishers, Inc.

related. This grouping allows the commonalities and differences of the associated drivers also to be grouped for ease of review.

Second-stage cost drivers measure the amount of activity resources used by the cost object—such as different procedures or patients. The activities must be isolated for each activity center. Then, the most appropriate cost driver must be selected. Examples of second-stage cost drivers for the ten different activity centers are shown in Exhibit 5–4. The cost drivers selected in this example are only possibilities. Each organization should make its own choices.

Note that the activity analysis methods described in the previous chapter may be applied to arrive at the activities for your own

organization. Again, the activities listed in this example are only possibilities. Each organization should conduct its own analysis and make its own choices.

COST CALCULATIONS

With conventional system cost calculations, direct costs are assigned. Hospital overhead, both departmental and general, must be allocated. In many conventional hospital cost accounting systems, overhead is allocated on a patient day basis, as illustrated in Exhibit 5–5. The cost of St. Joseph's two DRGs (DRG 1X1 and DRG 1X2) using the per patient day method described above is calculated in Table 5–1. The overhead amount allocated to the low-

Exhibit 5–4 Second-Stage Cost Drivers

ACTIVITY CENTER	ACTIVITIES	COST DRIVERS
1. Admit patients	Reservation/scheduling, inpatient registration, billing and insurance verification, admission testing, room/bed/medical assignment	Number of patients admitted
2. Cardiac catheterization	Scheduling, prepare patient, administer medication, cardiac catheterization, film processing, interpret results, patient education	Number of procedures by type*
3. Administer ECG tests	Scheduling, prepare patient, perform ECG procedure, interpret results	Number of tests
4. Provide meals/ nutritional service	Plan meals, purchase supplies, prepare food, deliver food, clean and sanitize	Number of meals by type[†]
5. Administer laboratory tests	Obtain specimens, perform tests, report results	Number of tests by type[‡]
6. Provide nursing care	Transport patients, update medical records, provide patient care, patient education, discharge planning, inservice training	Number of relative value units
7. Dispense medications	Purchase drugs and medical supplies, maintain records, fill medication orders, maintain inventory	Number of medication orders filled
8. Provide therapy	Schedule patients, evaluate patients, provide treatment, educate patients, maintain records	Number of hours by type
9. Perform diagnostic imaging	Schedule patients, perform procedures, develop film, interpret results, transport patient	Number of procedures by type[§]
10. Operate patients	Schedule patients; order supplies; maintain supplies, instruments, and equipment; provide nursing care; transport patient	Number of hours of surgery by surgical suite type

*Cardiac catheterization procedures include therapeutic procedures such as angioplasty, thrombolysis; and diagnostic procedures such as left heart catheterizations, ventriculography, and coronary angiograms.

[†]Different meal types include special meals, regular meals, and snacks.

[‡]Laboratory tests include pathological tests, chemical tests, blood tests, immunological tests, and nuclear medicine.

[§]Diagnostic imaging procedures include routine radiographs of spine, neck, chest, and extremities; mammography; and fluoroscopic procedures such as gastrointestinal series, barium enema, and gallbladder examinations.

Source: Reprinted from S. Udpa, Activity-Based Costing for Hospitals, *Health Care Management Review*, Vol. 21, No. 3, p. 92, © 1996, Aspen Publishers, Inc.

Exhibit 5–5 Overhead Allocated on a Per Patient Day Basis in a Conventional Cost System

Hospital Overhead Allocated Per Patient Day:

Hospital Overhead Costs / Number of Patient Days = Per Patient Day Allocation Unit

$10,832,673 Overhead Costs / 54,838 Patient Days = $197.54 Per Patient Day

Source: Data from S. Udpa, Activity-Based Costing for Hospitals, *Health Care Management Review,* Vol. 21, No. 3, p. 92, © 1996, Aspen Publishers, Inc.

Table 5–1 Cost under Conventional Cost Accounting System

	DRG 1X1	DRG 1X2
Patient days	5	5
Direct cost	$8,451.00	$2,421.00
Hospital cost allocated (5 patient days × 197.54)	987.70	987.70
Total Costs	$9,438.70	$3,408.70

Source: Reprinted from S. Udpa, Activity-Based Costing for Hospitals, *Health Care Management Review*, Vol. 21, No. 3, p. 94, © 1996, Aspen Publishers, Inc.

Exhibit 5–6 Activities Identified in the "Perform Diagnostic Imaging" Activity Center

> Schedule Procedure
>
> Perform Procedure
>
> Develop Film
>
> Interpret Results
>
> Transport Patients

Source: Data from S. Udpa, Activity-Based Costing for Hospitals, *Health Care Management Review*, Vol. 21, No. 3, p. 92, © 1996, Aspen Publishers, Inc.

acuity patient is the same as the overhead amount allocated to the high-acuity patient because the length of stay is the same for both.

In the ABC system, activity centers have been determined. Direct costs have been assigned to the activity centers. The overhead rate for each activity center has been calculated through the use of first-stage and second-stage cost drivers. These overhead rates have then been utilized to assign the cost of overhead based on the number of activity transactions.

A graphic example of St. Joseph's overhead costs as treated in ABC appears in Figure 5–1. A graphic example of the overhead cost allocated to a single activity center (perform diagnostic imaging) appears in Figure 5–2. The cost calculation steps utilized in Figures 5–1 and 5–2 are deconstructed in the following discussion.

First, identify activities contained in each activity center. The ten activity centers illustrated in Figure 5–1 have been previously identified in Exhibit 5–2. One of the ten activity centers is perform diagnostic imaging. This activity center has been selected for an illustrative cost calculation. The five activities identified in the perform diagnostic imaging activity center are illustrated in Exhibit 5–6.

Second, assign overhead cost to each activity center. First-stage cost drivers are used to assign blocks of overhead cost to specific activity centers. The first-stage cost drivers are summarized

in Exhibit 5–3. The distribution of $10,832,673 in hospital overhead cost among ten activity centers is illustrated in Figure 5–1. The perform diagnostic imaging activity center, for example, received $942,443 in assigned cost of the total $10,832,673.

Third, assign overhead cost within each activity center. Second-stage cost drivers used to assign overhead cost within the activity center are summarized in Exhibit 5–7. Of the five activities, four different types of drivers are used. Schedule procedure uses a number of

Exhibit 5–7 Second-Stage Cost Drivers Assign Cost within the "Perform Diagnostic Imaging" Activity Center

Schedule Procedure	$ 4.32 / test
Perform Procedure	$12.00 / RVU
Develop Film	$ 7.00 / film
Interpret Results	$ 1.67 / film
Transport Patient	$ 3.10 / minute

Source: Data from S. Udpa, Activity-Based Costing for Hospitals, *Health Care Management Review*, Vol. 21, No. 3, p. 92, © 1996, Aspen Publishers, Inc.

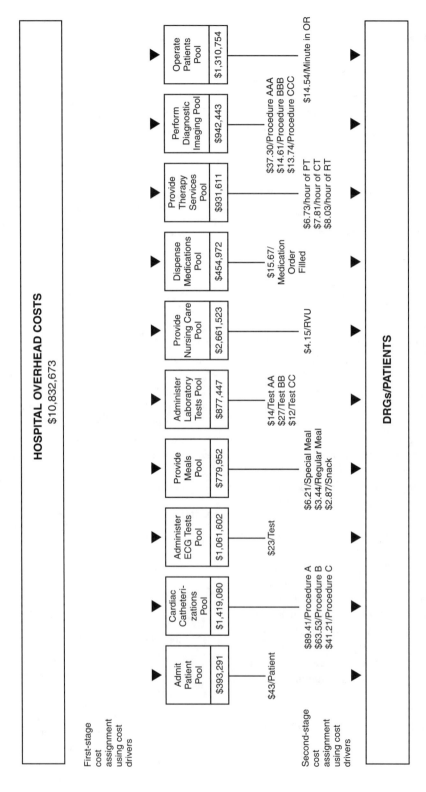

Figure 5–1 Graphic Example of Activity-Based Costing. *Source:* Reprinted from S. Udpa, Activity-Based Costing for Hospitals, *Health Care Management Review*, Vol. 21, No. 3, p. 90, © 1996, Aspen Publishers, Inc.

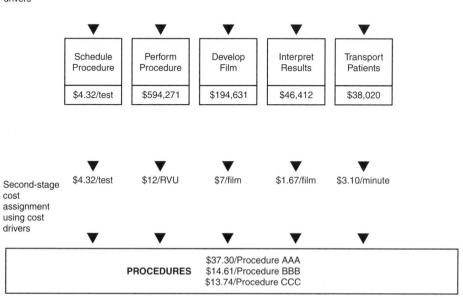

ACTIVITY POOL: PERFORM DIAGNOSTIC IMAGING
Overhead cost allocated: $942,443*

First-stage
cost
assignment
using cost
drivers

Schedule Procedure	Perform Procedure	Develop Film	Interpret Results	Transport Patients
$4.32/test	$594,271	$194,631	$46,412	$38,020

Second-stage
cost
assignment
using cost
drivers

$4.32/test $12/RVU $7/film $1.67/film $3.10/minute

PROCEDURES $37.30/Procedure AAA
$14.61/Procedure BBB
$13.74/Procedure CCC

*These are overhead costs relating to the activity center. Direct costs such as salaries of the radiologists, technologists, technicians, and staff, cost of supplies and depreciation, and maintenance of screening equipment, etc. are directly assigned to the activity pools.

Figure 5–2 Graphic Example of ABC Activity Center: Perform Diagnostic Imaging Pool. *Source:* Data from S. Udpa, Activity-Based Costing for Hospitals, *Health Care Management Review*, Vol. 21, No. 3, p. 93, © 1996, Aspen Publishers, Inc.

tests as its second-stage cost driver. Perform procedure uses a relative value unit (RVU) measure, whereas transport patients uses a per-minute count of employee labor as the driver. The remaining two activities—develop film and interpret results—both use film as the driver.

Fourth, accumulate costs by procedure within the activity center. Overhead costs were assigned to activities in the previous step. Now these costs are accumulated, or assembled, by procedure within this activity center. Each procedure will utilize a specific amount of the activities. This amount is quantified and assembled. See

Exhibit 5–8 for a summary of the three procedures illustrated in Figure 5–2. The three procedures are labeled AAA, BBB, and CCC for purposes of this example. They would, of course, be specifically and properly labeled by name in a real-life instance.

The accumulation of costs by procedure results in a different total cost for each type of procedure. In our example, procedure AAA at $37.30 displays a cost more than double that of the other two procedures. Procedure BBB has been assigned an overhead cost of $14.61 and procedure CCC has been assigned a cost of $13.74.

Exhibit 5–8 Overhead Costs Accumulated into Procedures in the "Perform Diagnostic Imaging" Activity Center*

Procedure AAA = $37.30
Procedure BBB = $14.61
Procedure CCC = $13.74

Designations of "AAA," "BBB," and "CCC" are used for purposes of example. Diagnostic imaging procedures include (1) routine radiographs of spine, neck, chest, and extremities; (2) mammography; and (3) fluoroscopic procedures such as gastrointestinal series, barium enema, and gallbladder examinations.

*See Figure 5–2.

Source: Data from S. Udpa, Activity-Based Costing for Hospitals, *Health Care Management Review,* Vol. 21, No. 3, p. 94, © 1996, Aspen Publishers, Inc.

Fifth, assemble transactions by activity center into overhead cost per DRG. To complete this example of activity-based costing calculations, the overhead costs have been assembled into DRGs. Table 5–2 illustrates the assembling of costs into DRG 1X1 and DRG 1X2. Note that

the various activity centers now have the word *pool* following; in our example, *perform diagnostic imaging* is now *perform diagnostic imaging pool.* This terminology refers to a cost pool. Also note that the result of action by a driver is called a transaction. Thus, procedures in our example of *perform diagnostic imaging* would be measured as a transaction, whereas patients would be measured as a transaction in the *admit patients pool.* The terms *transaction* and *pool* are adopted as uniform designations.

Table 5–2 illustrates number of transactions, rate per transaction, and overhead cost for DRG 1X1 and for DRG 1X2. Calculation of the overhead cost for the perform diagnostic imaging activity center example is set out in Exhibit 5–9. Note that the rate per transaction is merely the overhead cost by procedure type, as previously illustrated in Exhibit 5–8. Thus, the overhead cost calculation consists of (1) selecting the type and number of procedures designated for the appropriate DRG (2 AAA for DRG 1X1 and 2 CCC for DRG 1X2); (2) picking up the appropriate rate per transaction ($37.30 for AAA and $13.74 for CCC); and (3) multiplying (1) times (2) to arrive at the overhead cost calculation

Exhibit 5–9 Rate per Transaction and Overhead Cost Calculation in the "Perform Diagnostic Imaging" Activity Center

Rate per Transaction:*
(Overhead Costs by Procedure Type)

Procedure AAA = $37.30

Procedure BBB = $14.61

Procedure CCC = $13.74

Overhead Cost Calculation for the "Perform Diagnostic Imaging" Activity Center:**

Col 1		Col 2		Col 3
Number of Transactions	×	Rate per Transaction	=	Overhead Cost Calculation
2 Procedures AAA		$37.30/procedure AAA		$74.60
2 Procedures CCC		$13.74/procedure CCC		$27.48

*See Exhibit 5–8.
**See Table 5–2.

Source: Data from S. Udpa, Activity-Based Costing for Hospitals, *Health Care Management Review,* Vol. 21, No. 3, p. 95, © 1996, Aspen Publishers, Inc.

Table 5–2 Overhead Cost per DRG

Activity Center	DRG 1X1			DRG 1X2		
	Number of Transactions	Rate per Transaction	Overhead Cost	Number of Transactions	Rate per Transaction	Overhead Cost
Admit patient pool	1 patient	$43/patient	$43.00	1 patient	$43/patient	$43.00
Cardiac catheterizations pool	2 procedure A	89.41/procedure A	178.82	1 procedure C	$41.21/procedure C	41.21
Administer ECG tests pool	7 tests	$23/test	161.00	4 tests	$23/test	92.00
Provide meals pool	9 special meals	$6.21/special meal	55.89	9 regular meals	$3.44/regular meal	30.96
	6 snacks	$2.87/snack	17.22	6 snacks	$2.87/snack	17.22
Administer laboratory tests pool	4 tests BB	$27/test BB	108.00	3 tests AA	$14/test AA	42.00
Provide nursing care pool	312 RVUs	$4.15/RVU	1,294.80	104 RVUs	$4.15/RVU	431.60
Dispense medications pool	14 medication orders	$15.67/medication order filled	219.38	6 medication orders	$15.67/medication order filled	94.02
Provide therapy sessions pool	7 hrs CT	$7.81/hour of CT	54.67	2 hrs CT	$7.81/hour of CT	15.62
Perform diagnostic imaging pool	2 procedures AAA	$37.30/procedure AAA	74.60	2 procedures CCC	$13.74/procedure CCC	27.48
Operate patients pool	1 hr in OR	$14.54/minute in OR	872.40			
			$3,079.78			$835.11

Source: Reprinted from S. Udpa, Activity-Based Costing for Hospitals, *Health Care Management Review*, Vol. 21, No. 3, p. 90, © 1996, Aspen Publishers, Inc.

Table 5–3 Cost per DRG under ABC and Conventional Cost Systems

	Activity-Based Costing		Conventional Cost System	
	DRG 1X1	DRG 1X2	DRG 1X1	DRG 1X2
Direct costs	8,451.00	2,421.00	8,451.00	2,421.00
Hospital overhead allocated	3,079.78	835.11	987.70	987.70
Total costs	11,530.78	3,256.11	9,438.70	3,408.70
			Undercosted by 22.16%	Overcosted by 4.47%

Source: Reprinted from S. Udpa, Activity-Based Costing for Hospitals, *Health Care Management Review*, Vol. 21, No. 3, p. 95, © 1996, Aspen Publishers, Inc.

($74.60 for DRG 1X1 and $27.48 for DRG 1X2). This particular example—the perform diagnostic imaging pool—is one of the ten activity centers line items that are combined to create the overall DRG cost in Table 5–2. When combined, activity-based costing has resulted in an overhead cost of $3,079.78 for DRG 1X1 versus $835.11 for DRG 1X2.

COMPARISON OF COST PER DRG UNDER ABC AND CONVENTIONAL COST SYSTEMS

The result of activity-based costing is summarized in Table 5–2. The result of conventional costing is summarized in Table 5–1. These results are compared in Table 5–3. The conventional system has undercosted overhead for the high-acuity patient (DRG 1X1) by 22.16 percent and has overcosted overhead for the low-acuity patient (DRG 1X2) by 4.47 percent. The ABC methodology has allowed management to obtain more accurate costing information. Management's decision making will utilize costing information for case-mix decisions, for staffing decisions, for pricing decisions, for capital budgeting decisions, and for strategic planning direction. Thus more accurate costing information takes on a high priority.

CONCLUSION

It should be noted that the activity centers themselves, the types of activities within each activity center, and the specific drivers (both first-stage and second-stage) that are selected to assign cost can all vary from one facility to another. A specific example of this variation can be found by comparing Canby's[2] activity map (concerning the X-ray process) to the activities for diagnostic imaging set out in this illustration. The variation is twofold. The cost objective can create such variation, as has been previously discussed. And the facility process can and will be different; thus creating such variations.

It should also be noted that the decision to accumulate costs by procedure and then assemble by DRG is a facility-specific decision. Cost objectives other than the DRGs that are illustrated in this example may well be chosen by other facilities.

NOTES

1. S. Udpa, "Activity-Based Costing for Hospitals," *Health Care Management Review* 21, no. 3 (1996): 83–96.

2. J.B. Canby IV, "Applying Activity-Based Costing to Healthcare Settings," *Healthcare Financial Management* (February 1995): 50–56.

## CHAPTER 6

Time Studies for Activity-Based Costing

Judith J. Baker with Patricia Chiverton and Victoria G. Hines

CHAPTER OUTLINE

What Is a Time Study?
ABC Application in Health Care: A New
　Approach
Activity Categories
The Time Study: Step by Step
Example: Strong Memorial Hospital Case
　Management Time Study
Conclusion

WHAT IS A TIME STUDY?

Measuring time is part of measuring activities. The time spent in various activities is captured in order to ultimately measure the resources that are consumed. Time studies and work sampling are performed in order to determine the number, type, and frequency or volume of activities. A time study employs continuous timed observations of a single person during a typical workday. That person is either followed continuously or records his or her continuous time to determine the proportion of time that is spent in performing a given activity. The duration of specific activities is then used to determine the average amount of staff time for each activity.

Work sampling is a different method. Work sampling uses discrete and instantaneous observations of routine activities performed by a

variety of staff personnel. A large number of random observations are made and used to determine the number and type of steps for a job in its normal operating mode.[1] Although both methods can be employed in order to determine the amount of time expended in particular activities, this chapter concentrates on the time study methodology.

ABC APPLICATION IN HEALTH CARE: A NEW APPROACH

Time studies themselves are not new in health care. Nursing research has a long history of nurse labor and workload studies. Fiscal intermediaries in the Medicare program have also accepted time studies as a documented basis for apportioning certain expenses. Thus, time studies are not a new concept to health care managers.

The approach, however, is new. We are now proposing to link the process revealed by the studies to cost in an ABC application. Health care managers have long struggled with the problem of matching resources with patient care requirements in a way that allows cost-effective quality care.[2] The time study performed as part of fact-finding for ABC can provide the basis for resource consumption information.

ACTIVITY CATEGORIES

Activity categories are necessary because activities must be defined and classified. This methodology is part of activity analysis, as discussed in Chapter 4. Breaking activities into their component parts is aided by the use of activity categories. A category is, of course, a division within a system of classification.[3] Thus, an *activity category* is a division within a classification of activities. In this case, we are contemplating components of service-related activities. It is not necessary to reinvent the wheel in order to establish health care activity categories. Existing sources can be found with methodologically sound and defensible activity categories.

The activity categories in appropriate existing sources can be adapted to your own data collection forms. We will look at two suitable examples, one for nursing staff in acute care and one for ambulatory care activities.

The study that resulted in these activity categories was intended to refine activity categories for nursing staff duties. The researchers felt that previous studies of such duties had created activity categories that were too broad to identify areas where changes could be implemented, particularly as to indirect care.[4] Exhibit 6–1 presents the definitions of activity categories for nursing staff that resulted from this research. Note that certain nonvalue-added time can readily be identified within this example. (Refer to the supplies category in Exhibit 6–1, which reads "Supplies: Time spent outside of the patient's room looking for or obtaining supplies, but not requisitioning.")

The study that used these activity categories was intended to quantify ambulatory care activity categories by both time and complexity (Exhibit 6–2).[5] This set of activities should serve as a guide for your own organization's activity categories, and the guide should be adapted for your own use. The *health maintenance teaching* and *teaching related to illness/ condition* sections, for example, might be adapted to your organization's required outcomes under managed care contracts. Reference to such examples will enhance the activity categories that are used in the time study for your own project.

THE TIME STUDY: STEP BY STEP

We will now examine a time study step by step. First is the activity measurement sequence. The time study sequence for activity measurement is set out in Figure 6–1. The entire sequence should be taken into account when planning the project. The six tasks in the time column relate to the time study. The six tasks in the costs column relate to the gathering and assembly of costing information. Note that the sixth and final task in both columns is *transfer to time and cost spreadsheet.* It is possible to create a project planning flowchart from the sequential tasks listed in Figure 6–1.

Second is planning the time study itself. The planning process requires a series of decisions. The ten subjects that are involved are set out in Figure 6–2.

The setting is the first subject. Ask: Will the time study be held in a single department? The logistics are more complex if the study covers more than one department simultaneously. Additional planning questions may include: Who will fund the study? Who are the managers with input? What are the expectations of management? Is the project team multidisciplinary? Is there sufficient support in terms of personnel and computer support?

The time frame is the second subject. Ask: How long will the time study run? The time period must be long enough to obtain the necessary data. Will the time study be run in a continuous period or will it start and stop? It is usual for the study to run in a continuous period. Is the time period chosen free of unusual demands on the personnel? If the surveyors have come into a nursing home, for example, that time period is not normal or routine. It would not be a suitable choice.

Personnel to be included is the third subject. Ask: Will all personnel be included? If not, how

Exhibit 6–1 Definitions of Nursing Staff Activity Categories

With Patient

All nurse/patient time, either in the patient's room or in hallway (transporting, ambulating, etc.).

Patient Chart

Any work with the chart. This will usually be writing nursing notes, developing the care plans, or reading the chart.

Preparation of Therapies

Time spent preparing intravenous therapy, medications, treatments, etc.

Shift Change Activities

Report, counting narcotics, getting assignments, and making patient rounds, either during report or afterwards.

Professional Interaction

All face-to-face communications, except communications with patient. For example: communications with visitors, doctors, social workers, other nurses, hospital staff, etc.

Miscellaneous, Clinical

Any clinical activity not listed above.

Checking Physician's Orders

Checking physician orders for tests, medications, etc., including cross-checking medication order against the medication book.

Unit-Oriented Inservice

Time spent on inservice education (for new policies or procedures, for example) or case conferences.

Paperwork

Filling out forms, incident reports, requisitions or any work with paper, other than physician orders or charting.

Phone Communications

Any use of the telephone.

Supplies

Time spent outside of the patient's room looking for or obtaining supplies, but not requisitioning.

Miscellaneous, Non-Clinical

Any non-clinical activity, not listed above. Meals and break time are included in this category.

Don't Know

Source: Reprinted with permission from *Journal of Nursing Administration*, Vol. 20, No. 3, © 1990, Lippincott-Raven Publishers.

will those participating be selected? Will they be selected on the basis of the duties they perform? Or will they be randomly selected? Will the usual complement of personnel be present? Have absences due to vacations and holidays been taken into account?

The reporting method is the fourth subject. Generally, the choice is between self-reporting and observation. In self-reporting, the individual records his or her own data; whereas, in observation, an observer records the data. Self-reporting allows a large quantity of data to be collected over a short time period. It is economical in that consultants do not have to be used. Self-reporting has the disadvantage of inaccurate reporting in three different circumstances: because the employees may become very busy; because instructions for recording data may not be clear; and because of potential skewing.[6] Observation has the advantage of objective data

Exhibit 6–2 Activity Categories for Ambulatory Care

AMBULATORY CARE CLASSIFICATION TOOL

ACTIVITY

Assessment/Planning

_____	01. Documents (organization of)	(6,16)
_____	02. Documents (review of)	(7,27)
_____	03. Measurements of physiological and growth indices	(5,15)
_____	04. Specimens (collection and/or testing)	(7,24)
_____	05. Eligibility screening/arranging payment for services	(10,35)
_____	06. Referral (evaluation of need for and arrangement of referral)	(12,38)
_____ *	07. Follow-up assessment of patient's status	(9,47)
_____ *	08. Triage/Screening of patient's problems in person or by phone	(12,60)
_____ *	09. General assessment (health, knowledge of health maintenance, psychosocial)	(12,57)
_____ *	10. History (complete health and social history)	(17,57)
_____	11. Physical (complete physical and/or developmental exam)	(21,68)

Physical Comfort/Safety

_____	12. Directing to location of other services	(3,12)
_____	13. Communication (provision of special communication assistance)	(13,34)
_____	14. Physical preparation of patient for exam	(5,18)
_____	15. Comfort (hunger, etc., information about reasons for delay)	(6,27)
_____	16. Chaperoning (physically present for comfort or legal reasons)	(10,15)
_____	17. Transporting of patient to other services	(8,11)

Medications/IV

_____	18. Medication by any route other than IV	(7,50)
_____	19. IV therapy, with or without medications	(26,63)
_____	20. IV medications	(12,62)
_____	21. Blood therapy (blood and blood products)	(47,70)

Procedures and Treatments

_____	22. Applications of any therapeutic treatments to body surfaces	(12,45)
_____	23. Assisting with procedures	(17,45)
_____	24. Dressings	(12,43)
_____	25. Surgical preparation (for procedures in surgery or outpatient)	(16,51)
_____	26. Coordination and timing of client's needs with providers/services	(14,43)
_____	27. Appliances (application and removal of casts, etc.)	(20,51)
_____	28. Invasive procedures (catheterizations, enemas, etc.)	(18,50)
_____	29. Recovery (from surgical or outpatient procedures or sedation)	(24,50)
_____	30. Protocol care (provision of care following protocols)	(16,61)

Health Maintenance Teaching

_____	31. Provide information about health and normal body functioning	(15,56)
_____	32. Health status support (reinforcement of good health practices)	(12,48)
_____	33. Preventive care instruction	(13,51)
_____	34. Health care maintenance (planned educational program)	(21,59)

continues

Exhibit 6–2 continued

ACTIVITY

Teaching Related to Illness/Condition

_____ 35. System (explanation of ambulatory care system and related services)	(10,32)
_____ 36. Standardized instructions (home and/or self care)	(16,46)
_____ 37. Plan of care (explaining, reinforcing)	(21,53)
_____ 38. Illness/Condition program (planned program about condition/disease)	(26,61)
_____ 39. Individualized instructions (unstandardized and non-routine)	(25,69)

Psychosocial

_____ 40. Procedure support (before or during)	(14,48)
_____ 41. Client advocacy (attention to patient needs or complaints regarding care)	(16,57)
_____ 42. Terminal/Chronic illness (support, guidance to patient/family)	(30,71)

Admission/Transfer

_____ 43. Admission to an inpatient unit	(25,41)
_____ 44. Transfer to another outpatient area or service	(11,32)

*Mutually exclusive

Note: Numbers in parentheses are mean time in minutes and mean complexity on a scale of 1–100 for each activity area.

Source: Reprinted from **Nursing Economic$**, 1992, Volume 10, Number 3, pp. 185–186. Reprinted with permission of the publisher, Jannetti Publications, Inc., East Holly Avenue Box 56, Pitman, NJ 08071-0056; Phone (609) 256-2300; FAX (609) 589-7463. (For a sample issue of the journal, contact the publisher.)

---

recording. The primary disadvantage is the expense involved in either using and training consultants or hiring already trained personnel to serve as observers and to record data. Another disadvantage is that the presence of an observer can cause employees to perform activities faster or slower than usual.[7]

Technology is the fifth subject. Electronic technology is available today. Some projects use light wands that record bar coding with a swipe. The data is downloaded at the end of the shift or the end of the day. In theory, light wands eliminate the extra data input step, because the data is downloaded directly into the computer. Another electronic choice is a hand-held computer. There are many models. Some recognize handwriting, or the input can be entered by touching a stylus to the hand-held computer screen. An alternative choice is to record with paper and pencil. The paper forms can be designed to be scanned.

The data collection form design is the sixth subject. Ask: Who will design your data collection forms? The technology that is chosen impacts the type of form to be designed. Has this choice been properly taken into account? Is someone sufficiently skilled in designing the forms? Do you plan a test run of the forms? This is highly recommended. Have the data input requirements been considered when designing the forms?

Study administration is the seventh subject. Ask: Who will administer the time study? Will the individual be external (not affiliated with the organization) or internal (employed by the organization)? If internal, will the administrator be from outside the department where the study will occur? Or will some level of departmental manager be responsible for administering the study? In either case, has sufficient training been provided for the manager? In addition, who will train the employees in recording tech-

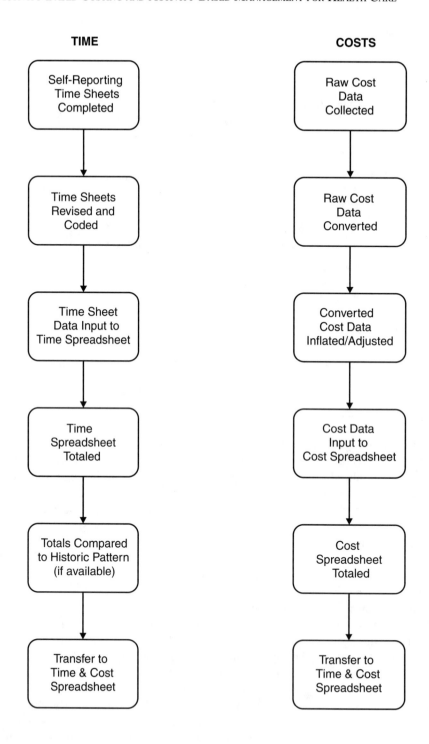

TIME

Self-Reporting
Time Sheets
Completed

Time Sheets
Revised and
Coded

Time Sheet
Data Input to
Time Spreadsheet

Time
Spreadsheet
Totaled

Totals Compared
to Historic Pattern
(if available)

Transfer to
Time & Cost
Spreadsheet

COSTS

Raw Cost
Data
Collected

Raw Cost
Data
Converted

Converted
Cost Data
Inflated/Adjusted

Cost Data
Input to
Cost Spreadsheet

Cost
Spreadsheet
Totaled

Transfer to
Time & Cost
Spreadsheet

Figure 6–1 Time Study Sequence for Activity Measurement. *Source:* Copyright © 1997, Resource Group, Ltd., Dallas, Texas.

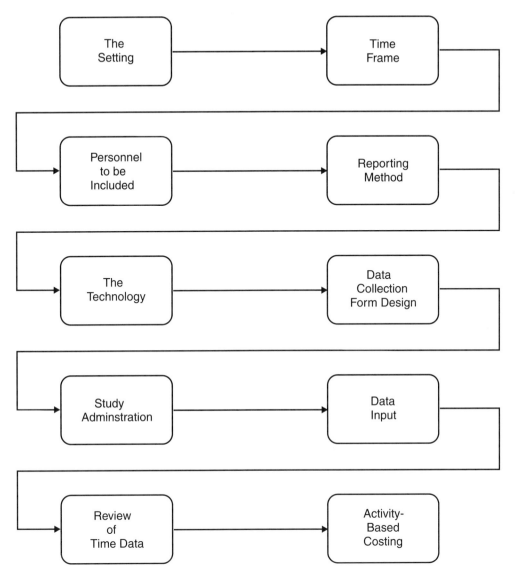

Figure 6–2 Planning the Time Study. *Source:* Copyright © 1997, Resource Group, Ltd., Dallas, Texas.

niques? Has a data entry guide been prepared? Will a training session be held? If so, who will be the trainer(s)? Has inter-rater reliability been considered? Inter-rater reliability expresses agreement among raters; a high level of agreement is expected. Who is responsible? How does that person intend to accomplish inter-rater reliability?

Data input is the eighth subject. Ask: If the forms have been subjected to a test run, has that test run extended to data input? This is highly recommended. Has the spreadsheet been designed in conjunction with the forms? Will input begin in batches? Is coding prior to input necessary? If so, who will perform the coding? How will accuracy of data input be tested? Is there a plan? Who will be responsible for completing the input? Who will be responsible for testing accuracy?

The review of time data is the ninth subject. Ask: Who will review the time-data spreadsheets after data input has been completed? Who is responsible for summarizing their contents? Who will review the data for uniformity and for validity?

Activity-based costing is the tenth subject. Ask: Who will attach the costing to the activity information obtained through the time study?

The questions posed above should all be answered in order to assemble a reliable and well-run time study project. Next we will examine a real-life example of a hospital time study.

EXAMPLE: STRONG MEMORIAL HOSPITAL CASE MANAGEMENT TIME STUDY

Strong Memorial Hospital, a 722-bed teaching hospital, is the University of Rochester's tertiary care referral center. Strong Memorial is part of a health system and has established its own HMO, Strong Care.

The psychiatric department of Strong Memorial believes in the case management concept. They proposed a postacute care psychiatric case management project. They obtained funding in the form of a research grant to run a pilot study for postacute psychiatric case management. The logistics of this time study are described throughout the remainder of the example.

All patients under postacute psychiatric case management included in the pilot study were to be captured over an 18-month period in this all-inclusive time study. Draft protocols of clinical activities (including both type of activity and projected time requirements) were developed to be tested during the pilot study. A short test run of procedures and forms was performed prior to the official start of the pilot study.

The projected time frame for the study was 18 months (although the actual study ran 19 months). All nurses participating in the pilot project were included in the time study.

Self-reporting was chosen as the reporting method to be used. Paper and pencil was chosen. No electronic technology was deemed necessary. Reasons included convenience and cost.

The activity categories that were selected were consistent with the expectations of this project. One reporting form was used per nurse per day. The time-reporting forms were designed to capture both direct and indirect time that was expended on a per-patient basis. (See Exhibit 6–3.) Mileage was also reported on a supplemental log. (See Exhibit 6–4.) Mileage was captured so it could be cross-referenced to travel time on the activity reporting forms. The data collection form was designed to record activities on a per-patient basis. The data collection for the time study was designed to interface with a database containing information about the patient's clinical condition. Another supplemental form recorded basic information about each nurse participating in the pilot study. This data included such items as education and years of experience.

Dr. Patricia Chiverton, Chief of Psychiatric Nursing for Strong Memorial Hospital, was designated as the study administrator. All personnel were instructed in proper procedures for self-reporting. Formal training sessions were held and quality assurance was maintained throughout the course of the study.

The data input spreadsheet was designed simultaneously with the data collection forms. The data collection forms were arranged in order to accommodate an easy input flow. The time study data was input into a Lotus spreadsheet. Review of the time data spreadsheets compared direct and indirect time. Individual personnel's direct and indirect times were reviewed against the mean and the median. Actual time incurred in the various activities was reviewed against what had been anticipated in the protocols. Travel time was also reviewed and cross-referenced to the mileage logs.

As the study was nearing completion, Strong Care, the hospital's HMO, needed a capitated rate for postacute care psychiatric case managed patients. Consequently, the activities deter-

Exhibit 6–3 Time Log

DIRECT/INDIRECT TIME LOG

Patient Name_____Total Direct/Indirect Time_____

Address_____Total Mileage _____

Home Care Nurse _____

Direct Time:

*Please indicate on time log if you have modified number of visits or telephone contacts over 5-week period, or if service was extended. Please add time accordingly.

Prior to Discharge: Initial Data Collection (Tools, Appointments)   _____

Week 1	Visit	_____
Week 2	Telephone	_____
Week 3	Visit	_____
Week 4	Telephone	_____
Week 5	Visit	_____

Direct Total _____

Indirect Time:

Initial Data Collection (Discharge Summary Care Map)   _____
Documentation:

Care Map I   _____

Care Map II   _____

Care Map III   _____

Care Map IV   _____

Care Map V   _____

Other telephone contacts, in addition to 2 telephone assessments
  (e.g., therapists, agencies, etc.)   _____

Any other time spent with case that is not directly with patient   _____

Travel Time (specify location below if different from address above)

Visit I (Date)	_____	Mileage	_____
Visit II (Date)	_____	Mileage	_____
Visit III (Date)	_____	Mileage	_____

Indirect Total _____

Courtesy of University of Rochester, School of Nursing, Rochester, New York.

Exhibit 6–4 Mileage Log

CUMULATIVE MILEAGE LOG

Specify Location If Different from Patient's Address

Total Mileage

Patient Name_____   _____

Address _____   _____

Date/Mileage   Visit I _____   Visit II _____   Visit III _____   =   _____

Patient Name_____   _____

Address _____   _____

Date/Mileage   Visit I _____   Visit II _____   Visit III _____   =   _____

Patient Name_____   _____

Address _____   _____

Date/Mileage   Visit I _____   Visit II _____   Visit III _____   =   _____

Patient Name_____   _____

Address _____   _____

Date/Mileage   Visit I _____   Visit II _____   Visit III _____   =   _____

Patient Name_____   _____

Address _____   _____

Date/Mileage   Visit I _____   Visit II _____   Visit III _____   =   _____

Patient Name_____   _____

Address _____   _____

Date/Mileage   Visit I _____   Visit II _____   Visit III _____   =   _____

Patient Name_____   _____

Address _____   _____

Date/Mileage   Visit I _____   Visit II _____   Visit III _____   =   _____

Patient Name_____   _____

Address _____   _____

Date/Mileage   Visit I _____   Visit II _____   Visit III _____   =   _____

Grand Total Mileage   _____

Courtesy of University of Rochester, School of Nursing, Rochester, New York.

mined by the time study data just described were utilized in calculating an activity-based cost. The ABC figure then became a base point for setting the proposed capitated rate. The team for the subsequent ABC project consisted of Victoria G. Hines, Associate Dean for Administration and Finance of the School of Nursing, Judith J. Baker, ABC Research Consultant, and Patricia Chiverton, Chief of Psychiatric Nursing and School of Nursing Associate Dean. The scope for ABC was determined by the ABC project team. Fixed and variable account designations were agreed on and direct and indirect costs were reviewed by the team. Labor costs for the case management pilot study were attached to activities that were reported through the time study. Training time was also costed. Training time included cost of time for the trainer and for the trainee. Labor costs were traced as just described. Other traced costs included:

- chargeable medical supplies
- drugs
- lab work
- additional tests and procedures
- consults
- physical therapy
- assistive devices

These costs are all direct care items that are separately billable. The Strong system can trace these items on a patient-specific/episode-specific basis. Thus, a sample of actual cases can yield the mean and median costs. Indirect costs were allocated with an algorithm. The start-up

costs for putting more case managers in the field was also calculated.

The outcome encompassed four results: (1) The patient population was categorized by risk level. (2) Activity-based costing was applied to arrive at the case management cost for each risk level. (3) A proposed capitation rate was calculated. (4) Upon completion of contract negotiations the rate was implemented.

CONCLUSION

The future may hold perpetual rolling time databases, thus making time studies obsolete (such a virtual time sheet is described in the Standards section of Chapter 12).[8] But until that point is reached, if ever, time studies will still be required, and it will still be necessary to justify them to management. One way to justify the studies is to emphasize their multiple management uses.

Although the primary focus of this chapter is utilizing time study data for purposes of activity-based costing and activity-based management, the time measurement data is also available for other management uses. Such uses by clinical management could include, for example, formulating and evaluating care plans, critical paths, care maps, and protocols; analyzing staffing patterns; and adjusting workloads.[9] The data can also be useful for strategic planning purposes. The data has even been used by an architectural firm while redesigning work stations. Such creative justification may well help sell your project's funding to your executive committee.

NOTES

1. C. Horngren et al., *Cost Accounting: A Managerial Emphasis*, 8th ed. (Englewood Cliffs, NJ: Prentice Hall, 1994), 479.

2. J.G. Schade and J.K. Austin, "Quantifying Ambulatory Care Activities by Time and Complexity," *Nursing Economics* 10, no. 3 (1992): 183.

3. *Merriam-Webster's Collegiate Dictionary*, 10th ed. (Springfield, MA: Merriam-Webster, Inc., 1996), 180.

4. G. Hendrickson et al., "How Do Nurses Use Their Time?" *Journal of Nursing Administration* 20, no. 3 (1990): 31.

5. Schade and Austin, "Quantifying Ambulatory Care Activities," 186.

6. A. Iglar et al., "Time and Cost Requirements for Decentralized Pharmacist Activities," *American Journal of Hospital Pharmacy* 47 (1990): 576.

7. Ibid., 576.

8. J.B. White, "Chrysler's Intranet: Promise vs. Reality," *The Wall Street Journal*, 13 May 1997, B1, B6.

9. N.J. Adler and M.L. Icenhour, "Analysis through Work Sampling of the Role of the Emergency Nurse," *Journal of Emergency Nursing* 19, no. 1 (1993): 32.

Structural Choices

Judith J. Baker

CHAPTER OUTLINE

INTRODUCTION

Structural choices determine your organization's costing framework. These choices determine how your costing framework will be constructed, and such choices begin with service lines. The composition of fixed versus variable costs is a structural choice, and the designation of direct versus indirect costs is a basic building block in costing systems. In ABC these designations have a particular impact because direct costs are traced and indirect costs are allocated.

The specificity of your ABC system will depend on the precision with which these distinctions are made. Cost drivers are an integral part of the ABC methodology. As such, they too impact structural choices. A number of different approaches to ABC have been developed for health care applications today. This overview of

structural choice is intended to clarify the composition of the costing framework.

SERVICE LINES

In traditional cost accounting circles, a product line is a grouping of similar products.[1] In the health care field many organizations opt instead for "service line" terminology. A service line is a grouping of similar services. Strategic planning sometimes sets out service lines. If your institution has set out service lines, then consider whether the distinctions are appropriate for your application of activity-based costing. One health system started with a blank sheet of paper and two basic designations: "Inpatient" and "Ambulatory." They wound up with eight service lines.

A number of hospitals have adopted the major diagnostic categories (MDCs) as service lines. MDCs serve as the classification system for diagnosis related groups (DRGs). A listing of the MDCs appears as Exhibit 7–1. The case study in Chapter 16 illustrates a hospital that is using MDCs as service lines. One advantage of MDCs is that they are a universal designation in the United States. MDCs also have the advantage of possessing a standard definition. In another case, a chief financial officer (CFO) reported that his hospital had recently updated their strategic plan. They had settled on five ser-

Exhibit 7–1 Major Diagnostic Categories

	DISEASES AND DISORDERS OF THE:
MDC 1	Nervous System
MDC 2	Eye
MDC 3	Ear, Nose, Mouth, and Throat
MDC 4	Respiratory System
MDC 5	Circulatory System
MDC 6	Digestive System
MDC 7	Hepatobiliary System and Pancreas
MDC 8	Musculoskeletal System and Connective Tissue
MDC 9	Skin, Subcutaneous Tissue, and Breast
MDC 10	Endocrine, Nutritional, and Metabolic
MDC 11	Kidney and Urinary Tract
MDC 12	Male Reproductive System
MDC 13	Female Reproductive System
MDC 14	Pregnancy, Childbirth, and the Puerperium
MDC 15	Newborns and Other Neonates with Conditions Originating in the Perinatal Period
MDC 16	Blood and Blood Forming Organs and Immunological Disorders
MDC 17	Myeloproliferative and Poorly and Differentiated Neoplasms
MDC 18	Infections and Parasitic Diseases (Systemic or Unspecified Sites)
MDC 19	Mental Diseases and Disorders
MDC 20	Alcohol/Drug Use and Alcohol/Drug Induced Organic Mental Disorders
MDC 21	Injuries, Poisonings, and Toxic Effect of Drugs
MDC 22	Burns
MDC 23	Factors Influencing Health Status and Other Contacts with Health Services

vice lines: (1) medical; (2) surgical; (3) women and children; (4) mental health; and (5) rehab, neuro-ortho rehab (Figure 7–1). Some health care organizations do use the product line terminology. For example, at the time of this writing, Columbia/HCA is reported to classify its services into eight product lines in a disease management approach. The eight product lines include: (1) cancer, (2) cardiology, (3) diabetes, (4) behavioral health, (5) workers' compensation, (6) women's services, (7) senior care, and (8) emergency services.

We often recommend that a continuing care retirement community (CCRC) consider using various levels of care as their starting point. Thus, the CCRC might have four service lines, listed in the descending order of resident acuity: (1) skilled nursing facility, (2) nursing facility, (3) assisted living, and (4) independent living.

The skilled nursing facility would provide services for the highest level of resident acuity and the independent living would provide services for the lowest level of resident acuity. One adjustment to this approach would include isolating subacute services separately from the remainder of skilled nursing facility services. Another adjustment to this approach might involve splitting independent living into two categories; one for HUD-subsidized independent housing and the other for private-pay independent housing. Figure 7–2 illustrates CCRC service lines by acuity level.

Numerous categories of service delivery can be present under the "home care" umbrella. A practical example appears in the Chapter 18 home care case study. This home care entity, part of a health system, arrived at what they call their "key functions." These key functions can

HOSPITAL SERVICE LINE EXAMPLE

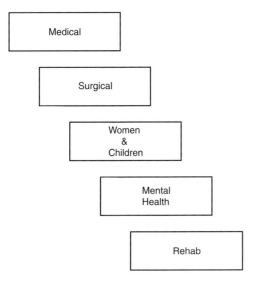

Figure 7–1 Hospital Service Lines. *Source:* Copyright © 1997, Resource Group, Ltd., Dallas, Texas.

in turn be converted to service lines. (See Figure 7–3).

Service delivery for physician groups will vary, of course, with the nature of the group itself. A generic set of service lines is presented in Figure 7–4.

Each service line will be comprised of an array of services. We have called this array "components." For example, in the case study appearing in Chapter 23, the cardiac service line has three major groupings and thirteen individual DRG components. It is reproduced here as Exhibit 7–2.

An example of the components of a standard home care service line appears in Chapter 18. The seven components are reproduced here as Exhibit 7–3.

To repeat: Service lines are an important part of ABC structural choices.

FIXED VERSUS VARIABLE COSTS

The designation of fixed or variable is basic to the application of activity-based costing. The ABC definition of a fixed cost is "a cost element of an activity that does not vary with changes in the volume of cost drivers or activity drivers." The depreciation of a machine, for example, may be direct to a particular activity, but it is fixed with respect to changes in the number of units of the activity driver. As with any fixed expense, the designation of a cost as fixed versus variable may vary depending on the time frame of the decision in question; a cost is fixed over a given time period. And the designation of fixed cost can also vary depending on the extent to which the volume of pro-

CONTINUING CARE RETIREMENT COMMUNITY (CCRC) SERVICE LINE EXAMPLE

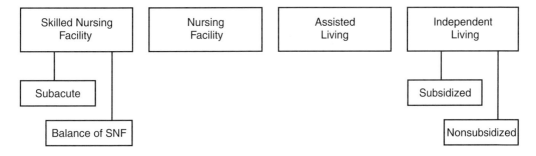

Figure 7–2 Long-Term Care Service Lines. *Source:* Copyright © 1997, Resource Group, Ltd., Dallas, Texas.

HOME CARE SERVICE LINE EXAMPLE

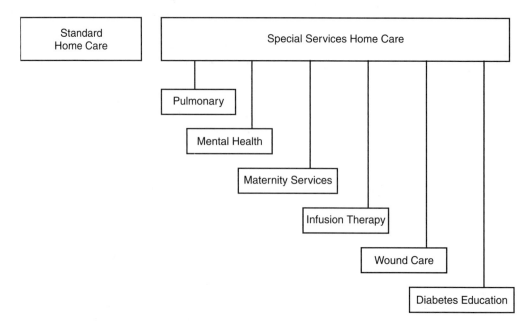

Figure 7–3 Home Care Service Lines. *Source:* Copyright © 1997, Resource Group, Ltd., Dallas, Texas.

duction, activity drivers, or cost drivers may change. The ABC definition of a variable cost is "a cost element of an activity that varies with changes in volume of cost drivers and activity drivers." The cost of supplies handling to an activity, for example, will vary depending on the number of material deliveries and pickups to and from that activity. An illustration of fixed and variable cost distribution in a family practice is illustrated in Exhibit 7–4. (The case study about this family practice appears in Chapter 13.)

An illustration of fixed and variable cost distribution in a hospital operating room is illustrated in Exhibit 7–5. (The case study about this operating room appears in Chapter 15.)

As previously stated, it should be understood that costs are not intrinsically fixed or variable.[3] Managerial analysis with ABC affords a clear picture of cost variability. The end result is an opportunity to reduce demands on resources of the organization.

DIRECT VERSUS INDIRECT COSTS

The main criticism of health care cost accounting by traditional methods is aimed at the inadequate methods for allocating indirect costs.[4] Activity-based costing uses a different methodology for dealing with indirect costs. ABC segregates indirect costs and support resources by activities.[5] This difference in method is the heart of ABC. The ABC definition of a *direct cost* is "a cost that is traced directly to an activity of a cost object." For example, the supplies issued for a particular procedure and the operating room nurse time devoted to that procedure are direct costs to the procedure (service) delivered. The ABC definition of an *indirect cost* is "the cost that is allocated—as opposed to being traced—to an activity or cost object." For example, the costs of supervision may be allocated to an activity on the basis of direct labor hours. Whereas direct costs are traced, indirect costs are allocated. This struc-

**PHYSICIANS GROUP
SERVICE LINE EXAMPLE**

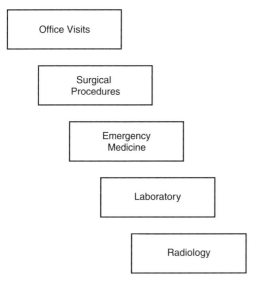

Figure 7–4 Physicians Group Service Lines. *Source:* Copyright © 1997, Resource Group, Ltd., Dallas, Texas.

tural methodology is the heart of activity-based costing. The degree of tracing versus the amount of allocating directly affects the precision of the resulting ABC system. Indirect costs are allocated using cost drivers. The use of cost drivers is another inherent characteristic of activity-based costing. Cost drivers are discussed in the following section.

COST DRIVERS

In an ABC system, the allocation bases that are used for applying costs to services or procedures are called *cost drivers*. Cost drivers include any causal factor that increases the total costs of an activity. Both volume-related allocations bases and other nonvolume-related allocation bases can be used as cost drivers in an ABC system.[6] (The use of a multitude of allocation bases that can be either volume-related or nonvolume-related is a major distinction of the ABC system.)

A cost driver is typically defined in ABC as "any factor that causes a change in the cost of an activity." An activity may—and usually does—have multiple cost drivers associated with it. Each organization must decide (1) how many cost drivers to use and (2) which cost drivers to use. These decisions are structural choices and are of paramount importance to the specificity of the resulting ABC system. Among the factors that affect the choices are the desired accuracy and specificity of reported service and product costs, the diversity of the services delivered, the relative costs of the activities to be traced, and the degree of volume diversity present in the organization.[7]

An illustration of operating room overhead cost drivers is illustrated in Exhibit 7–6. (The case study about this operating room appears in Chapter 15.) There are 14 different types of cost drivers listed for the operating room overhead in this particular hospital.

ABC methodology generally uses cost drivers in a two-stage allocation. First-stage cost drivers are utilized to trace the cost of inputs into cost pools for each activity center.[8] (Direct costs go directly to the activity center through tracing. The indirect costs must be allocated through the use of cost drivers.) An example of first-stage cost drivers is presented in Exhibit 7–7. Note that the hospital overhead costs in Exhibit 7–7 are gathered into four types of related groupings: labor-related, equipment-related, space-related, and service-related.

After indirect costs have arrived at the activity center through use of the first-stage cost drivers, second-stage cost drivers are utilized to provide a measure of the amount of activity resources consumed by the different elements present in that activity center—procedures, patients, and so forth. An example of second-stage cost drivers is presented in Exhibit 7–8. In this example, the activity center is a DRG—or more specifically, the group of procedures that make up a DRG.

Note that the activities are specified for each numbered line item whereas the particular cost driver for that line item is listed at the far right

Exhibit 7–2 Components in a Hospital Cardiac Service Line

Cardiac Pacemaker Services
    DRG 115, Permanent Cardiac Pacemaker with Acute Myocardial Infarction, Heart Failure, and Shock
    DRG 116, Other Permanent Cardiac Pacemaker Implant
    DRG 117, Cardiac Pacemaker Revision Except Device Replacement
    DRG 118, Cardiac Pacemaker Device Replacement
Cardiac Disorders
    DRG 121, Circulatory Disorders with Acute Myocardial Infarction and Cardiovascular Complication, Discharged Alive
    DRG 122, Circulatory Disorders with Acute Myocardial Infarction without Cardiovascular Complication, Discharged Alive
    DRG 123, Circulatory Disorders with Acute Myocardial Infarction, Expired
    DRG 124, Circulatory Disorders Except Acute Myocardial Infarction with Cardiac Catheterization and Complex Diagnosis
    DRG 125, Circulatory Disorders Except Acute Myocardial Infarction with Cardiac Catheterization and Complex Diagnosis
    DRG 126, Acute and Subacute Endocarditis
    DRG 127, Heart Failure and Shock
Chest Pain
    DRG 140, Chest Pain
    DRG 143, Chest Pain

Courtesy of Ryerson Management Associates, Inc., Akron, Ohio.

---

of the exhibit. Number five, administer laboratory tests, for example, has three activities listed while the lab test cost driver is number of tests by type. A multitude of choices are required when selecting cost drivers. It is imperative to follow a uniform methodology.

A STRUCTURAL VIEW OF ANCILLARY COSTING BY PROCEDURE

The framework of the costing spreadsheets illustrated in this example can be utilized, with few modifications, by activity-based costing applications. Most ABC examples emphasize the allocation of indirect costs because this aspect of ABC is the unique portion of its methodology and because it is the portion that is likely to be unfamiliar. Most ABC examples do not carry through to illustrate how the overall costing spreadsheet for a procedure appears in its entirety. The overview is usually missing. The costing spreadsheets in this example provide an overview of structural choices. In particular they reveal the relationship of direct and indirect costs by procedure. They also reveal how both direct and indirect costs can be either fixed or variable and how the components fit together as a whole.

Exhibit 7–3 Components in a Standard Home Care Service Line

Skilled Visit
Aide Visit
Rehab Visit—Physical Therapy
Rehab Visit—Occupational Therapy
Rehab Visit—Speech Therapy
Medical Social Services
Dietician Visit

Source: Copyright © 1997, Resource Group, Ltd., Dallas, Texas.

Exhibit 7–4 Distribution of Fixed and Variable Expenses—Northwest Family Physicians Ltd.

	FY 1995–1996 TOTAL		VARIABLE		FIXED	
Account	Amount	Allocation	Amount	Allocation	Amount	Allocation
Doctors' Salary	$280,500	$7.69	$280,500	$7.69		
Employees' Salary	$162,264	$9.40	$162,264	$9.40		
Payroll Taxes	$30,187	$1.75	$30,187	$1.75		
Rent	$69,384	$4.02			$69,384	$4.02
Supplies	$44,161	$2.56	$44,161	$2.56		
Office Supply						
computer	$8,010	$0.46			$8,010	$0.46
supply	$14,110	$0.82			$14,110	$0.82
postage	$7,644	$0.44	$7,644	$0.44		
print	$4,315	$0.25			$4,315	$0.25
Service						
act	$14,545	$0.84			$14,545	$0.84
computer	$4,217	$0.24			$4,217	$0.24
legal	$1,615	$0.09			$1,615	$0.09
other	$14,884	$0.86			$14,884	$0.86
payroll	$1,966	$0.11			$1,966	$0.11
Malpractice Insurance	$16,479	$0.95			$16,479	$0.95
Gen Insurance	$3,034	$0.18			$3,034	$0.18
Rental Equipment	$1,415	$0.08			$1,415	$0.08
Maintenance	$1,320	$0.08			$1,320	$0.08
Telephone	$11,305	$0.66			$11,305	$0.66
Subscriptions	$1,363	$0.08			$1,363	$0.08
Taxes	$713	$0.04			$713	$0.04
Depreciation	$21,643	$1.25			$21,643	$1.25
Non-shared Expenses	$86,014	$4.98			$86,014	$4.98
Total	$801,088		$524,756		$276,332	

These statements are examples of structural treatment per procedure in an ancillary department.[9] The structural treatment (direct-indirect, then fixed-variable) is laid out for a procedure in a radiology department. It is important to remember that under ABC costs are accumulated for activities that consume resources. These accumulated costs are then applied to procedures on the basis of the activities that are required to deliver the service that is represented by that particular procedure.[10] The spreadsheets for the resulting costs will be structured similarly to the examples presented here. In other words, direct costs will be traced and indirect costs will be allocated. Fixed and variable cost designations will have been made. ABC methodology will be applied to determine appropriate drivers. The spreadsheets will then reveal the layout for direct-indirect and/or fixed-variable.

Five spreadsheets are presented. They include examples of (1) nonrevenue cost centers allocated to revenue-producing cost centers; (2) a typical cost summary; (3) allocation of cost component expenses to the specific procedure; (4) total cost per procedure, by cost component; and (5) average cost per procedure, by cost component. Entries on the spreadsheets are

Exhibit 7–5 Fixed and Variable Cost Distribution—Operating Room

Account	Equipment	Fixed	Variable	Total
SOC SEC			60,517	60,517
PENSION			22,696	22,696
HEALTH INS			18,422	18,422
CHILD CARE			4,564	4,564
DEPR-EQ	87,378			87,378
DEPR-BLDG		41,377		41,377
AMORT-INT		(5,819)		(5,819)
INSURANCE		4,216		4,216
ADMIN		56,966		56,966
MED STAFF		1,722		1,722
COMM REL		40,813		40,813
MAT MGNT		64,573		64,573
HUM RES		19,045		19,045
NURS ADMIN		82,471		82,471
DP		17,815		17,815
FISCAL		17,700		17,700
PT ACCTG			155,356	155,356
ADMITTING			110,254	110,254
TELEPHONE		2,839		2,839
UTILITIES		26,406		26,406
PLANT		77,597		77,597
ENV SVC		32,874		32,874
DIETARY			35,526	35,526
UTILIZATION REVIEW			0	0
MED RECORDS			93,718	93,718
SAFETY		2,016		2,016
QUAL MGMT		10,016		10,016
MED STAFF		9,444		9,444
CQI		4,895		4,895
MED WASTE			2,377	2,377
EE HLTH		569		569
STERILE PROC			78,720	78,720
LAUNDRY			40,693	40,693
TOTAL ALLOCATED	87,378	507,535	622,843	1,217,756
ALL OTHER EXPENSES				1,211,608
TOTAL EXPENSE				2,429,364

deconstructed in order to reveal their structural framework. An example of nonrevenue cost centers allocated to revenue-producing cost centers is found in Table 7–1. This table allocates four indirect cost centers (transporters, receptionists, file room clerks, and managers) to five radiology department cost centers (CCs); CC# 557, 558, 559, 560, and 561. The total to be allocated is in the left-hand column labeled total indirect costs. The four indirect cost centers' total costs will be allocated by use of three allocation bases indicated in the next column. The three bases are volumes (A), direct cost (B), and number of films (C). The statistics for

Exhibit 7–6 Operating Room Overhead Cost Drivers

Account	Driver	Total
SOC SEC	Salary Expense	60,517
PENSION	Salary Expense	22,696
HEALTH INS	FTE Level	18,422
CHILD CARE	FTE Level	4,564
DEPR-EQ	Fixed Asset Subledger	87,378
DEPR-BLDG	Square Feet	41,377
AMORT-INT	Square Feet	(5,819)
INSURANCE	Square Feet	4,216
ADMIN	FTE Level	56,966
MED STAFF	Revenue Level	1,722
COMM REL	Revenue Level	40,813
MAT MGNT	Supply Level	64,573
HUM RES	FTE Level	19,045
NURS ADMIN	FTE Level	82,471
DP	# of Ports	17,815
FISCAL	Area Managers	17,700
PT ACCTG	Revenue Level	155,356
ADMITTING	Revenue Level	110,254
TELEPHONE	# of Extensions	2,839
UTILITIES	Square Feet	26,406
PLANT	Square Feet	77,597
ENV SVC	Time Survey	32,874
DIETARY	# of Meals Served	35,526
MED RECORDS	Time Survey	93,718
SAFETY	Area Managers	2,016
QUAL MGMT	Area Managers	10,016
MED STAFF	Revenue Level	9,444
CQI	Area Managers	4,895
MED WASTE	# of Red Bags	2,377
EE HLTH	FTE Level	569
STERILE PROC	Time Survey	78,720
LAUNDRY	# of Pounds Laundry	40,693
TOTAL ALLOCATED		1,217,756
ALL OTHER EXPENSES		1,211,608
TOTAL EXPENSE		2,429,364

each allocation basis are found at the bottom of the table.

Thus, for CC #557 the allocation basis for transporters is A: volume of 100,000 against 500,000 total, or 20 percent. Thus 20 percent of $550,000, or $110,000, is allocated to CC #557. The allocation basis for receptionists is B: direct cost of $1,000,000 against $6,000,000 total, or one-sixth. The allocation basis B is used twice, once for receptionists and once for managers. For receptionists, one-sixth of the indirect cost of $360,000 is allocated to CC #557, or $60,000. For managers, one-sixth of the indirect cost of $240,000 is allocated to CC #557, or $40,000. The allocation basis for file room clerks is C: number of films 400,000 against a total of 520,000, or approximately 77 percent. Thus 77 percent of $117,000 is allocated to CC

#557, or $90,000 (rounded). The total of the four costs allocated to CC #557 ($110,000 + $60,000 +$90,000 +$40,000) is $300,000.

An example of a typical cost summary is found in Table 7–2. This cost summary is for the radiology cost center (CC) #557. It illustrates the interrelationship of direct and indirect with fixed and variable costs. Reading down vertically, note that CC #557 costs are grouped into three categories, labeled *direct costs*; *intradepartmental overheads*, which consists entirely of indirect labor within the department; and *institutional overheads*, which consists of overhead costs outside the department.

The first column of figures consists of the total amount per general ledger, and is the direct cost charged directly to CC #557, amounting to $1,000,000. The next column is labeled *transfer amount*, and represents amounts allocated to CC

#557. There are two groups of amounts allocated to CC #557. The first grouping is the *intradepartmental overhead*, which is entirely indirect labor within the department. Note that the amounts transferred to CC #557 here are the four amounts that we deconstructed in Table 7–1; they total $300,000. The second grouping is the *institutional overhead*, which has been transferred to CC #557 from outside the department; this group totals $700,000. The two transfer groups ($300,000 + $700,000) total $1,000,000. The third column of figures is labeled *adjusted amount* and is the sum of column 1 and column 2. The proof total under *total expense* for the third column is $2,000,000 ($1,000,000 total column 1 + $1,000,000 total column 2).

Now note the column headings for the remainder of Table 7–2. There is *direct labor, indirect labor, nonchargeable materials, other*

Exhibit 7–7 First-Stage Cost Drivers

	Hospital overhead costs	First-stage cost drivers
Labor-related	Supervision	Number of employees/payroll dollars
	Personnel services	Number of employees
Equipment-related	Insurance on equipment	Value of equipment
	Taxes on equipment	Value of equipment
	Medical equipment depreciation	Value of equipment/equipment hours used
	Medical equipment maintenance	Number of maintenance hours
Space-related	Building rental	Space occupied
	Building insurance	Space occupied
	Power costs	Space occupied, volume occupied
	Building maintenance	Space occupied
Service-related	Central administration*	Number of employees/patient volume
	Central service†	Quantity/value of supplies
	Medical records, and billing/ accounting	Number of documents generated/patient volume
	Cafeteria	Number of meals/number of employees
	Information system	Value of computer equipment/number of programming hours
	Laundry	Weight of laundry washed
	Marketing	Patient volume

*Central administration costs include salaries of the president, vice president, and other central administrative staff.

†Central service costs include supplying, reclaiming, and sterilizing supplies such as gloves, needles, glassware, syringes, linens, surgical packs, and instruments.

Source: Reprinted from S. Udpa, Activity-Based Costing for Hospitals, *Health Care Management Review*, Vol. 21, No. 3, p. 91, © 1996, Aspen Publishers, Inc.

Exhibit 7–8 Second-Stage Cost Drivers

	Activity center	Activities	Cost drivers
1.	Admit patients	Reservation/scheduling, inpatient registration, billing and insurance verification, admission testing, room/bed/medical assignment	Number of patients admitted
2.	Cardiac catheterization	Scheduling, prepare patient, administer medication, cardiac catheterization, film processing, interpret results, patient education	Number of procedures by type*
3.	Administer ECG tests	Scheduling, prepare patient, perform ECG procedure, interpret results	Number of tests
4.	Provide meals/nutritional service	Plan meals, purchase supplies, prepare food, deliver food, clean and sanitize	Number of meals by type[†]
5.	Administer laboratory tests	Obtain specimens, perform tests, report results	Number of tests by type[‡]
6.	Provide nursing care	Transport patients, update medical records, provide patient care, patient education, discharge planning, inservice training	Number of Relative Value Units
7.	Dispense medications	Purchase drugs and medical supplies, maintain records, fill medication orders, maintain inventory	Number of medication orders filled
8.	Provide therapy	Schedule patients, evaluate patients, provide treatment, educate patients, maintain records	Number of hours by type
9.	Perform diagnostic imaging	Schedule patients, perform procedures, develop film, interpret results, transport patient	Number of procedures by type[§]
10.	Operate patients	Schedule patients; order supplies; maintain supplies, instruments, and equipment; provide nursing care, transport patient	Number of hours of surgery by surgical suite type

*Cardiac catheterization procedures include therapeutic procedures such as angioplasty, thrombolysis; and diagnostic procedures such as left heart catheterizations, ventriculography, and coronary angiograms.

[†]Different meal types include special meals, regular meals, and snacks.

[‡]Laboratory tests include pathological tests, chemical tests, blood tests, immunological tests, and nuclear medicine.

[§]Diagnostic imaging procedures include routine radiographs of spine, neck, chest, and extremities; mammography; and fluoroscopic procedures such as gastrointestinal series, barium enema, and gallbladder examinations.

Source: Reprinted from S. Udpa, Activity-Based Costing for Hospitals, *Health Care Management Review*, Vol. 21, No. 3, p. 92, © 1996, Aspen Publishers, Inc.

direct (expense), *equipment*, and *overhead*, plus three totals columns. This format lays out the direct/indirect expense configuration. Under each of the column headings just listed there are subheads. The subheads stipulate either *fixed* or *variable*. Thus, *direct labor* is all variable, whereas *indirect labor* has both fixed and variable subheads. Three individual *nonchargeable materials* subheads (all supplies) are all labeled variable. *Other direct* has both fixed and variable subheads. *Equipment* is only fixed; *over-head* has both fixed and variable subheads. The next two total columns accumulate expenses by either variable or fixed, and the final *total* column captures all expenses for a CC #557 *total* of $2,000,000. The format of the subheads lays out the fixed/variable configuration. Note that fixed/variable is subordinate to direct/indirect in this layout.

There are ten line items listed vertically under direct costs, and their subtotal in the third column, *adjusted amount*, is $1,000,000. We

Table 7–1 Example of Nonrevenue Cost Centers Allocated to Revenue Producing Cost Centers

SUMMARY OF INTRADEPARTMENTAL OVERHEAD

DEPT.—RADIOLOGY–DIAGNOSTIC   CC #557
COST SUMMARY—YEAR TO DATE NOVEMBER 19XX

ALLOCATION OF INDIRECT COSTS TO RADIOLOGY DEPARTMENTS

INDIRECT COST CENTERS	TOTAL INDIRECT COSTS	ALLOCATION BASIS	CC #557 DIAGNOSTIC RADIOLOGY	CC #558 ULTRA-SOUND	CC #559 NUCLEAR MEDICINE	CC #560 CT SCAN	CC #561 RADIATION THERAPY	TOTAL
TRANSPORTERS	550,000	A	110,000	132,000	88,000	154,000	66,000	550,000
RECEPTIONISTS	360,000	B	60,000	36,000	72,000	108,000	84,000	360,000
FILE ROOM CLERKS	117,000	C	90,000	3,375	13,500	4,500	5,625	117,000
MANAGERS	240,000	B	40,000	24,000	48,000	72,000	56,000	240,000
TOTALS	$1,267,000		$300,000	$195,375	$221,500	$338,500	$211,625	$1,267,000
	ALLOCATION BASIS:							
	A. VOLUMES		100,000	120,000	80,000	140,000	60,000	500,000
	B. DIRECT COST		$1,000,000	$600,000	$1,200,000	$1,800,000	$1,400,000	$6,000,000
	C. NUMBER OF FILMS		400,000	15,000	60,000	20,000	25,000	520,000

Source: Adapted from A. Baptist, A General Approach to Costing Procedures in Ancillary Departments, *Topics in Health Care Financing*, p. 36, © 1987, Aspen Publishers, Inc.

will now examine how these expenses are distributed across the direct and indirect column headings and the fixed and variable subheads. Account 4010, *direct labor variable*, is entirely distributed to the direct labor column for techs-variable. Account 4020, *indirect labor variable*, is entirely distributed to the indirect labor column subheaded variable, and account 4030, *indirect labor fixed*, is entirely distributed to the indirect labor column subheaded fixed.

The nonchargeable materials column heading has three types of supply subheads, all of which are labeled variable. Among these, account 4210, *office supplies*, is charged entirely to *general supplies variable*; account 4310, *film, chemicals, and med/surg supplies*, is charged entirely to *film and film supplies variable*; and account 4320, *diagnostic supplies*, is charged entirely to *specific supplies variable*.

The remaining four line items will all be charged to a fixed subhead. Of the four, account 4900, *misc., travel, paper, books*, is charged entirely to the *other direct* column and the fixed subhead. The remaining three line items—account 4700, *equipment service contracts*, account 4740, *equipment repairs and rentals*,

and account 5100, *depreciation expense*—are all charged entirely to the *equipment* column heading and the fixed subhead.

There are four line items listed vertically under intradepartmental overheads, and their subtotal in the third column, *adjusted amount*, is $300,000. These are the items we examined in Table 7–1, so we know how they arrived on Table 7–2. We will now examine how these expenses are distributed across the direct and indirect column headings and the fixed and variable subheads. Note that these four items are all distributed in the *indirect labor* column; two line items rest under the subhead variable and two line items rest under the subhead fixed. Thus, transporters and file room clerks are distributed entirely to the variable subhead of the indirect labor whereas receptionists and manager are distributed entirely to the fixed subhead of the indirect labor column.

There are six line items listed vertically under *institutional overheads*; and their subtotal in the third column, *adjusted amount*, is $700,000. These are the items charged to CC #557 from outside the department. We will now examine how these expenses are distributed across the direct and indirect column headings and the fixed and variable subheads. The first item, *depreciation–buildings*, is distributed entirely to the *overhead* column and to the fixed subhead. The second item, *benefits*, represents the fringe benefits (payroll taxes, health insurance, and so forth) paid for all labor. The $125,000 in fringe benefits is distributed across the three labor columns in amounts proportionate to the amount of labor found in each column. Thus $62,500 is distributed to the *direct labor: techs-variable* column; $37,500 to the *indirect labor: variable* column; and $25,000 to the *indirect labor: fixed* column—for a total of $125,000.

The next line item is *administration and general*. All of the $250,000 in this account is charged to the *overhead* column. Of this total, however, $202,500 is charged to the variable subhead and the remaining $47,500 is charged to the fixed subhead.

The final three columns on the right-hand side of the worksheet sum the variable total, the fixed total, and the grand total, respectively, for a proof total of $2,000,000.

An example of the allocation of total expense of each cost component to the procedure performed is found in Table 7–3. Table 7–3 illustrates how the cost of the CC #557 technicians' labor plus fringe benefits is spread over all types of procedures performed in the department. The technicians' labor plus fringe benefits totals $562,500, as shown at the bottom of the second column from the right side of the table. The same $562,500 can be found on Table 7–2. (It is the total of the fourth numerical column from the left on Table 7–2.)

In the case of Table 7–3, the $562,500 cost will be assigned by a combination of number of procedures and RVUs. One hundred thousand procedures have been performed in this department (see total of third column under *number procedures*). Thus, the overall departmental average cost per procedure is $5.62, or $562,500 total cost divided by 100,000 total procedures.

This average cost of $5.62 does not give us, however, a cost per type of procedure. The cost-

ing methodology used in this table is as follows: The time required to perform each type of procedure is listed in the two columns labeled *RVUs (hours) IP* and *RVUs (hours) OP*. These figures represent time as expressed in decimals for performing each type of procedure for an inpatient (IP) or an outpatient (OP). Thus, the service code 557140, time for a skull routine procedure, is listed at 0.33 hours for an inpatient procedure and 0.33 hours for an outpatient procedure—or 20 minutes apiece (0.33 = one-third of an hour; 60 minutes times 0.33 = 20 minutes).

The *weighted RVUs (hours)–(quantity RVUs)* represents the time spent for the reporting period for each type of procedure. Thus, the total hours for the reporting period for service code 557140, skull routine, is 1,848 hours. This column represents the number of procedures times the RVUs (hours). That is, 5,600 procedures times 0.33 hours or 20 minutes apiece equals 1,848 hours. (The actual cells in a spreadsheet formula would be IP procedures of 2,000 times 0.33 IP hours plus OP procedures of 3,600 times 0.33 OP hours; the previous sentence shortcuts this calculation because the hours in the example are the same for both IP and OP.) Total hours for the reporting period equal 27,182 (the column total). The column total is arrived at by summing the calculated results for each line item in the column.

The *allocated cost* column represents the total direct variable labor of the technicians and totals $562,500. The $562,500 is spread among the procedures pro rata using the weighted RVUs just calculated in the prior column. Thus, service code 557140, skull routine, has an allocated cost of $38,242, which equals 1,848 divided by 27,182 times $562,500 (rounded).

The *cost per procedure* in the final right-hand column is arrived at by dividing the allocated cost by the number of procedures. Thus, service code 557140, skull routine, has a cost per procedure of $6.83, which equals $38,242 divided by 5,600 (rounded).

An example of the total cost per procedure by cost component is found in Table 7–4. Table

Table 7–2 An Example of a Typical Cost Summary

DEPT.—RADIOLOGY–DIAGNOSTIC   CC #557
COST SUMMARY—YEAR TO DATE   NOVEMBER 19XX

ACCT. NUMBER	EXPENSE ACCOUNT DESCRIPTION	TOTAL AMT PER G/L	TRANSFER AMOUNT	ADJUSTED AMOUNT	DIR LABOR TECHS VARIABLE	INDIRECT LABOR VARIABLE	INDIRECT LABOR FIXED
	DIRECT COSTS						
4010	DIRECT LABOR VARIABLE	500,000	0	500,000	500,000		
4020	INDIRECT LABOR VARIABLE	100,000	0	100,000		100,000	
4030	INDIRECT LABOR FIXED	100,000	0	100,000			100,000
4210	OFFICE SUPPLIES	25,000	0	25,000			
4310	FILM, CHEM, MED/SURG SUPPL	90,000	0	90,000			
4320	DIAGNOSTIC EXPENSES	35,000	0	35,000			
4700	EQUIPMENT SERVICE CONTRACTS	50,000	0	50,000			
4740	EQUIP, REPAIRS, & RENTAL	10,000	0	10,000			
4900	MISC, TRAVEL, PAPER, BOOKS	10,000	0	10,000			
5100	DEPRECIATION EXPENSE	80,000	0	80,000			
	SUBTOTAL—DIRECT COSTS	1,000,000	0	1,000,000	500,000	100,000	100,000
	INTRADEPARTMENTAL OVERHEADS						
	TRANSPORTERS	0	110,000	110,000		110,000	
	RECEPTIONISTS	0	60,000	60,000			60,000
	FILE ROOM CLERKS	0	90,000	90,000		90,000	
	MANAGER	0	40,000	40,000			40,000
	SUBTOTAL—INDIRECT COSTS	0	300,000	300,000	0	200,000	100,000
	INSTITUTIONAL OVERHEADS						
	DEPRECIATION–BUILDINGS	0	75,000	75,000			
	BENEFITS	0	125,000	125,000	62,500	37,500	25,000
	ADMIN & GENERAL	0	250,000	250,000			
	SPACE COSTS	0	150,000	150,000			
	TEACHING–I & R	0	0	0			
	OTHER OVERHEAD	0	100,000	100,000			
	SUBTOTAL—ALLOC OVERHEADS	$0	$700,000	$700,000	$62,500	$37,500	$25,000
	TOTAL EXPENSE—DIAGNOSTIC RADIOLOGY	1,000,000	1,000,000	2,000,000	562,500	337,500	225,000
	REVENUE			2,500,000			
	VARIANCE			500,000			

Source: Adapted from A. Baptist, A General Approach to Costing Procedures in Ancillary Departments, *Topics in Health Care Financing*, pp. 38–39, © 1987, Aspen Publishers, Inc.

NONCHARGEABLE MATERIALS			OTHER DIRECT		EQUIP-MENT	OVERHEAD		TOTAL	TOTAL	TOTAL
FILM & FILM SUPPLIES VARIABLE	SPECIFIC SUPPLIES VARIABLE	GENERAL SUPPLIES VARIABLE	VARIABLE	FIXED	FIXED	VARIABLE	FIXED	VARIABLE	FIXED	DEPARTMENT
								500,000	0	500,000
								100,000	0	100,000
								0	100,000	100,000
		25,000						25,000	0	25,000
90,000								90,000	0	90,000
	35,000							35,000	0	35,000
					50,000			0	50,000	50,000
					10,000			0	10,000	10,000
				10,000	·			0	10,000	10,000
					80,000			0	80,000	80,000
90,000	35,000	25,000	0	10,000	140,000	0	0	750,000	250,000	1,000,000
						PERCENT VARIABLE/FIXED		75%	25%	100%
								110,000	0	110,000
								0	60,000	60,000
								90,000	0	90,000
								0	40,000	40,000
0	0	0	0	0	0	0	0	200,000	100,000	300,000
						PERCENT VARIABLE/FIXED		67%	33%	100%
							75,000	0	75,000	75,000
							0	100,000	25,000	125,000
						202,500	47,500	202,500	47,500	250,000
						0	150,000	0	150,000	150,000
						0	0	0	0	0
						0	100,000	0	100,000	100,000
$0	$0	$0	$0	$0	$0	202,500	372,500	302,500	397,500	700,000
						PERCENT VARIABLE/FIXED		43%	57%	100%
90,000	35,000	25,000	0	10,000	140,000	202,500	372,500	1,252,500	747,500	2,000,000
						PERCENT VARIABLE/FIXED		63%	37%	100%

Table 7–3 An Example of the Allocation of Total Expense of Each Cost Component to the Procedure Performed

DEPT.—RADIOLOGY–DIAGNOSTIC   CC #557

| | | NUMBER PROCEDURES | | | RVUs HOURS | | TECHNICIANS WEIGHTED | | |
SERVICE CODE	DESCRIPTION	IN	OUT	TOTAL	IP	OP	RVUs (HRS.) (QTY RVU)	ALLOC COST	COST/ PROC
557140	SKULL ROUTINE	2,000	3,600	5,600	0.33	0.33	1,848	38,242	6.83
557170	CHEST PA & LAT.	30,000	17,500	47,500	0.18	0.18	8,550	176,930	3.72
557210	RIBS UNILATERAL	1,800	1,800	3,600	0.18	0.18	648	13,409	3.72
557230	SPINE CERVICAL ROUT	1,600	4,400	6,000	0.32	0.32	1,920	39,732	6.62
557280	PELVIS	900	600	1,500	0.32	0.32	480	9,933	6.62
557320	LIMB SHOULDER	700	1,900	2,600	0.31	0.31	806	16,679	6.41
557330	LIMB UPPER ARM	250	400	650	0.31	0.31	202	4,170	6.41
557340	LIMB ELBOW	700	1,600	2,300	0.31	0.31	713	14,754	6.41
557350	LIMB FOREARM (RADIUS)	1,200	800	2,000	0.31	0.31	620	12,830	6.41
557360	LIMB WRIST	1,000	2,400	3,400	0.31	0.31	1,054	21,811	6.41
557370	LIMB HAND	1,500	2,300	3,800	0.31	0.31	1,178	24,377	6.41
557380	LIMB FINGER OR THUMB	200	4,800	5,000	0.31	0.31	1,550	32,075	6.41
557390	LIMB FINGER MULTIPLE	100	250	350	0.31	0.31	109	2,245	6.41
557400	LIMB HIP UNILATERAL	1,200	1,000	2,200	0.26	0.26	572	11,837	5.38
557410	LIMB HIP BILATERAL	200	450	650	0.26	0.26	169	3,497	5.38
557420	LIMB FEMUR	500	600	1,100	0.26	0.26	286	5,918	5.38
557430	LIMB KNEE ONLY	750	2,600	3,350	0.26	0.26	871	18,024	5.38
557790	SPECIAL PROCEDURES	1,400	300	1,700	2.00	2.00	3,400	70,358	41.39
	TOTAL ALL OTHER	4,000	2,700	6,700	0.33	0.33	2,207	45,679	6.82
	TOTAL	50,000	50,000	100,000			27,182	$562,500	$5.62

Source: Adapted from A. Baptist, A General Approach to Costing Procedures in Ancillary Departments, *Topics in Health Care Financing*, p. 41, © 1987, Aspen Publishers, Inc.

7–4 displays the service code, description, and number of procedures just as is found in Table 7–3. Table 7–4 also displays all the column headings for labor, materials, and overhead in the same layout as is found in Table 7–2. The cost summary for diagnostic radiology is now set out by procedure. That is, the $562,500 direct labor column for technicians spread to procedures in Table 7–3 ($38,242 for skull routine, etc.) is now transferred in its entirety to the direct labor variable column in Table 7–4 totaling $562,500. All other columns are now also spread to procedures in Table 7–4. Compare the column totals from Table 7–2. The $337,500 and $225,000 for indirect labor (variable and fixed, respectively) now appear as column totals in Table 7–4, with the detail spread to procedures. The same is true for all

other column totals: $90,000, $35,000, and $25,000 for direct nonchargeable materials; $10,000 for other direct; $140,000 for equipment; and $202,500 and $372,500 for overhead. The total costs of $2,000,000 are the same as Table 7–2, with the $2,000,000 now assigned in its entirety to diagnostic radiology procedures. Table 7–4 displays two additional columns at the far right side of the table. These are total revenue and variance (variance being the difference between total cost and revenue). Thus, this table summarizes the cost of each procedure by cost component.

An example of the average cost per procedure by cost component is found in Table 7–5. The final example, Table 7–5, replicates Table 7–4 in all vertical line items and in all horizontal column headings. The purpose of Table 7–5 is to convert the whole dollar amounts on Table 7–4 to the average cost of each procedure by cost component. The averages are calculated, of course, by dividing each cost item by the appropriate number of procedures to arrive at the average. Thus, this table provides supplemental information to support the prior Table 7–4. This set of examples provides an overview of how direct and indirect/fixed and variable interlock and interact in a full spreadsheet cost summary.

CONCLUSION

Structural choices determine your organization's costing framework. The precision and usefulness of an ABC system are substantially affected by the choices between direct costs to be traced and indirect costs to be allocated and by choices among the number and type of drivers to be used for purposes of that allocation. It is imperative to understand and respect ABC structure when making management decisions about ABC implementation.

Table 7–4 An Example of the Total Cost Per Procedure by Cost Component

DEPT.—RADIOLOGY–DIAGNOSTIC   CC #557

SERVICE CODE	DESCRIPTION	NUMBER OF PROCEDURES			DIRECT LABOR INDIRECT LABOR			DIRECT (NON-CHARGE) MATERIAL		
		IN	OUT	TOTAL	VARIABLE ($)	VARIABLE ($)	FIXED ($)	FILM/PHOTO VARIABLE ($)	CONTRAST VARIABLE ($)	GENERAL VARIABLE ($)
557140	SKULL ROUTINE	2,000	3,600	5,600	38,242	18,900	12,600	4,047	0	1,400
557170	CHEST PA & LAT.	30,000	17,500	47,500	176,930	160,313	106,875	36,549	0	11,875
557210	RIBS UNILATERAL	1,800	1,800	3,600	13,409	12,150	8,100	2,770	0	900
557230	SPINE CERVICAL ROUT	1,600	4,400	6,000	39,732	20,250	13,500	4,885	0	1,500
557280	PELVIS	900	600	1,500	9,933	5,063	3,375	1,154	0	375
557320	LIMB SHOULDER	700	1,900	2,600	16,679	8,775	5,850	1,293	0	650
557330	LIMB UPPER ARM	250	400	650	4,170	2,194	1,463	336	0	163
557340	LIMB ELBOW	700	1,600	2,300	14,754	7,763	5,175	831	0	575
557350	LIMB FOREARM (RADIUS)	1,200	800	2,000	12,830	6,750	4,500	506	0	500
557360	LIMB WRIST	1,000	2,400	3,400	21,811	11,475	7,650	1,843	0	850
557370	LIMB HAND	1,500	2,300	3,800	24,377	12,825	8,550	687	0	950
557380	LIMB FINGER OR THUMB	200	4,800	5,000	32,075	16,875	11,250	680	0	1,250
557390	LIMB FINGER MULTIPLE	100	250	350	2,245	1,181	788	63	0	88
557400	LIMB HIP UNILATERAL	1,200	1,000	2,200	11,837	7,425	4,950	1,244	0	550
557410	LIMB HIP BILATERAL	200	450	650	3,497	2,194	1,463	618	0	163
557420	LIMB FEMUR	500	600	1,100	5,918	3,713	2,475	1,045	0	275
557430	LIMB KNEE ONLY	750	2,600	3,350	18,024	11,306	7,538	1,211	0	838
557790	SPECIAL PROCEDURES	1,400	300	1,700	70,358	5,738	3,825	26,559	35,000	425
	TOTAL ALL OTHER	4,000	2,700	6,700	45,679	22,613	15,075	3,681	0	1,675
	TOTAL	50,000	50,000	100,000	562,500	337,500	225,000	90,000	35,000	25,000

Source: Adapted from A. Baptist, A General Approach to Costing Procedures in Ancillary Departments, *Topics in Health Care Financing*, p. 44, © 1987, Aspen Publishers, Inc.

OTHER DIRECT	CAPITAL EQUIP.		OVERHEAD		TOTAL COSTS		TOTAL		
FIXED ($)	FIXED ($)	DIRECT EXPENSE SUBTOTAL ($)	VARIABLE ($)	FIXED ($)	VARIABLE ($)	FIXED ($)	DEPARTMENT ($)	TOTAL REVENUE ($)	VARIANCE ($)
560	6,551	82,299	11,695	21,513	74,284	41,224	115,508	140,000	24,492
4,750	55,565	552,856	78,564	144,518	464,230	311,708	775,938	950,000	174,062
360	4,211	41,901	5,954	10,953	35,184	23,624	58,808	72,000	13,192
600	7,019	87,485	12,432	22,889	78,798	43,988	122,786	210,000	87,214
150	1,755	21,804	3,098	5,700	19,623	10,979	30,602	30,000	(602)
260	3,041	36,549	5,194	9,554	32,591	18,705	51,296	78,000	26,704
65	760	9,150	1,300	2,392	8,162	4,680	12,842	13,000	158
230	2,691	32,019	4,550	8,370	28,473	16,465	44,938	46,000	1,062
200	2,340	27,625	3,926	7,221	24,512	14,261	38,773	30,000	(8,773)
340	3,977	47,946	6,813	12,533	42,792	24,501	67,293	68,000	707
380	4,445	52,214	7,420	13,649	46,258	27,024	73,282	57,000	(16,282)
500	5,849	68,479	9,731	17,901	60,611	35,500	96,111	80,000	(16,111)
35	409	4,809	683	1,257	4,261	2,489	6,750	7,000	250
220	2,574	28,799	4,093	7,528	25,148	15,272	40,420	88,000	47,580
65	750	8,759	1,245	2,290	7,716	4,577	12,293	13,000	707
110	1,287	14,823	2,106	3,875	13,057	7,746	20,804	33,000	12,196
335	3,919	43,170	6,135	11,285	37,513	23,076	60,589	100,500	39,911
170	25,010	167,085	23,744	43,676	161,823	72,682	234,505	255,000	20,495
670	7,838	97,230	13,817	25,416	87,464	48,999	136,463	229,500	93,037
10,000	140,000	1,425,000	202,500	372,500	1,252,500	747,500	2,000,000	2,500,000	500,000

Table 7–5 An Example of the Average Cost Per Procedure by Cost Component

DEPT.—RADIOLOGY–DIAGNOSTIC   CC #557

SERVICE CODE	DESCRIPTION	NUMBER PROCEDURES			DIR LABOR	INDIRECT LABOR		DIRECT (NON-CHARGE) MATERIAL		
		IN	OUT	TOTAL	VARIABLE ($)	VARIABLE ($)	FIXED ($)	FILM/PHOTO VARIABLE ($)	CONTRAST VARIABLE ($)	GENERAL VARIABLE ($)
557140	SKULL ROUTINE	2,000	3,600	5,600	6.83	3.38	2.25	0.72	0.00	0.25
557170	CHEST PA & LAT.	30,000	17,500	47,500	3.72	3.38	2.25	0.77	0.00	0.25
557210	RIBS UNILATERAL	1,800	1,800	3,600	3.72	3.38	2.25	0.77	0.00	0.25
557230	SPINE CERVICAL ROUT	1,600	4,400	6,000	6.62	3.38	2.25	0.81	0.00	0.25
557280	PELVIS	900	600	1,500	6.62	3.38	2.25	0.77	0.00	0.25
557320	LIMB SHOULDER	700	1,900	2,600	6.41	3.38	2.25	0.50	0.00	0.25
557330	LIMB UPPER ARM	250	400	650	6.41	3.38	2.25	0.52	0.00	0.25
557340	LIMB ELBOW	700	1,600	2,300	6.41	3.38	2.25	0.38	0.00	0.25
557350	LIMB FOREARM RADIUS	1,200	800	2,000	6.41	3.38	2.25	0.25	0.00	0.25
557360	LIMB WRIST	1,000	2,400	3,400	6.41	3.38	2.25	0.54	0.00	0.25
557370	LIMB HAND	1,500	2,300	3,800	6.41	3.38	2.25	0.18	0.00	0.25
557380	LIMB FINGER OR THUMB	200	4,800	5,000	6.41	3.38	2.25	0.14	0.00	0.25
557390	LIMB FINGER MULTIPLE	100	250	350	6.41	3.38	2.25	0.18	0.00	0.25
557400	LIMB HIP UNILATERAL	1,200	1,000	2,200	5.38	3.38	2.25	0.57	0.00	0.25
557410	LIMB HIP BILATERAL	200	450	650	5.38	3.38	2.25	0.95	0.00	0.25
557420	LIMB FEMUR	500	600	1,100	5.38	3.38	2.25	0.95	0.00	0.25
557430	LIMB KNEE ONLY	750	2,600	3,350	5.38	3.38	2.25	0.36	0.00	0.25
557790	SPECIAL PROCEDURES	1,400	300	1,700	41.39	3.38	2.25	15.62	20.59	0.25
	TOTAL ALL OTHER	4,000	2,700	6,700	6.82	3.38	2.25	0.55	0.00	0.25
	TOTAL	50,000	50,000	100,000	5.62	3.38	2.25	0.90	0.35	0.25

Source: Adapted from A. Baptist, A General Approach to Coding Procedures in Ancillary Departments, *Topics in Health Care Financing*, p. 44, © 1987, Aspen Publishers, Inc.

OTHER DIRECT	CAPITAL EQUIP.	OVERHEAD		TOTALS					
FIXED ($)	FIXED ($)	VARIABLE ($)	FIXED ($)	VARIABLE ($)	FIXED ($)	TOTAL ($)	AVERAGE PRICE ($)	VARIANCE ($)	% VARIANCE TO PRICE
0.10	1.17	2.09	3.84	13.26	7.36	20.63	25.00	4.37	17.5
0.10	1.17	1.65	3.04	9.77	6.56	16.34	20.00	3.66	18.3
0.10	1.17	1.65	3.04	9.77	6.56	16.34	20.00	3.66	18.3
0.10	1.17	2.07	3.81	13.13	7.33	20.46	35.00	14.54	41.5
0.10	1.17	2.07	3.80	13.08	7.32	20.40	20.00	−0.40	−2.0
0.10	1.17	2.00	3.67	12.53	7.19	19.73	30.00	10.27	34.2
0.10	1.17	2.00	3.68	12.56	7.20	19.75	20.00	0.24	1.2
0.10	1.17	1.98	3.64	12.38	7.16	19.54	20.00	0.48	2.3
0.10	1.17	1.98	3.61	12.26	7.13	19.39	15.00	−4.39	−29.2
0.10	1.17	2.00	3.69	12.59	7.21	19.79	20.00	0.21	1.0
0.10	1.17	1.95	3.59	12.17	7.11	19.28	15.00	−4.28	−28.6
0.10	1.17	1.95	3.58	12.12	7.10	19.22	18.00	−3.22	−20.1
0.10	1.17	1.95	3.59	12.17	7.11	19.28	20.00	0.72	3.6
0.10	1.17	1.86	3.42	11.43	6.94	18.37	40.00	21.63	54.1
0.10	1.17	1.91	3.52	11.87	7.04	18.91	20.00	1.09	5.4
0.10	1.17	1.91	3.52	11.87	7.04	18.91	30.00	11.09	37.0
0.10	1.17	1.83	3.37	11.20	6.89	18.09	30.00	11.91	39.7
0.10	14.71	13.97	25.69	95.19	42.75	137.94	150.00	12.06	8.0
0.10	1.17	2.06	3.79	13.05	7.31	20.37	34.25	13.89	40.5
0.10	1.40	2.03	3.73	12.53	7.48	20.00	25.00	5.00	

NOTES

1. C. Horngren et al., *Cost Accounting: A Managerial Emphasis*, 8th ed. (Englewood Cliffs, NJ: Prentice Hall, 1994), 116.

2. A. Sharpe and G. Jaffe, "Columbia/HCA Plans for More Big Changes in Health-Care World," *The Wall Street Journal*, 28 May 1997, A8.

3. R. Cooper and R.S. Kaplan, "Profit Priorities from Activity-Based Costing," *Harvard Business Review* (May–June 1991): 135.

4. Y. Goldschmidt and A. Gafni, "A Managerial Approach to Allocating Indirect Fixed Costs in Health Care Organizations," *Health Care Management Review* 15, no. 2 (1990): 43.

5. Cooper and Kaplan, "Profit Priorities," 131.

6. Y. Chan, "Improving Hospital Cost Accounting with Activity-Based Costing," *Health Care Management Review* 18, no. 1 (1993): 72.

7. R. Cooper, "The Rise of Activity-Based Costing—Part Three: How Many Cost Drivers Do You Need, and How Do You Select Them?" *Cost Management* (winter 1989): 34.

8. S. Udpa, "Activity-Based Costing for Hospitals," *Health Care Management Review* 21, no. 3 (1996): 86.

9. A. Baptist, "A General Approach to Costing Procedures in Ancillary Departments," *Topics in Health Care Financing* (summer 1987): 36, 38–39, 41, 44–45.

10. Chan, "Improving Hospital Cost Accounting," 73.

## CHAPTER 8

Reporting with Activity-Based Management

Judith J. Baker with John F. Congelli and Charles A. Keil

CHAPTER OUTLINE

INTRODUCTION

Activity-based management (ABM) has two basic components. It identifies the activities performed in an organization and it determines their cost and performance in terms of both time and quality.[1] ABM uses the results of ABC (see Chapter 2).

The purpose of activity-based management is the effective, consistent organization of the activities of the facility or the health system in order to use its available resources in the best possible manner to achieve its objectives.[2] Thus, ABM is specific to the organization. Each facility or health system must make choices about how to use its own available resources in the best possible manner to achieve its own objectives at this point in time. This chapter examines the role of ABM reporting in support of these organizational choices.

AN ABM REPORTING PERSPECTIVE

Activity-based management reporting for a specific organization should reflect that organization's own strategic planning and budgeting processes. It is helpful to view such reporting from a management control systems perspective. Management control systems consist of three phases, all of which are interrelated: preoperational, operational, and postoperational.[3] The preoperational phase consists of strategic planning, programming, and budgeting. The operational phase consists of actual operations and the measurement of results. The postoperational phase consists of performance evaluation, performance reporting, and performance auditing.[4]

Reporting is after the fact—postoperational. But reporting is interactive with operations. Reporting is also interactive with the preoperational phase's strategic planning, programming, and budgeting. Thus, activity-based management reporting for a specific organization, although reflecting the activity-based methodology, must also reflect the framework of that organization's own strategic planning processes.

ABM reporting for health care organizations is a particular challenge because the health care field is so highly complex. Williamson et al., in an introduction to strategic planning, summarize some of the reasons:

- Health care organizations provide services vital to society and to the individual at an immediate, fundamental level, often in nonpostponable situations.
- The work product must be highly individualized, often confounding managerial attempts to improve efficiency.
- The quality of the work performed is difficult to evaluate. Just defining quality here is challenging.[5]

And when ABM reporting also undertakes to profile physicians, the complexity increases once again, because "physicians control the amount and degree of much of the work output in health care organizations, yet they remain largely outside management's control."[6]

MULTIPLE USES AND ORGANIZATIONAL GOALS

The ABC-ABM system provides ultimate flexibility because it creates measurements that are both financial and operational. ABC creates a database of actions, all of which have been costed and therefore can be used in a variety of ways.[7] It is up to the organization's ABM reporting to choose appropriate reporting methods. This multifaceted flexibility is what Kaplan means when he says that it is illogical to refer to ABC as a "general ledger" system.[8] It would be more appropriate to refer to the ABC-ABM system as a service delivery (production) system or an engineering (process) system or even a marketing system. The rationale stems from the integrated nature of ABC-ABM: "It is more accurate to view an ABC model as an economic model of the organization that integrates data from many information systems, financial and operational."[9] Thus, the organization itself must choose what to report from an array of financial and operational options. This choice will reflect the current emphasis of the organization's concerns. One view of these choices is illustrated in Figure 8–1.

The three areas of potential emphasis include the cost of care, care outcomes, and quality of care. Cost of care can be quantified with ABC and can be interpreted and managed with ABM. Care outcomes can be interrelated with ABC through care paths and critical paths (discussed in other chapters). Through this interrelationship, the care outcomes can also be quantified with ABC and interpreted and managed with ABM. Quality of care remains the most qualitative of the three areas, yet it can be interrelated with care outcomes and therefore with cost of care. The organization-specific positioning among these three areas tends to be reflected in the choice of ABM reporting formats.

The following examples include department reporting and physician profiling. The examples reflect Genesee Memorial's outreach to their physicians. Physician profiling interrelates ABC cost of service delivery with care practices, which can in turn reflect care outcomes.

Physician profiling is an effective ABM tool. One practitioner is Dr. Loop of the Cleveland Clinic Foundation, who advocates an activity-based costing system. He writes about how information from the costing system should be

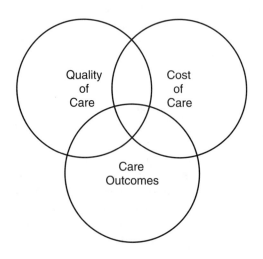

Figure 8–1 Health Care Information and Reporting Framework. *Source:* Copyright © 1997, Timothy D. West.

shared with physicians. He sees physician profiling as moving to an even higher level, where every physician is a utilization manager.[10]

The departmental reporting is laying the groundwork for linkage with care paths. That is, the ABM departmental reporting can serve as the developmental phase for care path linkage. The sequence of resource utilization for patient service delivery defines the treatment process.[11] These sequences can emerge and their framework can become more and more apparent as ABM departmental reporting criteria are adjusted and refined.

The choices in ABM reporting, exemplified by physician profiling or method of departmental reporting, must be coordinated with the current direction of the organization. Gareth Morgan commented that "managers and those involved in organization design always have choice, and . . . effective organization depends on the quality of choice."[12] We can paraphrase Morgan by saying that effective ABM reporting depends on the quality of choice in selecting what to report.

EXAMPLES: FIVE ABM REPORTS IN USE AT GENESEE MEMORIAL HOSPITAL

The following examples are contributed by John F. Congelli, Vice President of Finance, and Charles Keil, Cost Accountant, Genesee Memorial Hospital, Batavia, New York. Five types of reports are presented. The first is a specific procedure performance report that reveals activity accounting detail. The next two reports present types of physician profiling. The final two types of reports present reporting examples of inpatient costs (routine services and ancillary costs) and outpatient costs (ambulatory services).

Table 8–1 presents the performance report: cost details by procedure. Genesee management uses this report to determine a cost detail by procedure within a department for a particular case that can identify costly or efficient treatment patterns and physicians who have costs

per case higher or lower than average. Note the two blank columns for peer group information, which may be used if needed.

Table 8–2 presents the physician profitability report by case type within specific payer. Genesee management uses this report to analyze the total net profit or loss by individual case type within a specific payer. Management can use this data to identify unprofitable case types within specific payers, evaluate third-party proposals, and develop contracting strategies. This profitability report by payer can also be used to analyze profitability by physician for a particular payer or case type.

Table 8–3 presents the physician profitability report by payer within a specific case type. Genesee management uses this report to analyze the total net profit or loss by payer within a specific case type. Management can use this data to identify unprofitable payers within a case type, to evaluate third-party proposals, and to develop contracting strategies.

Exhibit 8–1 presents a key to payer names with contract types. It should be referred to in conjunction with both Table 8–2 and Table 8–3. Genesee management and medical directors use routine services and ancillary costs to assess the utilization and cost effect of individual physicians compared to all other physicians who have discharged an inpatient of that case type. (See Tables 8–4 and 8–5.) This data can identify costly or efficient treatment patterns and physicians who have costs per case higher or lower than average. This cost comparison highlights which physician or clinical service may be positively or negatively affecting overall case cost and profitability. Physicians who are practicing efficient yet effective medicine can indicate a potential "best demonstrates" clinical practice from a cost perspective, which can be conveyed to other physicians through medical staff participation in reviews and meetings.

Genesee management and medical directors use the ambulatory surgery costs to assess the utilization and cost effect of individual physicians compared to all other physicians who have treated an ambulatory surgery patient of

Table 8–1 Performance Report Cost Details by Procedure (Period Ended 12/31/96)

CLINICAL SERVICE: ALL PHYSICIANS
CASE TYPE: 8852 - ICD9 85.21
COST METHOD: ACTUAL

CLINICAL SERVICE
NO. OF CASES   36

CASE TYPE: 8852 LOCAL EXCIS BREAST LESION

COST CENTER BY PROCEDURE	PROCEDURES PER CASE			COST PER CASE			
	CLIN. SVC AVERAGE	PEER GROUP AVERAGE	VARIANCE	ACTUAL COST PER PROC	CLINICAL SERVICE	PEER GROUP	VARIANCE
206 OPERATING ROOM							
11 OR MIN1	0.52		0.52	64.93	33.76		33.76
12 OR MIN2	0.36		0.36	95.60	34.42		34.42
13 OR MAJ3	0.03		0.03	109.30	3.28		3.28
17 OR MIN	15.52		15.52	3.15	48.89		48.89
18 OR MIN	23.70		23.70	3.04	72.05		72.05
115 AMB SUR	1.00		1.00	25.38	25.38		25.38
116 AS EXT	0.27		0.27	58.54	15.81		15.81
300 LIN PACK	0.42		0.42	1.71	0.72		0.72
318 SKIN MAR	0.03		0.03	1.55	0.05		0.05
520 ES GR PK	1.00		1.00	3.51	3.51		3.51
581 ST DRAPE	0.03		0.03	8.15	0.24		0.24
584 D PENCIL	1.00		1.00	7.75	7.75		7.75
704 NS 2000	0.88		0.88	5.43	4.78		4.78
805 CON TUBE	0.09		0.09	0.65	0.06		0.06
827 SUC IN	0.06		0.06	0.65	0.04		0.04
1024 SM DRESS	0.27		0.27	4.53	1.22		1.22
1025 LG DRESS	0.09		0.09	6.99	0.63		0.63
1107 PED SHT	0.76		0.76	7.12	5.41		5.41
1111 LAPAR PK	0.15		0.15	14.75	2.21		2.21
1200 PACK-DIS	0.03		0.03	6.88	0.21		0.21
7001 IV START	0.18		0.18	9.44	1.70		1.70
7002 IV NURSE	0.18		0.18	9.83	1.77		1.77
999999 MSC OR	2.29		2.29	17.26	39.53		39.53
TOTAL COST CENTER	48.86	0.00	48.86		303.40	0.00	303.40
207 PACU							
1 OR RR	0.24		0.24	27.20	6.53		6.53
10 TELEMTR	0.48		0.48	12.60	6.05		6.05
20 PULS OX	0.64		0.64	11.74	7.51		7.51
999991 MSC RR	0.03		0.03	14.18	0.43		0.43
TOTAL COST CENTER	1.39	0.00	1.39		20.52	0.00	20.52

Table 8–2 Physician Profitability Report

PAYER/CASE
PERIOD ENDING 12/31/96

PHYSICIAN NUMBER: ALL
PAYER NUMBER: 028 MEDICARE INPAT PART A
CASE TYPE NUMBER: ALL   NUMBER OF DISCHARGES: 663

	TOTAL	PER CASE
GROSS REVENUE	5,628,739	8,490
NET REVENUE	3,010,802	4,541
VARIABLE COSTS	1,736,936	2,620
GROSS MARGIN	1,273,866	1,921
FIXED COSTS	1,808,745	2,728
NET INCOME	(534,879)	(807)

CASE TYPE	NO. OF DISCH.	REVENUE		COSTS			NET INCOME
		GROSS	NET	VARIABLE	FIXED	TOTAL	
0014 SPEC CV DISORD EX TIA	55	455,630	271,827	134,918	171,432	306,350	(34,523)
PER CASE		8,284	4,942	2,453	3,117	5,570	(628)
0015 TIA & PRECEREB OCC.	44	208,883	130,260	60,937	84,143	145,080	(14,820)
PER CASE		4,747	2,960	1,385	1,912	3,297	(337)
0088 CHRON OBSTRUC PULM DIS	53	416,016	218,863	113,970	125,193	239,163	(20,300)
PER CASE		7,849	4,129	2,150	2,362	4,513	(383)
0089 SIMP PNEU PLEUR>17 W/CC	113	1,016,490	551,560	303,676	324,456	628,132	(76,572)
PER CASE		8,995	4,881	2,687	2,871	5,559	(678)
0127 HEART FAIL & SHOCK	142	938,478	599,256	298,295	340,825	639,120	(39,864)
PER CASE		6,609	4,220	2,101	2,400	4,501	(281)
0132 ATHEROSCLEROSIS W/CC	71	371,545	198,607	123,609	138,278	261,887	(63,280)
PER CASE		5,233	2,797	1,741	1,948	3,689	(891)
0140 ANGINA PECTORIS	45	182,597	117,213	55,199	69,296	124,495	(7,282)
PER CASE		4,058	2,605	1,227	1,540	2,767	(162)
0182 ESOP G & MADD>17 W/CC	48	243,374	153,247	73,766	87,515	161,281	(8,034)
PER CASE		5,070	3,193	1,537	1,823	3,360	(167)
0209 MAJ JNT&LMB RETACH L/E	64	1,503,869	595,293	498,672	376,265	874,937	(279,644)
PER CASE		23,498	9,301	7,792	5,879	13,671	(4,369)
0210 HIP&FMR PRCXMJR JT>17 W/CC	19	252,635	142,346	66,206	81,503	147,709	(5,363)
PER CASE		13,297	7,492	3,485	4,290	7,774	(282)
0494 LAP CHOLECY W/O CC	9	39,222	32,330	7,688	9,839	17,527	14,803
PER CASE		4,358	3,592	854	1,093	1,947	1,645
TOTAL	663	5,628,739	3,010,802	1,736,936	1,808,745	3,545,681	(534,879)

Table 8–3 Physician Profitability Report by Payer (Period Ending 12/31/96)

PHYSICIAN NUMBER: ALL
PAYER NUMBER: ALL
CASE TYPE NUMBER: 0127 HEART FAIL & SHOCK   NUMBER OF DISCHARGE   163

	TOTAL	PER CASE
GROSS REVENUE	1,059,530	6,500
NET REVENUE	696,558	4,273
VARIABLE COSTS	332,338	2,039
GROSS MARGIN	364,220	2,234
FIXED COSTS	383,137	2,351
NET INCOME	(18,917)	(116)

		REVENUE		COSTS			
PAYER	NO. OF DISCH.	GROSS	NET	VARIABLE	FIXED	TOTAL	NET INCOME
OTH BC 1ST PLAN	1	12,479	4,571	3,237	4,091	7,328	(2,757)
PER CASE		12,479	4,571	3,237	4,091	7,328	(2,757)
BL CHOICE	3	21,636	13,714	5,434	6,382	11,826	1,888
PER CASE		7,212	4,571	1,811	2,131	3,942	629
COM PRIME	2	15,546	9,027	4,368	5,099	9,467	(440)
PER CASE		7,773	4,514	2,184	2,550	4,734	(220)
COMMUNITY BL	3	12,069	13,714	3,367	4,871	8,238	5,476
PER CASE		4,023	4,571	1,122	1,624	2,746	1,825
BC SPEC-1ST	1	2,922	4,571	782	939	1,721	2,850
PER CASE		2,922	4,571	782	939	1,721	2,850
CHAMPUS	1	9,455	3,838	2,358	3,025	5,383	(1,545)
PER CASE		9,455	3,838	2,358	3,025	5,383	(1,545)
COMMERCIAL 1ST	4	21,993	22,444	6,545	8,204	14,749	7,695
PER CASE		5,498	5,611	1,636	2,051	3,687	1,924
MEDICAID	3	15,518	13,145	5,214	5,723	10,937	2,208
PER CASE		5,173	4,382	1,738	1,908	3,646	736
MEDICARE I/P PART A	142	938,478	599,256	298,295	340,825	639,120	(38,864)
PER CASE		6,609	4,220	2,101	2,400	4,501	(281)
BC/BS PRIME	1	2,216	4,571	715	851	1,566	3,005
PER CASE		2,216	4,571	715	851	1,566	3,005
DEFAULT PAYER	2	7,218	7,707	2,023	3,117	5,140	2,567
PER CASE		3,609	3,854	1,012	1,559	2,570	1,284
TOTAL	163	1,059,530	696,558	332,338	383,137	715,475	(18,917)

Exhibit 8–1 Genesee Memorial Hospital Payer Names with Contract Types

Payer			Report Column		
Number	Description		Number	Description	
017	CHAMPUS ALL		1	MEDICARE	

Contract Types					
		Y/N			Y/N
1.	Medicare	Y	7.	Case Type Per Diem	Y
2.	Day Outliers	N	8.	Per Diem	Y
3.	Charge Outliers	N	9.	Capitation	Y
4.	Case Type	N	10.	Risk Sharing	N
5.	Charge Related	N	11.	Maximum Allowables	N
6.	Bad Debts	Y	12.	Cost Plus	Y

Payer			Report Column		
Number	Description		Number	Description	
029	PART B MEDICARE		1	MEDICARE	

Contract Types					
		Y/N			Y/N
1.	Medicare	Y	7.	Case Type Per Diem	N
2.	Day Outliers	N	8.	Per Diem	N
3.	Charge Outliers	N	9.	Capitation	N
4.	Case Type	N	10.	Risk Sharing	N
5.	Charge Related	N	11.	Maximum Allowables	N
6.	Bad Debts	Y	12.	Cost Plus	N

Courtesy of Genesee Memorial Hospital, Batavia, New York.

Table 8–4 Report of Inpatient Routine Service and Ancillary Costs

DRG#089 SIMPLE PNEU & PLEUR >17 W/CC
PERIOD ENDING 12/31/96

PHYSICIAN NO.	ALL	A	B	C	D	E
FEDERAL—MEDICARE	113	23	47	5	14	25
NON-FEDERAL	22	0	15	7	0	0
NO OF CASES	135	23	62	12	14	24
HOSPITAL ALOS	10.5	7.2	9.8	14.5	10.7	13.4
FEDERAL ALOS	6.2					
NON-FEDERAL ALOS	8.0					
EXPECTED NET REV—MEDICARE	4,592					

DEPT NAME	AVG COST / ALOS CASE		AVG COST / ALOS CASE		AVG COST / ALOS CASE		AVG COST / ALOS CASE		AVG COST / ALOS CASE		AVG COST / ALOS CASE	
ROOM & BOARD COST:												
MED/SURG	10.0	2,710	6.6	1,802	9.3	2,505	13.0	3,782	10.7	2,712	13.4	3,575
ICCU	0.5	268	0.6	346	0.5	288	1.5	865	0.0	0	0.0	0
TOTAL ROOM	10.5	2,978	7.2	2,148	9.8	2,793	14.5	4,647	10.7	2,712	13.4	3,575
AVG ROOM COST/DAY		284		298		286		320		254		267
ANCILLARY COST:												
OR		24		0		0		0		0		136
PACU		1		0		0		0		0		2
ANESTHESIA		1		0		0		0		0		4
ER		174		345		137		373		0		108
AMBULANCE		52		31		60		152		10		31
LAB		318		260		299		601		352		263
PATH		2		0		0		0		0		6
EKG		61		84		53		84		56		50
CARDIAC REHAB		12		0		0		0		16		60
RADIOLOGY		183		141		140		219		335		227
ECHOCARDIOLOGY		77		58		73		146		97		58
CAT SCAN		41		20		27		0		69		101
PULMONARY		336		349		253		630		283		420
PHYSICAL THERAPY		41		24		48		82		75		0
CENTRAL SUPPLY		54		32		63		43		74		43
PHARMACY		703		524		608		843		692		1,056
TOTAL ANCILLARY		2,080		1,868		1,761		3,173		2,059		2,565
AVG ANCILLARY COST/DAY		198		259		181		219		193		191
TOTAL COST PER CASE		5,058		4,016		4,554		7,820		4,771		6,140
NET INCOME/(LOSS) PER CASE		(466)		576		38		(3,228)		(179)		(1,548)
AVG COST/DAY		482		558		467		539		447		458

Table 8–5 Report of Inpatient Routine Service and Ancillary Costs

DRG#494 LAP CHOLECY W/O CDE W/O CC
PERIOD ENDING 12/31/96

PHYSICIAN NO.	ALL	A	B	C	D	E
FEDERAL—MEDICARE	9	2	2	1	2	2
NON-FEDERAL	82	12	9	6	16	39
NO OF CASES	91	14	11	7	18	41
HOSPITAL ALOS	1.5	3.6	1.3	1.0	1.0	1.2
FEDERAL ALOS	1.8					
NON-FEDERAL ALOS	2.0					
EXPECTED NET REVENUE	2,754					

DEPT NAME	AVG COST / ALOS CASE		AVG COST / ALOS CASE		AVG COST / ALOS CASE		AVG COST / ALOS CASE		AVG COST / ALOS CASE		AVG COST/ ALOS CASE	
ROOM & BOARD COST:												
MED/SURG	1.4	440	3.3	985	1.3	388	1.0	310	1.0	310	1.2	347
ICCU	0.1	26	0.3	173	0.0	0	0.0	0	0.0	0	0.0	0
TOTAL ROOM	1.5	466	3.6	1,158	1.3	388	1.0	310	1.0	310	1.2	347
AVG ROOM COST/DAY		311		322		310		310		310		297
ANCILLARY COST:												
OR		1,010		959		981		1,200		924		1,035
PACU		51		52		52		52		52		49
ANESTHESIA		34		33		34		37		37		33
ER		8		0		0		0		0		17
LAB		26		28		32		15		46		16
PATH		30		30		31		30		30		30
EKG		3		21		0		0		0		0
RADIOLOGY		8		24		23		0		0		3
CENTRAL SUPPLY		20		28		14		11		36		14
PHARMACY		55		69		52		45		45		57
TOTAL ANCILLARY		1,245		1,244		1,219		1,390		1,170		1,254
AVG ANCILLARY COST/DAY		830		346		975		1,390		1,170		1,072
TOTAL COST PER CASE		1,711		2,402		1,607		1,700		1,480		1,601
NET INCOME/(LOSS) PER CASE		1,043		352		1,147		1,054		1,274		1,153
AVG COST/DAY		1,141		667		1,286		1,700		1,480		1,368

Table 8–6 Report of Outpatient Ambulatory Surgery Costs

AMBULATORY SURGERY
ICD-9 85.21 LOCAL EXCIS BREAST LESION
PERIOD ENDING 12/31/96

PHYSICIAN NO.	ALL	A	B	C	D
NO OF CASES	36	3	5	9	19
OR MINUTES/CASE	39	40	45	33	40
EXPECTED NET REVENUE	538				

DEPT NAME	AVG COST PER CASE	AVG COST PER CASE	AVG COST PER CASE	AVG COST PER CASE	AVG COST PER CASE
OR	304	327	387	313	274
PACU	20	12	42	32	10
ANESTHESIA	13	11	20	11	11
LAB	37	0	38	56	34
PATH	33	45	40	31	30
RADIOLOGY	30	0	50	29	32
CENTRAL SUPPLY	1	0	3	0	0
PHARMACY	7	7	5	5	9
TOTAL COST PER CASE	445	402	585	477	400
NET INCOME/(LOSS) PER CASE	93	136	(47)	61	138

Table 8–7 Report of Outpatient Ambulatory Surgery Costs

AMBULATORY SURGERY
ICD-9 04.43 CARPAL TUNNEL RELEASE
PERIOD ENDING 12/31/96

PHYSICIAN NO.	ALL	A	B	C	D	E	F
NO OF CASES	110	10	2	2	32	29	35
OR MINUTES/CASE	38	43	35	25	32	30	51
EXPECTED NET REVENUE	554						

DEPT NAME	AVG COST PER CASE	AVG COST PER CASE	AVG COST PER CASE	AVG COST PER CASE	AVG COST PER CASE	AVG COST PER CASE	AVG COST PER CASE
OR	370	366	424	586	334	253	490
PACU	26	33	65	12	19	9	45
ANESTHESIA	14	15	20	11	13	11	18
PATH	5	5	0	0	3	0	10
EKG	1	0	42	0	0	0	2
CENTRAL SUPPLY	3	7	8	0	0	0	8
PHARMACY	6	4	6	2	6	2	11
TOTAL COST PER CASE	425	430	565	611	375	275	584
NET INCOME/(LOSS) PER CASE	129	124	(11)	(57)	179	279	(30)

that case type. (See Tables 8–6 and 8–7.) This data can identify costly or efficient treatment patterns and physicians who have costs per case higher or lower than average. This cost comparison highlights which physician or clinical service may be positively or negatively affecting overall case cost and profitability. Physicians practicing efficient yet effective medicine can indicate a potential "best demonstrates" clinical practice from a cost perspective, which can be conveyed to other physicians through medical staff participation in reviews and meetings.

CONCLUSION

In conclusion, we recognize that ABC provides a mix-and-match menu of costs and their financial and operational interrelationships. It is the responsibility of management to see that ABM reporting illustrates what the organization most wants to measure and manage.

As Peter Drucker said, "Reports...should focus only on the performance needed to achieve results in the key areas. To 'control' everything is to control nothing. And to attempt to control the irrelevant always misdirects."[13] This is a lesson we in ABC-ABM should take to heart.

NOTES

1. J. Brimson and J. Antos, *Activity-Based Management for Service Industries, Government Entities, and Nonprofit Organizations* (New York: John Wiley & Sons, 1994), 15.

2. J. Brimson, *Activity Accounting: An Activity-Based Costing Approach* (New York: John Wiley & Sons, 1991), 78.

3. M. Ziebell and D. DeCoster, *Management Control Systems in Nonprofit Organizations* (New York: Harcourt Brace Jovanovich, 1991), 45.

4. Ibid., 46.

5. S. Williamson et al., *Fundamentals of Strategic Planning for Healthcare Organizations* (Binghamton, NY: Haworth Press, 1997), 4.

6. Ibid., 4.

7. C.J. McNair, "Interdependence and Control: Traditional vs. Activity-Based Responsibility Accounting," *Cost Management* (summer 1990): 22.

8. R.S. Kaplan, "In Defense of Activity-Based Cost Management," *Management Accounting* (November 1992): 58.

9. Ibid., 58.

10. F. Loop, "You Are in Charge of Cost," *Annals of Thoracic Surgery* 60 (1995): 1510.

11. J.H. Evans III et al., "Cost Reduction and Process Reengineering in Hospitals," *Journal of Cost Management* (May–June 1997): 20.

12. G. Morgan, *Images of Organization* (Newbury Park, CA: Sage Publications, 1986), 73.

13. P.F. Drucker, *The Practice of Management* (New York: Harper & Row, 1954), 135.

## CHAPTER 9

Implementing a Resource Consumption-Based Income Statement for Health Care Organizations

Timothy D. West

CHAPTER OUTLINE

Introduction
Organizational Readiness for Change
The ABC Implementation Process
Conclusion

INTRODUCTION

What decisions does your organization's income statement enable you to make? This question was posed to a group of health care professionals during a recent conference. Attendees involved in administration[1] indicated that the information that is presented in their income statements assisted them in making decisions about cash flow, cost reduction, and asset deployment. Clinicians at the conference answered the same question by saying, "We receive income statements, but they do not affect how we do our jobs. They are irrelevant in terms of what we do on a day-to-day basis." This dialogue reflects the typical barriers that exist between "administrative people" and "clinical people" when they are trying to discuss costs and resource utilization. With the increasing importance of managed care as part of the health care landscape, organizations that fail to recognize this communication barrier are at risk in terms of how they manage the cost,

quality, and outcomes of care associated with capitated contracts.

This chapter demonstrates how to implement a resource consumption-based income statement. An income statement of this type provides a common ground for administrative and clinical people to discuss issues involving cost, quality, and outcomes. An activity-based costing (ABC) approach provides the information framework for such an income statement. Implementing ABC successfully, however, depends on (1) assessing readiness for change, and (2) developing a systematic and collaborative implementation process. The first half of this chapter describes how to assess your organization's change readiness. The second half presents a four-step process for developing a resource consumption-based income statement.

ORGANIZATIONAL READINESS FOR CHANGE

ABC systems represent an administrative innovation that has the potential to have an impact on, or change, a variety of factors, both behavioral (e.g., performance measurement) and organizational (e.g., resource allocation).[2] Accordingly, managers who propose the implementation of an ABC system should anticipate resistance to the proposal. Resistance to change stems from the underlying idea that change creates uncertainty and may be harmful. "Resisters to change" may attempt to protect themselves, both rationally and emotionally, from the perceived risks associated with an innovation that threatens organizational norms.

Understanding an organization's readiness for change and managing the subsequent change process are crucial to implementing ABC successfully.[3] Researchers in general have recognized the importance of change and transformational leadership.[4] Unfortunately, accounting researchers have not examined very thoroughly the role that transformational management plays in adopting and internalizing an administrative innovation such as ABC. Shields identified five factors that affect ABC implementation success in manufacturing: (1) organizational support and coherence, (2) training, (3) ABC system independence, (4) software, and (5) the accounting department's ownership of the ABC system.[5] None of these factors dealt with an organization's readiness for change. Furthermore, these factors explained only 50 percent of why ABC implementation efforts

succeed. Perhaps a better understanding of change readiness can provide additional insight into why administrative innovations like ABC may ultimately prove successful.

As in most organizations, more than one constituency is affected by any proposed administrative innovation. In health care, however, these constituencies can be classified generally as clinical and administrative. These two voices within an organization may perceive change from very different perspectives. Accordingly, their readiness for change may develop at different paces. An organization's readiness, therefore, may depend on how adaptable both constituencies are in general, and how accepting they are of the new idea, or change, that is being proposed.

Figure 9–1 presents a change readiness matrix that considers both the clinical and administrative constituencies. Change readiness of each constituency is depicted on the axes and can be assessed as high or low for each group. Once each group's readiness has been assessed, the current strategic focus of the organization can be classified as either: (1) existence-focused, (2) cost-focused, (3) quality-focused,

Figure 9–1 Change Readiness Matrix for Health Care Organizations. *Source:* Copyright © 1997, Timothy D. West.

or (4) outcomes-focused. By understanding where your organization fits in the matrix, you can design a plan to enhance your overall change readiness. Only by developing innovation adaptability among both the clinical and administrative voices of the organization can change become the norm rather than the exception to how things are usually done.

Figure 9–1 characterizes health care organizations as falling within one of the quadrants in a four-cell matrix. Before assessing where your organization falls within the matrix, however, you must decide how to measure the high and low dimensions of change readiness that are depicted on each axis. The flexibility of the matrix to accommodate alternative measures of change readiness makes it robust and generalizable to a wide range of organizations and theories of change.

Existence-focused organizations demonstrate a low readiness for change on both the clinical and administrative dimensions. Moreover, managers frequently believe that they lack the necessary resources for innovations. Two examples of this type of organization come to mind. First, some small rural hospitals with low occupancy levels have been unable to attract and retain physicians. They cannot justify the cost of the additional administrative staff necessary to pursue change initiatives. Second, some inner-city hospitals have aging facilities and limited resources. They lack the flexibility necessary to shift services from underutilized traditional points of service (e.g., inpatient referral) to overutilized points of service (e.g., emergency rooms and trauma centers). Their primary objective is self-preservation.

Quality-focused organizations reflect an environment that is driven by the clinical staff. In these organizations, clinicians adopt many of the principles associated with total quality management (TQM) and pursue a variety of quality initiatives. Unfortunately, the clinical managers who are responsible for these initiatives frequently act independently. Therefore, any improvements may not be shared across the organization. On the administrative side, change readiness is low. Their focus is on budgeting and financial reporting. In quality-focused organizations, administrators often challenge the value of improved clinical efficiency because they see no direct connection between process improvement and cost reduction.

Clinicians in this type of organization usually assume that improved quality can enhance patient satisfaction and ultimately reduce operating costs. Unfortunately, this may not be true or may not be in the best economic interest of the facility as a whole. Consider an emergency room where patient satisfaction is frequently determined by patient wait time.[6] Improved quality might require additional resources to reduce wait time; however, that increase in resources (cost) may not affect the ultimate outcome of patient care. If a patient comes to the emergency room with a sprained ankle, for example, how long that patient waits before being seen will affect satisfaction. The patient's recovery (treatment outcome) remains unaffected by emergency room wait time. Incurring more cost (e.g., physicians and nurses) to reduce waiting time may not improve the clinical outcome and ultimately may not be in the best interest of the organization.

Cost-focused organizations emphasize the importance of cost reductions and cost containment. Too often, they are driven by administrative or financial decisions without adequate consideration of the clinical implications. An organization of this type faces perhaps the greatest challenge because the emphasis on cost containment drives a wedge between the two voices of the organization. The clinical voices in the organization argue that lower cost will result in reduced quality of care. Alternatively, the administrative voices argue that reduced cost enables competitive contract bidding and long-term financial survival.

Consider the continuing emphasis being placed on cost containment initiatives such as nursing staff realignments or reductions in length of stay. Administrative directives of this type often occur without first-hand understanding of how these changes affect clinical operations. Fewer nurses and shorter lengths of stay may improve short-term profitability. However, they may fail to recognize the long-term consequences (e.g., cost) of subsequent readmission or potential malpractice liability. A cost-focused organization also may cause clinicians to resist innovations in treatment processes because they are afraid of losing additional resources.

Outcomes-focused organizations have succeeded in moving both their clinical and administrative staffs toward change readiness. These organizations have created a partnership between the clinical and administrative voices. As partners, both professional groups focus on cost management (not cost reduction) and outcome improvements (not independent quality initiatives). Clinical improvements are linked to costs (improved efficiency) but the focus is on long-term patient care (improved care effectiveness).

A hospital that successfully implements clinical pathways represents an example of an outcomes-focused organization. Development of a standardized clinical pathway for cardiac bypass surgery requires coordinated input from both surgeons and administrators. The surgeons must build consensus around the clinical procedures that should be followed to achieve the desired outcomes. Administrators should participate by demonstrating how reductions in process variation have an impact on both short-run (e.g., surgical supplies) and long-run (e.g., readmission for complications) costs. By focusing on high-quality outcomes, both groups can find a common ground for communication.

THE ABC IMPLEMENTATION PROCESS

This section of the chapter describes a four-stage implementation process for an ABC system that supports a resource consumption-based income statement. The process includes

1. identifying key resources
2. identifying activity drivers
3. relating key resources to activity drivers
4. developing a resource consumption-based income statement

Originally, ABC systems were described as a two-stage cost assignment process. In the first stage, costs were identified with cost pools (resources). The second stage used activity drivers to link resource consumption with individual products. This manufacturing-based model, however, underestimates the complexity of cost assignment in health care.

Figure 9–2 should help to clarify the assignment of costs in health care. As indicated previously, the implementation of ABC in health care can be viewed as a four-stage costing process. Stage one involves the selection of key resources (cost pools). For example, nursing staff, medical supplies, and physical facilities should not be in the same cost pool. Each is a key resource. Stage two links resources (costs) with clinical procedures by identifying a measure (activity driver) of how each key resource is consumed by procedures. Each clinical procedure may consume several key resources (e.g., nursing evaluations of patients require nursing time, medical supplies, and facilities). Stage three of the costing process develops procedural ties to clinical pathways. Pathways represent treatment processes that require several individual procedures (i.e., a recipe for care or a bill of procedures). The cost of a process (or pathway) represents the sum of the costs of the individual procedures. Finally, stage four recognizes that patient care is a function of proper diagnosis and treatment for individual patients. Similar to the costing of processes or pathways, the cost of patient care is the total of the individual processes provided for the individual patient. As shown in Figure 9–2, the linkage between stage one and stage two is the resource consumption for each procedure (i.e., activity drivers). The link between stage two and stage three is the specification of efficient clinical pathways that clinicians utilize. The final link between stage three and stage four is the effectiveness of the clinical pathways in delivering the expected patient care outcome.

Health care organizations, and hospitals in particular, are some of the most complex organizations in the world. The purpose of these

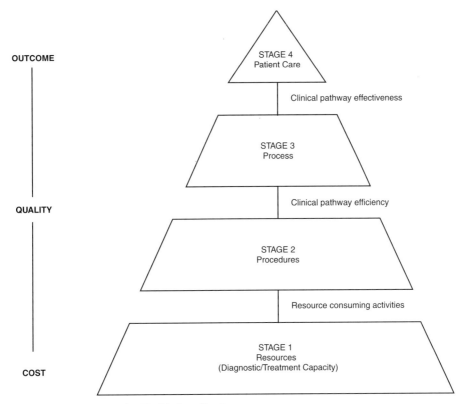

Figure 9–2 Four-Stage Process for Health Care Costing

organizations is to bring together, or identify, the resources necessary to deliver the highest quality patient care. These resources are massive. However, each year an organization can focus on only a limited number of key resources associated with select strategic initiatives. Key strategic resources are: (1) resources that provide the facility with unique expertise (e.g., cardiac care center, oncology, or pediatric intensive care unit), or (2) resources that potentially could constrain the facility's delivery of care (e.g., emergency room capacity or obsolete technology).

In the first case, unique clinical expertise can provide the facility with a competitive advantage and set it apart from other health care organizations in the marketplace. In order to attract more patients and physicians, admin-

istrators would focus on making resources increasingly available to support that expertise. In the second case, certain resources may be outdated or in short supply (e.g., specialty physicians or nurses with required levels of expertise). This inadequacy could place a facility at a competitive disadvantage because it cannot offer some essential services. In these cases, administrators must consider whether to increase available resources in this key area or, alternatively, eliminate the delivery of services that depend on these constrained resources. In either situation, organizational strategy is shaped by the type of care being delivered and the availability of key resources necessary to deliver that care.

Key resources can be classified as patient care or administrative services. These classifi-

Table 9–1 Identification of Key Resources and Corresponding Activity Drivers

Key Resources	Total Cost Pool	% of Net Patient Fees	Proposed Activity Drivers
Patient care resources:			
Nursing staff	$38,000,000	38.00%	Acuity adjusted patient days
Medical supplies	10,500,000	10.50%	Directly traceable
Equipment	7,300,000	7.30%	Number of procedures requested
Imaging	7,000,000	7.00%	Number of X-rays
Facilities	6,200,000	6.20%	Patient days
Pharmacy	5,000,000	5.00%	Directly traceable
Laboratory	4,200,000	4.20%	Relative value of lab tests
Staff physicians	2,500,000	2.50%	ICD-9 based RVU scale
Other patient care resources	5,800,000	5.80%	Not applicable
Total patient care resources	$86,500,000	86.50%	
Administrative resources:			
Medical records/information systems	$2,800,000	2.80%	Acuity adjusted patient days
Accounting/billing/purchasing	2,500,000	2.50%	Number of patients
Human resources/education	1,200,000	1.20%	Number of employees
Other administrative resources	3,200,000	3.20%	Not applicable
Total administrative resources	$9,700,000	9.70%	

cations serve as a reminder that an organization's competitive advantage depends on sufficient clinical and administrative expertise. For example, Table 9–1 identifies eight key patient care resources and four key administrative resources for a 250-bed tertiary hospital. Additionally, the costs associated with each resource are accumulated in cost pools in an effort to determine the relative significance of each resource. Nursing staff represents the largest single cost pool. Staff physicians are a key resource also, not because of the relative costs associated with these doctors, but because of the referral network these physicians must develop and maintain for the hospital to thrive.

Finally, not all costs can be identified with key resources. The benefit of an ABC system and its resource consumption-based income statement does not depend on matching each cost with a unique resource or cost pool. Accordingly, a category of other resources is included in both the patient care and administrative resource categories. Additional general ledger detail should exist to support the expenses in these categories. The expenses, however, can be monitored by looking at trends and exceptions.

The inevitable question is how many resources should be identified as "key." Is six enough? Is twenty too many? The answer depends on two issues: (1) experience of administrative and clinical staff at linking care delivery with resource consumption, and (2) capability and capacity of the facility's information system to develop, deliver, and maintain information in this format. Initially, the identification of five to fifteen key resources or cost pools should be sufficient. With more than fifteen, your system may be too cumbersome and system users may become overloaded with information. With fewer than five, the new system may lack sufficient detail to assist clinicians in their understanding of cost at the procedure level. Regardless of how many key resources your system contains, identifying them will always require: (1) negotiation between clinicians and administration, (2) consensus among the groups, and (3) acceptance of the role that estimation plays in the costing process.

The key resources consumed in each clinical procedure are measured by identifying the reason why each resource is required. These measures are referred to as activity drivers. For example, imaging/X-ray represents a key resource in many hospitals. This resource exists to perform X-rays and process films. One choice of an activity driver would be the number of films processed. Alternatively, an acuity adjusted measure for the number of X-ray films could also be used as an activity driver because some imaging/X-ray procedures are more difficult (costly) than others. In either case, the objective is to identify the cost of the key resource with an activity that represents how that resource is used in clinical or administrative operations.

Implementation of an ABC system requires the specification of resource (cost) categories and the selection of activity drivers. Costing accuracy, however, depends on trade-offs among four potential sources of error in the design of new cost systems: (1) specification error (resource cost pool/activity driver proportionality), (2) aggregation error (cost pool homogeneity), (3) errors in cost pool measurement, and (4) errors in product specific activity driver measurement.[7] Although each of the four sources of error can affect the ultimate accuracy of the costing process, the cost pool–activity driver proportionality assumption is critical to the development of a resource consumption-based income statement.

The problem of specification error occurs when a resource cost pool does not change proportionally with its corresponding activity driver. Specification error represents a potentially significant problem for each key resource cost pool that is specified in the ABC system.

Proportionality means that as the activity drivers increase or decrease, resource costs will change accordingly. By assuming cost pool–activity driver proportionality, system designers could compute individual cost pool rates for each key resource as follows:

> Cost pool rate = Estimated key resource cost ÷ Estimated number of activities

Acceptance of the proportionality assumption implies that resource costs vary with their activity drivers. In terms of cost behavior, therefore, the cost pool rate represents the marginal cost of performing one more activity. The calculation of procedure-level costs when cost pool rates are computed under the above assumption implies the following cost equation:

> Procedure cost = Σ (Cost per activity $\times$ Activities per procedure)

In this traditional calculation of cost pool rates, no allowance is made for those resource costs that might be fixed relative to a cost pool's activity driver. Accordingly, no fixed cost component exists in the cost equation. In health care, however, a significant percentage of a facility's costs are fixed regardless of the measure of volume selected as an activity driver. For example, if an organization specified imaging/X-ray as a key resource, certain costs (e.g., depreciation) will remain unchanged regardless of the number of X-rays performed. These fixed costs are incurred whether any procedures are run on the equipment or not. They represent the cost of providing a certain level of diagnostic-treatment capacity within the facility. In fee-for-service environments, managers encourage clinicians to increase their utilization of fixed resources, thereby increasing the number of treatments and the level of reimbursement without incurring significant additional costs. Under capitation, however, managers have an incentive to reduce volume because decreased resource utilization results in lower total costs. Therefore, a facility's income statement that separates each key resource into variable and

Table 9–2 Example Regression Analysis of Cost Pool–Activity Driver Relationships

	Cost of Nursing Staff	Acuity Adjusted Patient Days
January	$3,331,000	8,400
February	$3,217,000	7,200
March	$3,180,000	6,800
April	$3,141,000	6,400
May	$3,199,000	6,700
June	$3,198,000	7,000
July	$3,028,000	5,200
August	$3,103,000	6,000
September	$3,113,000	6,100
October	$3,103,000	6,000
November	$3,132,000	6,300
December	$3,255,000	7,900
	$38,000,000	80,000

Variable cost per patient day = $90.77 (or ~$91.00)

Fixed cost per month = $2,561,520

$r^2 = 0.98$

fixed costs could enable managers to make better decisions concerning how available resources are consumed.

Simple regression methods frequently are used to test the proportionality assumption. Using statistical packages[8] or spreadsheet software,[9] managers can analyze the proportionality of their resource cost pool–activity driver relationships. As shown in Table 9–2, twelve months of cost pool and activity driver data can provide a basis for testing this relationship. The monthly cost data represent the dependent variable (Y) and corresponding activity driver data represent the independent (or explanatory) variable (X). A regression analysis can be performed by entering the monthly data into a spreadsheet table, and selecting the regression command option from the package's tool bar.

In Table 9–2, for example, the monthly cost of nursing is compared to the monthly acuity adjusted patient volume. Applying regression techniques to these data allows a manager to investigate the applicability of the following cost behaviors:

Resource cost = Fixed costs + Variable cost per activity (Number of activities)

If a cost pool is perfectly proportional, fixed costs are zero, variable cost per activity is constant, and total resource cost is directly correlated with the number of activities. In terms of nursing, however, some costs are fixed relative to activities (e.g., minimum staffing for ICU) and some are variable (e.g., on-call nursing). The results of the regression analysis[10] indicate that monthly costs associated with nursing staff can be depicted by the following cost equation:

Nurse staffing cost = $2,561,520 + $91 (Acuity adjusted patient days)

Monthly fixed costs of $2,561,520 (or approximately $30.4 million) represent minimum staffing requirements. The variable cost of nurse staffing is $91 for each acuity adjusted patient day.

By applying regression analysis to each cost pool–activity driver relationship, managers can also obtain information about the strength of the relationship that is depicted by the cost equation. The regression results obtained from either statistical or spreadsheet software also compute a coefficient of determination (r^2). The coefficient indicates how much of the variation in cost is explained by the activity driver. For example, the nursing staff regression analysis resulted in an $r^2 = 0.98$. This result indicates that 98 percent of the monthly nurse staffing costs are explained by the cost equation specified in the analysis.[11]

Typically, an organization's control and performance measurement systems include the income statement as a key component. Unfortunately, ABC systems frequently fall short of managers' expectations because the system, and specifically the resulting income statement, are not integrated with a company's control systems.[12] Cooper and Kaplan first addressed this issue by developing a resource consumption-based income statement in support of ABC.[13] They recognized that, in reality, cost behaviors within each cost pool may be either variable or fixed and seldom are perfectly variable (such as specification error) as is often assumed by designers of ABC systems. Specification error is a continuing inadequacy in many ABC system designs. Instead of discarding ABC results because of this error, however, the results can be used to develop a resource consumption-based income statement.

With an ABC income statement perspective, variable resource costs represent marginal costs whereas fixed resource costs represent diagnostic-treatment capacity available for patients whether or not they use the facility. Traditionally, income statements rarely focus users on capacity management issues involving strategic resources.[14] In contrast, a resource consumption-based income statement offers users the opportunity to monitor cost changes at both the variable (marginal) level and the fixed (capacity) level. An example of this type of income statement is presented in the next sections of this chapter (see Tables 9–3, 9–4, and 9–5). Managers, both clinical and administrative, can use an ABC type of income statement for additional analyses (e.g., breakeven), and perhaps more importantly for bidding on managed care contracts.

As shown in Table 9–3, the key resources for Example Hospital initially have been classified as either patient care or administrative resources. Eight patient care and three administrative key resource categories are identified (see Tables 9–4 and 9–5). In both patient care and administrative categories, the costs that are incurred for nonkey resources are grouped together as other unanalyzed costs. These eleven key resources provide a basis for developing more accurate cost information without overloading the information user. Furthermore, as an organization becomes more accustomed to managing along these resource lines, additional resources may be isolated from the unanalyzed category. Subsequently, therefore, the income statement may reflect still greater resource consumption specificity.

The eleven key resources are analyzed individually using regression to identify the variable and fixed components of each. The supporting income statement schedules can be used to identify and investigate trends that may appear for both variable (Table 9–4) and fixed (Table 9–5) components of each resource. Additional analysis is performed on the fixed resource portion of each resource. As shown in Table 9–4, an attempt was made to identify the practical capacity associated with each resource. Practical capacity is used in this anal-

---

Table 9–3 Resource Consumption-Based Income Statement

	Used	Unused	
Net patient fees (250 beds, 50% occupancy)			$100,000,000
Variable resources (See Table 9–4):			
Patient care resources			34,945,000
Administrative resources			4,195,000
Resource contribution margin			60,860,000
Resource contribution margin %			60.86%
	Capacity		
Fixed resources (See Table 9–5):	*Used*	*Unused*	
Patient care resources	39,455,750	12,099,250	51,555,000
Administrative resources	4,681,250	823,750	5,505,000
Total fixed resources	44,137,000	12,923,000	57,060,000
Net operating income			$3,800,000
Net operating margin			3.80%

Table 9–4 Schedule of Variable Resources

		Variable resources as a % of	
		Total variable resources	Total net patient fees
Variable patient care resources:			
Medical supplies	$9,450,000	27.04%	9.45%
Nursing staff	7,600,000	21.75%	7.60%
Pharmacy	4,250,000	12.16%	4.25%
Laboratory	3,360,000	9.62%	3.36%
Imaging	2,100,000	6.01%	2.10%
Staff physicians	1,250,000	3.58%	1.25%
Equipment	1,095,000	3.13%	1.10%
Facilities	620,000	1.77%	0.62%
Other unanalyzed	5,220,000	14.94%	5.22%
Total variable patient care resources	$34,945,000	100.00%	34.95%
Variable administrative resources:			
Medical records/information systems	$700,000	16.69%	0.70%
Accounting/billing/purchasing	375,000	8.94%	0.38%
Human resources/education	240,000	5.72%	0.24%
Other unanalyzed	2,880,000	68.65%	2.88%
Total variable administrative resources	$4,195,000	100.00%	4.20%

ysis because it represents the currently attainable level of efficiency for each key resource. By increasing practical capacity, a facility can accomplish more without requiring additional resources. Available capacity becomes increasingly important when assessing managed care contracts.

Based on the patient care-administrative and variable-fixed categories of cost, a resource consumption-based income statement can be developed. In more traditional income statements, costs are determined to be variable or fixed relative to a single measure of volume such as acuity adjusted patient days. The variable resources in the proposed ABC income statement are variable relative to the activity drivers specified for each key resource. The resulting income statement provides greater flexibility when defining *volume*, and provides managers with more options when they are searching for cost-effective process improvement.

Fixed costs are separated into used and unused capacities. This dichotomy is important because it prevents the cost of activities actually performed or patients actually served from being distorted by absorbing full costs (used and unused capacity). For reporting purposes, full costs are recognized. Costing at the procedure, process, or patient level (that is, cost object) considers only variable costs (resources consumed) and the cost object's share of fixed costs (resource capacity) actually used. As capitation becomes more prominent, managers will focus on reducing volume, thereby freeing up available capacity. If cost per treatment under capitation is still computed by dividing total variable and fixed costs by a smaller level of volume, the facility's cost per patient or treatment will increase regard-

Table 9–5 Schedule of Fixed Resources

| | Capacity | | | Capacity Utilization |
	Used	Unused	Total	% *(A)**
Fixed patient care resources:				
Nursing staff	$25,840,000	$4,560,000	$30,400,000	85.00%
Equipment	3,412,750	2,792,250	6,205,000	55.00%
Facilities	2,790,000	2,790,000	5,580,000	50.00%
Imaging	4,165,000	735,000	4,900,000	85.00%
Staff physicians	750,000	500,000	1,250,000	60.00%
Medical supplies	945,000	105,000	1,050,000	90.00%
Laboratory	588,000	252,000	840,000	70.00%
Pharmacy	675,000	75,000	750,000	90.00%
Other unanalyzed	290,000	290,000	580,000	50.00%
Total fixed patient care resources	$39,455,750	$12,099,250	$51,555,000	76.53%
Fixed administrative resources:				
Accounting/billing/purchasing	$1,806,250	$318,750	$2,125,000	85.00%
Medical records/information systems	1,995,000	105,000	2,100,000	95.00%
Human resources/education	720,000	240,000	960,000	75.00%
Other unanalyzed	160,000	160,000	320,000	50.00%
Total fixed administrative resources	$4,681,250	$823,750	$5,505,000	85.04%

*Note: (A) Capacity utilization % = Used capacity ÷ Practical capacity

less of the improvements made in patient care. In the extreme, for example, if volume were reduced to one, total variable and fixed costs of the entire hospital would be assigned to a single patient.

In contrast, a resource consumption-based income statement provides information that can enable managers to avoid cost distortions. More accurate costing is essential to profitable managed care contract bidding. If too high, an organization may be unsuccessful in bidding on contracts. If too low, the organization may obtain contracts that prove unprofitable.

CONCLUSION

Implementation of ABC and use of a resource consumption-based income statement offer managers four distinct benefits. First, identification of key resources and corresponding activity drivers provides clinicians and administrators with a common language to discuss how costs and procedures link together. Second, evaluating the resource–activity driver relationship allows managers to accommodate a broader definition of *volume*, and identify the variable and fixed cost components of each key resource. Third, identification of the variable cost per activity provides a benchmark for managers that links process improvement with cost reduction. Finally, distinguishing between used and unused capacity enables managers to acknowledge process improvements that free up capacity even though costs are not eliminated. Managers may then better understand which key resources are constraints when managing costs or bidding on future managed care contracts.

NOTES

1. In this chapter, administration is used to include accounting and finance as well as other nonclinical managerial staff.

2. M.D. Shields and S.M. Young, "A Behavioral Model for Implementing Cost Management Systems," *Journal of Cost Management* (winter 1989): 17–27.

3. C. Argyris and R.S. Kaplan, "Commentary—Implementing New Knowledge: The Case of Activity-Based Costing," *Accounting Horizons* (September 1994): 83–105.

4. See J.P. Kotter, *Leading Change* (Boston: Harvard Business School Press, 1996); J. Seltzer and B.M. Bass, "Transformational Leadership: Beyond Initiation and Consideration," *Journal of Management* 16 (1990): 693–703; W. Bennis and B. Nanus, *Leaders: The Strategies of Taking Charge* (New York: Harper & Row, 1985).

5. M.D. Shields, "An Empirical Analysis of Firms' Implementation Experiences with Activity-Based Costing," *Journal of Management Accounting Research* (fall 1995): 148–166.

6. M.F. Hall and I. Press, "Keys to Patient Satisfaction in the Emergency Department: Results of a Multiple Facility Study," *Hospital & Health Services Administration* (winter 1996): 515–532.

7. S. Datar and M. Gupta, "Aggregation, Specification and Measurement Errors in Product Costing," *The Accounting Review* (October 1994): 567–591.

8. Frequently used statistical packages include: Minitab, SPSS, SAS, and JMP.

9. All major spreadsheets (e.g., Excel and Lotus 123) have regression functions as part of their data analysis capabilities.

10. Lotus 123, Release 5, was used in this analysis. The regression command is available as part of the /Range, Analyze function.

11. When interpreting r^2, consider values of 1.00–0.70 as high values, 0.70–0.30 as moderate values, and below 0.30 as low values. The higher the value, the more confidence can be placed in the cost equation. Therefore, the activity driver is a good predictor of resource cost.

12. See Y.T. Mak and M.L. Roush, "Commentary–Flexible Budgeting and Variance Analysis in an Activity-Based Costing Environment," *Accounting Horizons* (June 1994): 93–103; Shields, "An Empirical Analysis," 148–166.

13. R. Cooper and R.S. Kaplan, "Activity-Based Systems: Measuring the Costs of Resource Usage," *Accounting Horizons* (September 1992): 1–13.

14. See C.J. McNair, "The Hidden Costs of Capacity," *Journal of Cost Management* (spring 1994): 12–24; P.R. Sopariwala, "How Much Does Excess Inpatient Capacity Really Cost?" *Healthcare Financial Management* (April 1997): 54–60.

## CHAPTER 10

Performance Measurement with Activity-Based Management

Judith J. Baker with Cynthia McClard and Mec B. Cothron

CHAPTER OUTLINE

Introduction
Outcomes as Performance Measures
Business Process Improvement as
    Performance Measures
Activity Improvement as Performance
    Measures
Conclusion: Adding Quality Measures to
    the Equation

INTRODUCTION

Performance measures represent the operational and the financial statistics that are used to determine an organization's performance. The three key measures consist of cost, time, and quality. Thus, performance measures for activity-based management (ABM) can be financial or nonfinancial or a combination of both. Performance information makes up part of the attributes of an activity. (Attributes being the characteristics of an activity.) Therefore, because the performance information is available, it would follow that measures of such performance can and should be made.[1]

The primary aim of performance measures is to monitor cost, time, and quality. The managers who are accountable and whose responsibilities are being measured may be part of a purely financial, purely nonfinancial (clinical, for example), or multidisciplinary management team that cuts across both the financial and nonfinancial aspects of performance. Activity-based management accommodates all of these performance measurement scenarios. Brimson summarized the aim of performance measurement in ABM as follows: "In activity accounting, performance is measured as the cost per output. Performance measures are monitored to determine their trend, and the people responsible for each activity are made accountable for continually improving the performance."[2]

Health care integrated delivery systems (IDSs) are excellent prospects for uniform coordinated performance measures under ABM. The integrated delivery system will encompass different levels of care and different types of service delivery providers. ABC and ABM provide a uniform base unit of performance measurement for resource use across the system.[3] We will examine three examples of performance measures. The first example is a pharmacy department that created outcome performance measures. The second example concerns business process improvement and uses the food service process in an integrated delivery system. The third example is about activity performance measurement in a family practice. The chapter ends with a discussion of quality measures.

OUTCOMES AS PERFORMANCE MEASURES

As managed care becomes more entrenched, service delivery outcomes become a distinct and an important element of ABM performance measures. Service delivery outcomes are the measures of performance on this year's contract. And this year's outcomes become part of the basis for negotiating next year's contract.

Outcome measurement in ABM can be multidisciplinary. Outcome measurement is often used in conjunction with care paths or critical paths, where the documenting of such outcomes is part of the care path process (along with variance analysis for deviations from the accepted path). Take, for example, the pharmacy at Columbia/HCA Hendersonville Hospital.[4]

The pharmacy outcomes performance report (Exhibit 10–1) includes the intervention by the pharmacist, the specific drug involved, the benefit (those elements that prevent or limit adverse drug events in the patient), the length of therapy (generally tied to the acute care length of stay), and the dosage. The outcomes performance report also includes the drug cost, the nursing and distribution costs, the physician involved in the intervention, and a "loss" or "savings" to the transaction. In addition, the report includes identification of the specific pharmacist and the cost of that pharmacist's time.

The key terms on the pharmacy outcomes performance report are defined in Exhibit 10–2. Note, for example, that the column labeled *nursing and distribution costs* on the outcomes performance report represents the cost of time spent by nurse, pharmacist, and technician for nursing and distribution. Note also that the column labeled *RPH cost* represents time spent by the registered pharmacist investigating the intervention and contacting the physician or nurse. The activities recorded on the performance report appear in the intervention column of Exhibit 10–1. In other words, the interventions represent the activities for purposes of ABM performance measurement. Exhibit 10–3 presents these intervention codes—the fourteen identified intervention activities. These activities range from consultation and chart audit review to inservice provided.

Supplemental information supporting the pharmacy outcomes performance report includes pharmacy intervention statistics. (See Exhibit 10–4.) This run includes the code for the type of intervention, the count for each type, the applicable number of elapsed minutes, and the actual time.

Other supplemental information includes the pharmacy intervention list. (See Exhibit 10–5.) This run includes a patient-specific entry for each intervention. Three examples are illustrated on the exhibit: Jones, Smith, and Black (all fictitious entries). The patient-specific detail records date, time required, user, status, type of intervention (first by code and then spelled out), staff type (generally an MD), staff member, the drug (first by acronym and then spelled out), the generic equivalent, class, keywords (for search purposes), related Rx (if applicable), patient name and account number, a severity score, and an outcome. The final space on the report, coded as text allows for narrative comments to be inserted. The level of detail available in pharmacy defined activities that are tied to time, cost, outcome, and to patient-specific supplemental information, allows for the outcome performance measurement for ABM.

A word in closing about departmental outcome performance measures is necessary: We might do well to ask, "Whose performance is being measured? The department's? The responsibility accounting manager's?" If the manager bears the brunt of the performance measure, a key question is: "How well does the performance measure capture this manager's ability to influence the desired results?"[5] Change in organizational behavior can often be expected from the ABM. A switch to multidisciplinary responsibility for ABM outcome performance measures would evidence a desirable organizational behavior change.

Exhibit 10–1 Pharmacy Cost and Outcomes Report

Intervention	Drug	Benefit	Length	Drug Cost	Nurs/dist	MD	Loss	Savings	RPH	RPH cost
Duplicate Therapy	Ancef 1Gm & Vantin 200mg		V-2 da	$ 5.74	$13.50	180-R	$19.24	$ —	CSS	$ 6.25
Duplicate Therapy	Ventolin Neb-Ventolin Inhale		N/A	$ 2.00	$ 6.75	895-A		$ 8.75	AMA	$ 6.25
Duplicate Therapy	Isosorbid 5/Monoket 10mg		4es	$ 4.16	$54.00	639-A		$58.16	CSS	$ 4.16
	TOTAL			$11.90	$74.25			$66.91		$16.66
Consultation	Zosyn chx to q6h + Cleocin 900mg q8h for gangrene	appropriate antibio				110-A			CSS	$12.50
Consultation	Once a day-Gentamicin dosing for dc for NH ptx4d	dec incid of nephtox				930-A			MAC	$62.50
Consultation	MRSA in nasal-recBactroban, BactrimDS & rifampin	appropriate antibio				705-A			AMA	$12.50
Consultation	Rocky MT-onFloxin/Claforan 1Gm waiting to chx on titer	appropriate antibio				206-W			CSS	$25.00
		TOTAL								$112.50
CRCI Dosing	Floxin 400 from q12 to q24h		3es	$ 8.37	$20.25	782-A		$38.16	AMA	$ 6.25
CRCI Dosing	Floxin 300mg from q12h to q24h		3es	$ 7.60	$20.25			$27.85	AMA	$ 6.25
CRCI Dosing	Claforan 1Gm to 500mg q8h		3es	$15.75		750-A		$15.75	AMA	$ 6.25
CRCI Dosing	Allopurinol 300 mg to 100mg qd		4es	$ 0.80		705-A		$ 0.80	CSS	$ 6.25
		TOTAL		$32.52	$40.50			$82.56		$25.00
Chart Audit Rev									AMA	$ 50.00
Chart Audit Rev									AMA	$175.00
								TOTAL		$225.00
Amino/Vanco Mon	Gentamicin 60mg q8h to 100mg q12h		3es	$ 4.20	$20.25	875-A		$24.45	CSS	$ 10.00
Amino/Vanco Mon	Gentamicin 80mg q8h to 100mg q8h		3es	$ (1.30)		354-A		$ (1.30)	CSS	$ 10.40
Amino/Vanco Mon	Ordered Gentamicin Peak and trough	appropriate monitor							AMA	$ 2.10

continues

Exhibit 10–1 continued

Intervention	Drug	Benefit	Length	Drug Cost	Nurs/dist	MD Loss	Savings	RPH	RPH cost
Amino/Vanco Mon	Gentamicin 80mg q8h to 100mg q8h		3es	$ (1.30)		875-A	$ (1.30)	AMA	$ 12.50
		TOTAL		$ 1.60	$ 20.25		$ 21.85		$ 35.00
Inservice Provided RN								AMA	$ 12.50
Inservice Provided Nursing Orientaton								AMA	$ 12.50
		TOTAL							$ 25.00
Formulary switch	Zantac 50mg q8 to 150mg IV qd		4es	$ 22.00	$ 40.50	110-A	$ 62.50	CSS	$ 6.25
Formulary switch	Cipro 500mg IV chx to Floxin 400mg IV		3es	$ 54.30		103-A	$ 54.30	CSS	$ 6.25
Formulary switch	Cipro 500mg po chx to Floxin 400mg po		9d	$ 1.35		293-A	$ 1.35	AMA	$ 6.25
		TOTAL		$ 77.65	$ 40.50		$ 118.15		$18.75
Invest of situation	High WBC/pt not on antibiotics-called-ectopic preg	tx infection if need						AMA	$ 8.35
Invest of situation	Low Na-checked meds for hyponatremia effects	dec potential adv eff						AMA	$ 8.35
Invest of situation	Valium IV ordered-PO given SOE invest&completed	med error						AMA	$ 6.25
Invest of situation	Serax 7.5mg-Clarified&gave 1/2 15mg tab	ppro administ						AMA	$ 6.25
		TOTAL							$29.20
Switch IV to PO	Floxin IV to PO		8d	$ 134.10		250-A		AMA	$ 6.25
Switch IV to PO	Lasix IV to PO		4da	$ 1.92		250-A		AMA	$ 6.25
Switch IV to PO	Tagamet IV to PO		11d	$ 77.55		110-A		AMA	$ 6.25
Switch IV to PO	Zantac IV to PO		4es	$ 24.58	$ 54.00	705-A	$ 78.58	AMA	$ 6.25
				$ 238.15	$ 54.00		$ 78.58		$25.00

Order incomplete	No strength-Hytrin-3calls, 3 days-no response		355-?	AMA	$ 8.35
Order incomplete	Pt tx-meds not reordered-called reordered		286-A	AMA	$ 8.35
Order incomplete	Dilaudid-no strength		354	CSS	$ 2.08
				TOTAL	$18.78
Inapp dose	Toradol 60mg IV q6h-Max dose 120mg	dec potential adv eff	286-R	AMA	$ 6.25
Inapp dose	Toradol 30mg IM q6h-PT 74yo-dose should be dec	dec potential adv eff	715-R	AMA	$ 4.20
Inapp dose	Diflucan 150mg qd ordered for vag inf-inapp	inapp length of thera	639-R	CSS	$ 6.25
Inapp dose	Cefotan 1gm q8h to q12h	dec potential adv eff	642-A	CSS	$ 6.25
				TOTAL	$22.95
Interaction	Dyazide-Motrin-May cause renal failure	dec potential adv eff	275-R	CSS	$ 2.10
Interaction	Catapres-Lopressor potentiation	dec potential adv eff	355-R	CSS	$ 6.25
Interaction	Coumadin-Erythromycin-PT not ordered	dec potential adv eff	352-R	AMA	$ 6.25
Interaction	Biaxin-Theo-Dur-Theophylline IV monitored	dec potential adv eff	286-A	AMA	$ 6.25
				TOTAL	$20.85
C&S Reviewed	DC gentamicin-Start Cleocin 600mg q8h-Contancef	appropriate antibiot	355-A	CSS	$12.50

Courtesy of Columbia Hendersonville Hospital, Hendersonville, Tennessee.

Exibit 10–2 Key Terms in Pharmacy Cost and Outcomes Report

KEY TERMS

Intervention—Clinical activities of pharmacists that focus on appropriate usage, appropriate dosage, drug interactions, allergies, and drug monitoring in an effort to obtain optimum drug benefit.

Drug—Identifies specific drugs involved in the intervention.

Benefit—Those elements that prevent or limit adverse drug events in patients.

Length of Therapy—The average length of stay at Hendersonville is approximately four days. When specific data is not available, the length of therapy is estimated in days. When specific data is available, it is presented either in doses (d) or days (da, day).

Drug Cost—Actual cost of the drug to the facility. IV drugs also include, when applicable, the cost of the IV fluid.

Nursing and Distribution Costs—Cost of time spent by nurse, pharmacist, and technician.

MD—Identifies the physicians who were involved in the intervention.
　　A = The physician accepted the recommendation
　　R = The physician rejected the recommendation

Loss—It is considered a loss to the institution when the physician rejects the recommendation because the pharmacist's recommendation is considered to be of optimal benefit to the institution.

Savings—It is considered a savings to the institution when the physician accepts the recommendation.

RPH—Initials of pharmacist involved in the intervention.

RPH Cost—Time spent by the pharmacist investigating the intervention and contacting the physician and/or nurse.

Courtesy of Clinical Management Consultants, Inc., Brentwood, Tennessee.

Exhibit 10–3 Pharmacy Intervention Codes

INTERVENTION CODES

Duplicate Therapy—Indicates that two drugs of the same class are ordered on the same patient.

Consultation—Involves the pharmacist's assisting in developing optimal therapy regimens, dosing, assessing interactions and allergies, and monitoring medication ordered by physicians.

Creatinine Clearance—Records a pharmacist's dosing drugs that are renally eliminated that are dosed based on kidney function using the estimated creatinine clearance.

Chart Audit Review—Involves a pharmacist's reviewing charts to determine if charges are correct.

Aminoglycoside and Vancomycin Monitoring—The pharmacist monitors these drugs that are highly nephrotoxic to ensure that levels are drawn and the dose is appropriate.

Inservice Provided—The pharmacist is called upon to educate hospital personnel on drug usage.

Formulary Switch—The pharmacist calls the physician when a nonformulary drug is ordered and suggests a comparable drug that is on the formulary.

Investigation of Situation—Involves the pharmacist resolving issues that are discovered during monitoring activities.

Switch IV to PO—Involves switching IV medication to PO medication in patients who are already taking other oral medications. The drugs involved in the switch are those whose absorption is equivalent to IV.

Order Incomplete—The physician writes an order and fails to identify one or more of the following: strength, schedule, or reorder medications after transfer.

Inappropriate Dose—The pharmacist identifies drugs that have been prescribed at inappropriate doses and contacts the physician.

Interaction—The pharmacist identifies interactions based on severity level and notifies the physician.

C&S Reviewed—The pharmacist reviews cultures and sensitivities to determine if the antibiotic is appropriate.

Inappropriate Drug—The pharmacist identifies drug orders in which the drug is unavailable from a manufacturer, the patient is allergic to the drug, or the drug ordered is inappropriate for the patient's condition.

Courtesy of Clinical Management Consultants, Inc., Brentwood, Tennessee.

Exhibit 10–4 Pharmacy Intervention Statistics

Run Date: 04/20/9x   Pharmacy Live
Run Time: 0828   PHA INTERVENTION STATISTICS
                    From 08/01/9x Thru 08/31/9x

E.PHA.CSS - Smith, John

TYPE	COUNT	MINUTES	TIME
INV	1	15	0d 0h 15m
QUE	1	30	0d 0h 30m
ADR	5	90	0d 1h 30m
ADRR	2	30	0d 0h 30m
AMI/VAN	5	95	0d 1h 35m
CO	9	170	0d 2h 50m
COST	2	30	0d 0h 30m
CRCL	10	150	0d 2h 30m
CS	1	30	0d 0h 30m
DOSE	4	55	0d 0h 55m
DRUG	5	75	0d 1h 15m
DUP	2	25	0d 0h 25m
FOR	12	170	0d 2h 50m
INT	2	20	0d 0h 20m
INV	2	30	0d 0h 30m
ORD	2	15	0d 0h 15m
PO	8	125	0d 2h 05m
TOTAL	73	1155	0d 19h 15m

Courtesy of Columbia Hendersonville Hospital, Hendersonville, Tennessee.

Exhibit 10–5 Pharmacy Intervention List

Run Date: 04/20/9x   Pharmacy Live
Run Time: 0828   PHA INTERVENTION LIST
               From 08/01/9x Thru 08/31/9x

Date	Time Req.	User	Status	Intervention	Intervention Name
08/08/9x	15 min	E.PHA.CSS	Comp	CO	Consultation by Pharmacist

STAFF TYPE	STAFF MEMBER			
MD	xxx, Bill J.			
DRUG	DRUG NAME	GENERIC	CLASS	KEYWORDS RELATED Rx
ATENOT25	ATENOLOL 25 MG TABLET	ATENOLOL	24:04B	DI

PATIENT: Jones, B.   ACCT #: E000111222
SEVERITY: n/a
OUTCOME: n/a

TEXT:
PATIENT ON CATAPRES + TENORMIN—SENT INTERACTION PRINTOUT TO CHART

08/08/9x	30 min	E.PHA.AMA	Comp	CRCL	CREATININE CLEARANCE DOSING

STAFF TYPE	STAFF MEMBER			
MD	xxx, Jim E.			
DRUG	DRUG NAME	GENERIC	CLASS	KEYWORDS
FLOXIV4010	FLOXIN I.V. 40MG/ML VIAL	0FLOXACIN	08:22	CRCL

PATIENT: Smith, H.   ACCT#: E000222333
SEVERITY: n/a
OUTCOME: ACC

TEXT:
FLOXIN 400MG IV Q12H. BASED ON CRCL OF 26.35. IT SHOULD BE Q24H. NOTE PLACED ON
CHART @0830 ON 8-2. ORDER WRITTEN TO CHANGE TO Q12H ON 8-2. PATIENT ALREADY
ON Q12H. WE CALLED OFFICE TO CLARIFY
ALREADY ON Q12H. WE CALLED OFFICE ON 8-3 TO CLARIFY. ORDER THEN CHANGED TO
Q24H. BUT WAS OC'D BEFORE ANY DOSES GIVEN.

08/08/9x	10 min	E.PHA.CSS	Comp	CO	Consultation by Pharmacist

STAFF TYPE	STAFF MEMBER			
MD	xxx, Ron T.			
DRUG	DRUG NAME	GENERIC	CLASS	KEYWORDS
CORDOT200	CORDARONE 200 MG TABL	AMIODARON	DI	

PATIENT: Black, R.   ACCT #: E000333444
SEVERITY: n/a
OUTCOME: n/a

TEXT:
SENT CORDARONE/DIGOXIN INTERACTION PRINTOUT TO CHART

Courtesy of Columbia Hendersonville Hospital, Hendersonville, Tennessee.

BUSINESS PROCESS IMPROVEMENT AS PERFORMANCE MEASURES

Business process can primarily be improved through attention to synchronizing process. When work is handed off from one department or one division to another, process suffers. In other words, when accountability blurs, critical process issues fall through the cracks.[6] Expectations for business process improvement include: (1) minimizing unused capacity, (2) recognizing and removing root causes of process problems, (3) encouraging best practices, and (4) evaluating alternative resource use.[7] Performance measures can be set for these expectations.

Systemwide coordination needs particular attention in synchronizing business process, and performance measures can serve as a catalyst for the synchronization rationale. Activity-based costing can provide a clear picture of resource use not only across service lines but across the various providers within a system.[8] The ability to measure and assess the system's resource use affords opportunities for systemwide coordination.

The following example of a systemwide business process improvement measure, viewing food service activities from a business process perspective, has been contributed by James "Beau" Keyte of Branson, Inc. Whereas most delivery systems are focusing on major clinical and support areas for integrated improvements, some astute systems are discovering significant and nearly painless opportunities in a surprise location: food services. In fact, one of Branson's clients identified nearly $2 million in savings without downsizing the operations or compromising the quality of the food served.

Why bother looking at food services? Consider the reasons why most systems tend to overlook food services as a source for potential cost reductions:

- Food services represents approximately 2 percent of the budget of most delivery systems.

- Food issues can be political; everyone has an opinion about food and many people make it known.
- Benchmarking articles have not identified food services as a key department.
- Many providers have high levels of patient satisfaction regarding the meal activities.

Savings in food service can be quickly realized and deployed to more strategic initiatives. Although there are several reasons to put most of an integrated delivery system's available resources into redesigning service lines, it still might make sense to perform a due diligence of system food services. Some of the reasons are:

- Shifts in lengths of stay and outpatient volumes are reducing the need for extensive menus.
- Outsourced food services might not have appropriate incentives to reduce meal costs.
- Cafeteria meal subsidies, catering policies, and patient menus might vary among facilities.
- Best practices can easily be leveraged within a system perspective.

Most opportunities for savings can be achieved within several months, with savings deployed where they are needed the most: the strategic redesign of the system's service lines. In addition, if the system has self-insured employee health benefits, long-term gains can be achieved by restructuring cafeteria and catered meals to emphasize healthy foods.

A large integrated delivery system recently assessed their food services with a mission to identify activities that can benefit from a systemwide coordination. Key food service activities, such as patient meals, cafeteria meals, and catering, were analyzed, compared, and contrasted to quantify opportunities for improvement (see Figure 10–1). The significant findings included:

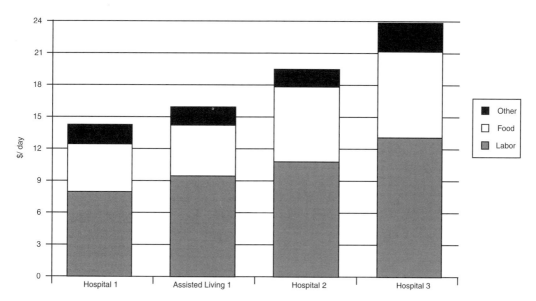

Figure 10–1 Patient Meal Cost per Patient Day. *Source:* Copyright © 1997, Branson, Inc. Further reproduction is strictly prohibited.

- patient meal cost variations, including floor stocks, of nearly 70 percent among similar facilities
- cafeteria meal discounts for employees ranging from 28–45 percent
- unmanaged catering policies resulting in as much as a 15 percent annual growth rate in catering expenses

The results of this analysis were developed within eight weeks. Food product cost opportunities are nearly $2 million and are being realized within 12 months by implementing straightforward recommendations. They are:

- Incorporate best practices, such as core menus, to reduce food costs without sacrificing quality or service.
- Develop a systemwide budget for cafeteria meal discounts that results in consistent menu prices.
- Incorporate menu incentives for healthy meals for patients and employees.

- Create a common catering policy that limits support beyond mealtime meetings.

Finding these opportunities in the delivery system involves:

- identifying and allocating activity costs to the major food service activities such as patient and cafeteria meals
- benchmarking these costs externally and within the system to quantify potential savings
- working with a systemwide food service team to identify and develop appropriate best practices
- establishing executive ownership of these activities
- measuring and communicating the success of the efforts at a system level

Although food services may not be a major player in system cost reduction, the opportunities can quickly be realized and may not involve the painful process of downsizing. Such an activity, if fully embraced and supported by management, can fund more costly and complex changes in the IDS and reduce long-term exposure of employee health costs for self-insured systems.

ACTIVITY IMPROVEMENT AS PERFORMANCE MEASURES

Activity improvement is a common performance measure in activity-based management. Activity improvement can and should improve working methods by simplifying tasks and methods, by eliminating duplication in tasks and other waste in work performance, and by encouraging best practices.[9] The great significance to activity improvement is this: Freeing up resources through activity improvement allows those resources to be deployed more effectively. Such benefits thoroughly support the use of activity improvement as a performance measure.

Activity analysis leads to activity improvement. When the pattern of activities is revealed, the inefficiencies are also revealed. The following example is excerpted from the extensive family practice case study appearing in Chapter 13. This example concerns a simple report processing activity analysis and subsequent activity improvement.

The example is family practice opportunities for activity improvement. The starting point is activity analysis (see Chapter 4). Activity analysis provides the basis for judging where to direct activity improvement efforts for performance measures. This family practice performed extensive activity analysis over a period of several years. The activity analysis was part of ongoing ABC and ABM implementation within the practice.

Activity improvement should be directed where the effort will yield the most benefit. Although this statement appears gratuitous, many performance measurement projects that utilize activity improvement use across-the-board measures that are not efficient. The results of such across-the-board measures do not yield as many clear-cut performance measures because they are not efficient.

This example represents the activity analysis for report processing in the family practice (see Table 10–1). The activity analysis involves three individuals: the receptionist, the doctor, and the medical assistant. The activity detail for each is presented in the activity column while the time incurred for each is presented in the hours column. (Minutes are expressed in decimals to aid spreadsheet calculations. Thus .10 = 60 minutes × .10 or 6 minutes.)

Table 10–1 Family Practice Reporting Processing

	A	B	C	D	E	F	G	H
1								
2				REPORT PROCESSING				
3	Actor	Activity	Hours	Hrly Rate	Total	Recpt	MA	Doctor
4	Recpt	Opens Report	0.05	$8.50	$0.43	$0.43		
5		Pulls Chart	0.10	$8.50	$0.85	$0.85		
6		Takes to Doctor						
7	Doctor	Evaluates Record	0.10	$54.15	$5.42			$5.42
8		Delegates to MA						
9	MA	Calls Patient	0.10	$12.00	$1.20		$1.20	
10		Files Chart	0.05	$12.00	$0.60		$0.60	
11	Total				$8.50	$1.28	$1.80	$5.42
12								

This example is costed out; thus the time expressed in the hours column is multiplied times the hourly rate to arrive at the total cost incurred. The cost items are then distributed to the appropriate individuals (receptionist, medical assistant, or doctor) in the remaining spreadsheet columns. (For a discussion of how the hourly rate amount for the doctor was calculated, see the full case study in Chapter 13.)

If the report processing activity was selected for activity improvement as a performance measure, the various facets of the activity would be examined for waste, repetition, and so forth. It is a desirable procedure to select activities that are worthy of the effort required. Pareto analysis (discussed in Chapter 12) is one method of selecting the appropriate areas for activity improvement as a performance measure.

It is important to remember that activities are defined in terms of both financial performance measures and nonfinancial performance measures.[10] Different views of the same activity are provided depending on which question is asked. These questions can involve the cost, the time, and/or the efficiency of activity performance. Thus, we may be viewing performance based on cost or quality of flexibility, but it is best to judge activity performance on a combination of all three attributes.[11]

CONCLUSION: ADDING QUALITY MEASURES TO THE EQUATION

Quality measures often take shape as continuous quality improvement (CQI). Continuous quality improvement allows a never-ending search for higher levels of performance within the organization; "if you're not going forward, you're going backward."[12] CQI represents W. E. Deming's philosophy. Deming was a pioneer in the development of process improvement. His process improvement concept is summarized in "Deming's wheel," which involves repeated application of the steps of PDCA: planning (P), doing (D), checking (C), and acting (A).[13] As the wheel revolves, the cycle is repeated over and over, illustrating the concept of continuous, or never-ending, improvement.

Quality measures can be added to the performance measurement equation by synchronizing ABC and CQI. This rationale is logical. ABC's activity analysis and cost driver analysis allows the exploration of process. This exploration of process from both the performance measurement and the costing aspects of ABC flows directly into the process improvement elements of continuous quality improvement. Thus, the highest and best uses for ABC and for CQI occur when the two initiatives are synchronized. Quality as well as time and cost can be measured.

NOTES

1. J. Brimson and J. Antos, *Activity-Based Management for Service Industries, Government Entities, and Nonprofit Organizations* (New York: John Wiley & Sons, 1994), 187.

2. J. Brimson, *Activity Accounting: An Activity-Based Costing Approach* (New York: John Wiley & Sons, 1991), 75.

3. J.J. Baker, "Activity-Based Costing for Integrated Delivery Systems," *Journal of Health Care Finance* 22, no. 2 (1995): 60.

4. Cynthia McClard, M.S., RPH and Mec Cothron, B.S., RPH contributed this Columbia/HCA Hendersonville, Tennessee pharmacy department example. Cynthia and Mec developed the Outcomes Performance Report for site-specific use at this hospital's pharmacy.

5. C. Horngren et al., *Cost Accounting: A Managerial Emphasis*, 8th ed. (Englewood Cliffs, NJ: Prentice Hall, 1994), 903.

6. Brimson and Antos, *Activity-Based Management*, 304.

7. Ibid., 305.

8. Baker, "Activity-Based Costing," 58

9. Brimson and Antos, *Activity-Based Management*, 305.

10. Brimson, *Activity Accounting*, 143.

11. Ibid., 144.

12. Horngren, *Cost Accounting*, 7.

13. J. Cryer and R. Miller, *Statistics for Business: Data Analysis and Modeling* (Boston: PWS-Kent Publishing, 1991), 12.

CHAPTER 11

Budgeting

Judith J. Baker

CHAPTER OUTLINE

INTRODUCTION

A budget is an organization-wide instrument. The organization's objectives define the specific activities to be performed, how they will be assembled, and the particular levels of operation, whereas the organization's performance standards or norms set out the anticipated levels of individual performance. The budget is the instrument through which activities are quantified into financial terms. The process of budgeting, then, requires managers to address questions such as:

- What is the proposed level of activity?
- What is the appropriate input (resources consumed) and output (services delivered) relationship?
- What is the appropriate dollar cost of the inputs?
- What resources will be available?
- How can these resources best be used to achieve the objectives?[1]

A health care standard view of budgeting is illustrated by the American Hospital Association's (AHA) four objectives for the budgeting process:

1. to provide a written expression, in quantitative terms, of a hospital's policies and plans
2. to provide a basis for the evaluation of financial performance in accordance with a hospital's policies and plans
3. to provide a useful tool for the control of costs
4. to create cost awareness throughout the organization[2]

STATIC VERSUS FLEXIBLE EXPENSE BUDGETING

A *static budget* is a budget that is based on a single level of output. It is not adjusted once it has been finalized.[3] A *variance* is the difference between an actual result and a budgeted amount when the budgeted amount is a financial variable reported by the accounting system. The variance may or may not be a standard amount. The variance may or may not be a benchmark amount.[4]

Actual results minus **static budget amount** equals **static budget variance**

The static budgeted expense amounts do not change in accordance with changes in levels of output. In the case of health care, we can use patient days as an example of level of output. Assume that the budget anticipated 400,000 patient days this year (patient days equating to output of service delivery; thus, 400,000 output units). Further assume that the revenue was budgeted for the expected 400,000 patient days and the expenses were also budgeted at an appropriate level for the expected 400,000 patient days. Now assume that only 360,000, or 90 percent, of the patient days are going to actually be achieved for the year. The budgeted revenues and expenses still reflect the original expectation of 400,000 patient days. This example is a static budget; it is geared toward only one level of activity. The original level of activity remains constant or static.

A *flexible budget* is one that is created using budgeted revenue and/or budgeted cost amounts. A flexible budget is adjusted, or flexed, to the actual level of output achieved (or perhaps expected to be achieved) during the budget period.[5] A flexible budget thus looks toward a range of activity (versus one level only in the static budget). Preparing a flexible budget involves four steps:

1. Determine the relevant range over which activity is expected to fluctuate during the coming period.
2. Analyze costs that will be incurred over the relevant range in terms of determining their cost patterns.
3. Separate costs by behavior.
4. Prepare a budget showing the costs that will be incurred at various points through the relevant range.[6]

Flexible budgets became important to health care when diagnosis-related groups (DRGs) were established in hospitals in the 1980s. The development of a flexible budget requires more time and effort than does the development of a static budget. If the organization is budgeting with workload standards, for example, the static budget projects expenses at a single normative level of workload activity, whereas the flexible budget projects expenses at various levels of workload activity.[7]

The concept of the flexible budget addresses workloads, control, and planning. Managers who are working with flexible budgets can readily adapt to ABC because the concepts of quantifying costs are already familiar to them.

VARIANCE ANALYSIS

In terms of variance analysis, a *variance* is the difference between standard prices and quantities and actual prices and quantities.[8] Flexible budgeting variance analysis was conceived by industry and subsequently discovered by health care. It provides a methodology to get more information about the composition of departmental expenses. The methodology subdivides total variance into three types: price, quantity, and volume.

The *price variance* is also known as the rate variance. The price or rate variance is the portion of the overall variance caused by a difference between the actual and expected price of an input. It is calculated as the difference between the actual and budgeted unit price, or hourly rate multiplied by the actual quantity of goods or labor consumed per unit of output and by the actual output level.

The *quantity variance* is also known as the use variance or efficiency variance. The quantity variance is the portion of the overall variance that is caused by a difference between the budgeted and actual quantity of input that is needed per unit of output. It is calculated as the difference between the actual quantity of inputs used per unit of output, multiplied by the actual output level and the budgeted unit price.

The *volume variance* is the portion of the overall variance that is caused by a difference between the expected workload and the actual workload. It is calculated as the difference between the total budgeted cost based on a predetermined, expected workload level and the amount that would have been budgeted had the actual workload been known in advance.[9]

Note that all three variable cost elements—that is, direct materials, direct labor, and variable overhead—can have a price variance and a quantity variance computed. But the variance is not known by the same name in all instances. For example:

Price Variance = Materials Price Variance (for direct materials)

Price Variance = Labor Rate Variance (for direct labor)

Price Variance = Overhead Spending Variance (for variable overhead)

Even though the names differ, the calculation for all three is the same. Note, too, that variance analysis is primarily a matter of input-output analysis. The inputs represent actual quantities of direct materials, direct labor, and variable overhead that are used. The outputs represent the services or products that are delivered (produced) for the applicable time period, expressed in terms of standard quantity (in the case of materials) or of standard hours (in the case of labor). In other words, the standard quantity or standard hours equates to what should have been used (the standard) rather than what was actually used.[10]

We will examine two examples of variance analyses from health care facilities using ABC. One example represents a hospital system and one example represents home care. We will then explore how activity-based budgets (ABBs) are created. Presenting the variance analysis first is intended to provide a frame of reference for the forthcoming budget assembly information. We suggest that you refer back to these examples from time to time as you review the ABB section.

We have previously examined the activity-based costing calculations for the diagnostic imaging activity pool for St. Joseph Hospital in Chapter 5. Exhibit 11–1 now examines an example of the hospital's variance analysis. The example deals with price variance and quantity variance. Note that the price variance is expressed in relative value units (RVUs). Note

also that the quantity variance is broken out into four subtypes: patient, caregiver, environmental, and efficiency variances, all of which are expressed in RVUs. The footnote on the example comments that a single cost driver (number of RVUs) is assumed to adequately capture the consumption of resources in this activity center for purposes of this example. In actual fact, a variety of cost drivers would be employed. It is also important to note that overhead costs for this activity center are assumed to be essentially variable in relation to the cost driver that is used. Finally, it is assumed that the budgeted activity level is equal to the standard activity level for purposes of this example.

The flexible budget calculation ($2,885,989) is based on actual quantity. When the $2,885,989 is compared to the actual cost of $2,661,523 for this activity center, a favorable price variance of $224,466 is realized. When the $2,885,989 is compared to the budgeted cost of $2,700,000 for this activity center, an unfavorable quantity variance of $(185,989) is realized.

There are two primary differences in this ABC variance analysis when compared to a traditional variance analysis. First, more causal cost drivers and more homogenous cost pools are used in the ABC variance analysis. This means that variance analysis is applied to each individual activity pool rather than to the entire hospital as would occur in the traditional method of analysis. Second, management is better able to locate weaknesses in service delivery and to focus improvement efforts when a more detailed variance analysis with emphasis on activity analysis is available to them under the ABC methodology.

The second example of ABC variance analysis concerns a home care agency, the Rush Home Care Network. Exhibit 11–2 illustrates variance analysis for the diagnostic category of diabetes patients.

The top one-quarter of the exhibit lists standard data. The six line items amount to a total standard cost of $1,980.15. The next one-quarter of the exhibit lists actual data. The six line

Exhibit 11–1 Illustrative Example of Variance Analysis Under an ABC System

Assume the following information for the nursing activity center of St. Joseph Hospital for the month of September:

Nursing Activity Center
Cost Driver = Number of Relative Value Units (RVUs)

Budget	**Actual**
Activity Level = 600,000 RVUs	Activity Level = 641,331 RVUs
Overhead Costs = $2,700,000	Overhead Costs = $2,661,523
Budgeted Cost per RVU = $4.50	Actual Cost per RVU = $4.15

Information obtained from the Variance Analysis Reports of all patients for the month of September.
Patient Variance = 8,231 RVUs
Caregiver Variance = 11,624 RVUs
Environmental Variance = 14,275 RVUs
Efficiency Variance = 7,201 RVUs

Summary Variance Report for Nursing Activity Center*

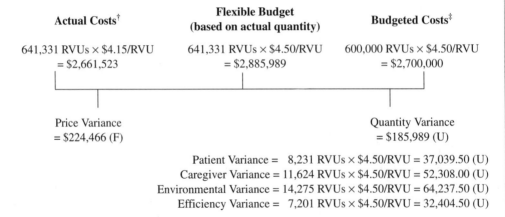

Actual Costs†	**Flexible Budget (based on actual quantity)**	**Budgeted Costs‡**
641,331 RVUs × $4.15/RVU	641,331 RVUs × $4.50/RVU	600,000 RVUs × $4.50/RVU
= $2,661,523	= $2,885,989	= $2,700,000

Price Variance = $224,466 (F)   Quantity Variance = $185,989 (U)

Patient Variance =   8,231 RVUs × $4.50/RVU = 37,039.50 (U)
Caregiver Variance = 11,624 RVUs × $4.50/RVU = 52,308.00 (U)
Environmental Variance = 14,275 RVUs × $4.50/RVU = 64,237.50 (U)
Efficiency Variance =   7,201 RVUs × $4.50/RVU = 32,404.50 (U)

*It is recommended that individual cost drivers be used for different activity pools in analyzing price and quantity variances. In this example, it is assumed that a single cost driver—number of RVUs—adequately captures the consumption of resources in this activity center.

†Here overhead costs for the Nursing Care Activity Center are assumed to be essentially variable in relation to the cost driver used (number of RVUs). For fixed costs, variances can be further divided into strategic and operational capacity variances.

‡For simplicity, budgeted activity level is assumed equal to standard activity level.

Source: Reprinted from S. Udpa, Activity-Based Costing for Hospitals, *Health Care Management Review*, Vol. 21, No. 3, p. 93, © 1996, Aspen Publishers, Inc.

items amount to a total actual cost of $4,790.00. The total unfavorable variance amounts to $(2,809.85), or (1,980.15 − 4,790.00 = 2,809.85).

The bottom one-half of the exhibit lists five types of variances utilized in this home care's ABC variance analysis system. The five types are (1) volume variance, (2) efficiency variance, (3) labor rate variance, (4) materials variance, and (5) profile variance. This exhibit illustrates the Rush Home Care Network's use of stan-

Exhibit 11–2 Variance Analysis

Given a standard profile of diabetes patients described below for the home care agency and assuming the corresponding standard costs, explain the variances between actual performance and standard. Assume the budgeted and actual monthly volume for this diagnostic category is 10.

Discipline	Profile volume	Visit time/h	Rate/h	Materials/ visit	Cost/visit	Monthly volume	Total cost
Standard data							
Skilled nursing	3.0	1.00	$17.00	$11.63	$28.63	31	$887.53
Physical therapy	9.0	0.75	15.50	0.00	11.63	92	1,069.37
Occupational therapy	0.2	0.75	15.50	0.00	11.63	2	23.25
Speech therapy	0.0	0.75	0.00	0.00	0.00	0	0.00
Social work	0.0	1.20	0.00	0.00	0.00	0	0.00
Home health aides	0.0	1.00	0.00	0.00	0.00	0	0.00
Totals	12.2					125	$1,980.15
Actual data							
Skilled nursing		1.20	$19.00	$3.00	$25.80	40	$1,032.00
Physical therapy		1.40	17.00	5.00	28.80	110	3,168.00
Occupational therapy		1.00	17.00	2.00	19.00	10	190.00
Speech therapy		1.00	14.00	2.00	16.00	10	160.00
Social work		1.50	12.00	0.00	8.00	5	90.00
Home health aides		1.00	7.00	3.00	10.00	15	150.00
Totals						190	$4,790.00

Total unfavorable variance $(2,809.85)

Explanation of variances

	Standard	Actual	Difference	Statistic	Totals
1. Volume variance					
Skilled nursing	31	40	(9)	$28.63	$(257.67)
Physical therapy	92	110	(18)	11.63	(209.34)
Occupational therapy	2	10	(8)	11.63	(93.04)
Totals					$(560.05)
2. Efficiency variance					
Skilled nursing	1.00	1.20	(0.20)	$680.00	$(136.00)
Physical therapy	0.75	1.40	(0.65)	1,705.00	(1,108.25)
Occupational therapy	0.75	1.00	(0.25)	155.00	(38.75)
Totals					$(1,283.00)
3. Labor rate variance					
Skilled nursing	$17.00	$19.00	$(2.00)	48	$(96.00)
Physical therapy	15.50	17.00	(1.50)	154	(231.00)
Occupational therapy	15.50	17.00	(1.50)	10	(15.00)
Totals					$(342.00)
4. Materials variance					
Skilled nursing	$11.63	$3.00	$8.63	40	$345.20
Physical therapy	0.00	5.00	(5.00)	110	(550.00)
Occupational therapy	0.00	2.00	(2.00)	10	(20.00)
Totals					$(224.80)

continues

Exhibit 11–2 continued

	Standard	Actual	Difference	Statistic	Totals
5. Profile variance					
Speech therapy	0	10	(10)	$16.00	$(160.00)
Social services	0	5	(5)	18.00	(90.00)
Home health aides	0	15	(15)	10.00	(150.00)
Totals					$(400.00)

Total variance $(2,809.85)

Source: Reprinted from T.A. Jendro and T.M. McNally, Managing Managed Care: A Comprehensive Costing and Contract Evaluation Model for an Era of Change, *Home Health Care Management Practices*, Vol. 9, No. 2, pp. 13–21, © 1997, Aspen Publishers, Inc.

dards of productivity: "At Rush these standards take the form of visiting time expressed as the average number of visits made in a given day. Standard cost accounting models also take into consideration labor rates paid, actual hours spent by caregivers, visit volume changes, and changes in the patient mix of services."[11] Using the ABC system, management is now able to monitor variances in departmental costs among standard amounts determined by budget volumes, productivity goals, and actual performance.

In closing, when should variances be investigated? Variances will fluctuate within some type of normal range. The trick is to separate normal randomness from those factors that require correction. The cost-benefit of variance analysis should be computed before undertaking the analysis.[12]

ACTIVITY-BASED BUDGETING: A NEW PERSPECTIVE

Activity-based budgeting is an approach to budgeting that focuses on the costs of activities that are necessary to produce and sell services or products. ABB is particularly valuable in the case of indirect costs; it separates indirect costs into individual cost pools. Management then identifies the specific cost drivers for each cost pool. One specific type of ABB integrates the

Kaizen approach. The *Kaizen* approach to ABB incorporates the concept of continuous improvement. That is, the budget is created by projecting costs on the basis of future improvements rather than on existing practices.[13]

The three key elements of ABB include: (1) the type of work to be done, (2) the quantity of work to be done, and (3) the cost of work to be done. Each of the key elements concerns activities. Each of the key elements also concerns workload. The determination of workload (see subsequent discussion) is integral to the ABB process.

An important goal of budgeting should be to improve each process on a continuous basis. The following eleven elements are all integral parts of activity-based budgeting. First, ABB sets improvement targets through activity process and business process. Second, ABB synchronizes activities to improve business process. Third, ABB sets business process improvement goals. These goals require joint efforts of employees from a variety of departments or cost centers; thus, helping departmental barriers crumble. Fourth, ABB, along with ABM, focuses on controlling the process to improve results. Fifth, ABB requires that the customer—the patient, the payer, and so forth—be consulted about their requirements. These requirements are then built into the improvement process. Sixth, ABB focuses on the output—not the input. The required resources are only a consequence of the activities. So the focus rests on the activities: what work is done, how the work is performed, and how much work is done. Seventh, ABB allows empowered employees to manage their own activities. Eighth, ABB accepts mistakes, but rejects a repetition of those same mistakes. Ninth, ABB uses a uniform language of the activities processes and business processes that everyone in the organization is using. Communication is enhanced. Tenth, ABB looks for consistency of the output. In other words, it is expected that an activity should be performed consistently over time in accordance with current best practices. Eleventh, ABB requires setting activity process and business process targets as a minimum level of performance—not the absolute level of such performance.[14]

The ABB process according to Brimson and Antos[15] is illustrated in Exhibit 11–3. The Brimson and Antos approach to ABB wraps around continuous improvement. That is, it both begins and ends with continuous improvement; thus, ABB is a cycle. The process steps as set out by Brimson and Antos[16] are summarized in the following discussion.

Step one: develop a strategy. Linking strategy and budgeting is essential to ABB. One of the areas of strategic management that is particularly emphasized is customer (patient and/or payer) requirements. An example of obtaining feedback for customer requirements is surveying customers. Table 11–1 illustrates an example of responding to such a survey with ABB. In this case, assume that the survey revealed that patients' families wanted the director and the assistant director of the intensive care unit (ICU) to spend more time communicating with them. An activity budget has been created in Table 11–1 to assess the cost of spending more time communicating with ICU patients' families. Assume that the director of the ICU and the assistant director of the ICU believe that they could spend more of such time if they did not have to perform as many inservices. Part one of Table 11–1 reflects the equivalent time (wages plus fringe benefits) that they could free up for communication instead of inservice duties. The supplies, telephone, depreciation, and space occupancy costs represent the other costs associated with the new activity. Total new communication cost is estimated at $10,210.

But the inservice is still required. It is assumed that an outsourcing fee could be paid to a former employee to perform the equivalent inservice at a cost of $6,000. The supplies, telephone, depreciation, and space occupancy costs represent the other costs associated with the outsourced inservice arrangement. Total outsourced inservice cost is estimated at $8,100. Management can now see the ABB cost—

Exhibit 11–3 The Activity-Based Budgeting Process

Develop a strategy

  Forecast the workload

    Establish specific activity level targets

      Coordinate interdepartmental projects

        Identify specific activity level projects

          Define, evaluate, select activity level projects

            Determine budgeted activities and workload for the coming year

Table 11–1 Activity-Based Budget Input for Proposed ICU Activity

1. For the activity "communicate with patient families"		2. For the activity "inservice"	
Salaries	$7,300	Outsourcing Fees	$6,000
Supplies	600	Supplies	600
Telephone	510	Telephone	510
Depreciation	1200	Depreciation	800
Space Occupancy	600	Space Occupancy	450
Total	$10,210	Total	$8,100
Grand Total			$18,310

$18,310—and can make a cost-benefit decision about whether to respond to the information from the customer survey.

Step two: forecast the workload. Forecasting the workload involves three separate levels: service-related and nonservice-related activity and/or business processes, plus special project activity and/or business processes. Detailing the bill of activities provides activity quantities by service lines for forecasting purposes.

Step three: establish specific activity level targets. To arrive at specific activity level targets, strategic objectives must first be set. Then the strategic objectives must be converted into performance targets. Price is set and performance targets for time, cost, and quality are established. Then, the performance targets can be converted into specific activity level targets.

Step four: coordinate interdepartmental projects. Interdepartmental projects must be coordinated. This step serves to eliminate duplicate activities being performed in more than one department. It also serves to better coordinate activities from an interdepartmental perspective.

Step five: identify specific activity level projects. The specific activity level targets must be converted into detail. That is, the activity level targets must now be translated into specific activity level projects. Improvement potential should be taken into account when developing projects at the activity level.

Step six: define, evaluate, select activity level projects. The projects must be compared against each other in order to make selections for the activity-based budget. One suggested methodology is to rank the projects. What should they be ranked against? One suggestion is to create a ranking system that compares project to customer (patient and/or payer) needs. Another approach would be to rank projects on a scale against the various aspects of continuous improvement that have been adopted by the organization's strategic objectives for the coming budget period. Still another suggestion is to classify the projects according to their level of support, using a four-stage ranking criteria. The four stages are current (cost of activities as presently performed), minimum (minimum level of service for an activity), intermediate (not a final solution), and expanded (enlarging level of service for this activity is recommended).

Step seven: determine budgeted activities and workload for the coming year. After the activity level projects are selected for the coming budget period, the selected projects are then translated into activities and related workloads. These activity and workload calculations are then collapsed into the approved activity-based budget.

As is fairly obvious, the activity-based budget process spends a great deal of time on improvement of business process. The unique aspect of ABB is that it allows improvement of specific activities as well as improvement of business process. By deconstructing to the activity level, ABB supports management's ability to view activity process; thus allowing capacity for managing specific improvement.

CONCLUSION

It is wise to recall from time to time that behavioral consequences as well as financial and technical consequences surround the budgeting process. "Budgeting, regardless of its framework, is accomplished through people. Its success or failure rests more with the behavioral considerations of the human processes than the technical considerations of schedule development. . . . A well-designed management control system . . . will ensure that the formalized procedures do not overwhelm the human aspects of budgeting."[17] If a participative budgeting approach is employed, many levels of management will be involved in the activity-based budgeting process. Thus, the budget for the organization as a whole becomes an interactive model. In conclusion: The activity-based budgeting process is ongoing. It can be quantified. It ties into strategy. It also is designed to work in tandem with continuous improvement efforts.

NOTES

1. M. Ziebell and D. DeCoster, *Management Control Systems in Nonprofit Organizations* (New York: Harcourt Brace Jovanovich, 1991), 50.

2. W.O. Cleverly, *Essentials of Health Care Finance* (Gaithersburg, MD: Aspen Publishers, Inc., 1992), 43.

3. C. Horngren et al., *Cost Accounting: A Managerial Emphasis*, 8th ed. (Englewood Cliffs, NJ: Prentice Hall, 1994), 228.

4. Ibid., 227.

5. Ibid., 228.

6. R. Garrison, *Managerial Accounting*, 6th ed. (Burr Ridge, IL: Richard D. Irwin, 1991), 411.

7. J.R. Pearson et al., "The Flexible Budget Process: A Tool for Cost Containment," *A. J. C. P.* 84, no. 2 (1985): 202.

8. Garrison, *Managerial Accounting*, 365.

9. S.A. Finkler, "Flexible Budget Variance Analysis Extended to Patient Acuity and DRGs," *Health Care Management Review* 10, no. 4 (1985): 24–26.

10. Garrison, *Managerial Accounting*, 365–366.

11. T.A. Jendro and T.M. McNally, "Managing Managed Care: A Comprehensive Costing and Contract Evaluation Model for an Era of Change," *Home Health Care Management Practices* 9, no. 2 (1997): 21.

12. Horngren et al., *Cost Accounting*, 247.

13. Ibid., 200.

14. J. Brimson and J. Antos, *Activity-Based Management for Service Industries, Government Entities, and Nonprofit Organizations* (New York: John Wiley & Sons, 1994), 264–267.

15. Ibid., 271.

16. Ibid., 271–291.

17. Ziebell and DeCoster, *Management Control Systems*, 242–243.

## CHAPTER 12

Standard Setting, Benchmarking, and Pareto Analysis

Judith J. Baker with Clark B. Bitzer

CHAPTER OUTLINE

Standards
Benchmarking
Pareto Analysis: A Tool for ABM

STANDARDS

A *standard* represents either a good level of performance or the best level of performance. A standard is usually developed from a careful study of the specific operation, and it is usually expressed on a per-unit basis.[1]

Health care managers need cost standards to determine how efficiently and profitably their institutions are operating.[2] A *standard cost* is the per-unit cost for a good level of performance or the best level of performance. A *standard input* is the set or allowed quantity of inputs (e.g., hours of labor) for one unit of input at a good level of performance or the best level of performance.[3]

It is important to recognize that different organizations vary in what they define as the good level of performance or the best level of performance.[4] The best level of performance under the best conceivable conditions, with no provision made for waste, spoilage, and so forth, is known as a *perfection standard*. A good level of performance, with provision made for waste, spoilage, and so forth, is known as a *currently attainable standard*.

There are three types of standards—engineered standards, customized standards, and continuous improvement standards. *Engineered costs* are costs that result specifically from a clear cause-and-effect relationship between inputs (such as nurse labor) and outputs (such as patients served). Inputs for engineered costs generally include direct labor cost and direct supply cost, along with other costs that can be traced. Engineered costs, in general, are best used for processes that are detailed and physically observable. The outputs for engineering costs generally include quantifiable services—services whose value can be determined and whose quality can be measured.[5]

Engineered standards emerge from the principles of engineered cost. Engineered labor standards, for example, should reflect the amount of work that a normal employee should be able to do on a particular task in order to produce work results of acceptable quality. Engineered labor standards are developed from a detailed study of the job and from observation, using statistically valid work sampling techniques. It can readily be seen that ABC and ABM fit exceptionally well with engineered labor standards.

Customized standards, as the name implies, are specific to a particular organization. The methods utilized are generally a blend of more than one type of methodology. A general characteristic of customized standards is wide variability.

The continuous improvement management philosophy incorporates the idea of continuous improvement in internal work processes (also known as *Kaizen*, which is the Japanese term for continuous improvement). The concept can be carried over into standards by setting continuous improvement standards. These represent standards set for process improvements yet to be made.[6] Thus, a *continuous improvement standard* cost represents a standard cost that is successively reduced over a series of succeeding time periods. Another term for continuous improvement standard cost is moving cost reduction standard cost.[7]

ABM performance measures can be utilized to adjust standards, or the standards themselves can be reconfigured to match activity-based costing parameters and activity-based management performance measures.

Engineered standards are an excellent match with ABC and with ABM performance measures. Engineered standards require a clear illustration of cause-and-effect between input (such as nurse labor) and output (such as patients served). ABC provides the cause-and-effect tracking, and ABM performance measures provide the data that is required to set or to adjust engineered standards.

Customized standards can also be a good match with ABC and with ABM performance measures. Customized standards should reflect the organization's unique management approach. ABC again can provide cause-and-effect tracking, and ABM performance measures can provide the data required to set or to adjust the customized standards.

An exceptional match of ABM performance measures with standards is in the area of continuous improvement standard cost setting. The usual method by which reductions are made in continuous improvement standard costs is through efficiency improvements. Because ABC and ABM provide substantial assistance in isolating the most favorable areas for efficiency improvement, they also provide equivalent assistance in setting continuous improvement standards.

Standards of productivity are desirable to ensure that the institution's resources are used in the most efficient manner.[8] Setting standards, or developing measures of efficient behavior, can be developed. First, have employees keep detailed records of their activity. (Specific methods are detailed in Chapter 6.) Averages of these activities are then used to set the standard. Second, have experienced outside observers monitor the employees and develop, through random observations, averages of these observations.[9]

If currently attainable standards are sought, then all employee performance would be averaged, or all employee performance except for predefined outliers would be averaged. If perfection standards are sought, then only best practices would be used for purposes of standard setting. If these are to be engineered standards, then statistically valid work sampling techniques should be used.

In a third method of setting standards, obtain data from similar organizations that have developed standards for their own operations. (This method must assume a close similarity between the two organizations.)[10] Some regulatory agencies use this methodology when developing comparison peer groups. Health care chains sometimes assign standard setting projects to particular facilities and then adopt the resulting standards for the balance of the facilities in the chain.

In a fourth method of setting standards, use historical data that has been generated by the existing management control system to establish standards.[11] This method is the weakest of the four, primarily because the so-called standard may be set without regard for any level of efficiency.

In conclusion, ABC enables health care managers to identify inefficiencies and assess the effect of management actions to correct these inefficiencies.[12] The ABC and ABM methodologies support true standard setting and can promote the pursuit of continuous improvement as embodied in the organization's standards.

Clark Bitzer is the Financial Analyst for the Lake Hospital System in Painesville, Ohio. He is responsible for the successful implementation of an ABC system that supports the cost and quality initiative for Lake Hospital System. He came to health care from industry, where he was Manager of Financial Analysis and Distribution Cost for a General Electric business group. We interviewed Clark about setting standards when he implemented a diagnosis-related group (DRG)-based activity accounting system at Lake Hospital System.

Q. *How did the project begin?*

A. The CEO and the Board of Trustees reviewed possible systems and made a choice. The CEO knew they (the hospital) would need activity accounting because managed care was coming. This was several years ago. He was right, of course.

Q. *When did you join the project?*

A. About three months after the system had been chosen. The hospital had been using an outside consultant. The CEO recruited me specifically to get the system operational and then to use it properly for the benefit of management

Q. *How did you decide to begin?*

A. We decided to do everything all at once.

Q. *Everything? Across the board?*

A. That's right. Everything.

Q. *How did you attack the standard setting?*

A. We divided each hospital into areas that would require different types of standards. The routine service areas, all the ancillary areas—then there was the pharmacy, the labs, and therapies: PT, OT, ST, RT, and outpatient. And the ER.

Q. *Then what?*

A. We used published standards for the pharmacy, the labs, and the therapies. We used published RVUs to set standards for procedures in the ancillaries. We worked with the directors of nursing (DONs) to develop the nursing labor standards. Some

of them are estimated. They are not engineered. Mostly two people worked at a time on this part.

Q. *And for material and supply standards?*

A. We worked from some bills of materials. We used published standards, too.

Q. *You mentioned that your nursing labor standards are not engineered. Are any of your standards engineered?*

A. No. We didn't approach it from that angle. It was a decision made at the beginning of the project.

Q. *And are your standards perfection standards or currently attainable standards?*

A. Currently attainable.

Q. *I had pretty much deduced that. How often do you review the standards now that the system has been running for some time?*

A. Mostly on an annual basis. If we break out a new procedure, we have to review the others that are related to it, though, because of the possible ripple effect on the others that are related.

Q. *One last question: If you had to do the whole thing over again, knowing what you do now, what would you do differently?*

A. I would spend more time on the standards at the beginning, before they were released. That's all.

BENCHMARKING

Benchmarking is the continuous process of measuring products, services, and activities against the best levels of performance. These best levels can be found either inside or outside the organization.[13]

There are three types of benchmarks:

1. a financial variable—reported in an accounting system
2. a financial variable—not reported in an accounting system
3. a nonfinancial variable[14]

Benchmarks are used to measure performance gaps. In the case of activity-based costing, there is another subset of four benchmarks:

1. a financial variable—reported in the general ledger accounting system
2. a financial variable—reported in the ABC accounting system
3. a financial variable—not reported in an accounting system
4. a nonfinancial variable—reported in the ABC activity analysis

The benchmarking methodology is predicated on the assumption that an exemplary process, similar to the process being examined, can be identified and examined to establish criteria for excellence.[15] Benchmarking can be accomplished in any one of several ways: (1) by studying the methods and end results of your prime competitors, (2) by examining analogous process of noncompetitors with a world-class reputation, or (3) by analyzing processes within your own organization (or health system) that are worthy of being emulated.[16] In any case, the required analysis will rely on one or both of the following methods: (1) parametric analysis, in which characteristics or attributes of similar services or products are examined; and (2) process

analysis, in which the process that serves as a standard for comparison is examined in detail to learn how and why it performs the way it does.[17] ABC and ABM can readily be applied to process analysis.

Benchmarking is used for opportunity assessment. Opportunity assessment, utilized for strategic planning and for process engineering, provides information about the way things should or possibly could be. Benchmarking is a primary information-gathering approach for opportunity assessment when it is used in this way.

Financial benchmarking in health care compares financial measures among benchmarking groups. This is the most common type of "peer group" health care benchmarking commonly in use. An example of a health care financial benchmarking report is illustrated in Table 12–1. The problem with this type of peer group benchmarking is that it does not go to the heart of good performance, let alone best performance. Although in theory the organizations that are being compared are like entities, the concept of efficient service deliv-

Table 12–1 Financial Benchmark Example

Indicator	Total	Upper-Quartile	Mid-Quartiles	Low-Quartile
Number of Hospitals	500.0	105.0	305.0	90.0
Total Margin (%)	4.1	11.0	4.5	−6.0
Occupancy (%)	64.5	65.7	64.0	56.1
Deductions from GPR (%)	29.0	28.5	29.2	31.3
Medicare (%GPR)	53.0	55.1	52.2	50.4
Medicaid (%GPR)	10.0	8.4	9.7	13.7
Self-pay (%GPR)	7.0	8.5	7.1	6.4
Managed Care Plans (%GPR)*	16.0	13.0	17.0	17.5
Other Third Party (%GPR)	14.0	15.0	14.0	12.0
Outpatient Revenue (%GPR)	22.0	25.0	21.8	17.7
# Days in Accounts Receivable	75.0	70.0	74.0	80.0
Cash Flow as a Percent of Total Debt	30.0	60.0	27.0	−0.5
Long-Term Debt as a Percent of Total Assets	35.0	26.0	36.0	42.0
Change in Admissions (1993–1997, %)	−7.0	−3.7	−6.3	−15.8
Change in Inpatient Days (1993–1997, %)	−6.0	−1.8	−6.5	−11.1

*Note: Managed Care Plans other than Title XVIII or Title XIX. All amounts are fictitious.

ery generally has not been sufficiently addressed. That is, an objective measure of commonalities and differences has not been made. Thus, full reliance on such financial benchmarking is substantially hampered.

Dr. Loop of the Cleveland Clinic Foundation speaks about motivation using benchmarking; and he utilizes a nonfinancial viewpoint:

> What is the best motivation to do better, to get from better to best? In my opinion, it has to begin nonfinancially. . . . The best motivator is a sense of competition generated through peer pressure, performance standards, personal recognition, and use of benchmark comparisons, both locally (within the department) and on a broader scale (institutionally and regionally). To get better every year, we stretch our expectations. Benchmarks serve as the denominator.[18]

Evans et al., support Dr. Loop's comment: "Physicians do respond to various types of profiling or benchmarking programs established by hospitals, even in the absence of direct links between these programs and monetary incentives."[19] A service delivery resource consumption approach will yield more information for decision making.

Service delivery resource consumption translates into benchmarking profiles. If several reasonably similar health care organizations have each implemented activity-based costing and are willing to share information, the potential for a useful benchmarking profile is greatly increased. If such circumstances are the case, measures of service delivery resource consumption can be translated into benchmarking profiles. The most common type of profile to date is generally product related. That is, it reflects the resource consumption for a particular health care service delivered. We predict that this type of useful benchmarking profile—which readily utilizes ABC and ABM—will become the profile of choice for future health care benchmarking.

A three-hospital ABC-ABM benchmarking report profile presents comparative data for a particular procedure. (See Exhibit 12–1.) Three hospitals use the same ABC-ABM system. Statistics on discharges, patient days, and average length of stay are presented, along with expected net revenue per case. Both routine service cost (room and board cost) and ancillary cost per case are presented. Routine service cost (room and board cost) is divided between med/surg and ICU. The average length of stay and the cost per case is shown for med/surg routine service and for ICU. The total ancillary cost per case is set out by ancillary department line items—CAT scan, echo, EEG, and so forth—as relevant to the particular type of case reflected in this profile. The total cost per case is summed (total of routine service costs and ancillary costs) and subtracted from the expected net revenue per case to arrive at an expected net income or loss.

The three hospitals are shown individually, followed by an average of the three. The final column of the profile illustrates the best practice equivalent figures for this type of case. The best practice figures are essential for this profile to be properly utilized by management.

To conclude, the benefit of comparing the individual organization's indicators to a benchmark based on efficient performance is that the comparison goes directly to efficiency analysis. For proper benchmarking there is always a common need to establish such objective measurement criteria for best practices purposes.

PARETO ANALYSIS: A TOOL FOR ABM

Creating standards and/or benchmarks, especially in an organization committed to continuous quality improvement, ultimately leads to management's exploring how to improve some step in a process. Pareto analysis is an analytical tool that employs the Pareto principle.

Pareto was a nineteenth-century economist who was a pioneer in applying mathematics to economic theory. His Pareto principle states that 80 percent of an organization's problems are

Exhibit 12–1 A Three-Hospital ABC/ABM Benchmarking Report

BENCHMARKING DATA
3rd Quarter

14 SPEC CV DISCORD EX TIA, ALL PAYERS

Description	Hospital A	Hospital B	Hospital C	Average	Best Practice
Discharges—Total	275	44	19	113	
Discharges—Medicare	197	41	13	84	
Patient Days	1,562	505	110	726	
ALOS	5.68	11.48	5.80	7.65	5.68
Expected Net Rev/Case	$4,777.00	$5,023.00	$5,834.00	$5,211.33	$5,834.00
Room & Board Cost					
Med/Surg ALOS	4.40	11.00	5.40	6.93	4.40
Cost/Case	$1,838.00	$2,960.00	$1,742.99	$2,180.33	$1,742.99
ICCU ALOS	1.30	0.48	0.42	0.73	0.42
Cost/Case	$749.00	$274.00	$393.30	$472.10	$274.00
Total Ancillary Cost/Case					
Operating Room	$2.00	$8.00	$10.47	$6.82	$2.00
PACU	$0.00	$1.00	$5.94	$2.31	$0.00
Anesthesia	$0.00	$1.00	$6.19	$2.40	$0.00
Emergency Dept	$293.00	$266.00	$246.05	$268.35	$246.05
Ambulance	$0.00	$128.00	$105.26	$77.75	$0.00
Radiology	$100.00	$132.00	$186.44	$139.48	$100.00
Laboratory	$234.00	$303.00	$305.79	$280.93	$234.00
Pharmacy	$342.00	$467.00	$396.44	$401.81	$342.00
Physical Therapy	$199.00	$206.00	$297.14	$234.05	$199.00
Renal	$0.00	$0.00		$0.00	$0.00
EKG	$68.00	$72.00	$60.41	$66.80	$66.40
Ultrasound	$36.00	$0.00		$18.00	$0.00
Cardiac Rehab	$0.00	$4.00		$2.00	$0.00
Central Supply	$6.00	$51.00	$69.95	$42.32	$6.00
Family Health	$0.00	$53.00		$26.50	$0.00
Pathology	$0.00	$1.00		$0.50	$0.00
Blood Processing	$0.00	$5.00	$6.52	$3.84	$0.00
CAT Scan	$213.00	$225.00	$201.08	$213.03	$201.08
Echo	$0.00	$124.00		$62.00	$0.00
Pulmonary	$83.00	$116.00	$170.52	$123.17	$83.00
			$15.47	$15.47	$0.00
EEG	$10.00	$31.00	$33.68	$24.89	$10.00
All Other	$208.00	$0.00		$104.00	$0.00
Vasc Cath	$50.00	$0.00		$25.00	$0.00
Total Ancillary Cost/Case	$1,844.00	$2,194.00	$2,117.35	$2,051.78	$1,489.53
Total Cost/Case	$4,431.00	$5,428.00	$4,253.64	$4,704.21	$3,506.52
Net Income/Loss	$346.00	($405.00)	$1,580.36	$507.12	$2,327.48

Courtesy of Ryerson Management Associates, Inc., Akron, Ohio.

caused by 20 percent of the possible causes: the 80/20 rule. Pareto's 80/20 rule holds true, for example, for cost drivers. In other words, just a few cost drivers (e.g., 20 percent) cause the majority of the effect (e.g., 80 percent). Or, in another example, 80 percent of the problems with a process may be caused by 20 percent of the activities.

The usual way to display a Pareto analysis is through the construction of a Pareto diagram. A Pareto diagram displays the important causes of variation as reflected in data collected on the causes of such variation. Exhibit 12–2 presents an example of a Pareto diagram. This example reinforces the idea behind the Pareto analysis— that the majority of problems are due to a small number of identifiable causes.[20]

The chief financial officer of XYZ Hospital believes that the billing and collection department is inefficient. Or, to be more specific, the process is probably inefficient. An activity analysis was conducted. It showed that the billing personnel were spending much time on unpro-ductive work. This Pareto diagram was constructed to display the activities involved in resubmitting denied bills. (Resubmitting denied bills is an inefficient and nonproductive activity.)

Constructing a Pareto diagram is quite simple.[21] The first step is to prepare a table that shows the activities that were recorded, the number of times that the activities were observed, and the percentage of the total number of times that was represented by each count. In Exhibit 12–2, the total number of times that these activities were observed is 43. The number of times that processing denied bills for resubmission (coded as PDB) were observed is 22. Thus 100 (22/43) = 51 percent. Similar calculations complete the table. The table of observations is shown in its entirety within the exhibit.

The Pareto diagram has two vertical axes, the left one corresponding to the number column in the table, the right one corresponding to the percent column in the table. On the horizontal axis, the activities are listed, creating bases of equal

Exhibit 12–2 Pareto Analysis of Billing Department Data

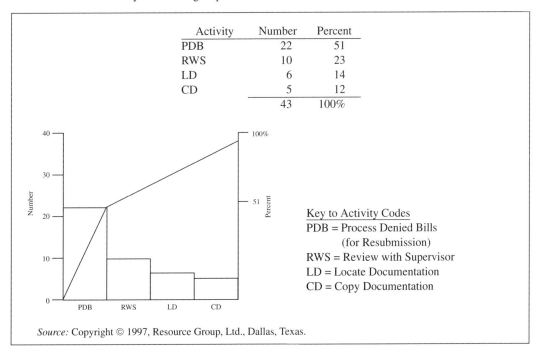

Activity	Number	Percent
PDB	22	51
RWS	10	23
LD	6	14
CD	5	12
	43	100%

Key to Activity Codes
PDB = Process Denied Bills
　　　(for Resubmission)
RWS = Review with Supervisor
LD = Locate Documentation
CD = Copy Documentation

Source: Copyright © 1997, Resource Group, Ltd., Dallas, Texas.

length for the rectangles shown in the diagram. The activities are listed in decreasing order of occurrence. Constructing the diagram in this manner means that the most frequently observed activity lies on the left extreme of the diagram, and the least frequently observed activity lies on the right extreme. The heights of the rectangles are drawn to show the frequencies of the activities, and then the sides of the rectangle are drawn.

The next step is to locate the cumulative percents of the activities using the right-hand axis. The cumulative percent for the first rectangle, labeled PDB, is 51 percent. (The calculation of the 51 percent was previously explained.) For the second rectangle from the left, labeled RWS, the cumulative percent is 51 + 23 = 74 percent. The 74 percent is plotted over the right-hand side of the rectangle labeled RWS. The next cumulative percent, for the third rectangle from the left, labeled LD, is 51 + 23 + 14 = 88 percent. The 88 percent is plotted over the right-hand side of the rectangle labeled LD. The last cumulative percent is, of course, 100 percent (51 + 23 + 14 + 12 = 100 percent), and it is plotted over the right-hand side of the last rectangle on the right, labeled CD.

Now draw straight lines between the plotted cumulative percents as shown in the exhibit.

The next step is to label the axes and add a title to the diagram. In Exhibit 12–2 the tallest rectangle could be lightly shaded to highlight the most frequent activity, suggesting the one that may deserve first priority in problem solving.

In general, the activities requiring priority attention, the "vital few," will appear on the left of the diagram where the slope of the curve is steepest. Pareto diagrams are often constructed before and after improvement efforts for comparative purposes. When comparing before and after, if the improvement measures are effective, either the order of the bars will change or the curve will be much flatter.

In conclusion, note that many authorities recommend that a Pareto analysis take the costs of the activities into account. The concern is that a very frequent problem may nevertheless imply less overall cost than a relatively rare but disastrous problem. Also, before basing a Pareto analysis on frequencies, as this example does, the analyst needs to decide that the seriousness of the problems is roughly proportional to the frequencies. If seriousness fails to satisfy this criterion, then activities should be measured in some other way. Exhibit 12–2 underlines the importance of judging the relevance of the measurements used in a Pareto analysis.

NOTES

1. C. Horngren et al., *Cost Accounting: A Managerial Emphasis*, 8th ed. (Englewood Cliffs, NJ: Prentice Hall, 1994), 226.

2. J.P. Bennett, "Standard Cost Systems Lead to Efficiency and Profitability," *Healthcare Financial Management* (September 1985): 46.

3. Horngren et al., *Cost Accounting*, 226–227.

4. Ibid., 234.

5. Ibid., 475, 477.

6. Ibid., 200.

7. Ibid., 246.

8. T.A. Jendro and T.M. McNally, "Managing Managed Care: A Comprehensive Costing and Contract Evaluation Model for an Era of Change," *Home Health Care Management Practices* 9, no. 2 (1997): 21.

9. M. Ziebell and D. DeCoster, *Management Control Systems in Nonprofit Organizations* (New York: Harcourt Brace Jovanovich, 1991), 186–187.

10. Ibid., 187.

11. Ibid., 187.

12. R.M. Dowless, "Using Activity-Based Costing to Guide Strategic Decision Making," *Healthcare Financial Management* (June 1997): 60.

13. Horngren et al., *Cost Accounting*, 903.

14. Ibid., 227.

15. L. Roberts, *Process Reengineering: The Key to Achieving Breakthrough Success* (Milwaukee, WI: ASQC Press, 1994), 60.

16. Ibid., 60.

17. Ibid.

18. F. Loop, "You Are In Charge of Cost," *Annals of Thoracic Surgery* 60 (1995): 1511.

19. J.H. Evans III et al., "Cost Reduction and Process Reengineering in Hospitals," *Journal of Cost Management* (May–June 1997): 27.

20. J. Cryer and R. Miller, *Statistics for Business: Data Analysis and Modeling* (Boston: PWS-Kent Publishing, 1991), 738, 740.

21. Example and instructions adapted and converted from Cryer and Miller, *Statistics for Business*, 738–740.

## CHAPTER 13

The Bottom-Up Approach to Process by Northwest Family Physicians

Ted J. Stuart, Jr. and Judith J. Baker

CHAPTER OUTLINE

Preface
Introduction
Methods
Results
Process Maps
Commentary

PREFACE

This case study is about a family practice physician's approach to ABC in his practice. He first implemented ABC in 1993, and has expanded and enhanced it during each succeeding year. The practice is a three-doctor family practice group located in Arizona. A significant portion of the practice's volume is managed care. The contributor, Ted Stuart, Jr., MD, is a family physician who practices full time in Glendale, Arizona. He is board certified by the American Board of Family Practice. He received his MBA degree from Arizona State University and his MD from Baylor Medical School. He is a past president of the Arizona Academy of Family Physicians.

Bottom up within the chapter title refers to Dr. Stuart's initial approach to his ABC project. He began by investigating process on a wide variety of activities within his practice. Thus, he went "bottom up" by focusing on the significant activities within the process and attaching cost to those activities. He believed that by concentrating on improving process he could better control and manage cost.

INTRODUCTION

I learned activity-based costing (ABC) so that I could determine the costs of treating patients in my family practice. I needed to know if I was making a profit on a specific service such as the routine office visit (99213). I wanted to make a profit on each item of service. If the revenue from a particular service did not provide a profit, then I would need to think about discontinuing that service or re-engineering it so that it was profitable. Physician practice costs are increasing and revenue is decreasing. During the past year, one of the capitated plans decreased physician reimbursement by 10 percent. Another health care plan reduced the reimbursement of a routine office visit (99213) from $46 to $36. Last week, my landlord raised my rent $24,000 per year. Another reason for using ABC is its help in the application of quality assurance. If the quality of a product or service is improved, then costs decrease because there are fewer mistakes, delays, and snags. If one is not measuring the cost, then one would not know that progress toward this end had been made.

If services are designed for quality, then the cost of the service must be one of the parameters that is used to evaluate the outcome. ABC is the most accurate means of measuring the cost of a product or service. I applied ABC to the processes in our three-doctor family practice group in Glendale, Arizona between 1993 and 1997. Since our inception, our group used a modified cash basis for its financial accounting statements. That method does not match revenue with costs because bills come in clumps and revenue comes in a steady stream.

ABC is a method of cost accounting, a tool used in the management of costs of products and services. I learned this method from a course in managerial accounting at Arizona State University West. In 1993, I used ABC to evaluate the routine office visit and was shocked to find out that Medicare payments did not cover the cost. Medicare reimbursement payments were determined by resource-based costing, a theory developed by Harvard professor Dr. Tsai. Medicare misapplied Dr. Tsai's work. It simply did not adequately cover the costs of overhead. The light dawned, and I realized that I would not be able to continue raising my fees to cover increasing costs as I had during the previous 25 years. Physician's services, including mine, became subject to the discipline of the marketplace.

The marketplace has changed rapidly in the last five years in my state. Managed care companies now dominate the health care field. Relationships have changed. In my practice, the customer is no longer the homogenous world of patients. Now the insurance company is the dominant customer and the patient is the consumer. True competition developed, and I became a price taker. Whatever the insurance company offered, I took (if I wanted to be paid). Once when I complained about reimbursement and slow payment to a medical director of one of the local managed health care plans, he told me, "If you don't like the reimbursement, go elsewhere." I needed effective financial tools to deal with the insurance companies in order to level the playing field somewhat.

ABC is an effective, simple tool to help the physician evaluate his or her financial relationship with a managed care company. It is an up-to-date technology on the cutting edge. It is simple to use and only requires the ability to read a profit and loss statement, the ability to use a spreadsheet, and the ability to map processes. Minimal resources are required: (1) total revenue from the managed care company, (2) explanation of benefit forms, (3) profit and loss monthly statement from his or her business, (4) a computer, and (5) software (spreadsheet, process mapping). ABC is a flexible process that can be used to calculate costs in either the fee-for-service arena or the capitated one.

Counterarguments to the use of ABC include: (1) Lack of flexibility—it is only updated yearly. The cost assumptions come from last year's data. (2) Resources—the person using the technique must have some education to apply the technique or else hire someone to perform it for him or her. (3) Simplistic—it is true that the process is simple but the average practitioner may be simply too busy to use it. (4) Cutting edge technology—so what? (5) Too expensive—what about the resources you are wasting?

METHODS

The source of my data gathering was my inside knowledge of the evaluation management process in the physician's office. I supplemented it with interviews of my office personnel and those of other offices. I diagrammed the process on paper and then transferred that diagram to the computer using software (Inspiration).

I used diagrams because I could not keep more than seven bits of information ± three bits in my conscious mind simultaneously. The diagram gave me a visual source of reference. I determined the average time necessary to perform the task and noted it on the map. I used monthly profit and loss forms from QuickBooks as well as the monthly statement from my accountant. I determined one year's total costs and then subtracted the variable costs; salaries for employees and physicians, medical supplies, drugs, laboratory supplies, and equipment. The amount left was the total sum of the fixed overhead. I applied this overhead to the average amount of time worked per year for all the doctors. The result was a figure of $16.08 per ten-minute slot. (We schedule appointments in ten-minute increments.)

I then calculated the variable costs per visit by determining the total amount of medical supplies, drugs, and so forth and dividing this by the total number of patients seen. This gave me a variable cost of $3.99 per patient seen. Labor cost was based on the total package cost per employee per hour, which includes salary, matching social security benefits, insurance, and so forth. I then used the process maps and Excel spreadsheets to calculate the costs for the following procedures:

- 99213 New patient
- 99213 Established patient

  - Simple office visit
  - With lab, X-ray, or consult
- 99214 Established patient
- 99215 Established patient
- Processing any report that requires chart coordination
- Phoning a prescription
- Cost to make an appointment (appointment scheduling)
- Cost to receive a patient (patient reception)
- Cost to check out and bill a patient (out processing)
- Cost of processing a simple consultation request
- Cost of processing a complex consultation request

RESULTS

The ABC results are summarized in two tables: (1) Cost per Service Provided (see Table 13–1) and (2) Cost per Combinations of Ser-

Table 13–1 Cost per Service Provided

COST PER SERVICE PROVIDED
(DETAILS)

NAME		FOH	Variable	DOCTOR	MA	RECPT	Other	Per/Svc TOTAL
99212		$16.08	$3.99	$9.09	$2.40	$5.15	$0.90	$37.61
99213		$16.08	$3.99	$9.09	$2.40	$5.15	$0.90	$37.61
99213F/U		$16.08	$3.99	$9.09	$2.40	$3.88	$0.90	$36.33
99213New		$16.08	$3.99	$9.09	$2.40	$6.00	$2.40	$39.96
99214		$32.16	$3.99	$28.84	$5.40	$9.40	$0.90	$80.69
99215		$48.24	$3.99	$38.09	$4.80	$14.55		$109.67
FPSS		$49.29	$3.99	$18.18	$13.80	$5.20		$90.46
XR Report		$0.00	$0.00	$5.42	$1.80	$1.28		$8.50
Report		$0.00	$0.00	$5.42	$1.80	$1.28		$8.50
Phone Rx		$0.00	$0.00	$5.42	$4.20	$2.12	$0.18	$11.92
Appoint		$0.00	$0.00			$2.15		$2.15
Phase I						$1.70	$0.27	$1.97
Phase II		$0.00				$0.85	0	$0.85
Phase III		$0.28				$2.60	$0.35	$3.23
Consult	Cmplx			$10.83	$1.20	$2.13	$10.38	$24.54
Consult	Simple			$5.42	$0.00	0	$5.63	$11.05

Table 13–2 Cost per Combination of Services Provided

| | COMBINATIONS | | | | | | | |
	E/M	X-Ray	Lab	ConsOrdr	Reports	Pap	MA	Total
99212	$37.61							$37.61
99213	$37.61							$37.61
99213	$37.61			$11.04	$8.50			$57.15
99213	$37.61		$8.50					$46.11
99213	$37.61	$8.50	$8.50					$54.61
99213	$37.61	$8.50	$8.50	$11.04	$8.50			$74.15
99213	$37.61	$8.50	$8.50	$23.13	$8.50			$86.24
99214	$80.69	incl	incl			incl		$80.69
99214	$80.69	incl	incl	$10.85	$8.50	incl		$100.04
99215	$109.67							$109.67
99215	$109.67			$11.04	$8.50			$129.21
99215	$109.67			$23.13	$8.50			$141.30
99215	$109.67			$11.04	$8.50	$8.50	$1.20	$137.71
99215	$109.67			$23.13	$8.50	$8.50	$1.20	$149.80

Source: CPT only © 1996 American Medical Association. All Rights Reserved.

vices Provided (see Table 13–2). The process maps follow. Examples of costing spreadsheets are provided within the Commentary section of this chapter.

The most startling thing that I discovered was that it cost me $74,800 per doctor per year to process paper! I only used $13,000 per year in resources to treat people over the phone. It costs me $27,000 per doctor per year to process the consultation requests. The cost is the same to process 600 complex consults or 1,200 simple consults. A simple consult is one where the doctor decides that it is indicated and orders it at the time of a visit. A complex consult is where the patient wants one and calls in the request. In this case the information is usually fragmentary and inaccurate. Time and effort are expended in clarifying the issues. The cost of other selected services per doctor per year are shown in Table 13–3.

An office visit for an established patient (99213) could cost me from $37.61 to $86.24 depending on what lab work or X-ray I ordered or if I requested a consultation. My reimbursement was $38.11 or less. The cost for a brief visit (99212) is the same as for a limited one

(99213) but the reimbursement is less. The intermediate office visit (99214) on an established patient costs me from $80.69 to $100.04 and the comprehensive evaluation (99215) costs me from $109.67 to $149.80. Some managed care companies downgraded my services from 99215 to 99213 and paid me $38.11 for what had cost me up to $149.80. I discontinued comprehensive evaluations of my patients. There is a need to achieve the objective of correct diagnosis and treatment without losing money. This led me to the belief that a new fundamentally

Table 13–3 Cost of Selected Services per Doctor per Year

Service	Cost Per Doctor Per Year
99213	$112,854
99213-Follow Up	$ 72,126
99213-New	$ 39,958
99214	$ 17,370
99215	$ 21,935
FPSS	$ 9,046
Report	$ 74,800
Phone Rx	$ 13,112

different way of evaluating patients is needed if the physician is to be compensated fairly, the patient to be treated properly, and the current marketplace is to determine the value of the service.

I realized that I needed business intelligence about the insurance companies and how they operate and handle claims. We profiled the various insurance companies with respect to what they paid for each procedure and determined our clinical approaches based on the revenue. The information from the ABC of my services leads directly into strategy and tactics. I quit performing 99215 exams because most of the companies would not pay for them. A refused claim only increases my costs. The cost of resubmission and documentation is not rewarded with enough revenue to justify its performance. If someone needed a complete evaluation and their insurance company reimbursement did not cover my costs, then I would refer the patient to a specialist. The insurance company would gladly pay the specialist more to do the work, the patient would get the necessary evaluation or treatment, and I would not lose money on poorly reimbursed processes.

PROCESS MAPS

The process maps commence with a generic process map. The remaining maps are divided into three categories: (1) revenue-producing patient service processes, (2) consult processes, and (3) front office processes.

Generic processes at Northwest Family Physicians (NWFP) are set out first. A summary of processes at NWFP is set out in Exhibit 13–1. The overall processes are grouped into three categories: (1) medical processes, (2) nonmedical processes, and (3) management activity. Selected office visit current procedural terminology (CPT) codes are defined for reference purposes in Exhibit 13–2.

The generic processes at Northwest Family Physicians are illustrated in Figure 13–1. The three categories summarized in Exhibit 13–1— medical processes, nonmedical processes, and

management activity—are further illustrated in Figure 13–1.

Revenue-producing patient service processes are set out next. Five revenue-producing patient service process maps are presented. The five NWFP patient services to be mapped include a simple office visit, another simple office visit with the lab processed in-house at NWFP, an annual exam for females, a complete physical exam, and an FPSS.

The process map for a simple office visit (99213) is illustrated in Figure 13–2. There are five columns across the top of the process map. Each column will contain the activities for a certain category of the process. In these maps, the far left column represents the patient's activ-

---

Exhibit 13–1 Summary of Processes at Northwest Family Practice

MEDICAL PROCESSES

Surgical Procedures
Emergency Medicine Activity
Clinical Testing
Injections
Patient Preparation
Review Outside Data
Medical Administration

NONMEDICAL PROCESSES

Consult
Billing
Document Intake
Phone Intake Plus Message
Filing In and Out

MANAGEMENT ACTIVITY

Finance
Marketing
Strategy
Human Resources
CIS

LABORATORY

Exhibit 13–2 Selected Office Visit Codes

Office visit for the evaluation and management of an established patient, which requires at least two of these three key components:

99212 [self-limited or minor]
    a problem focused history
    a problem focused examination
    straightforward medical decision making

99213 [low to moderate severity]
    an expanded problem focused history
    an expanded problem focused examination
    medical decision making of low complexity

99214 [moderate to high severity]
    a detailed history
    a detailed examination
    medical decision making of moderate complexity

99215 [moderate to high severity]
    a comprehensive history
    a comprehensive examination
    medical decision making of high complexity

Source: Adapted from CPT '97: Physicians' Current Procedural Terminology. American Medical Association, Chicago: 1996, pp. 11–13.

---

ities. The next column represents the receptionist's (front office) activities. The middle column represents the medical assistant's or nurse's activities. The next column represents the doctor's activities. The far right column heading represents a notation that the laboratory in this case is an outside service. Activities are mapped for each individual. Note that in this case lab activities are not mapped because it is an outside service and the process map is contained within the NWFP boundaries.

The process map for a simple office visit (99213) with lab processed in-house at NWFP is illustrated in Figure 13–3. Once again there are five column headings across the top of the process map. The first four headings remain the same as previously described. The far right column represents a notation that the laboratory in this case is processed in-house at NWFP. Activities are again mapped for each individual. Note that lab activities are mapped in this instance because it is now an inside service and is thus contained within the NWFP process boundaries.

The process map for an annual exam for females (99214) is illustrated in Figure 13–4. Note that there are many more activities contained in this process map. The annual exam for females requires multiple processing, which accounts for much of the excess activities present on the map. The additional activities translate into additional labor, which in turn translates into additional cost incurred for this process.

The process map for a complete physical examination (99215) is illustrated in Figure 13–5. Of the five revenue-producing patient services illustrated, the complete physical examination (CPE) is the most costly. Not surprisingly, it contains the most activities, as is revealed within this process map. Note the managed care payer paperwork requirements that are set out as part of the activities.

The process map for an FPSS is illustrated in Figure 13–6. The procedure reflected here is fairly straightforward when compared to the previous example. Maps such as Figure 13–6 can readily be used to show variations in practice patterns. Thus, different doctors may take different amounts of time to perform the various activities on this map. The graphic mapping illustration aids analysis and rapid comprehension of these variances.

Consult processes follow revenue-producing patient service processes. The process map for a generic consultation is illustrated in Figure 13–7. Note that the columns for activities now include a column for the managed care company (who has to approve the consult) and a column for the consultant (who is the other party within the process). This generic process

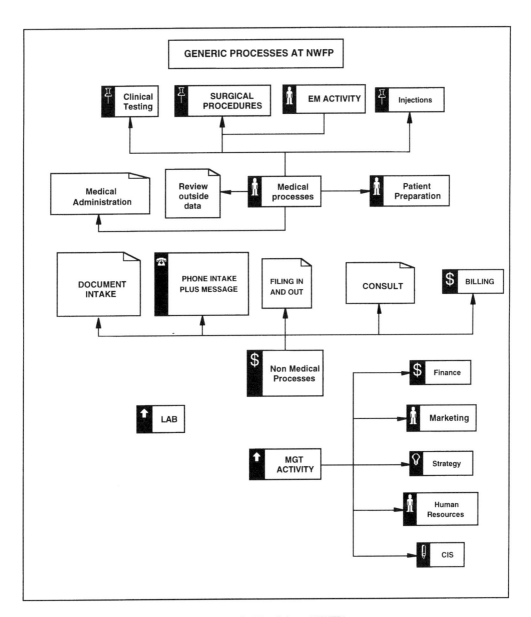

Figure 13–1 Generic Processes at Northwest Family Physicians (NWFP)

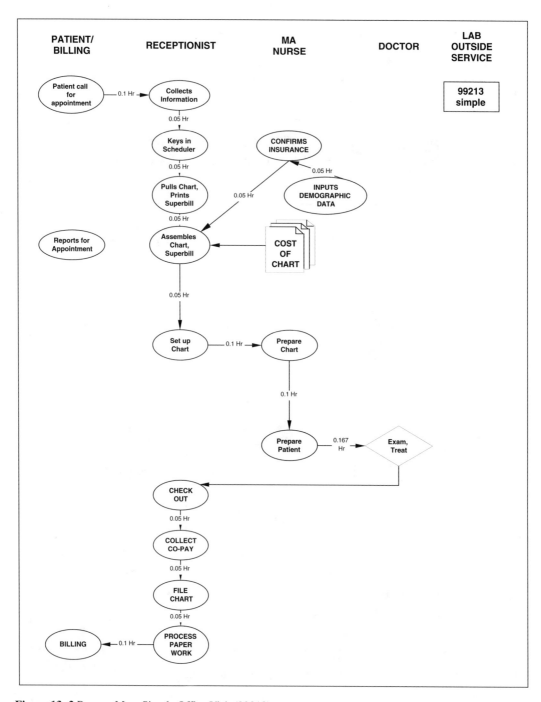

Figure 13–2 Process Map: Simple Office Visit (99213)

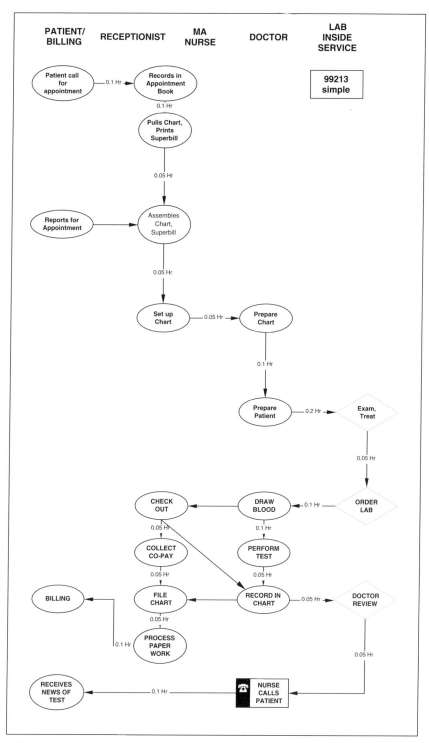

Figure 13–3 Process Map: Simple Office Visit (99213) with Lab Processed at NWFP

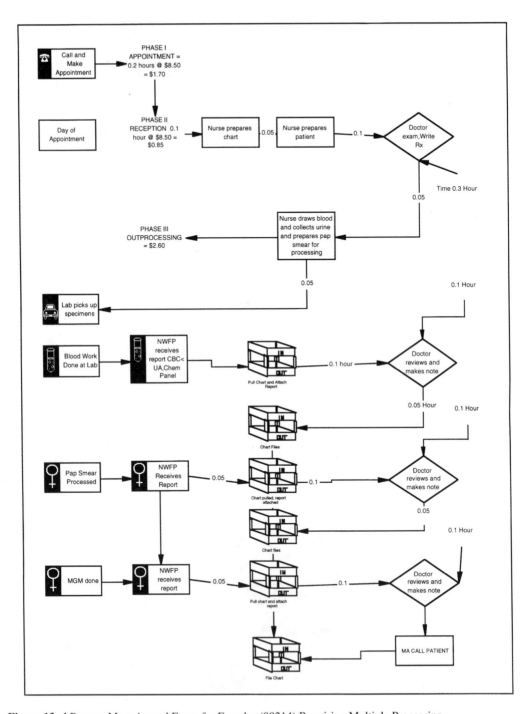

Figure 13–4 Process Map: Annual Exam for Females (99214) Requiring Multiple Processing

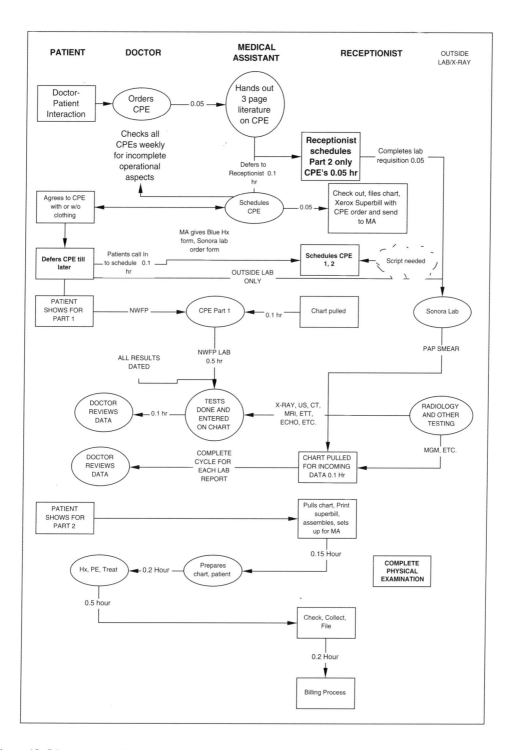

Figure 13–5 Process Map: Complete Physical Examination (99215)

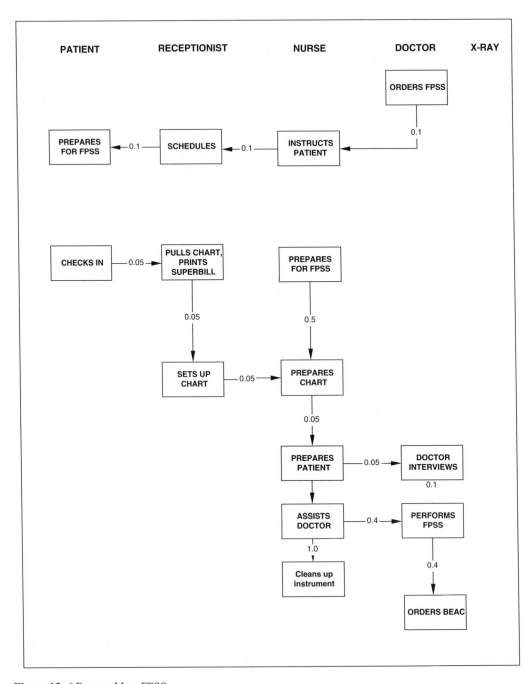

Figure 13–6 Process Map: FPSS

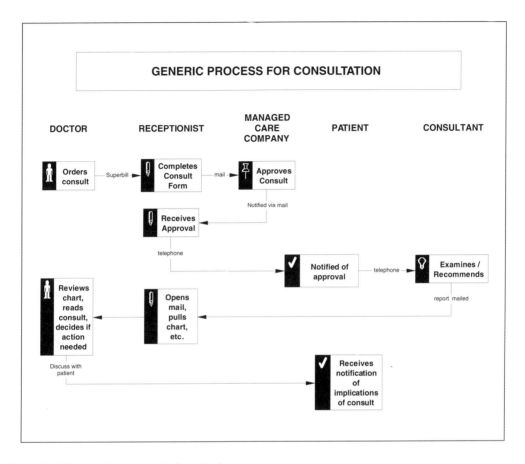

Figure 13–7 Process Map: Generic Consultation

map is a starting point. We will now examine two different consulting processes. One is more cost-effective and thus results in a minimal use of resources. One is not cost-effective and thus results in a maximum use of resources.

The process map for a consultation approval with the consult originating at the primary care physician (PCP) visit is illustrated in Figure 13–8. A consult originating at the PCP visit is more cost-effective. The minimal use of resources is thus illustrated in this process map. The cost of consultation approval with minimum resource use (e.g., the consult originating at the PCP visit) is illustrated in Figure 13–9.

The process map for a consultation approval with the consult originating outside the PCP is illustrated in Figure 13–10. A consult originating outside the PCP is not cost-effective. The maximum use of resources is illustrated in this process map and the difference can readily be seen by comparing Figure 13–10 with Figure 13–8. The cost of consultation approval with maximum resource use (e.g., the consult originating outside the PCP) is illustrated in Figure 13–11.

Finally, front office processes are presented in map form. The process map for phase one, appointment scheduling, is illustrated in Figure 13–12. The cost of this process is also set out in this figure. This information (process and cost) was used to assist in evaluating whether to install a new automated telephone system.

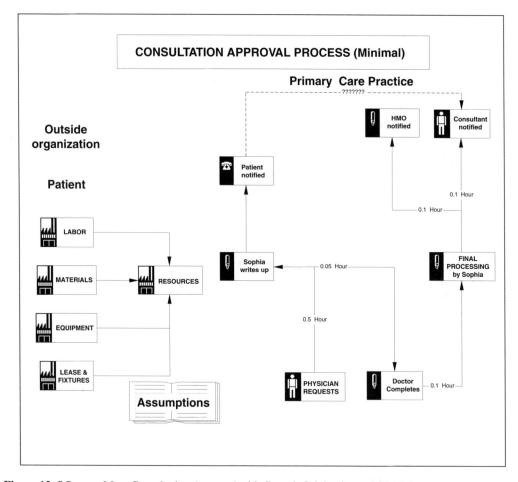

Figure 13–8 Process Map: Consultation Approval with Consult Originating at PCP Visit

The process map for phase two, patient reception, is illustrated in Figure 13–13. The cost of this process is again set out in this figure.

The process map for phase three, patient out processing, is illustrated in Figure 13–14. The cost of this process is once again set out in this figure. The three elements of front office interaction with the patient (phases one, two, and three) can now be combined in order to gain an overview of the total overall activities and costs that are involved in this particular process.

COMMENTARY

The distribution of fixed and variable expenses for NWFP, as described previously, is summarized in Exhibit 13–3. Salaries, payroll taxes, supplies, and postage were selected as variable expenses. Note that other practices might reflect a different distribution.

The established-patient routine office visit cost detail (Worksheet for 99213 [Routine Office Visit—Established Patient]) is set out in Table 13–4. The staff who are involved in the

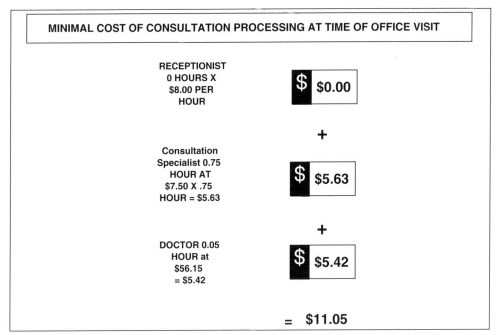

Figure 13–9 Cost of Consultation Approval with Minimum Resource Use

activities include the doctor, the medical assistant (MA), and the receptionist (see column 1; also columns 6, 7, and 8). The activities themselves are described in column 2. The time spent on the activity is recorded in column 3. The hourly rate for the particular individual identified as performing the activity is recorded in column 4. The total labor cost for the particular activity is recorded in column 5 (column 3 × column 4 = column 5). Columns 6, 7, and 8 distribute the labor cost arrived at in column 5 among the appropriate personnel. Finally, column 9, labeled other, contains all expenses other than the activity labor. The fixed overhead is added as a single figure, as is the allocated variable expense, to arrive at the total cost.

The new patient routine office visit cost detail (Worksheet for 99213 [Routine Office Visit—New Patient]) is set out in Table 13–5. The staff who are involved in the activities include the doctor, the MA, and the receptionist. The column labeled other contains expenses other than the activity labor. In this case—a new

patient—there are two additional expenses on the cost detail. There is a charge under other for materials as a new chart is set up for the new patient. There is an additional charge under labor as the receptionist inputs demographics for the new patient.

The annual female exam cost detail (Worksheet for 99214 [Annual Female Exam]) is set out in Table 13–6. The staff who are involved in the activities include the doctor, the MA, and the receptionist. The column labeled other contains expenses other than the activity labor. In this case—an annual female exam—there are multiple additional expenses on the cost detail. The activities increase, resulting in additional labor charges. There are additional line items in the MA activities column for chaperone and for process pap smear. The doctor's time is double that of a routine office visit, resulting in a greater labor charge. In addition, there is another entire array of activities for this exam listed on line items 27 through 35. These activities involve all three categories of personnel:

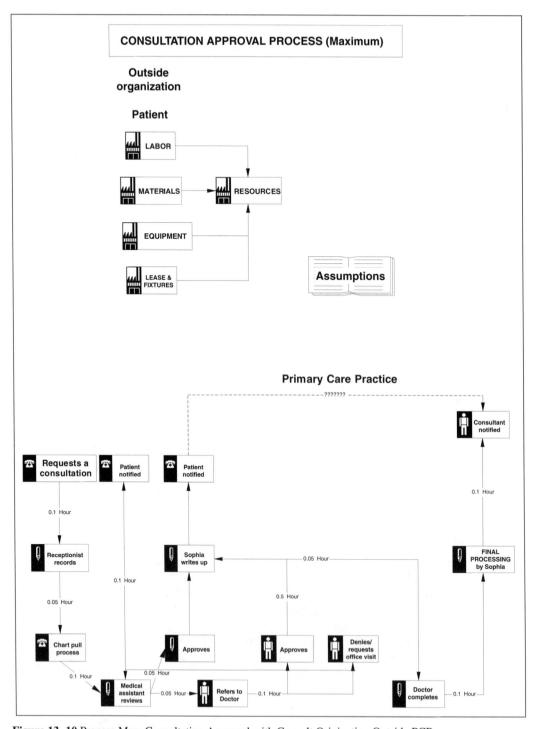

Figure 13–10 Process Map: Consultation Approval with Consult Originating Outside PCP

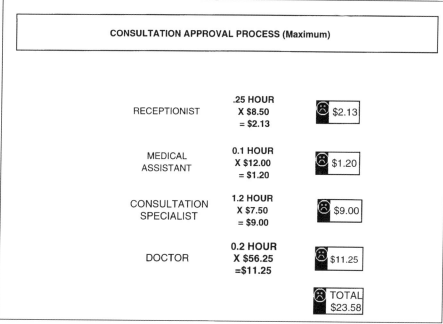

Figure 13–11 Cost of Consultation Approval with Maximum Resource Use

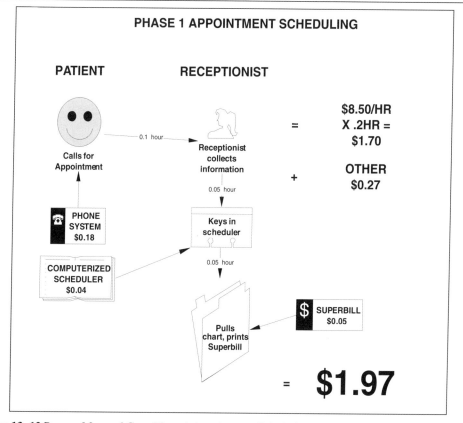

Figure 13–12 Process Map and Cost: Phase 1 Appointment Scheduling

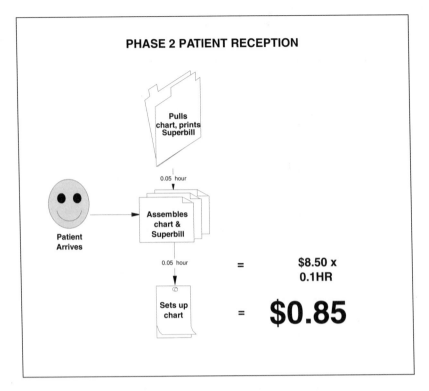

Figure 13–13 Process Map and Cost: Phase 2 Patient Reception

the doctor, the medical assistant, and the receptionist. The overall cost, of course, is increased by the cost of these additional activities.

The report processing cost detail (Worksheet for Report Processing) is set out in Table 13–7. This worksheet illustrates an internal office function. It reports labor cost only. All activities involved are listed in column B. This is a "pure" cost on Table 13–7; that is, it does not yet contain the additional charges for fixed overhead, variable expenses, and so forth. It is used by

NWFP to analyze internal processes for efficiency.

In conclusion, Dr. Stuart's emphasis is on process and process improvement. He is proactive and takes his findings to the payers as the rationale for contract negotiations. Since he implemented activity-based costing some years ago (in 1993), he has had the opportunity to demonstrate how it yields results in his practice. He continues to refine his ABC applications.

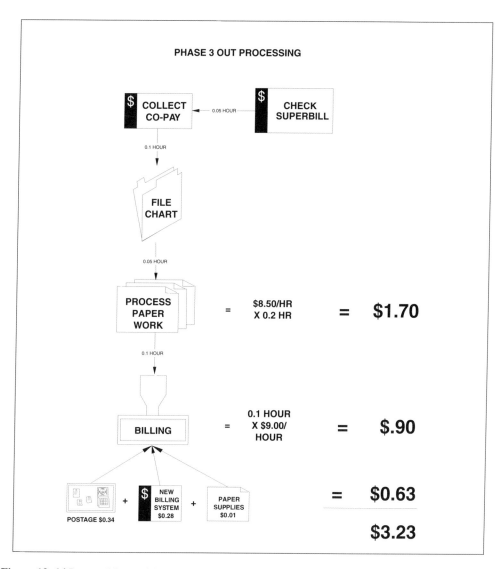

Figure 13–14 Process Map and Cost: Phase 3 Out Processing

Exhibit 13–3 Distribution of Fixed and Variable Expenses, NWFP

	FY 1995–1996					
	TOTAL		**VARIABLE**		**FIXED**	
Account	**Amount**	**Allocation**	**Amount**	**Allocation**	**Amount**	**Allocation**
Doctors' Salary	$280,500	$7.69	$280,500	$7.69		
Employees' Salary	$162,264	$9.40	$162,264	$9.40		
Payroll Taxes	$30,187	$1.75	$30,187	$1.75		
Rent	$69,384	$4.02			$69,384	$4.02
Supplies	$44,161	$2.56	$44,161	$2.56		
Office Supply						
computer	$8,010	$0.46			$8,010	$0.46
supply	$14,110	$0.82			$14,110	$0.82
postage	$7,644	$0.44	$7,644	$0.44		
print	$4,315	$0.25			$4,315	$0.25
Service						
accounting	$14,545	$0.84			$14,545	$0.84
computer	$4,217	$0.24			$4,217	$0.24
legal	$1,615	$0.09			$1,615	$0.09
other	$14,884	$0.86			$14,884	$0.86
payroll	$1,966	$0.11			$1,966	$0.11
Malpractice Insurance	$16,479	$0.95			$16,479	$0.95
Gen Insurance	$3,034	$0.18			$3,034	$0.18
Rental Equipment	$1,415	$0.08			$1,415	$0.08
Maintenance	$1,320	$0.08			$1,320	$0.08
Telephone	$11,305	$0.66			$11,305	$0.66
Subscriptions	$1,363	$0.08			$1,363	$0.08
Taxes	$713	$0.04			$713	$0.04
Depreciation	$21,643	$1.25			$21,643	$1.25
Nonshared Expenses	$86,014	$4.98			$86,014	$4.98
Total	$801,088		$524,756		$276,332	

Table 13–4 Worksheet for 99213 (Routine Office Visit—Established Patient)

Actor	Activity	Hours	Hrly Rate	Total	Recpt	MA	Doctor	Other
Patient	Calls NWFP							
Receptionist	Collects Information	0.10	$8.50	$0.85	$0.85			
	Keys into Scheduler	0.05	$8.50	$0.43	$0.43			
	Pulls Chart, Prn Superbill	0.05	$8.50	$0.43	$0.43			
PhoneSys	Per Call Received			$0.18				$0.18
Software	Per Appointment			$0.04				$0.04
Material	Superbill			$0.05				$0.05
Patient	Signs In							
Receptionist	Assembles Chart	0.05	$8.50	$0.43	$0.43			
	Sets up Chart	0.05	$8.50	$0.43	$0.43			
MA	Prepares Chart	0.1	$12.00	$1.20		$1.20		
	Prepares Patient	0.1	$12.00	$1.20		$1.20		
Doctor	Exam, Treat	0.167	$54.42	$9.09			$9.09	
Receptionist	Check Out	0.05	$8.50	$0.43	$0.43			
	Collect Co-Pay	0.05	$8.50	$0.43	$0.43			
	File Chart	0.05	$8.50	$0.43	$0.43			
	Process Paper	0.05	$8.50	$0.43	$0.43			
BillClerk	Billing	0.10	$9.00	$0.90	$0.90			
Source	Per Account Process			$0.28				$0.28
Postage	Per Bill			$0.34				$0.34
Supplies	Envelope, Paper			$0.01				$0.01
Total				**$17.54**	**$5.15**	**$2.40**	**$9.09**	**$0.90**
Fixed Overhead				$16.08				
Variable				$3.99				
Total				**$37.61**				

Table 13–5 Worksheet for 99213 (Routine Office Visit—New Patient)

Actor	Activity	Hours	Hrly Rate	Total	Recpt	MA	Doctor	Other
Patient	Calls NWFP							
Receptionist	Collects Information	0.10	$8.50	$0.85	$0.85			
	Keys into Scheduler	0.05	$8.50	$0.43	$0.43			
	Pulls Chart, Prn Superbill	0.05	$8.50	$0.43	$0.43			
PhoneSys	Per Call Received			$0.18				$0.18
Software	Per Appointment			$0.04				$0.04
Material	Superbill			$0.05				$0.05
Patient	Signs In							
Receptionist	Assembles Chart	0.05	$8.50	$0.43	$0.43			
	Confirms Insurance	0.05	$8.50	$0.43	$0.43			
	Inputs Demographics	0.05	$8.50	$0.43	$0.43			
Materials	Chart			$1.50				$1.50
	Sets up Chart	0.05	$8.50	$0.43	$0.43			
MA	Prepares Chart	0.1	$12.00	$1.20		$1.20		
	Prepares Patient	0.1	$12.00	$1.20		$1.20		
Doctor	Exam, Treat	0.167	$54.42	$9.09			$9.09	
Receptionist	Check Out	0.05	$8.50	$0.43	$0.43			
	Collect Co-Pay	0.05	$8.50	$0.43	$0.43			
	File Chart	0.05	$8.50	$0.43	$0.43			
	Process Paper	0.05	$8.50	$0.43	$0.43			
BillClerk	Billing	0.10	$9.00	$0.90	$0.90			
Source	Per Account Process			$0.28				$0.28
Postage	Per Bill			$0.34				$0.34
Supplies	Envelope, Paper			$0.01				$0.01
Total				**$19.89**	**$6.00**	**$2.40**	**$9.09**	**$2.40**
Fixed Overhead				$16.08				
Variable				$3.99				
Total				**$39.96**				

Table 13–6 Worksheet for 99214 (Annual Female Exam)

Actor	Activity	Hours	Hrly Rate	Total	Recpt	MA	Doctor	Other
Patient	Calls NWFP							
Receptionist	Collects Information	0.10	$8.50	$0.85	$0.85			
	Keys into Scheduler	0.05	$8.50	$0.43	$0.43			
	Pulls Chart, Prn Superbill	0.05	$8.50	$0.43	$0.43			
PhoneSys	Per Call Received			$0.18				$0.18
Software	Per Appointment			$0.04				$0.04
Materials	Superbill			$0.05				$0.05
Patient	Signs In							
Receptionist	Assembles Chart	0.05	$8.50	$0.43	$0.43			
	Sets up Chart	0.05	$8.50	$0.43	$0.43			
MA	Prepares Chart	0.1	$12.00	$1.20		$1.20		
	Prepares Patient	0.1	$12.00	$1.20		$1.20		
	Chaperone	0.1	$12.00	$1.20		$1.20		
Doctor	Exam, Treat, Order	0.33	$54.42	$17.96			$17.96	
MA	Process Pap	0.05	$12.00	$0.60		$0.60		
Receptionist	Check Out	0.05	$8.50	$0.43	$0.43			
	Collect Co-Pay	0.05	$8.50	$0.43	$0.43			
	File Chart	0.05	$8.50	$0.43	$0.43			
	Process Paper	0.05	$8.50	$0.43	$0.43			
BillClerk	Billing	0.1	$9.00	$0.90	$0.90			
Source	Per Account Process			$0.28				$0.28
Postage	Per Bill Sent			$0.34				$0.34
Supplies	Envelope, Paper			$0.01				$0.01
Receptionist	Open Mail, Pull Chart	0.1	$8.50	$0.85	$0.85			
Doctor	Review, Notes	0.1	$54.42	$5.44			$5.44	
Receptionist	Files Report, Chart	0.1	$8.50	$0.85	$0.85			
Receptionist	Open Mail, Pull Chart	0.1	$8.50	$0.85	$0.85			
Doctor	Review, Notes	0.05	$54.42	$2.72			$2.72	
Receptionist	Files Report, Chart	0.1	$8.50	$0.85	$0.85			
Receptionist	Open Mail, Pull Chart	0.1	$8.50	$0.85	$0.85			
Doctor	Review, Notes	0.05	$54.42	$2.72			$2.72	
MA	Calls Patient	0.1	$12.00	$1.20		$1.20		
Total				**$44.54**	**$9.40**	**$5.40**	**$28.84**	**$0.90**

Fixed Overhead		$32.16
Variable		$3.99
Total		**$80.69**

Table 13–7 Worksheet Report Processing

Actor	Activity	Hours	Hrly Rate	Total	Recpt	MA	Doctor
Recpt	Opens Report	0.05	$8.50	$0.43	$0.43		
	Pulls Chart	0.10	$8.50	$0.85	$0.85		
	Takes to Doctor						
Doctor	Evaluate Record	0.10	$54.15	$5.42			$5.42
	Delegates to MA						
MA	Calls Patient	0.10	$12.00	$1.20		$1.20	
	Files Chart	0.05	$12.00	$0.60		$0.60	
Total				**$8.50**	**$1.28**	**$1.80**	**$5.42**

## CHAPTER 14

The Top-Down Approach by Kentucky PrimeCare

Michael A. Fitzpatrick with Judith J. Baker

CHAPTER OUTLINE

Preface
Background
Initial Activity-Based Costing Pilot Project
Second Stage of Activity-Based Costing
Uses of ABC at PrimeCare
Commentary

PREFACE

This case study is about an overall view of activity-based costing (ABC) as implemented in a family practice. The initial pilot project was conducted in 1995 and was then followed by development and implementation of ABC for all CPT codes in the practice. The practice is a two-site family practice located in Kentucky, employing seven family physicians and two pediatricians. The contributor, Mike Fitzpatrick, MD, is chief financial officer of PrimeCare, a family practice professional service corporation (PSC) located in Elizabethtown, Kentucky. He also remains in private practice. In addition to his professional duties he is an Associate Clinical Professor at the University of Kentucky and at the University of Louisville. *Top down* within the chapter title refers to Dr. Fitzpatrick's initial approach to his ABC project. He began by choosing CPT codes as the structure on which to base his cost assignment. He went "top down" by choosing a financial data structure

(the CPT codes) and moving toward how to assign his various categories of costs. His approach reflects an inherent linking of the cause-and-effect relationship of cost and revenue. It is a financial management approach.

BACKGROUND

PrimeCare PSC is a primary care group practice located in central Kentucky, south of Louisville. It was formed by the merger of two existing group practices in January 1994. It now employs seven family physicians, two pediatricians, and two physician assistants to staff its offices in Elizabethtown, and Bardstown, Kentucky.

PrimeCare was formed as a result of the increasing penetration of managed care into the market in this area. It was believed that economies of scale could help keep costs down at a time when insurers and consumers were clamoring for decreased costs. Further, it was felt that by being progressive in approaching insurance companies, practicing physicians might be able to maintain their control over the clinical aspects of medicine. As a result, PrimeCare has attempted many projects to position itself for the marketplace in which it finds itself. We have begun the development of clinical pathways (and their monitoring) in ambulatory care practice. We have begun a detailed credentialing program that meets National Committee for Quality Assurance (NCQA) standards. We have also looked at the finances of medicine in a new way and used activity-based accounting as the method for determining the costs of providing various services.

INITIAL ACTIVITY-BASED COSTING PILOT PROJECT

The initial pilot project using ABC was conducted in 1995. At that time, the question asked was: "Is it cost-effective to perform laboratory studies in the office?" This question has frequently been asked by physicians in the era of managed care, and PrimeCare was interested in determining its own answer. In doing the study and using the data available at the time, there were two important discoveries. First, it was indeed cost-effective and profitable to perform in-office laboratory studies,[1] and second, there were some very real limitations to the accuracy of the study when only one portion of the office was considered in isolation.

SECOND STAGE OF ACTIVITY-BASED COSTING

The results of the pilot project compelled PrimeCare to move into the second stage of activity-based costing. At that point, the goal became to determine the cost of each CPT code for which PrimeCare billed. Although this project was far more complex than the pilot project, it also promised greater accuracy because places where overlap occurred, such as when a laboratory person performed work as a medical assistant (i.e., where someone was working outside his or her usual job description), could be dealt with more clearly.

Beginning in the second half of 1995, Prime-Care began the process of developing activity-based costing for all of its CPT codes. This required diagramming all the processes that occur in a primary care office.[2] This alone took two months. The diagramming allowed us to (1) cover all the steps needed, (2) assign steps to each CPT code, and (3) study activities to determine whether a particular CPT code might follow more than one pathway and therefore determine the relative frequencies of each and the amount of time and supplies involved in each activity.

In order to place costs where needed, Prime-Care has grouped the costs, dividing them into seven groups: overhead (or period) cost, network development cost, insurance and billing cost, front office cost, clinical cost, diagnostic cost, and provider cost. See Table 14–1 for examples of PrimeCare's activity-based costs. A discussion of the individual columns follows.

Overhead includes such things as rent, utilities, cleaning, and so forth. Allocating these costs are among the most difficult decisions in activity-based costing.[3] In the case of Prime-Care, these costs were spread out over each of the remaining six categories, based on the square footage that was used by each area in all the offices combined. This distribution was chosen because the cost of these items was, for the most part, proportional to the square footage that was used. For rent, this may seem obvious, but the cost of heating space and cleaning are also generally proportional to the amount of space to be heated or cleaned.

Network development cost represents the money that is invested by PrimeCare in growing the practice. It is mostly money spent on recruiting new providers (physicians and midlevel providers) and on enticing other practices to join with PrimeCare. Because these costs deal primarily with providers, the cost was divided evenly among each CPT code (based on frequency of billing) that includes the direct involvement of one of our providers. As of our latest figures, this amounts to $3.42 for all evaluation and management (E & M) codes and physician procedure codes. It was not added to the cost of codes involving injectables (done by medical assistants) or diagnostic tests (our physicians are not directly involved with the lab) or any other procedure where a physician was not directly and intimately involved.

In the insurance and billing cost group, it turned out that there were basically three classes of codes in use in PrimeCare. The first class represented those codes that were often used alone or were the point of service codes, such as most of the E & M codes. They were the most expensive because they were often sent alone to the insurer or were the first of several sent. They cost more because all the set up of insurance information must be done for sending in a single code or the first code in a list.

The second class represented the opposite extreme and were codes that were almost always sent in with other codes (or, in the case of allergy shots, were sent to the insurer in large numbers). This group was the least expensive because other codes ate up the set-up costs and these became incremental costs to the billing system.

The third class, and the smallest, were those codes where there was a large mix of times when the code was either sent alone or with others, or when a code had historically caused the practice to do extra work with insurers (such as those requiring reports). These occupied a middle level between the other two. It would be lengthy to go into the exact algorithms that were needed for us to develop the costs. The last data placed these three categories at roughly $3.55, $0.76, and $2.02, respectively. Thus, the insurance and billing cost of an office visit was roughly $3.55, of performing a lab test was $0.76, and of performing certain unusual procedures was $2.02.

The front office, clinical, and diagnostic cost categories became very complicated.

Front office cost reflects multiple factors in PrimeCare. It represents the amount of time and supplies that are used for answering phones, scheduling appointments (we were surprised to learn that the front office cost of scheduling patients and taking walk-ins without appointments was virtually identical for us), updating computer profiles on patients (insurance information, address, and so forth), checking patients out and collecting copayments and bills at the time of service, filing, transcription, pulling and filing charts for phone calls and for diagnostic studies when the results were not available at the time of service (this entire last step was shown to increase costs substantially at Prime-Care). Front office cost also includes, at Prime-Care, the cost of doing referrals (i.e., scheduling patients with specialists and arranging for appropriate insurance paperwork to be completed). There was no simple breakdown of how these costs turned out. Each CPT code represented the different percentages of activities that were performed at the different frequencies. This led to a wide variance, from just over $1.00 for some CPT codes, especially diagnostic tests, to almost $13.00 for certain procedures.

Clinical cost was very similar to front office cost. Clinical cost represents the amount of time spent by medical assistants in performing certain activities and the supplies they used in doing them. Once again the frequency of activities and the specific activities performed varied with the CPT code. The values here ranged from a few pennies (for CPT codes performed outside the office where the medical assistants' only time spent was in the occasional telephone call related to the out-of-office patient), to over $100 for those office procedures that were heavily time- or supply-intensive (such as an office endoscopy).

Diagnostic cost dealt with the costs of performing laboratory and radiology tests in office. The results were remarkably close to those obtained by the preliminary study, which was very gratifying. Once again, the amount of time needed by techs (or the cost of paying different types of techs) and the cost of supplies varied from one CPT code to another. As might be expected, it turned out in this area that the more frequently a particular test was performed the lower the cost tended to be. Current results show that lab tests cost between about $1.00 for the fastest, simplest, and most common to about $40.00 for the most intensive. X-rays ranged from about $20.00 to over $50.00, generally following the same pattern as the lab tests.

The last category of costs for our CPT codes was the provider cost. This was the only category of cost in which PrimeCare opted to depart from actual cost. Because PrimeCare is owned by its physicians, like most private medical practices, little of the earnings have been retained (traditionally). Thus, the more profitable the year, the larger the entire physician compensation becomes. The larger the entire physician compensation becomes, the more quickly the practice moves from being profitable to simply breaking even. Using these numbers for physician compensation in cost accounting means that the actual costs vary, depending on the profitability of the company. (Even more, this means that as a CPT code becomes more profitable, it costs more to perform it because the physician who is performing it is paid more; thus, it becomes less profitable. A paradox!)

It seemed unreasonable that the cost of a CPT code would vary based on its profitability. As a result, PrimeCare made the determination to base provider costs on an "ideal" provider, i.e., we estimated the cost of hiring an average provider in our area (based on data from *Medical Economics*) to take the place of each of our current providers. This total amount was then used instead of the actual amount. With nine months of data, the figures are surprisingly close (within 2.5 percent of each other). The ideal amount is then divided among the CPT codes— the actual time spent on each based on averages calculated using time study. Once again, wide variations seem to be the norm. Some CPT codes show no physician cost (such as lab tests—the cost of interpretation of studies is included in the E & M code) to over $250 for a highly time-intensive code.

For our purposes we then add all the categories together (and at the request of the physicians of PrimeCare a second total without the physician component is also calculated). This gives us the cost of providing a particular CPT code. These results show a reasonably close correlation with the Medicare relative value unit (RVU) system with a few notable differences. It also shows that, in our area at least, the Medicare reimbursement rate is about at the breakeven point for most CPT codes.

USES OF ABC AT PRIMECARE

During 1996, PrimeCare has used this information in dealing proactively with insurers as they attempted to adjust fee schedules. This information has been useful in determining the places where pressure could, and should, be applied and in determining whether a fee schedule was worth considering at all. In return, PrimeCare has found that many insurers were willing to attempt to adjust fee schedules in order to make them more accurately reflect the actual costs of physicians. In fact, PrimeCare has been impressed that insurers respond quite openly and honestly when faced with hard and well-researched numbers rather than anecdotal evidence and "gut feeling."

COMMENTARY

The seven family practice cost groupings utilized by PrimeCare are illustrated in Exhibit 14–1. These cost groupings are the particular choices made by PrimeCare for their practice. Dr. Fitzgerald's own footnote cautions readers not to extrapolate these results to their own office practices because each case is unique and must be determined on a case-by-case basis. He is correct.

Exhibit 14–1 Family Practice Cost Groupings

Network Development Costs
Insurance and Billing Costs
Front Office Costs
Clinical Costs
Provider Costs
Overhead Costs
Diagnostic Costs

The composition of the front office grouping is illustrated in Exhibit 14–2. Front office duties are considered support activities. Note that PrimeCare considers referral costs as front office costs. This is an individual choice and reflects a particular practice pattern.

The composition of the clinical costs, diagnostic costs, and provider costs is illustrated in Exhibit 14–3. Note that each of these designations measures the time that is expended by individuals whose services directly result in revenue. Also these individuals have received special training and certification to perform these duties. As a point of information, Prime-Care's physicians name the cost measurement for their time provider cost. Their rationale is that they—the physicians—provide the service. This terminology may, however, create confusion in other settings. Fiscal intermediaries and carriers consider the entity that is providing service delivery as the provider; hence, "provider number." In this case, because PrimeCare's information was designed for management use, there is no barrier to the use of the term in this manner.

Exhibit 14–2 Composition of Family Practice Front Office Costs

> **FRONT OFFICE COSTS**
>
> Time and Supplies to:
> Answer Phone
> Schedule Appointments
> Update Computer Profiles of Patients
> Check Out Patients
> Collect Copayments and Bills (at time of service)
> File
> Medical Records Transcription
> Pull/File Charts for Phone Calls
> Pull/File Charts for Diagnostic Studies (when results not available at time of service)
> Referral—Schedule Patients with Specialists
> Referral—Complete Insurance Paperwork
> *Source:* Copyright © 1997, Resource Group, Ltd., Dallas, Texas.

Exhibit 14–3 Composition of Family Practice Clinical, Diagnostic, and Provider Costs

> **Clinical Costs:** Time and Supplies Expended Primarily by Nursing Staff
>
> **Diagnostic Costs:** Time and Supplies Expended by Laboratory Technicians and Radiology Technicians (to perform laboratory and radiology tests in the office)
>
> **Provider Costs:** Time Expended by Practice Physicians
> *Source:* Copyright © 1997, Resource Group, Ltd., Dallas, Texas.

The composition of the overhead costs is illustrated in Exhibit 14–4. Note that the overhead example in PrimeCare's case primarily represents the costs of space occupancy. Dr. Fitzgerald says that allocating overhead costs is among the most difficult decisions in activity-based costing; he is correct.

The cost assignment method for each cost grouping is illustrated in Exhibit 14–5. Of the seven groupings, four are traced and three are allocated. Three of the four traced groupings used actual cost. The fourth (provider costs) uses standard cost rather than actual.

Each of the three allocated cost groupings uses a different allocation basis. This is proper in ABC methodology. (Note that some other organizations may use more than one allocation basis within a single cost grouping.) The allocation of insurance and billing cost was accomplished by examining activities and collapsing the activities into three categories for purposes

---

Exhibit 14–4 Composition of Family Practice Overhead Costs

> **Overhead Costs:** Examples include
>
> • Rent
> • Utilities
> • Cleaning

Exhibit 14–5 Family Practice Costs Assignment

COST ASSIGNMENT	
	Method
Network Development Costs	Allocated (evenly by CPT code volume)
Insurance and Billing Costs	Allocated (by 3 levels of resource consumption)
Front Office Costs	Traced (actual)
Clinical Costs	Traced (actual)
Diagnostic Costs	Traced (actual)
Provider Costs	Traced (using standard cost rather than actual—see text)
Overhead Costs	Allocated (by square feet)

of allocation. Each of the three categories represents a different level of resource consumption that can be generally described as high, moderate, or low. This methodology provides flexible allocation capability. The overhead is allocated by square feet. Whereas other practices may commonly use more than one allocation basis, Dr. Fitzgerald's rationale is set out in the text and reflects the true nature of his own practice's overhead composition. The network development costs are allocated evenly by CPT code volume. Again, Dr. Fitzgerald's rationale is set out in the text.

Dr. Fitzpatrick chose to assemble the costs by CPT code. This decision is an individual one to be made in the planning process. It is a vital decision because the output to be used for management decisions will appear in the chosen format.

Review Tables 14–1 through 14–5 (Prime-Care Costs by Procedure Code—Parts 1 through 5).

The new development cost (column 2) runs throughout Tables 14–1 and 14–2 and stops halfway through Table 14–3. The reason is this: The new development cost was charged against procedures that include the direct involvement of the physicians. It is not charged against procedures that include only the services of medical assistants (such as injectables) or only the services of technicians (such as certain laboratory tests and/or radiology exposures). The lat-

ter items are the costs that run through the second half of Table 14–3 and throughout Tables 14–4 and 14–5.

The insurance and billing cost (column 3) varies throughout Tables 14–1 through 14–5. Refer to Exhibit 14–5, illustrating the allocation of this cost category by three levels of resource consumption. The three levels appearing in Tables 14–1 through 14–5 are $3.50, $1.97, and $0.77.

The front office cost (column 4) reflects substantial variation in Tables 14–1 through 14–3 and the first half of Table 14–4. The remaining portion of Table 14–4 and all of Table 14–5 reflect a single figure of $1.20. This differential reflects the nature of the CPT codes (and their related resource consumption) in these respective portions of the tables.

The clinical cost (column 5) reflects variations throughout all five tables. The variations directly reflect whether nursing services were required for the particular line item. Also note that clinical costs, where applicable, ranged from a high of $115.83 to a low of $0.05.

The diagnostic cost (column 6) reflects zero until the middle of Table 14–4. The remaining portion of Table 14–4 and all of Table 14–5 reflect the varying costs for laboratory and radiology time and supplies.

The provider or MD cost (column 7) reflects varying costs through Tables 14–1 and 14–2 and the first half of Table 14–3. The remaining

Table 14–1 Selected PrimeCare Costs by Procedure Code—Part 1

CPT Code (1)	New Development (2)	Ins. & Billing (3)	Front Office (4)	Clinical (5)	Diagnostic (6)	Provider (MD) (7)	Total (8)	Net of MD (9)
99201	$2.57	$3.50	$6.73	$4.62	$0.00	$12.62	$30.60	$17.98
99202	$2.57	$3.50	$7.46	$5.15	$0.00	$19.84	$39.23	$19.39
99203	$2.57	$3.50	$8.18	$7.29	$0.00	$30.66	$53.16	$22.50
99204	$2.57	$3.50	$8.90	$10.50	$0.00	$43.28	$70.02	$26.74
99205	$2.57	$3.50	$9.62	$17.44	$0.00	$55.91	$90.69	$34.79
99211	$2.57	$3.50	$4.09	$4.62	$0.00	$2.71	$17.80	$15.10
99212	$2.57	$3.50	$4.81	$5.15	$0.00	$9.02	$25.51	$16.50
99213	$2.57	$3.50	$5.53	$6.22	$0.00	$16.23	$34.68	$18.45
99214	$2.57	$3.50	$6.25	$7.29	$0.00	$30.66	$51.20	$20.54
99215	$2.57	$3.50	$6.97	$9.96	$0.00	$45.09	$69.36	$24.27
99242	$2.57	$3.50	$6.97	$5.15	$0.00	$45.09	$64.46	$19.37
99243	$2.57	$3.50	$5.53	$6.22	$0.00	$59.52	$78.77	$19.25
99354	$2.58	$3.50	$2.16	$9.96	$0.00	$45.21	$64.58	$19.37
99355	$2.58	$3.50	$2.16	$9.96	$0.00	$45.21	$64.58	$19.37
99358	$2.57	$3.50	$1.20	$2.48	$0.00	$39.68	$50.34	$10.66
99360	$2.57	$3.50	$1.20	$7.29	$0.00	$37.87	$53.40	$15.53
99391	$2.57	$3.50	$4.81	$7.29	$0.00	$12.62	$31.36	$18.74
99392	$2.57	$3.50	$4.81	$7.29	$0.00	$12.62	$31.36	$18.74
99393	$2.57	$3.50	$4.81	$7.29	$0.00	$12.62	$31.36	$18.74
99394	$2.57	$3.50	$4.81	$7.29	$0.00	$12.62	$31.36	$18.74
99395	$2.57	$3.50	$4.81	$7.29	$0.00	$12.62	$31.36	$18.74
99396	$2.57	$3.50	$4.81	$7.29	$0.00	$12.62	$31.36	$18.74
99397	$2.57	$3.50	$4.81	$7.29	$0.00	$12.62	$31.36	$18.74
99396A	$2.57	$3.50	$6.01	$9.96	$0.00	$7.21	$29.80	$22.59
99396B	$2.57	$3.50	$6.73	$9.96	$0.00	$12.62	$36.05	$23.42
99396C	$2.57	$3.50	$7.46	$9.96	$0.00	$19.84	$44.13	$24.29
82270	$0.00	$0.77	$1.20	$0.53	$0.00	$0.18	$2.73	$2.55
99217	$2.57	$3.50	$0.24	$0.05	$0.00	$48.69	$56.08	$7.39
99218	$2.57	$3.50	$0.24	$0.05	$0.00	$54.11	$61.59	$7.49
99219	$2.57	$3.50	$0.24	$0.05	$0.00	$90.18	$98.33	$8.15
99220	$2.57	$3.50	$0.24	$0.05	$0.00	$119.03	$127.72	$8.69
99221	$2.57	$3.50	$0.24	$0.05	$0.00	$63.12	$70.78	$7.65
99222	$2.57	$3.50	$0.24	$0.05	$0.00	$91.98	$100.16	$8.19
99223	$2.57	$3.50	$0.24	$0.05	$0.00	$110.01	$118.53	$8.52
99231	$2.57	$3.50	$0.24	$0.05	$0.00	$30.66	$37.71	$7.05
99232	$2.57	$3.50	$0.24	$0.05	$0.00	$39.68	$46.90	$7.22
99233	$2.57	$3.50	$0.24	$0.05	$0.00	$70.34	$78.12	$7.79
99238	$2.57	$3.50	$0.24	$0.05	$0.00	$50.50	$57.92	$7.42
99251	$2.57	$3.50	$3.61	$0.05	$0.00	$12.63	$22.78	$10.15
99252	$2.57	$3.50	$0.24	$0.05	$0.00	$73.94	$81.80	$7.85
99253	$2.57	$3.50	$0.24	$0.05	$0.00	$93.78	$102.00	$8.22
99254	$2.57	$3.50	$0.24	$0.05	$0.00	$119.03	$127.72	$8.69
99255	$2.57	$3.50	$0.24	$0.05	$0.00	$162.32	$171.80	$9.49
99261	$2.57	$3.50	$0.24	$0.05	$0.00	$28.86	$35.88	$7.02
99262	$2.57	$3.50	$0.24	$0.05	$0.00	$45.09	$52.41	$7.32
99263	$2.57	$3.50	$0.24	$0.05	$0.00	$64.93	$72.61	$7.69
99281	$2.57	$3.50	$0.24	$0.05	$0.00	$32.46	$39.55	$7.09
99282	$2.57	$3.50	$0.24	$0.05	$0.00	$39.68	$46.90	$7.22
99283	$2.57	$3.50	$0.24	$0.05	$0.00	$50.50	$57.92	$7.42
99284	$2.57	$3.50	$0.24	$0.05	$0.00	$63.12	$70.78	$7.65
99285	$2.57	$3.50	$0.24	$0.05	$0.00	$81.16	$89.14	$7.99
99291	$2.57	$3.50	$0.24	$0.05	$0.00	$180.35	$190.17	$9.82
99292	$2.57	$3.50	$0.24	$0.05	$0.00	$75.75	$83.63	$7.89

Courtesy of PrimeCare, PSC, Elizabethtown, Kentucky.

Table 14–2 Selected PrimeCare Costs by Procedure Code—Part 2

CPT Code (1)	New Development (2)	Ins. & Billing (3)	Front Office (4)	Clinical (5)	Diagnostic (6)	Provider (MD) (7)	Total (8)	Net of MD (9)
99356	$2.57	$1.97	$0.24	$0.05	$0.00	$79.35	$85.75	$6.39
99357	$2.57	$1.97	$0.24	$0.05	$0.00	$79.35	$85.75	$6.39
99431	$2.57	$3.50	$0.24	$0.05	$0.00	$79.35	$87.31	$7.95
99433	$2.57	$3.50	$0.24	$0.05	$0.00	$32.46	$39.55	$7.09
99440	$2.57	$1.97	$0.24	$0.05	$0.00	$79.35	$85.75	$6.39
99301	$2.57	$3.50	$1.44	$10.69	$0.00	$30.66	$49.76	$19.11
99302	$2.57	$3.50	$1.44	$10.69	$0.00	$46.89	$66.30	$19.41
99303	$2.57	$3.50	$1.44	$10.69	$0.00	$63.12	$82.83	$19.70
99311	$2.57	$3.50	$1.44	$10.69	$0.00	$21.64	$40.58	$18.94
99312	$2.57	$3.50	$1.44	$10.69	$0.00	$28.86	$47.93	$19.07
99313	$2.57	$3.50	$1.44	$4.28	$0.00	$36.07	$48.74	$12.67
99321	$2.57	$3.50	$1.44	$4.28	$0.00	$19.84	$32.21	$12.37
99323	$2.57	$3.50	$1.44	$4.28	$0.00	$36.07	$48.74	$12.67
99333	$2.57	$3.50	$1.44	$4.28	$0.00	$36.07	$48.74	$12.67
99351	$2.57	$3.50	$1.44	$4.28	$0.00	$21.64	$34.05	$12.41
99352	$2.57	$3.50	$1.44	$4.28	$0.00	$37.87	$50.58	$12.71
99353	$0.00	$0.00	$0.00	$0.00	$0.00	$0.00	$0.00	$0.00
10040	$2.57	$3.50	$3.36	$53.20	$0.00	$126.25	$192.37	$66.12
10060	$2.57	$3.50	$0.00	$0.00	$0.00	$54.11	$100.84	$46.73
10061	$2.57	$3.50	$3.36	$53.20	$0.00	$126.25	$192.37	$66.12
10120	$2.57	$3.50	$3.36	$53.20	$0.00	$126.25	$192.37	$66.12
10121	$2.57	$3.50	$3.36	$53.20	$0.00	$126.30	$192.43	$66.13
10160	$2.57	$3.50	$3.36	$0.00	$0.00	$126.30	$138.25	$11.95
11000	$2.57	$3.50	$3.36	$23.08	$0.00	$36.07	$69.85	$33.78
11040	$2.57	$3.50	$13.23	$23.08	$0.00	$36.07	$79.90	$43.83
11050	$2.57	$3.50	$3.36	$35.46	$0.00	$54.11	$100.84	$46.73
11051	$2.57	$3.50	$3.36	$40.42	$0.00	$81.16	$133.44	$52.28
11052	$2.57	$3.50	$3.36	$40.42	$0.00	$108.21	$160.99	$52.78
11100	$2.57	$3.50	$13.23	$35.46	$0.00	$90.18	$147.63	$57.45
11101	$2.57	$3.50	$13.23	$35.46	$0.00	$46.89	$103.54	$56.65
11200	$2.57	$3.50	$3.36	$35.46	$0.00	$18.04	$64.10	$46.07
11201	$2.57	$1.97	$3.36	$35.46	$0.00	$18.04	$62.54	$44.50
11300	$2.57	$3.50	$3.36	$35.46	$0.00	$36.07	$82.47	$46.40
11301	$2.57	$3.50	$2.64	$27.45	$0.00	$27.05	$64.38	$37.33
11303	$2.57	$3.50	$3.36	$35.46	$0.00	$54.11	$100.84	$46.73
11305	$2.57	$3.50	$3.36	$35.46	$0.00	$18.04	$64.10	$46.07
11306	$2.57	$3.50	$3.36	$35.46	$0.00	$63.12	$110.02	$46.90
11310	$2.57	$3.50	$3.36	$35.46	$0.00	$18.04	$64.10	$46.07
11311	$2.57	$3.50	$3.36	$35.46	$0.00	$27.05	$73.28	$46.23
11400	$2.57	$3.50	$13.23	$35.46	$0.00	$54.11	$110.89	$56.78
11401	$2.57	$3.50	$13.23	$35.46	$0.00	$90.18	$147.63	$57.45
11402	$2.57	$3.50	$13.23	$35.46	$0.00	$108.21	$165.99	$57.78
11403	$2.57	$3.50	$13.23	$35.46	$0.00	$162.32	$221.10	$58.78
11406	$2.57	$3.50	$13.23	$35.46	$0.00	$216.42	$276.20	$59.78
11420	$2.57	$3.50	$13.23	$35.46	$0.00	$54.11	$110.89	$56.78
11421	$2.57	$3.50	$13.23	$35.46	$0.00	$81.16	$138.44	$57.28
11422	$2.57	$3.50	$13.23	$35.46	$0.00	$108.21	$165.99	$57.78
11423	$2.57	$3.50	$13.23	$35.46	$0.00	$162.32	$221.10	$58.78
11424	$2.57	$3.50	$13.23	$35.46	$0.00	$90.18	$147.63	$57.45
11440	$2.57	$3.50	$13.23	$35.46	$0.00	$108.21	$165.99	$57.78
11441	$2.57	$3.50	$13.23	$35.46	$0.00	$135.26	$193.55	$58.28
11442	$2.57	$3.50	$13.23	$35.46	$0.00	$162.32	$221.10	$58.78
11443	$2.57	$3.50	$13.23	$35.46	$0.00	$216.42	$276.20	$59.78

Courtesy of PrimeCare, PSC, Elizabethtown, Kentucky.

Table 14–3 Selected PrimeCare Costs by Procedure Code—Part 3

CPT Code (1)	New Development (2)	Ins. & Billing (3)	Front Office (4)	Clinical (5)	Diagnostic (6)	Provider (MD) (7)	Total (8)	Net of MD (9)
43200	$2.57	$3.50	$1.20	$0.00	$0.00	$81.16	$90.06	$8.91
43235	$2.57	$3.50	$1.20	$0.00	$0.00	$108.21	$117.62	$9.41
43239	$2.57	$3.50	$1.20	$0.00	$0.00	$126.25	$135.98	$9.74
45330	$2.57	$3.50	$13.23	$35.46	$0.00	$72.14	$129.26	$57.12
45331	$2.57	$3.50	$13.23	$35.46	$0.00	$90.18	$147.63	$57.45
45378	$2.57	$3.50	$1.20	$0.00	$0.00	$162.32	$172.72	$10.40
45380	$2.57	$3.50	$1.20	$0.00	$0.00	$180.35	$191.09	$10.74
45385	$2.57	$3.50	$1.20	$0.00	$0.00	$180.35	$191.09	$10.74
46083	$2.57	$3.50	$13.23	$30.12	$0.00	$54.11	$105.45	$51.34
46320	$2.57	$3.50	$3.36	$30.12	$0.00	$54.11	$95.39	$41.29
46600	$2.57	$3.50	$13.23	$30.12	$0.00	$18.04	$68.71	$50.67
51010	$2.57	$1.97	$3.36	$30.12	$0.00	$54.11	$93.83	$39.73
53670	$2.57	$1.97	$3.36	$23.08	$0.00	$36.07	$68.29	$32.22
53675	$2.57	$1.97	$3.36	$23.08	$0.00	$36.07	$68.29	$32.22
54150	$2.57	$3.50	$1.20	$0.00	$0.00	$54.11	$62.51	$8.41
56420	$2.57	$3.50	$1.20	$0.00	$0.00	$54.11	$62.51	$8.41
56501	$2.57	$3.50	$13.23	$24.77	$0.00	$54.11	$100.00	$45.90
57160	$2.57	$3.50	$3.36	$24.77	$0.00	$54.11	$89.95	$35.84
57454	$2.57	$3.50	$3.36	$35.46	$0.00	$162.32	$211.05	$48.73
57511	$2.57	$3.50	$3.36	$47.85	$0.00	$162.32	$223.66	$61.35
58100	$2.57	$3.50	$3.36	$0.00	$0.00	$72.14	$83.09	$10.95
58120	$2.57	$3.50	$1.20	$37.54	$0.00	$144.28	$192.59	$48.31
58301	$2.57	$3.50	$13.23	$12.39	$0.00	$36.07	$69.02	$32.95
62270	$2.57	$3.50	$3.36	$47.85	$0.00	$162.32	$223.66	$61.35
65205	$2.57	$3.50	$3.36	$23.08	$0.00	$72.14	$106.59	$34.45
65220	$2.57	$3.50	$3.36	$23.08	$0.00	$72.14	$106.59	$34.45
69000	$2.57	$3.50	$3.36	$23.08	$0.00	$90.18	$124.96	$34.78
69200	$2.57	$3.50	$13.23	$12.39	$0.00	$54.11	$87.39	$33.28
90780	$2.57	$3.50	$13.23	$12.39	$0.00	$72.14	$105.75	$33.61
90781	$2.57	$1.97	$13.23	$12.39	$0.00	$36.07	$67.46	$31.39
92499	$2.57	$3.50	$3.36	$35.46	$0.00	$21.64	$67.77	$46.13
15852	$0.00	$0.77	$5.53	$15.06	$0.00	$0.00	$21.75	$21.75
69210	$0.00	$0.77	$5.53	$23.08	$0.00	$0.00	$29.92	$29.92
86580	$0.00	$0.77	$1.20	$14.26	$0.00	$0.00	$16.52	$16.52
90700	$0.00	$0.77	$1.20	$14.26	$0.00	$0.00	$16.52	$16.52
90703	$0.00	$0.77	$1.20	$5.59	$0.00	$0.00	$7.69	$7.69
90705	$0.00	$0.77	$1.20	$68.91	$0.00	$0.00	$72.18	$72.18
90707	$0.00	$0.77	$1.20	$76.19	$0.00	$0.00	$79.60	$79.60
90711	$0.00	$0.77	$1.20	$63.81	$0.00	$0.00	$66.99	$66.99
90712	$0.00	$0.77	$1.20	$63.81	$0.00	$0.00	$66.99	$66.99
90713	$0.00	$0.77	$1.20	$63.81	$0.00	$0.00	$66.99	$66.99
90714	$0.00	$0.77	$1.20	$63.81	$0.00	$0.00	$66.99	$66.99
90716	$0.00	$0.77	$1.20	$63.81	$0.00	$0.00	$66.99	$66.99
90718	$0.00	$0.77	$1.20	$5.59	$0.00	$0.00	$7.69	$7.69
90719	$0.00	$0.77	$1.20	$5.59	$0.00	$0.00	$7.69	$7.69
90720	$0.00	$0.77	$1.20	$63.81	$0.00	$0.00	$66.99	$66.99
90724	$0.00	$0.77	$1.20	$14.26	$0.00	$0.00	$16.52	$16.52
90730	$0.00	$0.77	$1.20	$110.88	$0.00	$0.00	$114.93	$114.93
90731	$0.00	$0.77	$1.20	$110.88	$0.00	$0.00	$114.93	$114.93
90732	$0.00	$0.77	$1.20	$51.42	$0.00	$0.00	$54.37	$54.37
90733	$0.00	$0.77	$1.20	$115.83	$0.00	$0.00	$119.97	$119.97
90737	$0.00	$0.77	$1.20	$63.81	$0.00	$0.00	$66.99	$66.99
90744	$0.00	$0.77	$1.20	$105.92	$0.00	$0.00	$109.88	$109.88
90798	$0.00	$0.77	$1.20	$51.42	$0.00	$0.00	$54.37	$54.37

Courtesy of PrimeCare, PSC, Elizabethtown, Kentucky.

Table 14–4 Selected PrimeCare Costs by Procedure Code—Part 4

CPT Code (1)	New Development (2)	Ins. & Billing (3)	Front Office (4)	Clinical (5)	Diagnostic (6)	Provider (MD) (7)	Total (8)	Net of MD (9)
j1820	$0.00	$0.77	$1.20	$14.26	$0.00	$0.00	$16.52	$16.52
J1885	$0.00	$0.77	$1.20	$14.26	$0.00	$0.00	$16.52	$16.52
J1940	$0.00	$0.77	$1.20	$5.83	$0.00	$0.00	$7.94	$7.94
J2175	$0.00	$0.77	$1.20	$4.35	$0.00	$0.00	$6.43	$6.43
J2210	$0.00	$0.77	$1.20	$14.26	$0.00	$0.00	$16.52	$16.52
J2270	$0.00	$0.77	$1.20	$14.26	$0.00	$0.00	$16.52	$16.52
J2460	$0.00	$0.77	$1.20	$6.83	$0.00	$0.00	$8.95	$8.95
J2480	$0.00	$0.77	$1.20	$14.26	$0.00	$0.00	$16.52	$16.52
J2510	$0.00	$0.77	$1.20	$14.26	$0.00	$0.00	$16.52	$16.52
J2550	$0.00	$0.77	$1.20	$4.84	$0.00	$0.00	$6.93	$6.93
J2595	$0.00	$0.77	$1.20	$4.35	$0.00	$0.00	$6.43	$6.43
J2640	$0.00	$0.77	$1.20	$19.71	$0.00	$0.00	$22.07	$22.07
J2790	$0.00	$0.77	$1.20	$14.26	$0.00	$0.00	$16.52	$16.52
J2930	$0.00	$0.77	$1.20	$14.26	$0.00	$0.00	$16.52	$16.52
J2950	$0.00	$0.77	$1.20	$4.35	$0.00	$0.00	$6.43	$6.43
J3030	$0.00	$0.77	$1.20	$20.95	$0.00	$0.00	$23.33	$23.33
J3180	$0.00	$0.77	$1.20	$14.26	$0.00	$0.00	$16.52	$16.52
J3301	$0.00	$0.77	$1.20	$7.57	$0.00	$0.00	$9.71	$9.71
J3302	$0.00	$0.77	$1.20	$9.30	$0.00	$0.00	$11.47	$11.47
J3410	$0.00	$0.77	$1.20	$9.06	$0.00	$0.00	$11.22	$11.22
J3420	$0.00	$0.77	$1.20	$3.73	$0.00	$0.00	$5.80	$5.80
J3490	$0.00	$0.77	$1.20	$76.19	$0.00	$0.00	$79.60	$79.60
J7120	$0.00	$0.77	$1.20	$40.81	$0.00	$0.00	$43.56	$43.56
J7140	$0.00	$0.77	$1.20	$40.81	$0.00	$0.00	$43.56	$43.56
L4350	$0.00	$0.77	$1.20	$54.89	$0.00	$0.00	$57.91	$57.91
Q0124	$0.00	$0.77	$1.20	$14.26	$0.00	$0.00	$16.52	$16.52
WG313	$0.00	$0.77	$1.20	$14.51	$0.00	$0.00	$16.77	$16.77
WG664	$0.00	$0.77	$1.20	$36.56	$0.00	$0.00	$39.23	$39.23
WG665	$0.00	$0.77	$1.20	$36.56	$0.00	$0.00	$39.23	$39.23
WH386	$0.00	$0.77	$1.20	$9.30	$0.00	$0.00	$11.47	$11.47
36415	$0.00	$0.77	$1.20	$0.00	$0.78	$0.00	$2.79	$2.79
80002	$0.00	$0.77	$1.20	$0.00	$13.85	$0.00	$16.10	$16.10
80003	$0.00	$0.77	$1.20	$0.00	$13.85	$0.00	$16.10	$16.10
80005	$0.00	$0.77	$1.20	$0.00	$14.42	$0.00	$16.69	$16.69
80007	$0.00	$0.77	$1.20	$0.00	$14.42	$0.00	$16.69	$16.69
80008	$0.00	$0.77	$1.20	$0.00	$14.61	$0.00	$16.88	$16.88
80009	$0.00	$0.77	$1.20	$0.00	$14.80	$0.00	$17.07	$17.07
80010	$0.00	$0.77	$1.20	$0.00	$14.99	$0.00	$17.27	$17.27
80012	$0.00	$0.77	$1.20	$0.00	$27.54	$0.00	$30.04	$30.04
80015	$0.00	$0.77	$1.20	$0.00	$34.67	$0.00	$37.32	$37.32
80016	$0.00	$0.77	$1.20	$0.00	$34.67	$0.00	$37.32	$37.32
80018	$0.00	$0.77	$1.20	$0.00	$34.67	$0.00	$37.32	$37.32
80019	$0.00	$0.77	$1.20	$0.00	$34.67	$0.00	$37.32	$37.32
80058	$0.00	$0.77	$1.20	$0.00	$15.48	$0.00	$17.76	$17.76
80061	$0.00	$0.77	$1.20	$0.00	$16.43	$0.00	$18.74	$18.74
80091	$0.00	$0.77	$1.20	$0.00	$25.56	$0.00	$28.03	$28.03
80092	$0.00	$0.77	$1.20	$0.00	$48.06	$0.00	$50.95	$50.95
81000	$0.00	$0.77	$1.20	$0.00	$2.50	$0.00	$4.54	$4.54
81001	$0.00	$0.77	$1.20	$0.00	$2.50	$0.00	$4.54	$4.54
81002	$0.00	$0.77	$1.20	$0.00	$1.73	$0.00	$3.77	$3.77
81003	$0.00	$0.77	$1.20	$0.00	$1.73	$0.00	$3.77	$3.77
81025	$0.00	$0.77	$1.20	$0.00	$6.93	$0.00	$9.06	$9.06
81099	$0.00	$0.77	$1.20	$0.00	$3.21	$0.00	$5.27	$5.27
82040	$0.00	$0.77	$1.20	$0.00	$7.00	$0.00	$9.13	$9.13
82075	$0.00	$0.77	$1.20	$0.00	$12.49	$0.00	$14.72	$14.72

Courtesy of PrimeCare, PSC, Elizabethtown, Kentucky.

Table 14–5 Selected PrimeCare Costs by Procedure Code—Part 5

CPT Code (1)	New Development (2)	Ins. & Billing (3)	Front Office (4)	Clinical (5)	Diagnosic (6)	Provider (MD) (7)	Total (8)	Net of MD (9)
71020		$0.77	$1.20	$0.00	$38.32	$0.00	$41.03	$41.03
71022		$0.77	$1.20	$0.00	$30.92	$0.00	$33.49	$33.49
71030		$0.77	$1.20	$0.00	$30.91	$0.00	$33.48	$33.48
71100		$0.77	$1.20	$0.00	$45.59	$0.00	$48.43	$48.43
71101		$0.77	$1.20	$0.00	$45.59	$0.00	$48.43	$48.43
71111		$0.77	$1.20	$0.00	$52.21	$0.00	$55.17	$55.17
71120		$0.77	$1.20	$0.00	$28.05	$0.00	$30.57	$30.57
71130		$0.77	$1.20	$0.00	$28.05	$0.00	$30.57	$30.57
72020		$0.77	$1.20	$0.00	$25.40	$0.00	$27.87	$27.87
72040		$0.77	$1.20	$0.00	$28.05	$0.00	$30.57	$30.57
72050		$0.77	$1.20	$0.00	$34.84	$0.00	$37.48	$37.48
72070		$0.77	$1.20	$0.00	$39.47	$0.00	$42.20	$42.20
72090		$0.77	$1.20	$0.00	$58.50	$0.00	$61.58	$61.58
72100		$0.77	$1.20	$0.00	$58.50	$0.00	$61.58	$61.58
72110		$0.77	$1.20	$0.00	$55.05	$0.00	$58.07	$58.07
72114		$0.77	$1.20	$0.00	$55.05	$0.00	$58.07	$58.07
72170		$0.77	$1.20	$0.00	$39.47	$0.00	$42.20	$42.20
72190		$0.77	$1.20	$0.00	$58.50	$0.00	$61.58	$61.58
72200		$0.77	$1.20	$0.00	$25.57	$0.00	$28.04	$28.04
72202		$0.77	$1.20	$0.00	$25.57	$0.00	$28.04	$28.04
72220		$0.77	$1.20	$0.00	$25.57	$0.00	$28.04	$28.04
73000		$0.77	$1.20	$0.00	$19.11	$0.00	$21.46	$21.46
73010		$0.77	$1.20	$0.00	$50.27	$0.00	$53.20	$53.20
73020		$0.77	$1.20	$0.00	$50.27	$0.00	$53.20	$53.20
73030		$0.77	$1.20	$0.00	$25.57	$0.00	$28.04	$28.04
73050		$0.77	$1.20	$0.00	$25.57	$0.00	$28.04	$28.04
73060		$0.77	$1.20	$0.00	$37.37	$0.00	$40.06	$40.06
73070		$0.77	$1.20	$0.00	$19.11	$0.00	$21.46	$21.46
73080		$0.77	$1.20	$0.00	$37.37	$0.00	$40.06	$40.06
73090		$0.77	$1.20	$0.00	$19.11	$0.00	$21.46	$21.46
73100		$0.77	$1.20	$0.00	$19.11	$0.00	$21.46	$21.46
73110		$0.77	$1.20	$0.00	$25.37	$0.00	$27.84	$27.84
73120		$0.77	$1.20	$0.00	$19.69	$0.00	$22.05	$22.05
73130		$0.77	$1.20	$0.00	$31.06	$0.00	$33.64	$33.64
73140		$0.77	$1.20	$0.00	$17.99	$0.00	$20.32	$20.32
73510		$0.77	$1.20	$0.00	$48.93	$0.00	$51.84	$51.84
73550		$0.77	$1.20	$0.00	$25.57	$0.00	$28.04	$28.04
73560		$0.77	$1.20	$0.00	$25.57	$0.00	$28.04	$28.04
73562		$0.77	$1.20	$0.00	$25.95	$0.00	$28.43	$28.43
73564		$0.77	$1.20	$0.00	$26.14	$0.00	$28.62	$28.62
73565		$0.77	$1.20	$0.00	$50.27	$0.00	$53.20	$53.20
73590		$0.77	$1.20	$0.00	$37.18	$0.00	$39.86	$39.86
73600		$0.77	$1.20	$0.00	$19.69	$0.00	$22.05	$22.05
73610		$0.77	$1.20	$0.00	$19.88	$0.00	$22.25	$22.25
73620		$0.77	$1.20	$0.00	$25.18	$0.00	$27.65	$27.65
73630		$0.77	$1.20	$0.00	$23.73	$0.00	$26.17	$26.17
73650		$0.77	$1.20	$0.00	$18.18	$0.00	$20.52	$20.52
73660		$0.77	$1.20	$0.00	$18.18	$0.00	$20.52	$20.52
74000		$0.77	$1.20	$0.00	$25.59	$0.00	$28.06	$28.06
74010		$0.77	$1.20	$0.00	$25.59	$0.00	$28.06	$28.06
74020		$0.77	$1.20	$0.00	$37.37	$0.00	$40.06	$40.06
74022		$0.77	$1.20	$0.00	$20.79	$0.00	$23.18	$23.18
Total		$1.97	$3.05	$4.90	$4.65	$24.24	$26.87	

Courtesy of PrimeCare, PSC, Elizabethtown, Kentucky.

portion of Table 14–3 and all of Tables 14–4 and 14–5 reflect zero in this column because physicians are not involved in providing these procedures. Thus, no doctor cost is chargeable to them under PrimeCare's methodology.

The total cost (column 8, Tables 14–1 through 14–5) sums all items for a particular CPT code. This figure reflects all costs allocated or traced to this code.

The net of MD cost (column 9, Tables 14–1 through 14–5) sums all items for a particular CPT code except the doctor's time. Thus, this figure reflects costs net of physicians allocated or traced to this code. Dr. Fitzpatrick explained that this column was included in the report at the request of the PrimeCare physicians.

The final line on Table 14–5, labeled totals, represents averages for each column.

In conclusion, note that Dr. Fitzpatrick monitors the cost assignment bases (both for tracing and for allocation) and updates them semiannually. It is important to perform such periodic scheduled monitoring in order to maintain an updated ABC system.

NOTES

1. I caution readers not to extrapolate these results to their own office practices. Each case is unique and must be determined on a case-by-case basis.

2. It is assumed that the reader is familiar with the steps of activity-based costing. Only highlights of the general process are given here. Excellent books and seminars are available for anyone needing more detail.

3. Again, a detailed discussion of various options for dealing with overhead costs are beyond the scope of this chapter. The interested reader is again referred to texts and seminars dealing with activity-based costing.

## CHAPTER 15

ABC in the Operating Room at Valley View Hospital: A Case Study

Judith J. Baker with Georgia F. Boyd

CHAPTER OUTLINE

Preface
Background
ABC in the Operating Room
Operating Room Overhead and Cost Drivers
The Valley View OR ABC Model
Management Uses for the ABC Reports
Synchronizing ABC and CQI
Commentary

PREFACE

This case study presents an example of how one hospital reports the results of activity-based costing (ABC). It includes the composition and supporting assumptions of an ABC report for a particular procedure in the operating room (OR) and the management uses of the information that has been generated. It also describes how the continuous quality improvement (CQI) initiative at Valley View Hospital is synchronized with the ABC reporting. Valley View Hospital is a nonprofit community hospital in Glenwood Springs, Colorado. Glenwood Springs is situated in north-central Colorado. Valley View Hospital serves a three-county area and also operates a clinic in the town of Eagle, thirty miles to the east. Georgia Boyd is the cost accountant for Valley View Hospital where she continues to implement and develop procedure costs for product line profitability. Her original cost accounting experience was in the hardware and software industry.

BACKGROUND

Valley View's activity-based costing commenced about two years ago. The costing has been set up on a parallel system and is not integrated into the general ledger system. ABC can successfully function as a supplemental, or parallel, system. This is a great advantage, as the information system in place does not have to be disturbed.[1] ABC has been implemented internally department by department at Valley View.

ABC IN THE OPERATING ROOM

Consider the application of ABC to a single OR procedure. The overall cost of any OR procedure incorporates the direct labor and the direct supplies that are used, along with equipment cost for the specialty equipment utilized in the procedure. In addition, total procedure cost includes the particular procedure's portion of allocated costs for items such as administrative personnel. Finally, total procedure cost would include the institutional overhead that is attributable to the particular OR procedure.

The Valley View OR was converted to ABC within the last one-third of the hospital's departmental conversion process. OR costing is by type of procedure. Highest-volume procedures were converted first. Three reports most commonly used at Valley View to document costing in the OR are: (1) the Gross Margin Analysis Activity-Based Costing report, (2) the Bill of Activities report, and (3) the Specialty Capital Equipment (Technology) Costs report.

These three reports represent three levels of costing documentation. The Gross Margin Analysis Activity-Based Costing report represents a decision-making level of reporting. It uses the costing figures in conjunction with other decision-making information. The Bill of Activities report assembles the costing components that are used in the gross margin analysis. The Specialty Capital Equipment (Technology) Cost report presents the supporting line item detail for each item of specialty capital equipment that is directly associated with the procedure that is accounted for on a per-patient basis.

The OR cost information appears in the form of a Gross Margin Analysis Activity-Based Costing report. The procedure illustrated here is DRG 222: Knee Arthroscopy. Knee arthroscopy primary procedures are set out in Exhibit 15–1.

Exhibit 15–1 Knee Arthroscopy Primary Procedures

Operations on the Musculoskeletal System:

80.26   Arthroscopy—Knee
80.6   Excision of Semilunar Cartilage of Knee
81.47   Other Repair of Knee

Source: ICD-9-CM, Fifth Edition: Volume 3, Procedures. PMIC: Los Angeles, 1997.

The Gross Margin Analysis for Knee Arthroscopy is presented as Table 15–1. Recall that activity-based costing measures both cost and performance. This report format functions as a measure of both elements.

There are eight individual costing elements listed within the report:

1. Acuity three surgery per minute
2. Arthroscope
3. General closure suture/A

Table 15–1 Knee Arthroscopy Gross Margin Analysis

DRG 222   KNEE ARTHROSCOPY   SAMPLE = 47 PATIENTS
PRIM PROC 80.26, 80.6, 81.47

PROCEDURE NAME	PROC	CAT	AVG CT	UNIT CHG	STD COST	EXTD CHG	EXTD COST	GROSS MARGIN $	% OF TTL CHARGE
ACUITY 3 SURGERY/ MIN	36003176	360OR	55.9	18.00	9.27	1,006.20	518.19	488.01	
ARTHROSCOPE	36004042	360OR	1	188.50	3.40	188.50	3.40	185.10	
GENERAL CLOSURE SUTURE/A	36006502	360OR	1.4	19.40	0.42	27.16	0.59	26.57	
IV SET UP	36001303	360OR	1	20.30	2.52	20.30	2.52	17.78	
PHASE II RECOVERY	36001162	360OR	161.1	0.50	2.35	80.55	378.59	(298.04)	
SURGICAL PREPARATION	36003200	360OR	1	64.00	15.08	64.00	15.08	48.92	
TOURNIQUET EQUIPMENT	36006734	360OR	1	18.40	0.01	18.40	0.01	18.39	
VIDEO EQUIPMENT	36006752	360OR	1	78.00	23.41	78.00	23.41	54.59	
OPERATING ROOM						1,483.11	941.79	541.32	53.3%
GM %								36.5%	

4. IV set up
5. Phase two recovery
6. Surgical preparation
7. Tourniquet equipment
8. Video equipment

Activities include surgical preparation, IV set up, the surgery itself, and phase two recovery. Technology that is directly related to the activities for this procedure includes the arthroscope, the video equipment, and the tourniquet equipment. Each activity classification (surgical preparation, IV set up, the surgery itself, and phase two recovery) includes labor, supplies, equipment, and overhead costs.

The Gross Margin Analysis (GMA) report contains an average count column for each line item. The average count is multiplied by the relevant cost per unit column to arrive at the extended cost column. Thus, acuity three surgery per minute is listed at a cost of $9.27 per minute. The average count of 55.9 minutes for a knee arthroscopy is multiplied times the $9.27 cost per minute to arrive at the extended cost amount of $518.19. In a similar manner the average count is multiplied by the relevant

charge per unit column to arrive at the extended charge column. Thus, acuity three surgery per minute is listed at a charge of $18.00 per minute. The average count of 55.9 minutes for a knee arthroscopy is multiplied times the $18.00 charge per minute to arrive at the extended charge amount of $1,006.20. The difference between the extended charge amount of $1,006.20 and the extended cost amount of $518.19 accounts for the reported gross margin amount of $488.01 for this particular line item. Note that there can be both positive and negative amounts in the gross margin column. Further note that the overall gross margin calculated for this procedure is 36.5 percent ($1,483.11 less $941.79 equals $541.32; $541.32 divided by $1,483.11 equals 36.5 percent).

The bill of activities (BOA) for acuity three surgery per minute is presented as Table 15–2. A bill of activities is a list. In this case it is a list of the activities that are required and the associated costs of the resources consumed by a procedure.

This type of BOA is also called a service cost bill of activities. A service cost BOA represents

Table 15–2 Bill of Activity Cost Components

OR Acuity 3   Standard Unit Cost of $9.27 consists of the following Bill of Activity:

Cost Group	Resource	Usage	Direct Qty	Alloc Usage	Computed Std Cost
Direct Variable Labor	RN	Hour	1 min		0.37
Direct Variable Labor	RN, Cir Nurs	Hour		0.01	1.09
Direct Variable Labor	Scrub Nurs	Hour	1 min		0.32
Indirect Fixed Labor	Director			0.01	0.30
Equipment Direct		Usage	1		0.21
Equipment Allocated				1	0.30
Direct Variable Materials				1	0.33
Indirect Fixed Materials				1	0.56
Variable Overhead				1	3.19
Fixed Overhead				1	2.60
			Acuity Std Cost		$9.27 per min

all the activities necessary to provide a service.[2] Thus, for a hospital that is setting out the cost of an already developed service, the major costs to be found in a service cost BOA would include direct labor, supplies, and technology (including depreciation) along with associated support costs. That is true in the case of Valley View Hospital.

The terminology for this BOA—acuity three surgery per minute—reflects the OR acuity formula. The formula takes nurse skill level, skill mix, and quantity of staffing into account. In this case, acuity three surgery requires two RNs and a circulation nurse.

There are ten cost groups in the Table 15–2 BOA. They include:

1. Direct variable labor—RN
2. Direct variable labor—RN, Cir. nurse
3. Direct variable labor—Scrub nurse
4. Indirect fixed labor—Director
5. Equipment—direct
6. Equipment—allocated
7. Direct variable materials
8. Indirect fixed materials
9. Variable overhead
10. Fixed overhead

Assumptions regarding the OR acuity three bill of activity are summarized as follows:

First, direct variable labor (1, 2, and 3) represents the appropriate skill level, skill mix, and quantity of skill to meet the criteria for OR acuity three for this procedure. Second, indirect fixed labor (4) represents the director's time. Third, equipment—direct (5) requires a bit more explanation. All specialty equipment that is used in a procedure is directly charged to the patient as a separate line item. Thus, the arthroscope appears as a separate line item. However, there is also nonchargeable specialty equipment such as surgical table, OR lights, central warming cabinets, sterilizer, and so forth. This equipment is charged within the BOA as equipment—direct. Fourth, equipment—allocated (6) represents all other items such as instruments that are spread under an equipment allocation rather than being charged directly as specialty

equipment. Fifth, direct materials (7) are computed as a unit cost based on department supply expense levels. The actual supplies used are charged along with built-in overheads coming out of central supply; thus resulting in a "loaded" direct charge. Sixth, indirect materials (8) are computed as an allocated cost based on department supply expense levels. Seventh, variable and fixed overhead (9 and 10) are computed as unit costs based on overhead allocations. There are 33 elements of operating room overhead, each with its own driver and its own allocated unit cost.

The ten elements within the Table 15–2 BOA result in a $9.27 acuity standard cost per minute. This figure is carried forward to the GMA report. On the GMA the $9.27 per minute for OR acuity three is multiplied by the 55.9 minutes used for the knee arthroscopy procedure.

In an ABC system, the allocation bases that are used for applying costs to services or procedures are called cost drivers. Cost drivers include any causal factor that increases the total costs of an activity. Both volume-related allocations bases and other volume-unrelated allocation bases can be used as cost drivers in an ABC system.[3] (The use of a multitude of allocation bases that can be either volume-related or non-volume-related is a major distinction of the ABC system.) In this case, direct labor is the primary cost driver.

The OR direct materials assigned cost reconciliation is a proof sheet (see Exhibit 15–2). It tests the total cost of OR direct materials that are assigned through the ABC system against the total cost of OR direct materials as recorded by the purchasing department. Per the Exhibit 15–2 worksheet, $202,905 was assigned through the ABC system, contrasted to $205,515 recorded by the purchasing department. The difference of $2,610, or .01269 percent, is within the acceptable differential range and is passed. This type of proof sheet serves as a test of the bill of activities costing components. It indicates whether the system is functioning as expected.

Exhibit 15–2 OR Direct Materials

				INITIALS	DATE
PREPARED BY				GB	10/31/199X
APPROVED BY					

OR DIRECT MATERIALS

LINE No.	S.U.# Description	DVMAT PER S.U. (1)	Volumes (2)	Total Direct Materials Microcosted (3)	(4)	(5)
1	36002095 HIP	4003	17	68051.00		
2	36002103 KNEE	2775 40	22	61050.00		
3	36002111 LENS	185 00	47	8695.00		
4	36002228 MISC SURG	.07	14	.98		
5	ACUITY 1	.30	859	258.00		
6	SURGERY BLK	.07	6	.42		
7	ACUITY 2	.30	21398	6419.00		
8	ACUITY 3	.30	31139	9342.00		
9	ACUITY 4	.30	38900	11670.00		
10	ACUITY 5	.30	5307	1592.00		
11	36005577 PACEMAKER	8207.00	4	32828.00		
12	LASERS PER MINUTE	.01	83	.83		
13	EAR OX H	.01	1094	10.94		
14	6502 SUTURE	.42	5362	2252.00		
15	6504 SUTURE	.42	42	17.00		
16	6506 SUTURE	.42	4	1.68		
17	6559 ML II Inst.Fee	47.20	15	708.00		
18	8852 OTHER	.01	15	.15		
19	40278153 AccuCheck	.30	39	11.00		
20	66003689 CAST	.01	18	.18		
21	3770 "	.01	21	.21		
22	3861 "	.01	7	.07		
23	3952 "	.01	5	.05		
24						
25	Per S/A Service Units DVMAT Microcosted			202405.00		
26	Per MM Department Purchasing Activity Report			205515.00		
27						
28			Δ	2610.00	PASS	
29						

Specialty capital equipment (technology) costs include arthroscope equipment and video equipment.

The second line item in the knee arthroscopy gross margin analysis (Table 15–1) is listed as *arthroscope*. This entry indicates the arthroscope equipment that is used in the OR for the procedure. All specialty equipment that is utilized in a procedure is directly charged to a patient as a separate line item. An illustration of the direct charge for specialty capital equipment is composed of five line items as illustrated in Table 15–3.

Table 15–3 shows the asset acquired value and the annual depreciation cost for each of the five equipment line items. The annual usage for the past two years is set out. Then the annualized usage for the current year is set out. The final column calculates the current year cost per use. This figure is obtained by dividing the annual depreciation by the current year's annualized usage figure:

$930.60 annual depreciation divided by 274 annualized usage = $3.3964 Cost per Use

The knee arthroscopy gross margin analysis charges one unit for a single usage of the arthroscope. That is, one procedure performed equates to one unit. Note that Valley View's OR cost is at an advantage here. The arthroscopy camera—the most expensive item on the direct-

Table 15–3 Capital Equipment Charges: Arthroscope

Capital Equipment Charges: Operating Room 01.660—Arthroscope

			Asset	Annual				1996
		Service	Acquired	Depreciation	1994	1995	1996	Cost Per
Asst No.	Description	Unit No.	Value	Cost			Annualized	Use
	ARTHROSCOPE	36004042			229	266	274	
	Avg chg per product				$177.54	$181.20	$188.39	
(O) 000372	Arthroscopy Camera (fully deprec)		9,761.20	0.00				
(O) 000373	Telescope and Lenses		6,361.36	636.12				
(N) 000073	Duckbill Upbiter & basket punch		1,531.25	153.12				
(N) 000106	Forceps 3.4mm backbitter/ Arthrotek		905.45	90.60				
(N) 000289	Isometric Ligament Positioner		507.06	50.76				
			19,066.32	930.60			274	$3.3964

Annual Usage spans the 1994, 1995, and 1996 Annualized columns.

charge OR capital equipment charges (see Table 15–3)—is fully depreciated. Thus, the annualized cost per use for this year is one-half or less of what it would be if depreciation was still being charged for the arthroscopy camera.

The eighth line item in the knee arthroscopy gross margin analysis (Table 15–1) is listed as *video equipment*. This entry indicates the video equipment used in the OR for the procedure. All specialty equipment that is used in a procedure is directly charged to a patient as a separate line item. An illustration of the direct charge for specialty capital equipment is composed of fourteen line items as illustrated in Table 15–4.

Table 15–4 shows the asset acquired value and the annual depreciation cost for each of the fourteen equipment line items. The annual usage for the past two years is set out. Then the annualized usage for the current year is set out. The final column calculates the current year cost per use. This figure is obtained by dividing the annual depreciation by the current year's annualized usage figure:

$11,329.37 annual depreciation divided by 484 annualized usage = $23.4078 Cost per Use

The knee arthroscopy gross margin analysis charges one unit for a single usage of the video equipment. That is, one procedure performed equates to one unit. Note that Valley View's OR cost is again at an advantage here. Surgical video camera—the next-to-most expensive item on the direct-charge OR capital equipment charges (see Table 15–4)—is fully depreciated.

OPERATING ROOM OVERHEAD AND COST DRIVERS

Table 15–5 summarizes overhead costs for the OR. The 33 line items have been annualized. The current year annualized figures have then been compared to the prior year. The total allocated overhead is displayed at the bottom of the summary. The sum of all other expenses is added to the total allocated overhead to arrive at

Table 15–4 Capital Equipment Charges: Video Equipment

Capital Equipment Charges Operating Room 01.660–Video Equipment

Asst No.	Description	Service Unit No.	Asset Acquired Value	Annual Depreciation Cost	Annual Usage 1994	1995	1996 Annualized	1996 Cost Per Use
	VIDEO EQUIPMENT	36006752			212	510	484	
	Avg chg per product				$75.00	$75.00	$77.98	
(N) 000069	Arthroscopic Equip/Camera		34,876.24	3,487.68				
(N) 000076	Electronic Insufflator w/6 LT/MN		5,569.22	556.92				
(N) 000098	High Profile Cart w/drawers		1,346.67	89.76				
(N) 000121	19" Sony Monitor		1,586.50	226.68				
(N) 000305	Wolf Video Light		4,138.00	275.88				
(N) 000486	Camera Control Unit		6,522.25	1,304.52				
(N) 000487	(2) Camera + C-Mount		10,006.25	2,001.24				
(N) 000488	Printer HC-1600A		4,196.00	839.16				
(N) 000594	C-Mount Coupler		800.00	159.96				
(N) 000682	Wolf Insufflator		7,211.85	721.20				
(N) 000695	Light Source Dyonics		3,723.75	372.38				
(N) 000698	Video "Cool Cart"		3,220.00	643.99				
(N) 000704	Shaver System Dyonics		6,500.00	650.00				
(O) 000338	Surgical Video Camera (fully deprec)		11,300.00	0.00				
			100,996.73	11,329.37			484	$23.4078

total expense. The total expense amount is used as a proof figure.

The distribution of fixed and variable costs is presented in Table 15–6. Note that equipment depreciation is listed neither as fixed nor as variable. In this system the equipment depreciation is charged directly from the fixed asset sub-ledger and thus does not enter into these fixed or variable designations. The selection of fixed and variable labels for line item accounts is an important part of the costing procedure and has been further discussed in Chapter 7. Each organization should carefully make its own selections. The distribution of fixed and variable

costs is finalized with a proof sheet (see Exhibit 15–3). The proof sheet also displays the allocated variable unit cost and the allocated fixed unit cost.

The operating room overhead cost drivers are reflected in Table 15–7. Note that time surveys have been used for environmental services, sterile procedures, and medical records. Further note that, because telephone expense is allocated by number of extensions, this rationale is carried further by allocating data processing by the number of ports. This table could be further utilized by tying a key for the statistics of each driver to it.

Table 15–5 Operating Room Overhead

ACCOUNT	10-Month TOTAL	12-Month ANNUALIZED	Prior Year	Annual INCR(DECR)
SOC SEC	50,431	60,517	68,177	(7,660)
PENSION	17,229	20,675	23,473	(2,798)
HEALTH INS	7,018	8,422	18,507	(10,085)
CHILD CARE	3,803	4,564	4,334	230
DEPR-EQ	72,815	87,378	61,144	26,234
DEPR-BLDG	34,481	41,377	45,450	(4,073)
AMORT-INT	(4,849)	(5,819)	1,767	(7,586)
INSURANCE	3,513	4,216	7,836	(3,620)
ADMIN	48,305	57,966	56,309	1,657
MED STAFF	1,435	1,722	5,130	(3,408)
COMM REL	41,511	49,813	40,618	9,195
MAT MGNT	53,811	64,573	72,305	(7,732)
HUM RES	25,888	31,066	13,276	17,790
NURS ADMIN	68,726	82,471	92,666	(10,195)
DP	14,846	17,815	16,119	1,696
FISCAL	14,750	17,700	16,748	952
PT ACCTG	129,463	155,356	123,254	32,102
ADMITTING	91,878	110,254	101,040	9,214
TELEPHONE	2,366	2,839	2,569	270
UTILITIES	22,005	26,406	38,689	(12,283)
PLANT	64,664	77,597	84,128	(6,531)
ENV SVC	27,395	32,874	37,354	(4,480)
DIETARY	22,938	27,526	35,646	(8,120)
UTILIZATION REVIEW	0	0	0	0
MED RECORDS	76,432	91,718	94,304	(2,586)
SAFETY	1,680	2,016	2,179	(163)
QUAL MGMT	8,347	10,016	8,146	1,870
MED STAFF	7,870	9,444	9,391	53
CQI	4,079	4,895	0	4,895
MED WASTE	1,981	2,377	3,187	(810)
EE HLTH	474	569	1,513	(944)
STERILE PROC	65,600	78,720	70,725	7,995
LAUNDRY	33,911	40,693	40,463	230
TOTAL ALLOCATED	1,014,796	1,217,755	1,196,447	21,308
ALL OTHER EXPENSES	1,009,673	1,211,608	0	1,211,608
TOTAL EXPENSE	2,024,469	2,429,363	1,196,447	1,232,916

Table 15–6 Distribution of Fixed and Variable Costs

Account	Equipment	Fixed	Variable	Total
SOC SEC			60,517	60,517
PENSION			22,696	22,696
HEALTH INS			18,422	18,422
CHILD CARE			4,564	4,564
DEPR-EQ	87,378			87,378
DEPR-BLDG		41,377		41,377
AMORT-INT		(5,819)		(5,819)
INSURANCE		4,216		4,216
ADMIN		56,966		56,966
MED STAFF		1,722		1,722
COMM REL		40,813		40,813
MAT MGNT		64,573		64,573
HUM RES		19,045		19,045
NURS ADMIN		82,471		82,471
DP		17,815		17,815
FISCAL		17,700		17,700
PT ACCTG			155,356	155,356
ADMITTING			110,254	110,254
TELEPHONE		2,839		2,839
UTILITIES		26,406		26,406
PLANT		77,597		77,597
ENV SVC		32,874		32,874
DIETARY			35,526	35,526
UTILIZATION REVIEW			0	0
MED RECORDS			93,718	93,718
SAFETY		2,016		2,016
QUAL MGMT		10,016		10,016
MED STAFF		9,444		9,444
CQI		4,895		4,895
MED WASTE			2,377	2,377
EE HLTH		569		569
STERILE PROC			78,720	78,720
LAUNDRY			40,693	40,693
TOTAL ALLOCATED	87,378	507,535	622,843	1,217,756
ALL OTHER EXPENSES				1,211,608
TOTAL EXPENSE				2,429,364

Exhibit 15–3 Proof Sheet: Fixed and Variable Allocated Unit Cost

Variable   = $ 622,843 divided by 195,206
               equals $3.19 allocated unit cost
Fixed   = $ 507,535 divided by 195,206
               equals $2.60 allocated unit cost
[Note: Equipment depreciation of $87,378 charged directly; not allocated above]

Proof Totals:

          $ 622,843
            507,535
             87,378
          $1,217,756 per 12-month annualized
                     total, Table 15–5

THE VALLEY VIEW OR ABC MODEL

The Valley View OR ABC model is reflected in Figure 15–1. The major costing categories include labor, material or supplies, departmental equipment depreciation, and overhead. Each category has direct or indirect, or fixed or variable subgroup designations. This model illustrates the costing decisions made by a particular organization's management on behalf of a particular acute care facility. The management in other organizations may have a different focus that results in a variation to this ABC model.

MANAGEMENT USES FOR THE ABC REPORTS

Within ABC, the cost object drives the composition of the final cost reporting. A cost object is anything for which a separate measurement of costs is desired.[4] Brimson calls the cost object a "cost objective" and says that the cost objective depends on the management decision.[5] Thus, the cost objective influences the reporting objective and the reporting objective influences the cost objective.

Valley View management's primary use for the ABC reports is in four areas: (1) performance measurement and/or evaluation, (2) strategic planning, (3) managed care contract negotiations, and (4) managed care contract management. Valley View management's secondary use for the ABC reports is in two areas: (1) resource allocation and (2) cost control. Valley View management's future use for the ABC reports is in two additional areas: (1) departmental budgeting and (2) staffing decisions.

Management reports are at the procedure level in this OR example. The decision-making viewpoint is primarily from the service line, or product line, analysis. That is, the individual procedure that is reported on in this example is part of a service line. The management information presented in these reports fits into an overall service line analysis. It should be emphasized that there is no one right way for choosing cost objectives or reporting objectives. Each organization will respond according to its own situation.

SYNCHRONIZING ABC AND CQI

Valley View Hospital is committed to CQI. Continuous improvement allows a never-ending search for higher levels of performance within the organization: "If you're not going forward, you're going backwards."[6]

Deming's philosophy is taught to Valley View staff. W. E. Deming was a pioneer in the development of process improvement. His process improvement concept is summarized in Deming's wheel, which involves repeated application of the steps of PDCA: planning (P), doing (D), checking (C), and acting (A).[7] As the wheel revolves, the cycle is repeated over and over, illustrating the concept of continuous, or never-ending, improvement. The commitment of Valley View to CQI is best illustrated by this fact: There is a quality management line item within the array of general overhead expenses. This line item includes a budgeted amount available for CQI training.

Table 15–7 Operating Room Overhead Cost Drivers

Account	Driver	Total
SOC SEC	Salary Expense	60,517
PENSION	Salary Expense	22,696
HEALTH INS	FTE Level	18,422
CHILD CARE	FTE Level	4,564
DEPR-EQ	Fixed Asset Subledger	87,378
DEPR-BLDG	Square Feet	41,377
AMORT-INT	Square Feet	(5,819)
INSURANCE	Square Feet	4,216
ADMIN	FTE Level	56,966
MED STAFF	Revenue Level	1,722
COMM REL	Revenue Level	40,813
MAT MGNT	Supply Level	64,573
HUM RES	FTE Level	19,045
NURS ADMIN	FTE Level	82,471
DP	# of Ports	17,815
FISCAL	Area Managers	17,700
PT ACCTG	Revenue Level	155,356
ADMITTING	Revenue Level	110,254
TELEPHONE	# of Extensions	2,839
UTILITIES	Square Feet	26,406
PLANT	Square Feet	77,597
ENV SVC	Time Survey	32,874
DIETARY	# of Meals Served	35,526
MED RECORDS	Time Survey	93,718
SAFETY	Area Managers	2,016
QUAL MGMT	Area Managers	10,016
MED STAFF	Revenue Level	9,444
CQI	Area Managers	4,895
MED WASTE	# of Red Bags	2,377
EE HLTH	FTE Level	569
STERILE PROC	Time Survey	78,720
LAUNDRY	# of Pounds Laundry	40,693
TOTAL ALLOCATED		1,217,756
ALL OTHER EXPENSES		1,211,608
TOTAL EXPENSE		2,429,364

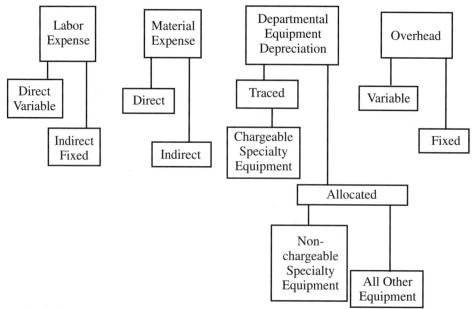

Figure 15–1 The Valley View OR ABC Model

Synchronizing ABC and CQI is logical. ABC's activity analysis and cost driver analysis allows for the exploration of process. This exploration of process from both the performance measurement and the costing aspects of ABC flows directly into the process improvement elements of continuous quality improvement. Thus, the highest and best use for ABC and for CQI occur when the two initiatives are synchronized.

COMMENTARY

The Valley View OR ABC reporting example demonstrates compliance with the three aims of a hospital cost accounting system. The underlying reporting objective is fulfilled in that the information that is provided can accomplish cost efficiency, can provide information for management to maximize resources, and can assist in continuous quality improvement.

NOTES

1. J.J. Baker, "Activity-Based Costing for Integrated Delivery Systems," *Journal of Health Care Finance* 22, no. 2 (1995): 59.

2. J. Brimson and J. Antos, *Activity-Based Management for Service Industries, Government Entities, and Non-profit Organizations* (New York: John Wiley & Sons, 1994), 240.

3. Y. Chan, "Improving Hospital Cost Accounting with Activity-Based Costing," *Health Care Management Review* 18, no. 1 (1993): 72.

4. C. Horngren et al., *Cost Accounting: A Managerial Emphasis*, 8th ed. (Englewood Cliffs, NJ: Prentice Hall, 1994), 248.

5. J. Brimson, *Activity Accounting: An Activity-Based Costing Approach* (New York: John Wiley & Sons, 1991), 161.

6. C. Horngren et al., *Cost Accounting*, 7.

7. J. Cryer and R. Miller, *Statistics for Business: Data Analysis and Modeling* (Boston: PWS-Kent Publishing Co., 1991), 12.

## CHAPTER 16

Comprehensive Implementation of ABC throughout the North River Hospital System: A Case Study

Judith J. Baker

CHAPTER OUTLINE

Preface
The Physical Setting
Organizational Environment
Implementing ABC
Specific Formats
Dos and Don'ts of Comprehensive
    Implementation

PREFACE

This case study comes from an actual hospital system and has been modified to keep the donor anonymous. "North River Hospital" is a fictitious name. This case study is of special interest for two reasons. The length of time that this activity accounting system has been in place is the first item of particular interest. It is unusual to find a hospital that was already implementing an activity accounting system in 1990. Since its initial implementation, this system has been enhanced on an ongoing basis. Second is that this activity accounting system represents a comprehensive application across all the health system operations. Many systems are rolled into place department by department; other systems never pick up all aspects of the operation. In this case, the costing for acute care, outpatient-ambulatory care, and skilled nursing facility–rehab care was put into place in one comprehensive implementation.

THE PHYSICAL SETTING

The health system consists of two medium-size acute care hospitals with strong outpatient and ambulatory services, an off-site same-day surgery clinic, a skilled nursing facility with subacute rehab, and a variety of community outreach programs. In the examples that follow, one hospital is designated as *North,* one is designated as *South,* and the off-site clinic is called *Waters.* All three designations are, again, fictitious.

ORGANIZATIONAL ENVIRONMENT

The hospitals' top management recognized the need for a costing system. They hired a financial analyst with cost accounting, quality assurance, budgeting, and measurement experience. He was hired from industry—from a Fortune 300 company. His charge was to install a costing system at the hospital. Management decision makers had predicted that managed care would impact their metropolitan area within the following three years. They wanted to prepare for increased managed care by implementing activity accounting. The CEO was also looking toward care paths and the report card approach and recognized that activity accounting would provide the necessary cost information to make his plans a reality.

IMPLEMENTING ABC

The initial implementation process of the costing system project began in 1989. Potential systems were reviewed and a selection was made. The system that was selected would run as a parallel system with product costing and departmental costing as the focus. The system was selected for its strength in product costing. The basic accounting system, consisting of the general ledger, payroll, and related accounts all ran on a hospital software accounting system that would remain in place. The data required for cost accounting would be exported to the stand-alone parallel cost accounting system.

Initial implementation took nine to ten months. The system crashed early in the process and a considerable amount of work had to be reconstructed. The reconstruction accounted for at least a month of the total implementation timeline. All aspects of the health system were costed at once; and all diagnosis-related groups (DRGs) and all procedures were costed at once. No reports were released until the entire health system was completed and ready to go. The individual in charge of implementation reports that there was good buy-in on the results from management and from physicians.

The output or reporting choices are specific to this particular organization. Other health care organizations would make different types of choices depending on their management and strategic planning focus. North River Hospitals chose to report by product and by product line. Results are reported by DRG and by procedure. North River Hospitals also chose to report by department. Departmental results are reported with expenses flagged as fixed or variable (see the details in the Specific Formats section).

The process of input is monthly, quarterly, and annually. General ledger, payroll, and related accounts are exported into the activity costing system on a monthly basis. The data transfer is accomplished using a modem and a commercial interface package. The data, once imported, is then converted by the costing system. This data is then used for the departmental reports, which are distributed on a monthly basis. Case mix data—cases, case type, and treatment profiles—are exported into the system via magnetic tapes. This data is transferred quarterly (rather than monthly) because of the large volume of records to be transferred. The data, once imported, is then converted by the costing system. This data is used for the physician profiles and payer reports, which are distributed on a quarterly basis. Standards are reviewed and adjusted annually. Budget modeling is performed annually. Some of the budget modeling is done using major diagnostic codes (MDCs) rather than DRGs. Overall tracing and allocation decisions and drivers are also reviewed and adjusted on an annual basis.

Note that some other organizations review and adjust standards on a semiannual or even a quarterly basis, and a few organizations use a perpetual rolling review-and-adjustment schedule. The choice is very specific to the particular organization.

SPECIFIC FORMATS

We will now examine the specific formats used by the activity accounting system. This system identifies the DRG and the procedure level.

The service lines, or product lines, are listed in Exhibit 16–1. This system uses MDCs for its service lines (see Chapter 7). Each line is assigned a number for cross-reference and reporting purposes. For example, immunology is number 16 and oncology is 17.

Case type names are tied to specific service lines, or product lines, in Exhibit 16–2. Thus, coagulation disorders, case type 397, is tied to product line number 16, or immunology. And radiotherapy, case type 409, is tied to product line 17, or oncology. The case types can thus be assembled by the appropriate MDC service line.

Each clinical service is described and assigned a number (Exhibit 16–3). Cardiology is 10, for example, and orthopedics is 65. These numbers are assigned for cross-reference and reporting purposes.

Exhibit 16–1 North River Hospital System Service Line Names File

Product Lines	
Number	**Name**
1	NERVOUS SYSTEM
2	EYE
3	ENT
4	RESPIRATORY SYSTEM
5	CIRCULATORY SYSTEM
6	DIGESTIVE SYSTEM
7	HEPATOBILIARY SYSTEM
8	MUSCULOSKELETAL
9	SKIN, SUBCUTANEOUS TISSUE
10	END, NUT, & META
11	KIDNEY & URINARY
12	MALE REPRODUCTION SYSTEM
13	FEMALE REPRODUCTION SYSTEM
14	OBSTETRICS
15	NEWBORNS
16	IMMUNOLOGY
17	ONCOLOGY
18	INFECTIOUS DISEASES
19	MENTAL DISEASES
20	SUBSTANCE USE
21	INJURY, POISON, & TOXIN
22	BURNS
23	OTHER HEALTH SERVICES
24	SPECIAL DRUGS
25	HIV
26	UNASSIGNED
59	OUTPATIENT

The clinical service names and numbers described in Exhibit 16–3 now reappear in Exhibit 16–4. Thus, particular doctors are tied to particular clinical services; doctor number 303 (the doctor's names are blank on this exhibit for purposes of anonymity) practices in cardiology, number 10, whereas doctor number 353 practices in orthopedics, number 65. This cross-referencing feature allows the system to produce physician profiling.

We will now look at certain cost allocation indicators. Exhibit 16–5 lists the cost center names and numbers. On the right side of the exhibit are identification numbers in both the fixed and the variable columns. These identification numbers indicate the code for grouping particular allocation bases. The particular expense classification pictured in Exhibit 16–5 is *global expense class option.*

An example of the chart of accounts appears as Exhibit 16–6. The cost center number, description, and type appear on the left side of the exhibit. The expense account classification, number, and description appear in the right center of the exhibit. The type of account appears as a number and a description toward the far right side of the exhibit. The far right column of the exhibit is labeled *F/V flag* and indicates whether the account is fixed or variable. Actually there are four possible codes: (1) F = fixed, (2) V = variable, (3) B = both (both fixed and variable can apply to this account), and (4) N = not applicable (not applicable because the account is allocated).

Thus, cost center number 506, *North—Same Day Stay,* which is a patient care cost center, has 17 expense accounts. Of these seventeen accounts, two—salaries and wages (10), and V/H/S (vacation/holiday/sick pay; 15)—are both fixed and variable (coded B). One account—capital costs (100)—is fixed (coded F). Ten accounts—consisting of various supplies and other expenses—are variable (coded V). Four accounts—all allocated overhead accounts—are not applicable (coded N) because they are allocated.

Exhibit 16–7 displays the cost assignment names and statistics. For activity accounting, this feature is used for cost assignment. In this particular illustration, the feature is used to display allocation bases, as the term on the computer run heading indicates. Thus, allocation base number 20, *nursing hours* is used for the 32 accounts listed on Exhibit 16–7. The total allocation base for nursing hours amounts to 61,404 hours for the current year to date. (The estimated annual total nursing hours for the full year is 736,850.)

Exhibit 16–2 North River Hospital System Case Type Names with Product Line Number

Case Type		Product Line	
Number	Description	Number	Description
392	SPLENECTOMY >17	16	IMMUNOLOGY
393	SPLENECTOMY 0-17	16	IMMUNOLOGY
394	OT O.R. PRC-BLD/BLD F	16	IMMUNOLOGY
395	RED BLD CELL DISORDER >17	16	IMMUNOLOGY
396	RED BLD CELL DIS 0-17	16	IMMUNOLOGY
397	COAGULATION DISORDERS	16	IMMUNOLOGY
398	RETITHELIAL/IMM DIS W/CC	16	IMMUNOLOGY
399	RETITHELIAL/IMM DIS WOCC	16	IMMUNOLOGY
400	LYMPHOM/LEUK W/MJ OR PRC	17	ONCOLOGY
401	LYMPH/N-A LK W/O O/R WCC	17	ONCOLOGY
402	LYMPH/N-A LK W/O O/R WOC	17	ONCOLOGY
403	LYMPH/NO-ACUTLEK W/CC	17	ONCOLOGY
404	LYMPH/NO-ACUTLEK W/O CC	17	ONCOLOGY
405	ACTE LEUK W/O MJ O/R 0-17	17	ONCOLOGY
406	MYPRF DSD/PDN MJ O/R CC	17	ONCOLOGY
407	MYPRF DSD/PDN MJ O/R W/O	17	ONCOLOGY
408	MYPRF DSD/PDN-OTH O/R	17	ONCOLOGY
409	RADIOTHERAPY	17	ONCOLOGY
410	CHEMO W/O AC LEUK SEC DG	17	ONCOLOGY
411	HIST MAL W/O ENDOSCOPY	17	ONCOLOGY
412	HIST MAL W/ENDOSCOPY	17	ONCOLOGY
413	OTH MY DIS/POND W/CC	17	ONCOLOGY
414	OTH MY DIS/POND W/O CC	17	ONCOLOGY
415	O/R - INFECT/PARASTC DIS	18	INFECTIOUS DIS
416	SEPTECEMIA >17	18	INFECTIOUS DIS
417	SEPTECEMIA 0-17	18	INFECTIOUS DIS
418	POSTOP/POSTRAUMA INFECT	18	INFECTIOUS DIS
419	FEVER-UKN ORIG >17W/C	18	INFECTIOUS DIS
420	FEVER-UKN ORIG >17W/OC	18	INFECTIOUS DIS
421	VIRAL ILLNESS >17	18	INFECTIOUS DIS
422	VIR ILL/FEVER UNK 0-17	18	INFECTIOUS DIS
423	OT INFECT/PARASTIC DX	18	INFECTIOUS DIS
4127	SNRU-HEART FAIL & SHOCK	5	CIRCULATORY SYS
4175	SNRU-GI HEMORR W/O CC	6	DIGESTIVE SYS
4189	SNRU-OTH DIG SYS	6	DIGESTIVE SYS
4236	SNRU-FRAC OF HIP & PELV	8	MUSCULOSKELETAL
4245	SNRU-BONE DIS/SP ARTH WO	8	MUSCULOSKELETAL
4256	SNRU-OTH MUSK SYS/CONN	8	MUSCULOSKELETAL
4335	SNRU-MAJ MALE PELV PROC	12	MALE REPROD SYS
4462	SNRU-REHABILITATION	23	OTHER HEALTH SVC
4464	SNRU-SIGNS/SYMPT W/O CC	23	OTHER HEALTH SVC
4466	SNRU-AFTCR W/O HIST MAL	23	OTHER HEALTH SVC
4467	SNRU-OTH FAC INFL HLTH	23	OTHER HEALTH SVC

Exhibit 16–3 North River Hospital System Clinical Service Names File

Clinical Service	
Number	Description
10	CARDIOLOGY
13	INF DIS
14	PREVENTIVE MED
15	INT MED/FP
16	NEPHRO
18	PULMONARY MED
23	ALLERGY/IMMUN.
25	ENT
30	GASTROENTEROL
40	HEMATOL/ONCOL
45	NEUROLOGY
50	NEUROSURGERY
55	SURGERY
63	DENTAL
64	PODIATRY
65	ORTHOPEDIC
66	PHYS MED/REHAB
70	EYE
75	UROLOGY
80	PLASTIC
85	PEDIATRICS
86	DERMATOLOGY
87	PATHOLOGY
88	RADIOLOGY
89	ANESTHESIA
90	OB/GYN
91	NEONATOLOGY
95	PSYCH
96	URGENT CARE
97	UNIDENTIFIED
98	EMERG
99	ALL OTHER

Per Exhibit 16–7, the nursing hours allocation base applied to cost center number 506, *North—same day stay,* for #1710, *clinical administration allocated overhead* will be 624 ÷ 61404.

Refer back to the chart of accounts in Exhibit 16–6. For cost center number 506, *North—same day stay,* account #1710, *clinical administration*

allocated overhead, the amount allocated on this line item will be allocated by the formula presented in the preceding paragraph.

Exhibit 16–8 presents procedure names and charges. For each cost center, a listing is provided of the number and description of each procedure that is acknowledged for that cost center, along with the charge. Thus, a right wrist X-ray at the South radiology department (procedure number 720081) has an associated charge of 80.75. This data is used for performance measures.

Job code names and salary or wage rates are presented in Exhibit 16–9. The cost center number and description are on the left of the exhibit and the number and description of the expense classification is in the middle. (The number and description of the expense classification is identical throughout the run because this is a salary run.) The job code number and description appears for every position present in the cost center. Thus, the North radiology department has four job code classifications: (1) RN (job code #3), (2) technician—patient care (job code #5), (3) technician—support (job code #6), and (4) clerical (job code #7). The hourly wage for each job code classification appears in the far right column. This type of arrangement allows activities to be related to particular job codes. The hourly wage related to that code can then be automatically attached.

Exhibit 16–10 shows the equipment ledger file. The full information on equipment for each cost center is present in the equipment ledger file. This type of system allows direct costing of specific items in the activity accounting tradition. The laboratory equipment (cost center number 526) appears in the middle of the page. A laboratory test example of ABC appears in Chapter 3. If this type of equipment ledger file were in place and recognized in that example, the specific items of equipment used for each specific lab test could be immediately isolated and appropriately costed.

The Valley View example in the preceding chapter uses equipment subledgers for individual cost centers. The information contained in

Exhibit 16–4 North River Hospital System Physician Names with Clinical Service File

Physician		Clinical Service	
Number	Name	Number	Description
286		88	RADIOLOGY
288		88	RADIOLOGY
289		15	INT MED/FP
300		45	NEUROLOGY
301		40	HEMATOL/ONCOL
302		16	NEPHRO
303		10	CARDIOLOGY
305		15	INT MED/FP
308		85	PEDIATRICS
31		97	UNIDENTIFIED
311		15	INT MED/FP
313		55	SURGERY
314		64	PODIATRY
32		96	URGENT CARE
321		15	INT MED/FP
324		63	DENTAL
325		65	ORTHOPEDIC
326		63	DENTAL
328		55	SURGERY
329		65	ORTHOPEDIC
33		18	PULMONARY MED
330		55	SURGERY
331		15	INT MED/FP
332		15	INT MED/FP
335		50	NEUROSURGERY
336		30	GASTROENTEROL
337		80	PLASTIC
338		90	OB/GYN
339		15	INT MED/FP
341		65	ORTHOPEDIC
344		80	PLASTIC
348		88	RADIOLOGY
349		65	ORTHOPEDIC
350		16	NEPHRO
352		55	SURGERY
353		65	ORTHOPEDIC
356		85	PEDIATRICS
358		89	ANESTHESIA
359		10	CARDIOLOGY
361		15	INT MED/FP
364		95	PSYCH
368		55	SURGERY
370		75	UROLOGY
372		25	ENT
373		18	PULMONARY MED
374		15	INT MED/FP
376		30	GASTROENTEROL
379		15	INT MED/FP

Exhibit 16–5 North River Hospital System Allocation Base Number Assignments

Cost Center		Expense Class		Assignment	
Number	Description	Number	Description	Variable	Fixed
100	GENERAL ADMINISTRATION	999999	GLOBAL EXPENSE CLASS OPTION	10	10
110	CLINICAL/NURS. ADM.	999999	GLOBAL EXPENSE CLASS OPTION	20	20
111	NURSING EDUCATION	999999	GLOBAL EXPENSE CLASS OPTION	20	20
112	P.A.T.	999999	GLOBAL EXPENSE CLASS OPTION	22	22
120	MEDICAL STAFF	999999	GLOBAL EXPENSE CLASS OPTION	25	25
130	FISCAL SERVICES	999999	GLOBAL EXPENSE CLASS OPTION	10	10
140	PATIENT ACCOUNTING	999999	GLOBAL EXPENSE CLASS OPTION	30	30
151	PATIENT REGISTRATION	999999	GLOBAL EXPENSE CLASS OPTION	30	30
160	EMPLOYEE BENEFITS	999999	GLOBAL EXPENSE CLASS OPTION	90	90
170	ADM. SVCS/H.R.	999999	GLOBAL EXPENSE CLASS OPTION	12	12
180	HLTH INFO MGMT	999999	GLOBAL EXPENSE CLASS OPTION	32	32
183	R.S./Q.A./LIBRARY	999999	GLOBAL EXPENSE CLASS OPTION	10	10
190	INFORMATION TECH.	999999	GLOBAL EXPENSE CLASS OPTION	10	10
200	CARE COORDINATION	999999	GLOBAL EXPENSE CLASS OPTION	42	42
210	PATIENT TRANSPORT	999999	GLOBAL EXPENSE CLASS OPTION	42	42
220	VOLUNTEERS	999999	GLOBAL EXPENSE CLASS OPTION	10	10
230	SECURITY	999999	GLOBAL EXPENSE CLASS OPTION	64	64
250	MATERIAL MGMT.	999999	GLOBAL EXPENSE CLASS OPTION	10	10
260	BLDG SERVICES	999999	GLOBAL EXPENSE CLASS OPTION	64	64
270	PLANT OPERATIONS	999999	GLOBAL EXPENSE CLASS OPTION	64	64
271	UTILITIES	999999	GLOBAL EXPENSE CLASS OPTION	64	64
273	BIOMEDICAL ENGINEERING	999999	GLOBAL EXPENSE CLASS OPTION	64	64
274	FACILITY MANAGEMENT	999999	GLOBAL EXPENSE CLASS OPTION	64	64
281	N-NUTRITION SERVICES	999999	GLOBAL EXPENSE CLASS OPTION	80	84
282	S-NUTRITION SERVICES	999999	GLOBAL EXPENSE CLASS OPTION	81	81
290	TELECOMMUNICATIONS	999999	GLOBAL EXPENSE CLASS OPTION	12	12
295	CENTRAL PROCESSING	999999	GLOBAL EXPENSE CLASS OPTION	50	50
299	DEPRECIATION	999999	GLOBAL EXPENSE CLASS OPTION	99	99
300	GENERAL	999999	GLOBAL EXPENSE CLASS OPTION	99	99
310	C-EMERGENCY CENTER	999999	GLOBAL EXPENSE CLASS OPTION	6	6
315	WOMEN/CHILDREN SERVICES	999999	GLOBAL EXPENSE CLASS OPTION	21	21
320	WATERS-ADM.	999999	GLOBAL EXPENSE CLASS OPTION	23	23

Exhibit 16-6 North River Hospital System Chart of Accounts

Cost Center			Expense Class				
Number	Type	Description	Number	Description	Type	Description	F/V Flag
500	03	PATIENT CARE	90	OTHER OPERATING EXP	15	OTHER EXPENSES	V
506	03	PATIENT CARE	10	SALARIES AND WAGES	11	LABOR	B
			15	V/H/S	12	BENEFITS	B
			21	DRUGS & IV'S	14	SUPPLIES	V
			22	FILM	14	SUPPLIES	V
			23	OTHER MED/SURG	14	SUPPLIES	V
			24	PT CHARGEABLE	14	SUPPLIES	V
			29	NON MEDICAL	14	SUPPLIES	V
			40	LINEN AND FOOD	14	SUPPLIES	V
			60	MARKETING	15	OTHER EXPENSES	V
			70	UTILITIES AND POSTAGE	15	OTHER EXPENSES	V
			80	PURCHASED SERVICE	15	OTHER EXPENSES	V
			90	OTHER OPERATING EXP	15	OTHER EXPENSES	V
			100	CAPITAL COSTS	16	EQUIPMENT	F
			1700	GEN ADMIN ALLOC OVHD	17	ALLOC OVERHEAD	N
			1710	CLIN ADMIN ALLOC OVHD	17	ALLOC OVERHEAD	N
			1720	PT SUPPORT ALLOC OVHD	17	ALLOC OVERHEAD	N
			1730	FAC SUPPORT ALLOC OVHD	17	ALLOC OVERHEAD	N
730	03	PATIENT CARE	10	SALARIES AND WAGES	11	LABOR	B
			15	V/H/S	12	BENEFITS	B
			21	DRUGS & IV'S	14	SUPPLIES	V
			22	FILM	14	SUPPLIES	V
			23	OTHER MED/SURG	14	SUPPLIES	V
			24	PT CHARGEABLE	14	SUPPLIES	V
			29	NON MEDICAL	14	SUPPLIES	V
			31	LEGAL AND OTHER FEES	15	OTHER EXPENSES	V
			40	LINEN AND FOOD	14	SUPPLIES	V
			60	MARKETING	15	OTHER EXPENSES	V
			70	UTILITIES AND POSTAGE	15	OTHER EXPENSES	V

80	PURCHASED SERVICE	15	OTHER EXPENSES	V
90	OTHER OPERATING EXP	15	OTHER EXPENSES	V
100	CAPITAL COSTS	16	EQUIPMENT	F
1700	GEN ADMIN ALLOC OVHD	17	ALLOC OVERHEAD	N
1710	CLIN ADMIN ALLOC OVHD	17	ALLOC OVERHEAD	N
1720	PT SUPPORT ALLOC OVHD	17	ALLOC OVERHEAD	N
1730	FAC SUPPORT ALLOC OVHD	17	ALLOC OVERHEAD	N
1740	EMP BENEFITS ALLOC OVHD	17	ALLOC OVERHEAD	N
1799	ALL OTHER ALLOC OVHD	17	ALLOC OVERHEAD	N

Exhibit 16–7 North River Hospital System Allocation Base Names and Statistics

Allocation Base		Cost Center		Expense Class		Annual Plan Statistic	Current Period Statistic
Number	Description	Number	Description	Number	Description		
020	NURSING HOURS						
		110	CLINICAL/NURS. ADM.	999999	GLOBAL EXPENSE CLASS OPT	8143	679
		112	P.A.T.	999999	GLOBAL EXPENSE CLASS OPT	3744	312
		310	C-EMERGENCY CENTER	999999	GLOBAL EXPENSE CLASS OPT	2080	170
		506	N-SAME DAY STAY	1710	CLIN ADMIN ALLOC OVHD	7488	624
		507	N-ENDOSCOPY/M. SURG	1710	CLIN ADMIN ALLOC OVHD	6760	563
		508	S-SAME DAY STAY	1710	CLIN ADMIN ALLOC OVHD	9048	754
		509	S-ENDOSCOPY/M. SURG	1710	CLIN ADMIN ALLOC OVHD	10088	841
		510	OTHER REHAB/DIAG.	1710	CLIN ADMIN ALLOC OVHD	9776	815
		514	S-VASCULAR CATH.	1710	CLIN ADMIN ALLOC OVHD	5824	485
		518	N-EMERGENCY CENTER	1710	CLIN ADMIN ALLOC OVHD	48942	4079
		519	S-EMERGENCY CENTER	1710	CLIN ADMIN ALLOC OVHD	52250	4354
		545	N-OPERATING ROOM	1710	CLIN ADMIN ALLOC OVHD	22256	1855
		546	S-OPERATING ROOM	1710	CLIN ADMIN ALLOC OVHD	39375	3281
		560	N-POST ANESTH CARE UNIT	1710	CLIN ADMIN ALLOC OVHD	8528	711
		561	S-POST ANESTH CARE UNIT	1710	CLIN ADMIN ALLOC OVHD	16120	1343
		565	N-RADIOLOGY	1710	CLIN ADMIN ALLOC OVHD	957	80
		590	O/P TREAT. UNIT	1710	CLIN ADMIN ALLOC OVHD	4680	390
		600	S-MED-SURG DIV 4	1710	CLIN ADMIN ALLOC OVHD	63232	5269
		605	S-NEURO	1710	CLIN ADMIN ALLOC OVHD	12688	1057
		620	S-MED-SURG DIV 5	1710	CLIN ADMIN ALLOC OVHD	72509	6042
		630	N-MED-SURG DIV B	1710	CLIN ADMIN ALLOC OVHD	40248	3354
		640	N-MED SURG DIV D	1710	CLIN ADMIN ALLOC OVHD	42182	3515
		645	N-INTENSIVE CARE UNIT	1710	CLIN ADMIN ALLOC OVHD	55952	4663
		655	S-INTENSIVE CARE UNIT	1710	CLIN ADMIN ALLOC OVHD	52000	4333
		660	S-SURG. ICU	1710	CLIN ADMIN ALLOC OVHD	21840	1820
		665	S-STEPDOWN	1710	CLIN ADMIN ALLOC OVHD	52208	4351

680	WATERS-DIAG.	1710	CLIN ADMIN ALLOC OVHD	2288	191
685	WATERS-SURG.	1710	CLIN ADMIN ALLOC OVHD	39000	3250
695	WATERS-OPHTH	1710	CLIN ADMIN ALLOC OVHD	1040	87
701	PAIN MGMT	1710	CLIN ADMIN ALLOC OVHD	2974	248
725	NR OCC. HLTH	1710	CLIN ADMIN ALLOC OVHD	2080	173
730	SUB-ACUTE REHAB	1710	CLIN ADMIN ALLOC OVHD	20550	1713
	TOTAL ALLOCATION BASE NO. 020			736850	61404
042	TOTAL I/P DISCH.				
530	N-NURSERY	1720	PT SUPPORT ALLOC OVHD	1312	109
600	S-MED-SURG DIV 4	1720	PT SUPPORT ALLOC OVHD	2485	207
605	S-NEURO	1720	PT SUPPORT ALLOC OVHD	98	8
620	S-MED-SURG DIV 5	1720	PT SUPPORT ALLOC OVHD	2695	225
630	N-MED-SURG DIV B	1720	PT SUPPORT ALLOC OVHD	1720	143
635	N-OBSTETRICS DIV C	1720	PT SUPPORT ALLOCOVHD	1343	112
640	N-MED SURG DIV D	1720	PT SUPPORT ALLOC OVHD	1635	136
645	N-INTENSIVE CARE UNIT	1720	PT SUPPORT ALLOC OVHD	694	58
655	S-INTENSIVE CARE UNIT	1720	PT SUPPORT ALLOC OVHD	275	23
660	S-SURG. ICU	1720	PT SUPPORT ALLOC OVHD	72	6
665	S-STEPDOWN	1720	PT SUPPORT ALLOC OVHD	1220	102
730	SUB-ACUTE REHAB	1720	PT SUPPORT ALLOC OVHD	409	34
	TOTAL ALLOCATION BASE NO. 042			13958	1163

Exhibit 16–8 North River Hospital System Procedure Names/Charges

Cost Center		Procedure		Charge		
Number	Description	Number	Description	Pre-Adj	Adjusted	Day Rate
556	S-CPS	610001	JET NEB CONTINUOUS	122.5		
556	S-CPS	610002	IPPB TREATMENT	39		
556	S-CPS	610007	OXYGEN	56.75		
556	S-CPS	610011	MECHANICAL VENTILATOR	358.25		
556	S-CPS	610018	ARTERIAL PUNCTURE	27.25		
556	S-CPS	610023	AEROSOL TREATMENT	28.25		
556	S-CPS	610026	CHEST PHYSIOTHPY/CLAP	48.5		
556	S-CPS	610027	CONTINUOUS CPAP	347.75		
556	S-CPS	610056	B&A PFT	147		
556	S-CPS	610065	PULMONARY MECHANICS	48.5		
556	S-CPS	610071	INHALER	11.75		
556	S-CPS	610080	OXIMETRY SINGLE	53.5		
556	S-CPS	610081	OXIMETRY MONITORING	158.5		
556	S-CPS	610102	CPAP TREATMENT	47.5		
556	S-CPS	612003	OXYGEN INITIAL	44.5		
556	S-CPS	612007	AEROSOL TREATMENT INIT	44.5		
556	S-CPS	612008	INCENTIVE SPIROMETRY IN	44.5		
556	S-CPS	612013	INHALER INITIAL	36.5		
556	S-CPS	612014	OX PER SHIFT INITIAL	95		
556	S-CPS	612015	OX MON INITIAL	95		
556	S-CPS	880003	EKG	82.25		
556	S-CPS	880006	HOLTER	178.75		
556	S-CPS	880008	CST	295.25		
556	S-CPS	880010	ECHOCARDIOGRAM	478.25		
556	S-CPS	880012	CST WITH THALIUM	319.75		
556	S-CPS	880013	CARDIAC DOPPLER STUDY	123.5		
558	S-CPS	880015	DOPPLER COLOR FLOW MAP	95		
556	S-CPS	880019	STRESS ECHOCARDIOGRAM	531.75		
556	S-CPS	885000	LOWER EXT ARTERIAL EXAM	360.25		
556	S-CPS	999996	REV ADJ			
556	S-CPS	999998	ALL OTHER	46.32		
567	RADIATION THERAPY	999998	ALL OTHER	304.22		
568	S-RADIOLOGY	720012	FACIAL BONES COMPLETE	115		
568	S-RADIOLOGY	720018	PARANASAL SINUSES	115		
588	S-RADIOLOGY	720030	PORTABLE CHEST	97.75		
588	S-RADIOLOGY	720032	CHEST 1 VIEW	69.25		
588	S-RADIOLOGY	720033	CHEST 2 VIEWS	92.25		
568	S-RADIOLOGY	720043	RIBS UNILATERAL AND LV CH	99.5		
568	S-RADIOLOGY	720049	THOR SP WITH SHIMMER	96.75		
568	S-RADIOLOGY	720050	L-S SPINE 2 VIEWS	99.5		

continues

Exhibit 16–8 continued

Cost Center		Procedure		Charge		
Number	Description	Number	Description	Pre-Adj	Adjusted	Day Rate
568	S-RADIOLOGY	720056	PELVIS AP ONLY	78		
568	S-RADIOLOGY	720061	LUMBAR MYELO COMPLETE	290		
588	S-RADIOLOGY	720069	RIGHT SHOULDER	85		
568	S-RADIOLOGY	720070	LEFT SHOULDER	85		
568	S-RADIOLOGY	720081	RIGHT WRIST	80.75		
568	S-RADIOLOGY	720082	LEFT WRIST	80.75		
568	S-RADIOLOGY	720083	RIGHT HAND	80.75		
568	S-RADIOLOGY	720084	LEFT HAND	80.75		
568	S-RADIOLOGY	720085	FINGERS RIGHT HAND	62		
568	S-RADIOLOGY	720099	RIGHT ANKLE	80.75		
568	S-RADIOLOGY	720100	LEFT ANKLE	80.75		
568	S-RADIOLOGY	720101	RIGHT FOOT	80.75		
568	S-RADIOLOGY	720102	LEFT FOOT	80.75		
568	S-RADIOLOGY	720107	ABDOMEN KUB	78		
568	S-RADIOLOGY	720108	ABD AP DECUB/ERECT	92.25		
568	S-RADIOLOGY	720109	ACUTE ABD W/PA CHEST	108.25		
568	S-RADIOLOGY	720110	ESOPHAGUS	172.75		
568	S-RADIOLOGY	720115	COLON BARIUM ENEMA	250.75		
588	S-RADIOLOGY	720116	BARIUM ENEMA W/AIR	327		
568	S-RADIOLOGY	720118	CHOLANG OPERA	284		
568	S-RADIOLOGY	720123	INTRA PYELOGRAM	191.75		
568	S-RADIOLOGY	720184	MAMMOGRAMS BI-LATERAL	193		
568	S-RADIOLOGY	720201	RIGHT KNEE 4 VIEWS	85		
568	S-RADIOLOGY	720202	LEFT KNEE 4 VIEWS	85		
568	S-RADIOLOGY	720267	FLUOROSCOPY	165.75		
568	S-RADIOLOGY	720272	ERCP	462.5		
568	S-RADIOLOGY	720282	UROGRAM W/TOMOS	312.5		
568	S-RADIOLOGY	720290	PORTABLE	33.25		
568	S-RADIOLOGY	720295	MAMMOGRAM UNILATERAL	96.75		
568	S-RADIOLOGY	720297	BREAST SURGICAL SPECIMEN	216.25		
568	S-RADIOLOGY	720298	SCREENING MAMMOGRAM	60		
568	S-RADIOLOGY	720304	CERVICAL SPINE 4 VIEWS	115		
568	S-RADIOLOGY	720350	RIGHT HIP 1 VIEW	69		
568	S-RADIOLOGY	720386	UGI AIR CON W/KUB	276.5		
568	S-RADIOLOGY	720388	UGI AIR CON 2/KUB SM B	310		
568	S-RADIOLOGY	720445	SPINE SINGLE VIEW SHOOT TH	89.25		
568	S-RADIOLOGY	999996	REV ADJ			
568	S-RADIOLOGY	999998	ALL OTHER	98.57		
570	S-MRI	700002	BRAIN	769.25		
570	S-MRI	700010	CERVICAL SPINE	782.5		

Exhibit 16–9 North River Hospital System Job Code Names/Rate

Cost Center		Expense Class		Job Code		Hourly Wage
Number	Description	Number	Description	Number	Description	
190	INFORMATION TECH.	10	SALARIES AND WAGES	1	MGR/DIRECTOR	46.6542
190	INFORMATION TECH.	10	SALARIES AND WAGES	2	SUPERVISORS	22.4197
190	INFORMATION TECH.	10	SALARIES AND WAGES	5	TECH-PT CARE	17.1739
190	INFORMATION TECH.	10	SALARIES AND WAGES	6	TECH-SUPPORT	14.1473
190	INFORMATION TECH.	10	SALARIES AND WAGES	7	CLERICAL	12.4334
190	INFORMATION TECH.	10	SALARIES AND WAGES	8	OTHER	8.0587
282	S-NUTRITION SERVICES	10	SALARIES AND WAGES	2	SUPERVISORS	18.5728
282	S-NUTRITION SERVICES	10	SALARIES AND WAGES	6	TECH-SUPPORT	9.038
282	S-NUTRITION SERVICES	10	SALARIES AND WAGES	7	CLERICAL	9.2338
290	TELECOMMUNICATIONS	10	SALARIES AND WAGES	6	TECH-SUPPORT	10.4415
290	TELECOMMUNICATIONS	10	SALARIES AND WAGES	7	CLERICAL	8.6
295	CENTRAL PROCESSING	10	SALARIES AND WAGES	2	SUPERVISORS	19.8175
295	CENTRAL PROCESSING	10	SALARIES AND WAGES	6	TECH-SUPPORT	10.7241
295	CENTRAL PROCESSING	10	SALARIES AND WAGES	7	CLERICAL	12.0667
565	N-RADIOLOGY	10	SALARIES AND WAGES	3	RN	19.242
565	N-RADIOLOGY	10	SALARIES AND WAGES	5	TECH-PT CARE	15.2892
565	N-RADIOLOGY	10	SALARIES AND WAGES	6	TECH-SUPPORT	10.3622
565	N-RADIOLOGY	10	SALARIES AND WAGES	7	CLERICAL	11.2937
600	S-MED-SURG DIV 4	10	SALARIES AND WAGES	2	SUPERVISORS	21.6916
600	S-MED-SURG DIV 4	10	SALARIES AND WAGES	3	RN	18.8356
600	S-MED-SURG DIV 4	10	SALARIES AND WAGES	4	LPN	13.1108
600	S-MED-SURG DIV 4	10	SALARIES AND WAGES	5	TECH-PT CARE	7.6563
600	S-MED-SURG DIV 4	10	SALARIES AND WAGES	6	TECH-SUPPORT	9.4815
600	S-MED-SURG DIV 4	10	SALARIES AND WAGES	7	CLERICAL	10.302
600	S-MED-SURG DIV 4	10	SALARIES AND WAGES	9	NURSE AIDE	9.375
620	S-MED-SURG DIV 5	10	SALARIES AND WAGES	1	MGR/DIRECTOR	26.2416
620	S-MED-SURG DIV 5	10	SALARIES AND WAGES	2	SUPERVISORS	22.6265
620	S-MED-SURG DIV 5	10	SALARIES AND WAGES	3	RN	19.3024
620	S-MED-SURG DIV 5	10	SALARIES AND WAGES	4	LPN	13.2968

620	S-MED-SURG DIV 5	10	SALARIES AND WAGES	5	TECH-PT CARE	8.1581
620	S-MED-SURG DIV 5	10	SALARIES AND WAGES	6	TECH-SUPPORT	9.3192
620	S-MED-SURG DIV 5	10	SALARIES AND WAGES	7	CLERICAL	9.8539
620	S-MED-SURG DIV 5	10	SALARIES AND WAGES	9	NURSE AIDE	8.2769
645	N-INTENSIVE CARE UNIT	10	SALARIES AND WAGES	2	SUPERVISORS	25.0413
645	N-INTENSIVE CARE UNIT	10	SALARIES AND WAGES	3	RN	19.953
645	N-INTENSIVE CARE UNIT	10	SALARIES AND WAGES	4	LPN	13.8593
645	N-INTENSIVE CARE UNIT	10	SALARIES AND WAGES	5	TECH-PT CARE	17.3318
645	N-INTENSIVE CARE UNIT	10	SALARIES AND WAGES	6	TECH-SUPPORT	10.1458
645	N-INTENSIVE CARE UNIT	10	SALARIES AND WAGES	7	CLERICAL	10.0713
645	N-INTENSIVE CARE UNIT	10	SALARIES AND WAGES	9	NURSE AIDE	8

their subledger is similar to the information displayed in Exhibit 16–10. However, Valley View also has a replacement cost feature in their subledgers that was not shown in the case study.

Exhibit 16–11 shows one page of the matrix allocation totals report. This exhibit illustrates the first pass, the second pass, and the third pass in the reciprocal step-down costing process. The beginning amount in the left hand column represents the total amount of overhead to be allocated. These beginning amount totals are contained in cost centers from number 100 through number 320. (You may review the names of these cost centers as listed in Exhibit 16–5.) The allocated amounts are shown on each of the following line items by cost center number and by classification number. Computers are excellent tools for step-down allocations. (For a further explanation of step-down allocation, see Chapter 3.)

Exhibit 16–11 shows the ability of this system to apply reciprocal step-down matrix allocation for both fixed and variable items. This flexibility is desirable for the purposes of activity accounting.

DOs AND DON'Ts OF COMPREHENSIVE IMPLEMENTATION

The individual in charge of implementation strongly supported comprehensive implementation. He says that because of comprehensive implementation there is no chance of perceived favoritism ("your department was costed first; mine wasn't"). The sense of suspense is eliminated. He believes that the CEO accomplished his vision with the comprehensive implementation: costs were managed and reduced and length of stay (LOS) was reduced while treatment practices were revealed and analyzed. The costing results have been put to good use for general management as well as for use in managed care negotiations and tracking.

When asked what he would do differently in the implementation, knowing what he does today, this individual had only one comment. He would have fine tuned the standards up front (before release) instead of adjusting them after the fact. When asked what was on his wish list for the future, he reported that APGs (ambulatory practice groups) were on the top of his list.

Exhibit 16-10 North River Hospital System Equipment Ledger File

Cost Center		Expense Class		Equipment		Historical Cost	MMYY Purch.	Annual Depr.
Number	Description	Number	Description	Number	Description			
518	N-EMERGENCY CENTER	100	CAPITAL COSTS	92060	DEFIBRILLATOR M	8870	01/94	1109
518	N-EMERGENCY CENTER	100	CAPITAL COSTS	93020	COPIER NP4050	6525	01/94	1305
518	N-EMERGENCY CENTER	100	CAPITAL COSTS	94001	ER CARTS-STRETCHERS	12554	01/94	1255
518	N-EMERGENCY CENTER	100	CAPITAL COSTS	500120	PASSPORT IREL MN	8168	01/95	1167
518	N-EMERGENCY CENTER	100	CAPITAL COSTS	930530	E/R ROOM FURNITURE	18162	01/95	1513
518	N-EMERGENCY CENTER	100	CAPITAL COSTS	999999	ALL OTHER			19330
519	S-EMERGENCY CENTER	100	CAPITAL COSTS	90026	LIFEPACK 10	9649	01/90	1206
519	S-EMERGENCY CENTER	100	CAPITAL COSTS	95072	ESCORT MONITORS	14000	01/95	2800
519	S-EMERGENCY CENTER	100	CAPITAL COSTS	96037	PASSPORT MONITOR	215761	01/96	30823
519	S-EMERGENCY CENTER	100	CAPITAL COSTS	510700	HYD STRETCHERS	14668	01/95	1467
519	S-EMERGENCY CENTER	100	CAPITAL COSTS	999999	ALL OTHER			530
526	LABORATORY	100	CAPITAL COSTS	87202	EKTACHEM 700	111119	01/87	5556
526	LABORATORY	100	CAPITAL COSTS	89259	PARKS FLO-LAB	31650	01/89	3165
526	LABORATORY	100	CAPITAL COSTS	90016	CHEMICAL ANALYZER	126046	01/91	15756
526	LABORATORY	100	CAPITAL COSTS	90017	REP HELENA ANALYSIS	47316	01/91	5915
526	LABORATORY	100	CAPITAL COSTS	91008	LAB ORDER E HDWE	17338	01/93	3468
526	LABORATORY	100	CAPITAL COSTS	91014	AUTOSCAN WLK	81000	01/91	10125
526	LABORATORY	100	CAPITAL COSTS	93029	HEMATOL ANALYZER	84067	01/94	10508
526	LABORATORY	100	CAPITAL COSTS	93128	LAB INFORMATION SYSTEM	111391	01/93	22278
526	LABORATORY	100	CAPITAL COSTS	94105	COAG ANALYZER	30000	01/95	6000
526	LABORATORY	100	CAPITAL COSTS	94404	RENOVATE LAB	399646	01/95	39965
526	LABORATORY	100	CAPITAL COSTS	100801	CABLING-PILOT 5W	40170	01/93	4017
526	LABORATORY	100	CAPITAL COSTS	100805	SUNQUEST NET EQ	27694	01/95	5539
526	LABORATORY	100	CAPITAL COSTS	910080	COMPUTER	15785	01/93	3157
526	LABORATORY	100	CAPITAL COSTS	910804	LAB INFORMATION SYSTEM	25000	01/94	5000
526	LABORATORY	100	CAPITAL COSTS	920240	HORMONE ANALYZER	27500	01/94	3929
526	LABORATORY	100	CAPITAL COSTS	930270	COMPUTERS, ETC.	17169	01/93	3434
526	LABORATORY	100	CAPITAL COSTS	930290	HEMATOL ANALYZER	67555	01/94	8444

continues

Exhibit 16–10 continued

Cost Center		Expense Class		Equipment		Historical Cost	MMYY Purch.	Annual Depr.
Number	Description	Number	Description	Number	Description			
526	LABORATORY	100	CAPITAL COSTS	930905	VIDEO WRKSTAT	19538	01/94	3908
526	LABORATORY	100	CAPITAL COSTS	932906	TISSUE PROCESSOR	33038	01/94	3304
526	LABORATORY	100	CAPITAL COSTS	999999	ALL OTHER			39745
530	N-NURSERY	100	CAPITAL COSTS	94407	ECG MONITORS	48900	01/94	6986
530	N-NURSERY	100	CAPITAL COSTS	96066	DATA SCOPE INFANT	7786	01/96	1112
530	N-NURSERY	100	CAPITAL COSTS	944073	INCUBATORS	24222	01/94	2422
530	N-NURSERY	100	CAPITAL COSTS	999999	ALL OTHER			71247
535	N-DELIVERY ROOM	100	CAPITAL COSTS	92081	EC6 MONITORS	18113	01/93	2588
535	N-DELIVERY ROOM	100	CAPITAL COSTS	93101	ULTRAS LE15018	38800	01/93	5543
535	N-DELIVERY ROOM	100	CAPITAL COSTS	95122	FETAL MONITORS	69534	01/96	9933
535	N-DELIVERY ROOM	100	CAPITAL COSTS	999999	ALL OTHER			129
560	N-POST ANESTHOLOGY CARE UNIT	100	CAPITAL COSTS	999999	ALL OTHER			9634
561	S-POST ANESTHOLOGY CARE UNIT	100	CAPITAL COSTS	90012	MON/RECORDER	10001	01/91	1429
561	S-POST ANESTHOLOGY CARE UNIT	100	CAPITAL COSTS	91108	ECG ESCORT MON	8847	01/92	1264
561	S-POST ANESTHOLOGY CARE UNIT	100	CAPITAL COSTS	92042	PNEUMATIC STRETCHER	17832	01/92	1189
561	S-POST ANESTHOLOGY CARE UNIT	100	CAPITAL COSTS	92043	MONITORS	103633	01/93	14805
561	S-POST ANESTHOLOGY CARE UNIT	100	CAPITAL COSTS	92045	PNEUMATIC STRETCHER	21440	01/92	1429
561	S-POST ANESTHOLOGY CARE UNIT	100	CAPITAL COSTS	95062	BP MONITORS-NIV	7480	01/96	1247
561	S-POST ANESTHOLOGY CARE UNIT	100	CAPITAL COSTS	999999	ALL OTHER			5301

Exhibit 16–11 North River Hospital System Matrix Allocation Totals Report for Fiscal Period Ending 03/31/97

		GL Costs: Actual Period Beginning Amounts		1st Pass Totals		2nd Pass Totals		3rd Pass Totals	
CC#	Class #	Fixed Amount	Variable Amount	Fixed Amount	Variable Amount	Fixed Amount	Variable Amount	Fixed Amount	Variable Amount
100	999999	727020.00		212302.80		71092.56			
110	999999	130262.00		54284.20		16330.62			
111	999999	24439.00		10520.46		3018.35			
112	999999	22186.00		13772.68		5098.65			
120	999999	14657.00		11508.72		4702.48			
130	999999	62825.00		26163.07		7218.90			
140	999999	80738.00		62500.90		17179.18			
151	999999	47677.00		31628.56		9424.30			
160	999999	930586.00		184129.07		53023.37			
170	999999	136619.00		29272.96		8459.76			
180	999999	122499.00		60409.53		18264.68			
183	999999	30527.00		39799.61		8529.65			
190	999999	157590.00		76476.17		21948.27			
200	999999	63448.00		34616.54		9766.79			
210	999999	16374.00		11716.34		3441.54			
220	999999	8541.00		6244.67		2166.39			
230	999999	51235.00		8806.48		2582.32			
250	999999	195472.00		60314.28		18342.66			
260	999999	114883.00		165674.67		64731.88			
270	999999	149856.00		56040.04		15618.23			
271	998999	168139.00		33336.82		9599.95			
273	999999	22623.00		11161.33		3265.74			
274	999999	33363.00		6681.56		1844.55			
281	999999	124109.00		105802.19		51447.85			
282	999999	117974.00		91855.48		38533.93			
290	999999	66236.00		24783.55		7181.58			
295	999999	94250.00		42924.94		13697.30			
299	999999	329021.00		71942.46		20717.16			
300	999999	493973.00		94124.79		27104.97			
310	999999	44472.00		12657.11		3631.68			
315	999999	61007.00		15940.91		4520.13			
320	999999	24276.00		58585.42		28266.18			
506	1700			3406.25		4519.30		4990.38	
506	1710			2379.59		3560.79		3976.56	
506	1720			5416.31		8536.67		9888.24	
506	1730			5306.33		8073.97		9646.81	
506	1740			4066.44		4871.04		5172.58	
506	1799			1754.52		2108.55		2347.27	
507	1700			3531.00		4721.53		5212.86	
507	1710			1490.01		2140.10		2352.77	
507	1720			2505.48		3921.65		4629.04	
507	1730			1029.11		1565.86		1870.90	
507	1740			2148.93		2574.13		2733.48	
507	1799			2132.42		2562.71		2852.85	
508	1700			3922.69		5201.36		5743.61	

continues

Exhibit 16–11 continued

CC#	Class #	Beginning Amounts Fixed Amount	Beginning Amounts Variable Amount	1st Pass Totals Fixed Amount	1st Pass Totals Variable Amount	2nd Pass Totals Fixed Amount	2nd Pass Totals Variable Amount	3rd Pass Totals Fixed Amount	3rd Pass Totals Variable Amount
508	1710			2784.75		4140.89		4613.65	
508	1720			10533.90		16076.69		18226.14	
508	1730			15372.29		23390.05		27946.51	
508	1740			4859.89		5821.49		6181.87	
508	1799			1993.68		2395.97		2667.23	
509	1700			5498.13		7347.92		8112.66	
509	1710			2234.14		3213.11		3534.03	
509	1720			3077.41		4935.78		5784.21	
509	1730			980.87		1492.46		1783.20	
509	1740			3570.53		4277.01		4541.78	
509	1799			3286.34		3949.47		4396.60	
510	1700			6790.49		9015.40		9955.02	
510	1710			2132.16		3054.52		3354.67	
510	1720			1886.55		3314.63		4263.01	
510	1730			1929.58		2935.99		3507.93	
510	1740			7769.21		9306.46		9882.58	
510	1799			3548.91		4265.03		4747.89	
514	1700			15525.47		20834.01		23000.41	
514	1710			2127.32		3263.15		3676.94	
514	1720			4310.20		7448.55		8673.54	
514	1730			1945.82		2960.46		3537.16	
514	1740			5289.68		6336.31		6728.57	
514	1799			10007.31		12026.63		13388.22	
518	1700			67755.50		89496.81		98534.19	
518	1710			11159.30		16157.76		17819.02	
518	1720			12842.28		21993.01		26779.26	
518	1730			8892.13		13530.02		16165.71	
518	1740			24034.97		28790.61		30572.92	
518	1799			28046.59		33705.95		37521.93	
519	1700			70128.08		92677.38		102075.56	
519	1710			11842.83		17123.61		18874.02	
519	1720			13726.20		23317.17		27649.83	
519	1730			12059.85		18349.94		21924.56	
519	1740			25026.78		29978.67		31834.53	
519	1799			29548.05		35510.38		39530.65	
520	1700			563.42		759.48		838.38	
520	1710			16.24		29.00		34.31	
520	1720			142.31		246.63		277.55	
520	1730			627.11		954.20		1140.08	
520	1740								
520	1799			392.30		471.46		524.84	
526	1700			44823.28		59759.77		65982 50	
526	1710			1365.57		2437.82		2884.33	
526	1720			16629.30		29307.46		36045.37	
526	1730			27094.46		41226.19		49257.19	
526	1740			37206.39		44568.18		47237.21	
526	1799			25562.65		30720.79		34198.81	
530	1700			5352.43		7120.27		7862.05	
530	1710			5619.03		7154.54		7808.63	

Planning for Managed Care with ABC—Meridia's Home Health Agency Model for Chronic Illness Care: A Case Study

Patricia Hinton Walker, Judith J. Baker, Christine A. Pierce,
Cindyleigh Mocilnikar, and Jan Steinel

CHAPTER OUTLINE

PREFACE

This case study examines a comparison of chronic obstructive pulmonary disease (COPD), wound care, diabetes education, and regular care in a home health agency for managed care purposes. The case study revolves around these three specialty care types and regular care. This chapter explores the process of providing that care and the time analysis portion of the project. Chapter 18 is concerned with implementing the necessary activity data-driven cost components.

A unique aspect of this case study is the effort to isolate and identify the specific activities that make up the specialty care versus regular care. The information is vital for strategic planning and for future pricing in the managed

care arena. Note also that a small pilot study (ten patients) was conducted prior to undertaking the larger study. This is desirable methodology.

Meridia Home Care Services is part of the Meridia Health System. The Cleveland-based health system is comprised of four hospitals, the home care division and multiple outpatient centers, and medical office facilities. Over 1,200 private practice physicians are associated with the health system and residency programs.

INTRODUCTION

Escalating costs of health care in all sectors have stimulated the need for providers, purchasers, and regulators of health care to develop methods for cost containment. Home health care providers are preparing for significant change in this era of cost containment. One of the methods now being considered for home health care is prospective payment. Although the Medicare Prospective Payment System (PPS) has been effective in reducing the number of hospital admissions and length of stay, the cost savings are questionable because some of the reduction has been achieved by shifting care to posthospital settings, such as home health agencies (HHAs).[1] The potential implementation of PPS is causing home health providers to explore new approaches to care in order to change their economic behavior as new incentives challenge old systems of care. Moving from a fee-for-visit reimbursement system to a per-patient or per-episode payment system creates an obvious incentive to reduce the number of visits. It is anticipated that in the future, this reduction of utilization will create incentives for new disease-specific, case management models of care. These models may include increased use of longer, less frequent visits, telemedicine, video, and medical equipment.[2] This chapter highlights the exploration of new models of care for patients with chronic illness diagnoses in the context of this new health care reimbursement environment.

Diagnosis has been the principal factor used in determining hospital payment under PPS, but there is a concern in the home health industry that International Classification of Diseases, Ninth Revision, Clinical Modification (ICD-9) codes alone are not good predictors of utilization of services. Studies show that other factors such as age, functional limitations, and the availability of informal caregivers in the home contribute to the utilization of service. However, it is important for home health agencies to develop and evaluate new approaches to care for chronically ill patients, particularly high users of service. It is estimated that nearly ten million Americans require home care services annually.[3] The last National Medical Expenditure Survey[4] characterized the home care population at more than 50 percent over the age of 65 with 40 percent having functional limitations in one or more activities of daily living.

The 1994 National Home and Hospice Care Survey from the National Center for Health Statistics[5] illustrates the top home care diagnoses to be diseases of the circulatory system—heart disease comprising 20 percent of this total—with diabetes, stroke, and hypertension all running a close second. With these statistics, it becomes readily apparent that addressing the costs and outcomes of diabetes, heart disease,

and peripheral circulation problems is a necessary component of good home health business management. A study conducted in New Jersey[6] reflects other national data regarding chronically ill patients and the relationship of diagnosis to the number of home care visits. In this report, in rank ordering of number of patients by diagnosis, the top diagnosis groups were: circulatory, neoplasm, injuries or poisonings, musculoskeletal, endocrine/metabolic diseases such as diabetes, and respiratory. Rank ordering of diagnosis groupings based on number of visits included: number three—injuries or poisonings, and neoplasms (which may involve wound or ostomy care); number six—endocrine disorders, which includes diabetes; and number seven—respiratory disorders. More recent data supports these trends: cerebral vascular disease, followed by hip fractures, diabetes, circulatory system disease, or malignant neoplasms were the most costly. COPD patients were less costly when ranked only by primary diagnosis; however, comorbidities among the patients with chronic disease respiratory problems contribute to higher utilization of services than many other diagnoses.[7]

It is necessary to examine high cost/high utilization diagnosis for which inpatient hospitals are seeking alternate care venues and to plan for improved community management. Diabetic patients are frequent re-visitors to the hospital—often due to complications that result from noncompliance or inadequate education regarding the management of their chronic disease. Patients with circulatory disorders may develop peripheral ulcers that require long-term and intensive wound management while their condition renders them immobile and unavailable for ambulatory clinics.[8] COPD[9] patients may frequent the emergency room with dyspnea, respiratory infections, and the like—perhaps ending up in the intensive care unit for management—when prevention and education may have been successful through home care.[10] As the health care industry becomes more competitive, new product development and accurate pricing of services within the context of managed care is a key to survival in the future.

MANAGED CARE CONTEXT

One of the most significant challenges for health care providers in all types of health care delivery systems is the rapidly changing competition in the managed care marketplace. This market-driven reform is moving at a rapid rate, causing buyers and sellers in the marketplace to scramble for ways to decrease costs in the system, develop new cost-effective programs, and initiate methods of measuring costs in order to respond to the market. Competitive pricing and reducing risk of financial failure depend on understanding the nature, needs, and utilization patterns of the clients being served as well as determining ways to identify and manage costs. It is clear that some form of managed care is here to stay, and this is evidenced, in part, by the number of consolidations, mergers, and joint ventures in urban areas across the country.[11] Home health agencies have not escaped this buying and selling frenzy, and the survivors will be those organizations that "gain knowledge and control of true costs."[12]

Cost containment is the name of the game, but it is not the only factor that must be considered. The reality of today's health care market is that health care professionals must carefully balance resources against acceptable patient outcomes. Commonly attributed to managed care, this balancing act is having a particularly dramatic impact on the staff and operations of home health agencies that have historically operated within the cost-reimbursement environment of traditional Medicare. Throughout the last five years, commercial insurance carriers have gradually moved from fee for service reimbursement, through discounted fee for service, to per diem, and finally to capitation. Enrollment in senior HMOs is steadily increasing, shifting the traditional Medicare base of home health reimbursement to a managed care model, and the Health Care Finance Adminis-

tration (HCFA) proposes implementation of a prospective payment system by 1999.

Mauser and Miller report that "home health users utilize significantly more health care services than non-users. Seventy percent of Medicare home health users in 1992 were hospitalized at some point during the year, while only 13 percent of non-users were hospitalized."[13] Therefore, it is not surprising that home health care users' overall expenditures were higher than nonusers. As discussed previously, most of these high users are older, and many have chronic conditions. As cost constraints continue across the health care industry, it becomes increasingly necessary to manage these chronic cases in a proactive, cost-effective manner, while continuing to achieve satisfactory outcomes. Today's home health agency must not only be prepared to care for these types of cases, but must be willing to compare their costs and outcomes against more traditional delivery systems (hospitals), illustrate positive results, and be prepared to continue generating their results with less and less financial resources as managed care progresses. Home care must now be managed as it has never been managed before.

BACKGROUND ON MERIDIA

Meridia Home Care Services is an integrated home health delivery system that includes a Medicare certified home health agency, an infusion pharmacy, a high risk pregnancy service, a medical equipment and supply company, and a Lifeline emergency response service. The home care operation is affiliated with Meridia Health System, a large community-based health care delivery system situated in the eastern suburbs of metropolitan Cleveland, Ohio. The health system consists of four hospitals, multiple outpatient centers and medical office facilities, and employs nearly 5,000 individuals. Over 1,200 private practice physicians associated with the health system and residency programs for both doctors of medicine (MDs) and doctors of osteopathy (DOs) are housed here.

Home care in the Meridia Health System began in 1977 prior to the integration of the community hospitals under one system. As a department of what was then Hillcrest Hospital (Hillcrest Hospital Coordinated Home Care Program), the home health agency started with fewer than ten employees and the mission was to service discharged patients within a ten-mile radius of that facility. Only 652 visits were made during that first year of service. Agency growth between 1978 and 1982 averaged 29.5 percent, then declined to less than 1 percent between 1983 and 1987. In 1988, the home care agency ownership was transferred from the hospital to the postacute and for-profit division of the health system and was physically relocated into a freestanding facility.

Over the next seven years the agency's volume grew at nearly three times the industry average (30 percent), approaching 170,000 visits in 1996, and staff expanded to nearly 300. In 1995, the affiliated businesses of home infusion, pharmacy, medical equipment and supplies, perinatal services, and Lifeline emergency response systems were effectively integrated into the home health agency. In order to better position the agency for managed care, the introduction of disease specialty management teams, case managers, managed care specialists, and nontraditional services (homemakers, sitters, and so forth) are but a few of the changes that the agency is undergoing in order to respond to the rapid changes in the Cleveland market. Three of the disease specific approaches to managing chronically ill patients are highlighted in this chapter: care of COPD patients by registered nurses (RNs) with respiratory therapy credentials, care of diabetic patients by registered nurses certified as diabetic educators, and care of patients with wounds and/or ostomies by registered nurses who are enterostomal therapists.

EXPLORING THE OPPORTUNITIES

Within the context of a changing health care market in the Cleveland area and a shift to man-

aged care, Meridia Home Care Services was exploring new approaches to the health care of chronically ill populations. Effective management of populations with chronic conditions such as COPD, diabetes, colostomies, and wound care are critical for home health agencies in order to control costs. To be proactive in a changing market and to explore new ways to manage these high costs and high frequency users of services, the Meridia Home Health leadership facilitated the development and evaluation of new models of care. By using RNs with specialty preparation in caring for disease-specific populations in a new case management approach, it was anticipated that more effective clinical management would decrease the numbers of readmissions, the numbers of emergency room visits, and the length of stay. However, it was important that the new models of care be structured and evaluated in the context of cost and quality.

Although the focus of these new models of care was to increase cost savings while maintaining quality of care, one of the most important components of the evaluation of this new approach was to identify the actual cost of the new model(s) of care. Cost savings of a new model of care could only be determined by clarifying and defining this new model and establishing data collection measures to determine actual costs. Activity-based costing was the methodology chosen for this project. The first challenge, however, was to understand and describe the new model of care that would be delivered by an RN with specialty preparation related to disease management of a specific chronically ill population. The next step was to compare and contrast this approach with the traditional model of home health service, using RNs who did not have specialty background and/or certification to provide care to a similar population.

THE MODEL(S) OF CARE

Three new models of care were clarified and defined for the purposes of this project, and the traditional model of care was also clarified and defined for comparison purposes. The new models of care were intensive case management models of specific populations by specialty prepared RNs. The common factor in each of the new models was disease specific assessment, planning, and case management beyond the traditional role of the home health nurse. Patients selected for management in these new models of care included: those in advanced stages of the disease, those with multiple diagnoses, those who were noncompliant with the medical regimen, those with poor support networks—frequently with a lack of reliable caregivers, and the elderly. For the purposes of this project, RNs with specialty preparation related to the three chronic illness were interviewed in order to describe, define, and develop activity-based costing data-collection instruments to track activities related to the new models of care. Also, traditional home health nurses were interviewed in order to design an instrument for tracking activities related to the traditional model of care.

During the interviews, questions were asked regarding the activities occurring during the client-focused time (actual home care time), activities immediately before and after the home health visit, subsequent case management activities, and activities related to administration or office time specific to the home health agency responsibilities. For most of the nurses, the activities immediately before and after the home care visits were similar, along with duties related to administration and daily work at the home health agency. Differences in the new models of care primarily focused on the care provided during the home health visit and case management activities between visits, during the follow-up of the patient related to MD specialist care, and during readmissions to the hospital.

The following sections present a detailed view of the overall model of care that was provided to each chronically ill population chosen for this study: the traditional model of care; and home health care of patients with COPD, diabetes, and ostomies and/or wound care needs.

Traditional Model of Care

Home health care provided by RNs for the traditional model of care are probably fairly similar across home health agency settings. For the purpose of this project, however, and specifically for the design of the instruments for data collection related to activity-based costing, it was important to identify and clarify detailed client-focused activities, secondary activities, and administrative activities (see Figure 17–1). Presented below is the outline of specific responsibilities that were identified during the interview process. Subsequent to this interview, the data collection instruments for the traditional model of care were developed, pilot tested by the nurses providing traditional care, and used for activity-based costing data collection.

First are home health visit activities or client-focused activities. Activities before the home health visit included:

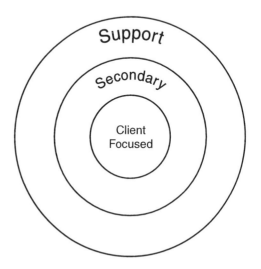

Figure 17–1 Classifying Activities: The Modified Target Method. *Source:* Copyright © 1997, Resource Group, Ltd., Dallas, Texas.

- Call the patient and/or client to set up and/or confirm the time of the visit.
- Call a significant other to confirm the time if relevant.
- Obtain and prepare supplies for the visit related to diagnosis and specific patient needs.
- Communicate with other home health staff as necessary if other staff members have made a visit or handled calls related to the patient while the regular home health nurse was not available.
- Review the chart for new orders.
- Recertify patient and/or rewrite orders as necessary for ongoing patients.
- Travel to the patient's home, record mileage, time out, and time entering the home.

Activities during the home health visit included:

- Wash hands and open in-home charting forms.
- Converse with the patient to assess changes since last home health visit, such as possible emergency room visits, visits to the physician and/or hospitalizations, and changes in condition or care.
- Take vital signs.
- Observe patient signs and symptoms related to the specific diagnosis. For example, with the pulmonary patient assess color and nail beds for signs of cyanosis; assess respirations and symptoms of shortness of breath (SOB); assess lung sounds and coughing; assess medications compliance; do a complete systems assessment, especially of related body systems for other diagnoses; and generally check equipment, such as O_2 and nebulizers.
- Give patient education interventions for both patient and family and/or caregiver as needed; review O_2 precautions.
- Assess readiness to learn.
- Review pathophysiology related to disease process as indicated.

- Give medication education and compliance teaching.
- Encourage use of Lifeline and/or portable phone for emergency situations.
- Encourage and provide emotional support.
- Talk with patient and family.
- Provide support to the family and/or caregiver.
- Continue to assess patient, caregiver stress, and environment during this time.
- Close and recap visit.
- As needed, telephone MD from home or supervisor at the HHA for major changes.
- Complete charting in the home as required by HHA.
- Schedule next visit or tentatively set up date and times for the future.
- Wash hands and put away home health bag and supplies.

Activities after the visit included:

- Complete the physician's orders in the car as needed.
- Log in time of completion of visit.
- If family members need to be called, may complete call after leaving the home while in the car.
- Travel to the laboratory to turn in specimens as needed.
- Travel to the next patient, office, or home, depending on the time of day.

Second are activities related to secondary aspects of care. These activities still relate to the patient visit but are generally performed in the office after the visit. Most of these activities involve telephone calls. The calls may be case management calls about the patient's clinical care and/or physician calls. Or the calls may be about insurance reimbursement or recertification for care. The calls may also be to the patient or the caregiver. Activities other than telephone calls included completing forms in the patient record and the occasional hospital visit when the home care patients were hospitalized.

Third are activities related to administration or staff responsibilities. These activities are unrelated to a specific patient visit. Instead, they are part of the administrative or staff responsibilities at the home health agency. Clinical-related activities include consults on specialty care. Other nonspecific visit-related activities include scheduling patients, completing day sheets, attending inservice programs for staff about specialty care, attending quality improvement meetings and staff meetings, marketing with specialists, and seeing to "professional growth responsibility," meaning such activities as continuing professional education.

COPD Model

Home health care for COPD patients is performed by the RN/Pulmonary Specialist—a registered nurse who is also a registered respiratory therapist (RRT). This RN/RRT designed a case management program for chronically ill, pulmonary patients—specifically those patients who were frequent users of the emergency department and who had more than three hospital admissions in the previous 12 months. Based on the interviews with all of the providers, it became clear that the activities before and after the home visit were essentially the same across all provider groups. However, the activities were significantly different during the home health visit for each of the RN specialist groups of care providers. Consequently, the following process of care will only focus on the activities during the home health visit, and this process of care was subsequently used to develop the instruments used for data collection related to COPD specialty care.

Home health visit activities or client-focused activities included activities before, during, and after a visit. Activities before the home health visit were similar to the traditional model of care.

Activities during the home health visit included:

- assessing respiratory functioning—observing skin and mental status
- greeting and warm-up phase of communication
- washing hands
- explaining all consents, forms, home health agency if the patient was new
- completing systems assessment checklist or assessment of the problem targeted for the call
- detailing pulmonary assessment and care, including a pulse oximetry; an O_2 check when relevant; an equipment check; an assessment for noncompliance issues, such as medications and/or treatment compliance; and assessing for prescription refills and the ability of the patient or family to accomplish compliance
- checking the functioning of any other respiratory equipment
- checking the medications supply and review of medication box
- assessing nocturnal therapies
- cleaning and caring for equipment (with patient or family)
- assessing ability to use and/or do the following: metered dose inhalers, tracheostomy tube care if relevant, postural drainage and chest physiotherapy, aerosol therapy, breathing retraining, early signs and symptoms of exacerbations, hand-held nebulizer treatment, oxygen therapy, relaxation and panic control, and any other relevant procedures or equipment
- telephoning the physician as appropriate to discuss changing medications and/or treatment if required and initiating medications change as ordered
- calling the durable medical equipment (DME) supplier, home health agency, or family member if needed
- educating for relevant health care including the use of equipment, safety issues related to having O_2 in the home, and return demonstrations on any procedure and equipment in home that seems to be a compliance issue or area of difficulty; if

this is an initial visit, then all new equipment and procedures will be taught and return demonstrated

- checking of last minute needs or assistance
- initiating and answering patient questions
- charting and documentation session in the home
- suggesting and reinforcing self-care
- decision making regarding quality of life issues and determining whether staying in the home, ER, or hospitalization is desired if there are emergency difficulties

Activities after the visit were similar to the traditional model of care.

Diabetic Model

Home health care for diabetic patients is performed by the RN/Certified Diabetes Educator (RN/CDE)—a registered nurse who is also certified as a diabetes educator with specialty training in caring for diabetic patients. The RN/CDEs also participated in a case management program specifically designed for chronically ill, diabetic patients. The specifics of care were tailored to the specific needs of the population that was evidenced by the differences in care provided to this population by the RN/CDEs versus the traditional RNs in the same home health agency. As mentioned previously, based on the interviews with all of the providers, it became clear that the activities before and after the home visit were essentially the same across all provider groups. However, the activities were significantly different during the home health visit for each of the RN specialist groups, in this case the RN/CDE care providers. Consequently, the following process of care will only focus on the activities during the home health visit. This process of care was subsequently used to develop the instruments used for data collection related to management of the diabetic population by the RN/Diabetic Specialist (RN/DS).

Home health visit activities or client-focused activities included activities before, during, and after a visit. Activities before the home health

visit were similar to the traditional model of care.

Activities during the home health visit began with an introduction and/or ice breakers and greetings. Other activities included:

- Familiarize yourself with the house, check the supplies bag or box.
- Explain about all consents, forms, home health agency, and so forth if the patient is new.
- Assess the need for the caregiver to assist diabetic patient with medications.
- Review medication history and pattern (with attention to diabetes medications).
- Assess the dexterity and ability of the patient to administer own insulin and calibrate glucometer.
- Assess glucometer and perform or observe hands-on monitoring of blood sugar.
- Calibrate the glucometer or observe return demonstration by patient or family.
- Review intake information.
- Observe self-care and administration of medications.
- Perform physical assessment system by system by assessing feet for wounds and/or ulcerations and assessing for complications such as decreased vision, mobility, and coordination.
- Initiate patient teaching and/or review of diabetes related care by observing self-care of feet and review teaching regarding the importance of foot care, by reviewing signs and symptoms of hypoglycemia, and by reviewing safety and correct disposal of sharps (provide container as necessary).
- Plan diet and review nutrition and meal planning.
- Obtain laboratory specimens as needed.
- Provide emotional support and reassurance to patient and/or family caregiver by giving attention to relationship building with caregivers as needed and relationship between patient and family.
- Order supplies as needed to last until next visit.

- Summarize and plan frequency of future visits based on needs, assessment, and compliance.
- Ask questions, review answers, and close.
- Perform in-home charting and documentation.
- Contact physician as needed to change medications as necessary, to order pre-filled syringes as necessary, and to obtain the necessary lab specimens as ordered.

Activities after the visit were similar to the traditional model of care.

Ostomy and Wound Care Model

Home health care for ostomy and wound care patients is performed by the RN/Enterostomal Therapist—a registered nurse who is also a certified enterostomal therapist (ET). The RN/ETs developed a similar case management program for chronically ill patients, specifically those patients who needed ostomy care or wound care and who were frequent users of the emergency departments or had frequent hospitalizations. As mentioned previously, based on the interviews with all of the providers, the activities before and after the home visit were essentially the same across all provider groups. However, the activities were significantly different during the home health visit for each of the RN specialist groups such as the RN/ET care providers. Consequently, the following process of care will only focus on the activities during the home health visit, and this was subsequently used to develop the instruments used for data collection related to specialty care for ostomy patients and those needing wound care.

Home health visit activities or client-focused activities included activities before, during, and after a visit. Activities before the home health visit were similar to the traditional model of care.

Activities during the home health visit involved introductions and getting acquainted. Other activities included:

- Introduce home health agency and obtain relevant consents.
- Interview patient and determine causal event for the wound and/or ostomy, such as an accident or a surgical procedure.
- Assess wound and/or ostomy, including clinical decision making regarding wound care and type of dressing, measuring wounds at least two times per week and recording, and taking photographs as necessary.
- Perform physical assessment if relevant.
- Telephone physician in order to review findings and obtain relevant orders or consultation.
- Assess the need for DME supplies and order as needed.
- Assess and/or set up basic work area and rearrange furniture as necessary (assist patient and/or caregiver).
- Assess medications record and compliance.
- Obtain necessary lab specimens.
- Provide reassurance and emotional support to patient and family in their acceptance of ostomy and/or wound, in their grief and/or feelings related to the causal event, and in their difficulty with social acceptability.
- Initiate patient teaching and/or return demonstration of wound care.
- Write and/or review wound care instructions.
- Teach and/or review physiology of wound with emphasis on what is normal and abnormal as well as self-care techniques and responsibilities.
- Review related dietary issues.
- Perform in-home charting and documentation.
- Ask questions, give answers, and close.

Activities after the visit were similar to the traditional model of care.

DESIGNING THE SYSTEM

In order to compare the costs and cost-savings of these new experimental models of home health care for chronically ill populations, a study was designed to identify costs according to activity-based costing methodology across the specialty groups compared with the traditional model of home health care delivery. Using a participative research process, each provider group was interviewed. Following the interviews, data collection instruments were developed for activity-based costing data collection.

Data were also identified from patient records and from electronic billing records to identify the number of hospitalizations, lengths of stay, and number of emergency room visits for patients seen within the Meridia Health Care System. Using ICD-9 codes, the design of the study was to determine the risk adjustment of the specific patient populations (COPD, diabetic, and ostomy/wound care) to compare those patients in the new case management specialist models of care with a matching cohort of clients cared for by RNs in the traditional model of care. Preliminary data related to care of a small group of COPD patients are included in the last section of this chapter (Implications for Cost Savings). This methodology and the details of this portion of the study will not be presented here. The focus of this chapter is the detailed process of developing the activity-based costing studies.

Data collection instruments for time studies based on activity-based costing were designed for nurses who were providing the traditional model of care. (See Exhibits 17–1, 17–2, 17–3, and 17–4). Exhibit 17–1 reflects the activities provided immediately before, during, and after the home health visit. Exhibit 17–2 reflects the activities involved in the follow-up of care away from the patient's home and includes telephone management with physicians, insurers, durable medical equipment, and so forth. Exhibit 17–3 reflects the activities related to agency requirements, administrative needs, and so forth. These include staff meetings, research done related to a specific patient's needs, conferences with other home health nurses, continuing education, and so forth. Exhibit 17–4 gathers the information into a daily time summary.

The Standard Practice RN Data Collection Instrument: Patient Visit Sheet (Exhibit 17–1) was specifically designed for the traditional model of care. The remaining forms (Exhibits 17–2, 17–3, and 17–4) represent forms designed to be uniform across all standard practice and specialty positions.

Data collection instruments for activity-based costing time studies were designed for nurses who were providing the RN/specialist models of care also based on participative research interviews. Each group of nurses were interviewed by the primary investigator and differences and similarities in the experimental models and the traditional model of care were identified. As mentioned previously, the before and after activities, as well as the activities related to working at the home health agency, were essentially the same for the traditional model of care. Consequently, some of the data collection instrumentation is similar for the specialty nurses and the traditional group. However, the specific process of care by the specialist groups (which occurred during the home health visit) were each very different. Also, it is anticipated that the data will indicate differences in the amount and type of telephone case management based on how the experimental models were designed.

To prevent confusion both in data collection and data entry, after the study format was completed, the forms were reproduced on different colored paper for each group of RN/specialty nurses and for the nurses providing the traditional model of care. Exhibit 17–5 is an example of the data collection instrument for the RN/RRT who provided the experimental model of care to the COPD patient population. The data collection instrument used by the RN/ET specialists who provided care (in the experimental model) to ostomy and wound care patient populations is presented in Exhibit 17–6. Finally, the data collection instrument for the RN/CDE who provided the experimental model of care for the diabetic population is provided in Exhibit 17–7. Each of these specialized instruments was used in conjunction with the standard forms illustrated as Exhibits 17–2, 17–3, and 17–4. Thus, a complete set of four forms was reproduced on different colored paper for the traditional care RN, the RN/RRT, the RN/ET, and the RN/CDE in order to prevent confusion.

Once the data collection instruments were designed, the nurses at Meridia Home Care Services had the opportunity to test the instruments in a pilot program to make sure that each group understood the data collection procedures and use of the instruments. Meetings were held with the supervisor to make sure that the period of time for data collection was understood and that questions could be answered as necessary on site. Then data collection was initiated. All groups of registered nurses completed the activity-based costing data collection through self-report. Forms were completed during the day for each patient home health visit that was made or at the end of the day. Data collection continued for at least ten days for each nurse who was participating in the study. This included nurses in each experimental group, RN/RRT, RN/DS, RN/ET, and the nurses providing the traditional model of care. At the end of the data collection period, the instruments were collected and reviewed by the primary investigator (Patricia Hinton Walker, PhD, RN) and the research consultant (Judith J. Baker, PhD, CPA). Data were then entered into an Excel spreadsheet for analysis and inclusion of salary information from the Meridia Home Health Budget.

IMPLICATIONS FOR COST SAVINGS

An experimental case management model pilot study for COPD patients similar to the one described in this chapter was initiated prior to the beginning of this study. The pilot study was small (n=10), admitting patients who met the following criteria: (1) A chronic pulmonary disorder that affected the patient's ability to engage in independent activities of daily living (IADLs).

(2) The patient is a frequent user of the emergency department and/or has had more than three admissions in the last 12 months for an exacerbation of their chronic pulmonary disease. (3) The patient is at high risk for the development of an exacerbation of their pulmonary disorder because of advanced stages of the disease, multiple diagnoses, frail elderly condition, noncompliance with medical regimen, poor support network—lack of reliable caregivers, and malnourishment and/or dehydration. (4) Professional support in the home would enable the patient and family to provide the necessary care needed by the patient. (5) The patient's home medical regimen includes the use of respiratory care modalities. (6) Home professional services are required to monitor the patient's response to care and alert the physician of any needed modifications to the home care plan of treatment. (7) The patient is agreeable to program admission and demonstrates compliance with the plan of treatment.

For the purposes of this pilot study, there was no matching cohort group against which the data were measured. The number of admissions, emergency visits, and total number of hospital days were identified for this patient population, and this data were compared retrospectively for five years (from 1990–1996), prior to instituting the experimental pulmonary case management specialist model of care (SMOC). Preliminary results indicate the potential cost savings of this specialist model of care. In most of the cases, not only were the number of admissions reduced, but the average number of days hospitalized was also reduced. These results showed the potential for cost savings of the new experimental model of care; however, the results were inconclusive because there were no data related to the actual cost of this new specialty approach to care, nor was the design of the study rigorous enough to ensure that these results could be generalized. The cost-savings potential could not be ignored, however. Hence, a study was designed that served as the basis for this planning chapter and its companion costing implementation chapter (see Chapter 18).

Exhibit 17–1 HHA Standard Practice RN Data Collection Instrument—Patient Visit Sheet

---

STANDARD PRACTICE RN—PATIENT VISIT SHEET

Your Name_____Today's Date_____

Patient Name_____ID#_____

_____

BEFORE   No. Minutes

Review patient's previous problems   _____

Telephone contact to schedule visit (reconfirm time)   _____

Gather or replenish supplies   _____

Check voice mail reports on patient from other nurses   _____

Travel-related activities: to visit   _____

DURING

Introductory activities   _____

Obtain paperwork/consent signatures   _____

Assessment/observation of immediate condition   _____

Do assessment—systems by systems checklist   _____

Perform clinical care as necessary   _____

Draw lab work and complete requisitions   _____

Initiate charting in the home during visit   _____

Check medications supplies; review medications box   _____

Supervise care and cleaning of equipment   _____

Telephone calls from the home for clinical purposes:

    Physician   _____

    DME supplier   _____

    Home health agency   _____

    Members of family (as needed)   _____

Patient education   _____

Care of caregiver   _____

AFTER

Travel-related activities: from visit   _____

Log-in time spent   _____

Charting if needed   _____

Return follow-up telephone calls:

    Physician   _____

    DME   _____

    Members of family (not reached while in home)   _____

    Other case management calls re this patient   _____

Drop off specimens at the lab when necessary   _____

    Total Minutes (carry forward to Summary Sheet)   _____

Source: Copyright © 1997, Judith J. Baker, Ph.D. and Patricia Hinton Walker, Ph.D.

Exhibit 17–2 HHA Data Collection Instrument—Subsequent Visit-Related Activities

---

SUBSEQUENT VISIT-RELATED ACTIVITIES

Your Name_____Today's Date_____

	Today's Total Time
Telephone: Case Management Calls re Patient Clinical Care	(in minutes)

Telephone: Case Management Calls re Patient Clinical Care　　Today's Total Time (in minutes)

Patient Name_____　　_____

Patient Name_____　　_____

Patient Name_____　　_____

Patient Name_____　　_____

Patient Name_____　　_____　　_____

Telephone: Physician Calls

Patient Name_____　　_____

Patient Name_____　　_____

Patient Name_____　　_____

Patient Name_____　　_____

Patient Name_____　　_____　　_____

Telephone: Patient or Caregiver

Patient Name_____　　_____

Patient Name_____　　_____

Patient Name_____　　_____

Patient Name_____　　_____

Patient Name_____　　_____　　_____

Telephone: Insurance-Reimbursement-Recertification

Patient Name_____　　_____

Patient Name_____　　_____

Patient Name_____　　_____

Patient Name_____　　_____

Patient Name_____　　_____　　_____

Telephone: Other Visit-Related

(describe)_____　　　　　　　_____

Complete Forms in the Patient Record　　　　　　　_____

Submit Daily Visit Reports　　　　　　　_____

Hospital Visits (when patients are hospitalized)

Patient Name_____　　_____

Patient Name_____　　_____　　_____

Total Minutes (carry forward to Summary Sheet)　　_____

Source: Copyright © 1997, Judith J. Baker, Ph.D. and Patricia Hinton Walker, Ph.D.

Exhibit 17–3 HHA Data Collection Instrument—Nonvisit Related Activities

---

NONVISIT RELATED ACTIVITIES

Your Name_____Today's Date _____

                                                        Today's Total Time
                                                        (in minutes)

CONSULTS ON SPECIALTY CARE (enter time on lines below)

_____   _____

_____   _____

_____   _____

_____   _____

_____   _____

_____   _____

_____   _____

ALL OTHER NONSPECIFIC-VISIT RELATED (enter time on lines below)

Boarding Patients   _____

Complete Day Sheets   _____

Inservice Programs for Staff Members re Specialty Care   _____

Quality Improvement Meetings   _____

Staff Meetings   _____

Marketing with Specialists   _____

Professional Growth Responsibility   _____

Other (describe)_____   _____

Other (describe)_____   _____

Personal (describe)_____   _____

Personal (describe)_____   _____

           Total Minutes (carry forward to Summary Sheet)   _____

Source: Copyright © 1997, Judith J. Baker, Ph.D. and Patricia Hinton Walker, Ph.D.

Exhibit 17–4 HHA Data Collection Instrument--Daily Time Summary

---

DAILY TIME SUMMARY

Your Name_____Today's Date_____

Begin Time_____End Time_____ = Total Time*_____

	Today's Total Time (in minutes)

VISIT SUMMARY: (totals from Pt Visit Supplemental Sheets for this date)

(enter name below)   (minutes)

Visit:_____ (suppl sheet #)_____   = _____

Visit:_____ (suppl sheet #)_____   = _____

Visit:_____ (suppl sheet #)_____   = _____

Visit:_____ (suppl sheet #)_____   = _____

Visit:_____ (suppl sheet #)_____   = _____

Visit:_____ (suppl sheet #)_____   = _____

Visit:_____ (suppl sheet #)_____   = _____

Visit:_____ (suppl sheet #)_____   = _____

TOTAL MINUTES ALL VISITS ABOVE: = _____
(Sum of minutes from all Sheets #2 for the day as listed above)

SUMMARY OF SUBSEQUENT VISIT-RELATED ACTIVITIES: = _____
(Enter total minutes from Sheet #3)

SUMMARY OF NONAPPOINTMENT ACTIVITIES: = _____
(Enter total minutes from Sheet #4)

Total Minutes   = _____

(*Note: Total Minutes should equal Total Time at top of this sheet)

Source: Copyright © 1997, Judith J. Baker, Ph.D. and Patricia Hinton Walker, Ph.D.

Exhibit 17–5 HHA RN-Respiratory Therapist Data Collection Instrument—Patient Visit Sheet

---

RN-RESPIRATORY THERAPIST—PATIENT VISIT SHEET

Your Name_____Today's Date_____

Patient Name_____ID#_____

BEFORE	No. Minutes
Review patient's previous problems	_____
Telephone contact to schedule visit (reconfirm time)	_____
Gather or replenish supplies	_____
Check voice mail reports on patient from other nurses	_____
Travel-related activities: to visit	_____

DURING	
Introductory activities	_____
Obtain paperwork/consent signatures	_____
Assessment/observation of immediate condition	_____
Do assessment—systems by systems checklist	_____
Focused pulmonary assessment:	_____
– Pulse Oximetry	_____
– Check O_2 when relevant	_____
– Check other respiratory equipment	_____
– Assess use of nocturnal therapies	_____
Perform clinical care as necessary	_____
Draw lab work and complete requisitions	_____
Initiate charting in the home during visit	_____
Check medications supplies; review medications box	_____
Supervise care and cleaning of equipment	_____
Telephone calls from the home for clinical purposes:	_____
Physician	_____
DME supplier	_____
Home health agency	_____
Members of family (as needed)	_____
Patient education	_____
Care of caregiver	_____
Other_____	_____

AFTER	
Travel-related activities—from visit	_____
Log-in time spent	_____
Charting if needed	_____
Return follow-up telephone calls:	_____
Physician	_____
DME	_____
Members of family (not reached while in home)	_____
Other case management calls re this patient	_____
Drop off specimens at the lab when necessary	_____
Total Minutes (carry forward to Summary Sheet)	_____

Source: Copyright © 1997, Judith J. Baker, Ph.D. and Patricia Hinton Walker, Ph.D.

Exhibt 17–6 HHA Enterostomal Therapist Data Collection Instrument—Patient Visit Sheet

ENTEROSTOMAL THERAPIST—PATIENT VISIT SHEET

Your Name_____Today's Date_____

Patient Name_____ID#_____

	No. Minutes
BEFORE	
Review patient's previous problems	_____
Telephone contact to schedule visit (reconfirm time)	_____
Gather or replenish supplies	_____
Check voice mail reports on patient from other nurses	_____
Travel-related activities: to visit	_____
DURING	
Introductory activities	_____
Obtain paperwork/consent signatures	_____
Assessment/observation of immediate condition	_____
Do assessment—systems by systems checklist	_____
Focused assessment related to wound or ostomy:	_____
– Assess need for special supplies/equip for wound care	_____
– Measure wound	_____
– Take photos (when relevant)	_____
– Assist patient/family to make home user-friendly for wound care	_____
– Complete risk assessment sheet for wound care	_____
Perform clinical care as necessary	_____
Draw lab work and complete requisitions	_____
Initiate charting in the home during visit	_____
Check medications supplies; review medications box	_____
Supervise care and cleaning of equipment	_____
Telephone calls from the home for clinical purposes:	_____
Physician	_____
DME supplier	_____
Home health agency	_____
Members of family (as needed)	_____
Patient education	_____
Care of caregiver	_____
Other_____	_____
AFTER	
Travel-related activities—from visit	_____
Log-in time spent	_____
Charting if needed	_____
Return follow-up telephone calls:	
Physician	_____
DME	_____
Members of family (not reached while in home)	_____
Other case management calls re this patient	_____
Drop off specimens at the lab when necessary	_____
Total Minutes (carry forward to Summary Sheet)	_____

Source: Copyright © 1997, Judith J. Baker, Ph.D. and Patricia Hinton Walker, Ph.D.

Exhibit 17–7 HHA Diabetes Educator Data Collection Instrument—Patient Visit Sheet

---

DIABETES EDUCATOR—PATIENT VISIT SHEET

Your Name_____Today's Date_____

Patient Name_____ID#_____

	No. Minutes
BEFORE	
Review patient's previous problems	_____
Telephone contact to schedule visit (reconfirm time)	_____
Gather or replenish supplies	_____
Check voice mail reports on patient from other nurses	_____
Travel-related activities: to visit	_____
DURING	
Introductory activities	_____
Obtain paperwork/consent signatures	_____
Assessment/observation of immediate condition	_____
Do assessment—systems by systems checklist	_____
Focused diabetes related assessment:	_____
– Assess glucometer	_____
– Hands-on monitoring of blood sugar	_____
– Order and/or calibrate machine	_____
– Observe insulin administration (when necessary)	_____
– Check safety and disposal of sharps	_____
– Discuss diet and diet planning	_____
– Assess for complications related to diabetes	_____
– Assess for complications related to other comorbidities	_____
Perform clinical care as necessary	_____
Draw lab work and complete requisitions	_____
Initiate charting in the home during visit	_____
Check medications supplies; review medications box	_____
Supervise care and cleaning of equipment	_____
Telephone calls from the home for clinical purposes:	_____
Physician	_____
DME supplier	_____
Home health agency	_____
Members of family (as needed)	_____
Patient education	_____
Care of caregiver	_____
Other_____	_____
AFTER	
Travel-related activities—from visit	_____
Log-in time spent	_____
Charting if needed	_____
Return follow-up telephone calls:	_____
Physician	_____
DME	_____
Members of family (not reached while in home)	_____
Other case management calls re this patient	_____
Drop off specimens at the lab when necessary	_____
Total Minutes (carry forward to Summary Sheet)	_____

Source: Copyright © 1997, Judith J. Baker, Ph.D. and Patricia Hinton Walker, Ph.D.

NOTES

1. M.B. Taylor, "An Examination of Relationships between Home Health Service Use and Primary Diagnosis of Patient," *Home Health Care Services Quarterly* 9, no. 4 (1989): 47–60.

2. P. Hoffman, "Prospering under PPS: A Guide for Financial Managers," *Caring* 16, no. 2 (1997): 46–52.

3. National Association for Home Care, *Basic Statistics About Home Care 1996* (Washington DC: National Association for Home Care, 1996).

4. B. Altman and D. Walden, *Home Health Care Use, Expenditures and Sources of Payment*, National Medical Expenditure Survey Research Findings 15 (Rockville, MD: Agency for Health Care Policy and Research Publication, 1993).

5. G.W. Strahan, *An Overview of Home Health and Hospice Care Patients: 1994 National Home Health and Hospice Care Survey*, U.S. Department of Health and Human Services Publication, no. 274 (Washington, DC: U.S. Department of Health and Human Services, 1996).

6. Taylor, "An Examination of Relationships," 47–60.

7. L.G. Branch et al., "Medicare Home Health: A Description of Total Episodes of Care," *Health Care Financing Review* 14, no. 4 (summer 1993): 59–74.

8. S.M. Robinson, "Advancing Home Care Nursing Practice with an ET Clinical Nurse Specialist," *Home Healthcare Nurse* 14, no. 4 (1996): 269–274.

9. B.J. Munderloh, "Using Respiratory Therapists as Primary Care Managers," *AARC Times* 20, no. 6 (1996): 22–28.

10. L. Dennis et al., "The Relationship between Hospital Readmissions of Medicare Beneficiaries with Chronic Illnesses and Home Care Nursing Interventions," *Home Healthcare Nurse* 14, no. 4 (1996): 303–309.

11. M. England, *Managed Care Strategies 1996*, ed. Maria R. Traska (New York: Faulkner & Gray, 1995), vii.

12. Hoffman, "Prospering Under PPS," 46–52.

13. E. Mauser and N. Miller, "A Profile of Home Health Users in 1992," *Health Care Financing Review* 19, no. 1 (1994): 17–33.

## CHAPTER 18

Implementing Activity Data-Driven Cost Components for Meridia's Home Health Agency Service Delivery: A Case Study

Judith J. Baker, Patricia Hinton Walker, Christine A. Pierce, and John J. Brocketti

CHAPTER OUTLINE

PREFACE

This case study examines a comparison of chronic obstructive pulmonary disease (COPD), wound care, diabetes education, and regular care in a home health agency for managed care purposes. The case study revolves around specialty care for COPD, for wound care, and for diabetes education compared to regular or standard care. This chapter explores implementing the necessary activity data-driven cost components. Chapter 17 set out the process for providing that care and the activity analysis portion of the project.

A unique aspect of this case study is the effort to isolate and identify the specific activities that make up the specialty care versus regular care. The information is vital for strategic planning and future pricing in the managed care arena. Note also that a small pilot study (ten patients) was conducted prior to undertaking the larger study. This is desirable methodology.

Meridia Home Care Services is part of the Meridia Health System. The Cleveland-based health system is comprised of four hospitals, the home care division, and multiple outpatient centers and medical office facilities. Over 1,200 private practice physicians are associated with the health system and residency programs.

INTRODUCTION

During the past several years, the changes in the health care industry have caused managers to become more cost conscious and care to become more economically than clinically driven. Hospital administrators recognized the need for data-driven decision making when the Medicare Prospective Payment System (PPS) was implemented. However, many of the other delivery systems, such as home health care, historically have been somewhat sheltered from the economic pressures caused by PPS. The demands of consumers and purchasers of care in this new managed care environment "requiring quality care coupled with cost efficiency are making home health care agencies more cognizant of data such as product costing, clinical profiling, and the economic effect of a proposed managed care contract."[1]

According to Hoffman,[2] although leaders in home care have discussed implementation of PPS for the past ten years, legislative deficit-cutting, budget-balancing pressures in Washington and the growth of Medicare expenditures are rapidly making PPS a reality. He warns that one of the most obvious changes will be the loss of incentives for cost-shifting. The National Home Health Agency Demonstration Project currently being implemented in five states (California, Florida, Illinois, Massachusetts, and Texas) will have significant implications for the home health industry in the near future. Data generated from this project promise to change economic behavior and help control costs in a rapidly changing, managed care market. "PPS and capitation systems are viewed as complementary ways to redirect incentives from the current cost-based system, with its traditional inflationary incentives, to more cost-conscious behavior among providers."[3]

Increasing demand for home care also drives the policy makers' view of PPS. It is estimated that nearly ten million Americans require home care services annually.[4] The last National Medical Expenditures Survey[5] characterized the home care population as more than 50 percent over the age of 65 years with 40 percent having functional limitations in one or more activities of daily living.

An important major incentive of PPS is not only to reduce utilization but also to reduce costs. This requires managers to become more sophisticated in understanding cost and determining true costs of care. Additionally, because managed care will require home health agencies to accept much greater risk than in the current system, cost conscious, price conscious behavior will be needed to survive in an ever-changing, competitive marketplace. Success in the managed care environment requires increasing sophistication in financial and resource management by everyone.[6] Development of product costing models is the key to the successful pric-

ing and managing of risk. These costing models will need to establish on a microlevel "costs on a per-visit, per-discipline basis; on a macrolevel, these per-visit costs will be aggregated to a per-episode cost, distinguishable by payor and by diagnostic category."[7]

Unfortunately, current costing methods frequently do not provide accurate and reliable data for determining costs and setting prices. Agencies must better understand the relationships between direct and indirect components as well as between variable versus fixed costs. According to Hoffman,[8] agencies must consider restructuring their operating systems and accounting systems to capture detailed visit data according to clinical indicators, functional status, provider, and so forth. Data that are collected and analyzed must be able to demonstrate that cost-efficient care is being provided, that cost savings can be monitored, and that quality care is delivered.

One of the models to consider when developing costing models and ensuring appropriate product pricing is activity-based costing. "Generally speaking, activity-based costing models depart from the traditional classification of expenses into cost centers and examine the activities that are performed."[9] Studies must be conducted that capture all of the activities—direct care as well as indirect care and administrative costs. One study reported that nurses spent 47 percent of their time in direct patient care, 18 percent of their time documenting the care, 12 percent in other activities, and 22 percent of their time traveling.[10] Another study reported similar results: 47 percent of time in direct patient care, 18 percent documentation care, and 19 percent of their time traveling. The remaining 16 percent did not represent comparable activities.[11]

Development of costing models based on data-driven cost components such as the one described in this chapter can not only assist home health agencies in determining "true" costs but can also provide critical data for the development of managed care proposals. Other benefits include the ability to calculate breakeven analysis in the aggregate for the agency as well as by service discipline or provider group.[12] Finally, activity-based analysis of activities can assist managers in evaluating and revising the expectations of providers in the context of the number of visits expected, types and nature of documentation, staffing models, and other managerial activities that may be costing the agency unnecessarily. Some authors state that very little is known about the actual effectiveness of home health care in the context of cost and quality. "Quality must be translated into terms to let payers know what they are getting for their money. Improving quality of care may be a stated goal, but cost savings also must be proven."[13]

BACKGROUND ON MERIDIA

Meridia Home Care Services were "established in order to provide easy access to the highest quality services at competitive prices utilizing the newest available technologies."[14] This home health agency is committed to providing comprehensive services for health care needs outside the hospital setting and offers a variety of services. (See detailed history and description of the integrated delivery system in Chapter 17.) This home health operation has always been predominantly funded through conventional Medicare (88.7 percent), giving rise to clinical processes that were in concert with the cost reimbursement environment.

Over the past two years, a need to reevaluate those processes has occurred. This need is primarily driven by three factors: (1) the advent of senior HMOs moving traditional Medicare patients into a managed care environment, (2) the growth of integrated delivery systems, and (3) the health systems' broad examination of the high cost, high utilization diagnoses that occupy the inpatient acute care facilities and resultant goal to move patients into cost-effective care settings. The growth of integrated delivery systems as illustrated in the case of the Meridia Health System requires a level of integrated decision making. Resource use is the heart of decision-making support,[15] so a reevaluation of

processes leads to an evaluation of resource use. Skilled care is provided by professional nurses, physical therapists, occupational therapists, speech therapists, and medical social workers. Additionally, "specialized care is provided by diabetic educators, registered dieticians, enterostomal therapists, respiratory therapists, behavioral health specialists and others."[16] Data as related to the activity-based costing study of three of these specialized care roles (diabetic educators, respiratory therapists, and enterostomal therapists) are the source of data for this chapter.

PLANNING THE COSTING FRAMEWORK

Planning the costing framework involves four steps:

1. Identify the structure to be costed.
2. Identify available statistical data.
3. Identify available financial data.
4. Link available clinical data (as required).

The specific composition of the project depends on the discoveries that are made during the planning phase. If data are not available in the precise configuration desired, for example, it may be possible to substitute an alternative. Finding all the potential problems up front is highly recommended. The planning that is built around these discoveries will result in a customized costing framework that is specific to the organization where it will be implemented.

Identifying the structure to be costed is first. The structure of the system must be identified. A major decision revolves around what portion of the system should be costed and how that portion should be classified. To that end the team addressed key functions.

The team verified Meridia Home Care Services' key functions as illustrated in Exhibit 18–1. The key functions are distinguished as standard home care and six special services, including pulmonary, mental health, maternity, infusion therapy, wound care, and diabetes edu-

Exhibit 18–1 Home Care Key Functions

KEY FUNCTIONS
Standard Home Care
Special Services: Pulmonary
Special Services: Mental Health
Special Services: Maternity
Special Services: Infusion Therapy
Special Services: Wound Care
Special Services: Diabetes Education

Source: Copyright © 1997, Resource Group, Ltd., Dallas, Texas.

Exhibit 18–2 Elements Contained in Standard Home Care

STANDARD HOME CARE
Skilled Visit
Aide Visit
Rehab Visit—Physical Therapy
Rehab Visit—Occupational Therapy
Rehab Visit—Speech Therapy
Medical Social Services
Dietician Visit

Source: Copyright © 1997, Resource Group, Ltd., Dallas, Texas.

cation. The elements contained in Standard Home Care are illustrated in Exhibit 18–2. Each element is designated as a type of visit: a skilled visit, an aide visit, a rehab visit (physical therapy, speech therapy, occupational therapy), a medical social services visit, and a dietitian visit. The elements included in each of the six special services were also identified. The methods for so doing are described in Chapter 17. The service request forms for special services are illustrated in Appendixes 18–A and 18–B.

A small pulmonary pilot study was carried out as special services were being defined. The pilot was important from the standpoint of management decision making about program development. The pilot was also important from the standpoint of structuring output for the implementation of activity-based costing components. In other words, management decided which indicators and outcomes were important and those decisions shaped the structuring of the cost component implementation.

Appendix 18–C contains three exhibits from a poster session. The poster session presented the results of the Pulmonary Services Pilot Study. Exhibit 18–C.1 illustrates inpatient admissions and emergency room visits for a four-year period. Exhibit 18–C.2 summarizes the program screening criteria. Exhibit 18–C.3 presents an inpatient admissions analysis for the pilot project. The findings from this pilot

study supported management's decision to expand with the special services concept.

Identifying the available statistical data is second. Statistical data are necessary for measurement and for analytical purposes. It is important to identify available statistical data early on in the process of implementing activity-based costing components. This step is another part of structuring the project. Sometimes desired statistical data is simply not available. If this is the case and the problem is discovered early on in the project, a search can be instituted for another source. Another problem arises if the available data are too old to use. Still another problem occurs if the data are aggregated and cannot be accessed for detailed breakouts. If these problems cannot be solved, an alternative set of statistics may have to be adopted. It is wise to uncover such statistical problems early enough to adjust planned analyses.

If the statistical data can be accessed, it is usual for an ABC component implementation team to request special custom runs for purposes of the project. The statistics that are requested may include such information as the number of visits by type, primary diagnoses, secondary diagnoses, and so forth. Exhibit 18–3 illustrates headings for a typical custom statistical computer run. In this case, the statistics are assembled by ICD-9 code for primary diagno-

Exhibit 18–3 Meridia Home Care Services Visits by ICD-9 Codes—19xx Sorted by ICD-9

Primary ICD-9	2nd ICD-9	3rd ICD-9	Total Patients	Total Visits	Avg Visits per Pt
496			15	486	32.4
496	185		2	77	38.5
496	389	25001	1	17	17.0
496	391	9721	1	24	24.0
496	486		6	50	8.3
496	486	311	1	26	26.0
496	486	486	1	25	25.0
496	486	1629	1	12	12.0
496	486	2113	1	7	7.0

Courtesy of Meridia Home Care Services, Mayfield Village, Ohio.

sis. The example shows COPD code 496 as the primary diagnosis, followed by the second ICD-9 code and the third ICD-9 code. The total number of patients for each set of three codes is shown, followed by total visits and average visits per patient.

The statistical information, once delivered, must be reviewed and analyzed. There is usually a certain amount of supporting information that must be requested before the computer run can be understood and properly analyzed. An example of such supporting information is presented in Exhibit 18–4. This exhibit represents the key to the discharge codes, a column appearing in the custom computer run appearing in Exhibit 18–3.

Identifying available financial data is third. Financial data necessary to the project will almost always involve the general ledger and the personnel records. Other subledgers and

Exhibit 18–4 Discharge Codes

Code	Discharge Reason
01	Improved or condition stable
02	Entered the hospital
03	Expired
04	Entered long-term care facility
05	Patient/physician/family requests or refuses service
06	Unsafe conditions or environment
07	Referred to other home health or similar agency
08	No source of reimbursement
09	Moved from the geographic service area
10	Change in reimbursement source
11	Lack of progress
12	Other

Courtesy of Meridia Home Care Services, Mayfield Village, Ohio.

journals will probably be consulted. Detailed analyses of selected subaccounts will almost always be required. It is possible that the financial data will not be readily available. A backlog in the accounting department may mean that current financial data may not be accessible for a matter of additional weeks or even, in extreme cases, months. It is always wise to verify exactly what can be accessed, in what level of detail, and exactly when it can be accessed. The project timeline may have to be adjusted accordingly.

Linking available clinical data is fourth. The linking of available clinical data is necessary when the project requires case mix data or other measures of patient conditions and/or clinical outcomes. The use of the clinical data in relation to the costing framework must be clearly defined. When activity-based costing components are implemented, what will be linked? How will it be linked?

In the future, we may have the luxury of integrated databases where medical record clinical data reside alongside reimbursement and costing data on a patient-specific basis. In real life today, we usually find that two or more freestanding databases have to be linked in order to match desired clinical data with ABC projects. At any rate, the issue of availability must be taken into account in the planning process.

GENERAL LEDGER CATEGORIES

After the planning steps are completed, it is necessary to examine general ledger categories. In the Meridia ABC cost component implementation project, general ledger categories were explored in three ways: (1) the actual account structure was examined, (2) an overall review was performed, and (3) project-specific decisions were made.

The Meridia general ledger uses a 14-number account structure. The first two digits represent the company. In our case, the company is Home Health, which is Company 21. The next four digits represent the expense category (for example, payroll is 7000). The next four digits represent the subaccount. This is the place where different types of employees (such as RNs, PTs, and so forth) are differentiated. The last four digits indicate the department (home health aides is 7151). The basic account structure is illustrated in Exhibit 18–5.

Typical available general ledger categories are illustrated in Exhibit 18–6. The use of Meridia's general ledger account structure can best be illustrated by an example. A per-visit RN (that is, a registered nurse compensated on a per-visit basis) would have his or her wages coded to:

21-7000-2200-7151

Refer to Exhibit 18–6 to prove out this coding example.

A broad-based review encompassed how the home health portion of the general ledger fit into the overall structure of the Meridia Health System general ledger. After the broad-based review was completed, we reviewed the accounts for our project-specific use. We found that the Meridia Health System general ledger created distinct categories for the majority of the information that was required for this project. The project-specific approach to categories creates a plan-to-group cost. This con-

---

Exhibit 18–5 General Ledger Account Structure

General Ledger 14-Digit Account Structure:			
XX	**XXXX**	**XXXX**	**XXXX**
Company	Expense Category	Subaccount	Department

Courtesy of Meridia Home Care Services, Mayfield Village, Ohio.

Exhibit 18–6 General Ledger Categories

Subacct-Dept	G/L Designation	Position
0000-7151	Regular Time Mgmt	HHA Direct Care
2000-7151	Regular Time Prof-MDCL	Professional Medical
2100-7151	Agency Fees Prof Med	Registry Nurses
2200-7151	Reg Time—Prof Med Per Visit	Regular Per-Visit Nurses
2300-7151	Reg Hour—RN IV Per Visit	IV Specialists Per Visit
2400-7151	Reg Hour—RN ET Per Visit	ET Specialists Per Visit
3000-7151	Reg Time—Prof Nmed	LPNs
3200-7151	Reg Time—Prof Nmed Per Visit	Medical Social Workers
4000-7151	Reg Time—Tech-MDC	Speech Therapists
4100-7151	Agency Fees—Tech Med	Registry Speech Therapists
4200-7151	Reg Time—Tech Med Per Visit	Physical Therapists
5200-7151	Reg Time—Tech Nmed Per Visit	Occupational Therapists
6000-7151	Reg Time—Clerc—Med	Medical Clerical (Team Clerks)
7000-7151	Reg Time—Clerc—Nonmed	Nonmedical Clerical (incl. Billing/Collecting)
7100-7151	Agency Fees Clerc—Nonmed	Registry Nonmedical Clerical
8000-7151	Reg Time—Service—MDCL	Supply Clerk and Receptionist
8100-7151	Agency Fees—Service Med	Registry Supply Clerk
8200-7151	Serv Med—Per Visit	Home Health Aides
9000-7151	Reg Time—Service Nonmed	Equiv. of Supply Clerk

Courtesy of Meridia Home Care Services, Mayfield Village, Ohio

cept is expanded in the following section, wherein the discussion centers on aspects of the general ledger. Detailed budget data may also be helpful in an ABC account review. Such budget data will reveal, for example, the planned expenditures for new program development.

GROUPING COSTS

The Meridia costs for this project fell into three groups: (1) home health cost, (2) other related costs, and (3) home office costs. The inclusion-exclusion rationale will be discussed. A specific example of detailed grouping for personnel classification will be also be presented.

Home health cost relates to the cost that is incurred to provide home care. It can be thought of as a departmental cost concept, especially because the final four digits of the 14-digit gen-

eral ledger account code (7151) are the department. Or it can be thought of as a cost center.

Other related costs include compensation and fringe benefits for upper level home health management, such as the corporate director and related administrative staff. Although their costs are collected in a different four-digit account code, these individuals contribute to the home health agency's day-to-day operations. They should be included when costing for the ABC project.

Home office cost represents that portion of the health system's central office costs that are allocated to home care. The central office provides accounting services, marketing services, and so forth to the health system. The total central office costs are allocated across the health system. The allocation bases are consistent with home office Medicare regulations (see the discussion of traditional health care costing systems in Chapter 3).

Inclusion-exclusion rationale is important to the structuring of the activity-based costing components for implementation, which should include a rationale for the inclusion or exclusion of certain types of cost. In this instance, the general ledger arrangement assists with these decisions. Review of account content reveals that home health aides (7151) can be adopted as the basic aggregation for ABC, to then be designated as direct-indirect and/or fixed-variable in accordance with ABC principles. Other related costs

for management will also be adopted because it is part of the day-to-day home health operations.

A comment should be made here about account review. The amount of review time to expend can be related to the cost-benefit of such review. An account that is used three to four times per year, for example, may not qualify for the extent of review that is accorded to commonly used accounts. In other words, an account used once a quarter may not necessarily be the type to be reviewed. Exhibit 18–7 is a

Exhibit 18–7 Extract Listing—Most Commonly Used Account Numbers

MERIDIA HOME CARE SERVICES

Procedure for Coding Monthly Expenditures
Extract Listing—Most Commonly Used Numbers

Company Name	Company Number	Cost Center
Meridia Sleep Disorder Center	21	7188
Meridia Home Health	21	7151
Meridia LifeLine	21	7152
Meridia Home Care Services Office	21	8511
Meridia Health Equipment and Supplies	21	9045
HCM Infusion Services	73	xxxx
HCM Perinatal Services West	92	7050
HCM Perinatal Services East	98	xxxx
HCM Health Care Office	92	xxxx
Meridia Private Duty (Proposed Numbers)	21	7153

Commonly Used Prime Numbers and General Categories

Description	Sub	Prime#
Salary and Wage—Professional Medical Agency—per Visit	2100	7000
Salary and Wage—RN IV per Visit	2300	7000
Salary and Wage—Technical Medical Agency	4100	7000
Purchased Services—Medical	0000	8000
Purchased Services—Nonmedical	0000	8100
Supplies—Medical	0000	8200
Supplies—Nonmedical	0000	8300
Repairs and Maintenance	0000	8400
Utilities	0000	8500
Insurance*	0000	8600*
Lease and Rental	0000	8700
Depreciation*	0000	8800*
Interest*	0000	8900*

*Note: Those account numbers marked with an * are most commonly used by accounting and finance and should rarely be used at the departmental or company reporting level. Courtesy of Meridia Home Care Services, Mayfield Village, Ohio.

useful reference for this purpose; it is an internal listing showing most commonly used account numbers within this organization.

For this ABC components project we will not use the home office cost. The exclusion rationale is simple. Philosophically, the allocation for home office cannot be controlled by home health management. Operationally, a precedent has already been set in Meridia for this home office rationale. It has been the reporting habit of home health when preparing internal analyses to actually calculate two levels of cost; one with home office, termed full cost, and one net of home cost, termed without overhead. Our project followed the existing precedent.

Detail-specific steps of personnel classification are presented in Exhibit 18–8, which presents company and department, or cost center, classifications across the health system. Seven types of labor appear. These personnel classifications are cut fine enough to be of assistance in the ABC component implementation project.

DIRECT-INDIRECT AND FIXED-VARIABLE CLASSIFICATIONS

The fixed and variable classifications will be defined in accordance with the activity-based costing definitions—that is, fixed cost is a cost element that does not vary with changes in the volume of cost drivers or activity drivers, while variable cost does vary with such changes. The direct and indirect classifications will also be defined in accordance with the activity-based costing definitions—that is, direct cost is traced directly to an activity or cost object while indirect cost is allocated to the activity or cost object. Thus, the other related cost—the cost of

---

Exhibit 18–8 Subaccount Structure for Employee Identification

MERIDIA HOME CARE SERVICES

Subaccount Structure for Employee Identification

Administration
  0000 Management
  1000 Physicians
  1100 Agency (nonmedical)
  2000 Professional—Medical
  2100 Professional—Medical—Agency
  6000 Clerical—Medical
  6100 Clerical—Medical—Agency
  7000 Clerical—Nonmedical
  7100 Clerical—Nonmedical—Agency
  8000 Service—Medical
  8100 Service—Medical—Agency
  9000 Service—Nonmedical
  9100 Service—Nonmedical—Agency
  9999 Allocation

Skilled Nursing (SN)
  2200 RN per Visit
  2300 RN IV per Visit

2400 RN ET per Visit
3000 Other Nursing per Visit
3100 Nursing—Agency

Physical Therapy (PT)
  4200 PT per Visit
  5000
  5100 PT per visit—Agency

Speech Therapy (ST)
  4000 SP per Visit
  4100 PT per Visit—Agency

Occupational Therapy (OT)
  5200 OT per Visit

Medical Social Worker (MSW)
  3200 MSW per Visit

Home Health Aides (HHA)
  8200 HHA per Visit

Courtesy of Meridia Home Care Services, Mayfield Village, Ohio.

home health management and related administrative staff that was discussed in a prior section—will be termed fixed for purposes of the ABC project, irrespective of its usual designation.

OVERVIEW OF COST COMPONENTS

To summarize, the sequence for assembling the ABC components was as follows: (1) assign all possible cost through drivers, (2) directly attribute as much remaining cost as possible, (3) allocate as a last resort. Maintain a cost-benefit relationship on the decisions to assign, attribute, and allocate.

Five different data sources were used for this project. They are illustrated in Figure 18–1. The activity-based costing components, when assembled, produced the costing information that represented project output. Five data sources are pictured as contributing to the activity-based costing component model. They are listed in the order of importance for analysis: (1) the activity analysis, which is essential to the project; (2) the

general ledger breakout, necessary in order to extract base working data; (3) the detailed budget data, used to support the previous two elements; (4) patient-specific clinical data, used to obtain statistics about circumstances of patient care; and (5) patient-specific billing data, used to obtain statistics about number and type of visits and ICD-9 diagnoses.

Another organization's system will differ as to how the data are extracted and reassembled for ABC components. The sequence of review and examination steps must be followed in order to determine what to retrieve and how to properly assemble it in order to properly create the activity-based costing components.

CONCLUSION

We were able to extract sufficient cost data and reconfigure it for the purposes of this activity-based costing component project. The concept of home care special services is a vital one for the managed care arena. Attaching an activity-based cost to the special services project cre-

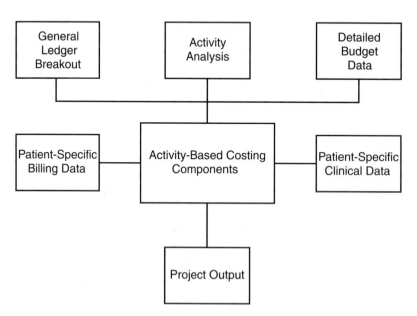

Figure 18–1 Activity-Based Costing Components—Meridia Model. *Source:* Copyright © 1997, Resource Group, Ltd., Dallas, Texas.

atcs a powerful tool for management decision making. It also creates the quantified costing information needed for managed care negotiations.

NOTES

1. T.A. Jendro and T.M. McNally, "Managing Managed Care: A Comprehensive Costing and Contract Evaluation Model for an Era of Change," *Home Health Care Management and Practice* 9, no. 2 (1997): 13–21.
2. P. Hoffman, "Prospering under PPS: A Guide for Financial Managers," *Caring* 16, no. 2 (1997): 46–52.
3. L.G. Branch et al., "Medicare Home Health: A Description of Total Episodes of Care," *Health Care Financing Review* 14, no. 4 (summer 1993): 59–74.
4. National Association for Home Care, *Basic Statistics about Home Care 1996* (Washington DC: National Association for Home Care, 1996).
5. B. Altman and D. Walden, *Home Health Care Use, Expenditures and Sources of Payment*, National Medical Expenditure Survey Research Findings 15 (Rockville, MD: Agency for Health Care Policy and Research Publication, 1993).
6. A. Bender, "Bringing Managed Care Home: Strategies for Success," *Home Healthcare Nurse* 15, no. 2 (1997): 133–138.
7. Jendro and McNally, "Managing Managed Care," 14.
8. Hoffman, "Prospering under PPS," 46–52.
9. Jendro and McNally, "Managing Managed Care," 18.
10. C.S. Hedtcke et al., "How Do Home Health Nurses Spend Their Time?" *Journal of Nursing Administration* 22, no. 1 (1992): 18–22.
11. J. Caie-Lawrence, A Time Study of Home Care Nurses (Poster presentation, Sixth National Nursing Symposium—Home Health Care, May, 1990).
12. Jendro and McNally, "Managing Managed Care," 14.
13. Bender, "Bringing Managed Care Home," 133–138.
14. Meridia Home Care Services, Meridia Brochure, 1–6.
15. J.J. Baker, "Activity-Based Costing for Integrated Delivery Systems," *Journal of Health Care Finance* 22, no. 2 (1995): 59.
16. Meridia Home Care Services, Meridia Brochure, 1–6.

BIBLIOGRAPHY

Altman, B., and D. Walden. *Home Health Care Use, Expenditures, and Sources of Payment*, National Medical Expenditure Survey Research Findings 15. Rockville, MD: Agency for Health Care Policy and Research Publication, 1993.

Baker, J.J. "Activity-Based Costing for Integrated Delivery Systems." *Journal of Health Care Finance* 22, no. 2 (1995): 59.

Bender, A. "Bringing Managed Care Home: Strategies for Success." *Home Healthcare Nurse* 15, no. 2 (1997): 133–138.

Branch, L.G. et al. "Medicare Home Health: A Description of Total Episodes of Care." *Health Care Financing Review* 14, no. 4 (Summer 1993): 59–74.

Caie-Lawrence, J. *A Time Study of Home Care Nurses*. Poster presentation, Sixth National Nursing Symposium—Home Health Care, May, 1990.

Dennis, L. et al. "The Relationship Between Hospital Readmissions of Medicare Beneficiaries with Chronic Illnesses and Home Care Nursing Interventions." *Home Healthcare Nurse* 14, no. 4 (1996): 303–309.

England, M. *Managed Care Strategies,* ed. Maria R. Traska. New York: Faulkner & Gray, 1995.

Goldbert, H.B. "Prospective Payment in Action: The National Home Health Agency Demonstration." *Caring* 16, no. 2 (1997): 14–27.

Hedtcke, C.S. et al. "How Do Home Health Nurses Spend Their Time?" *Journal of Nursing Administration* 22, no. 1 (1992): 18–22.

Hoffman, P. "Prospering under PPS: A Guide for Financial Managers." *Caring* 16, no. 2 (1997): 46–52.

Irwin, R. "The Impact of Prospective Payment on Medicare Patients." *Caring* 16, no. 2 (1997): 54–64.

Jendro, T.A., and T.M. McNally. "Managing Managed Care: A Comprehensive Costing and Contract Evaluation Model for an Era of Change." *Home Health Care Management and Practice* 9, no. 2 (1997): 13–21.

Kertland, K. "Home Care Past, Present, and Future: Opportunities and Challenges in a Managed Care Environment." *Home Care Provider* 1, no. 6 (1996): 316–19.

Mauser, E., and N. Miller. "A Profile of Home Health Users in 1992." *Health Care Financing Review* 19, no. 1 (1994): 17–33.

Munderloh, B.J. "Using Respiratory Therapists As Primary Care Managers." *AARC Times* 20, no. 6 (1996): 22–28.

National Association for Home Care. *Basic Statistics about Home Care 1996*. Washington DC: National Association for Home Care, 1996.

Robinson, S.M. "Advancing Home Care Nursing Practice with an ET Clinical Nurse Specialist." *Home Healthcare Nurse* 14, no. 4 (1996): 269–274.

Strahan, G.W. *An Overview of Home Health and Hospice Care Patients: 1994 National Home Health and Hospice Care Survey*, U.S. Department of Health and Human Services Publication, no. 274. Washington, DC: U.S. Department of Health and Human Services, 1996.

Taylor, M.B. "An Examination of Relationships between Home Health Service Use and Primary Diagnosis of Patient." *Home Health Care Services Quarterly* 9, no. 4 (1989): 47–60.

Request for Pulmonary Services

MERIDIA HOME HEALTH REQUEST FOR NURSING PROGRAMS AND SERVICES			TEAM 1 2 3 4 5 6 7
Affix Patient Information Label Here	SOC DATE:		
	HOME CARE AIDE: Yes No		
	CARE MANAGER:		

CIRCLE REQUESTED SERVICE(S)			
Mental Health	Pulmonary	Geriatric	Infusion Therapy
Request Date: __Primary Physician __Other Physician:	Request Date: __Primary Physician __Other Physician:	Request Date: __Primary Physician __Other Physician:	Request Date: __Primary Physician __Other Physician:

REASON(S)SERVICE REQUESTED			
EMERGENCY __Evidence of depression (Sad mood, diminished interest, insomnia/ hypersomnia, psychomotor agitation/retardation, excessive/ inappropriate guilt, recurrent thoughts of death/suicidal ideation) __Mania (Persistent elevated/irratio-nal mood, inflated self-esteem, flight of ideas) __Mood swings __Unrealistic/excessive anxiety/ worry __Psychotic symptoms (Delusions, hallucinations, flat or grossly inap-propriate affect, social isolation) __Dysfunctional grieving __Substance abuse __Other:	__Complex respira-tory Rx regimen __Aerosol therapy instruction __Oxygen therapy instruction __CPAP/BiPAP __Assess supplemen-tal oxygen needs __Trach management __Pulmonary hygiene __Evaluate for fol-low-up by pulmo-nary services program __Other:	__Consultation with care manager __Home visit: __Multiple chronic illness __Malnourished/ dehydrated __Re-admitted to acute care facility with same illness up to 3 most after D/C __Other:	__Very difficult blood draw __Monthly port flush __Placement of access device __Patient education re: _____ __Assess appropri-ateness of patient for home infusion __Type:_____ __Other:
Assigned to: Date:	Assigned to: Date:	Assigned to: Date:	Assigned to: Date:
Date completed:	Date completed:	Date completed:	Date completed:

Courtesy of Meridia Home Care Services, Mayfield Village, Ohio.

Request for ET and DE Services

MERIDIA HOME HEALTH **REQUEST FOR NURSING SPECIALTY/DIETICIAN SERVICE**			TEAM 1 2 3 4 5 6 7
Affix Patient Information Label Here	SOC DATE:		DIET:
	HOME CARE AIDE: Yes No		
	CARE MANAGER:		

CIRCLE REQUESTED SERVICE(S)			
ET	DE	Standard	Dietician
Request Date: __Primary Physician __Other Physician:	Request Date: __Primary Physician __Other Physician:	Request Date: __Primary Physician __Other Physician:	Request Date: __Primary Physician __Other Physician:

REASON(S) SERVICE REQUESTED			

__Home visit for:
  __Wound/wound care
    assessment & direc-
    tion
  __Ostomy instruction
  __Other:
 	
__Consultation with care
  manager
__Poor wound healing
__Wound deterioration
__Extensive wound
__Ostomy (new)
__Ostomy of _____
  inadequate pt/cg
  management
__Other:
	__Home visit for:
	  __Assess need for DE
	    and instruction
	  __DE
	  __Other:
	
	__Consultation with care
	  manager
	__New Dx diabetes
	__Pt new to insulin
	__Uncontrolled DM
	__Poor wound healing d/t
	  poor diabetes
	  management
	__Other:
		__Assmnt & mgmt of:
		  __CP __GI
		  __GU__Neuro
		  __Bowel/bladder
		__Irrigation of:
		  _____
		__Injection:
		  _____
		  _____
		__Foley management
		__Peg tube
		__Trach
		__Ng
		__Med instruction
		__Pt. care management
		__Pain management
		__Terminal care
		__Wound assessment/
		  treatment
		__Other:
			__Home visit
			__Consult
			__Newly Dx diabetes
			__Nutritional/diet coun-
			  seling
			__Pt. malnourished
			__Electrolyte imbalance
			__Fluid retention
			__Nausea/Vomiting
			__Difficulty swallowing
			__Pt. new to insulin
			__Pt. overweight
			__Wound healing
			__Tube feedings
			__Ostomy
			__Uncontrolled diabetes
			__Dehydration
			__Constipation
			__Other:

ET assigned: Date: 	DE assigned: Date: 	RN assigned: Date: 	RD assigned: Date:
Date completed:	Date completed:	Date completed:	Date completed:

Courtesy of Meridia Home Care Services, Mayfield Village, Ohio.

Pulmonary Services Pilot Study

Exhibit 18–C.1 Pulmonary Pilot Study: Inpatient Admissions and ER Visits

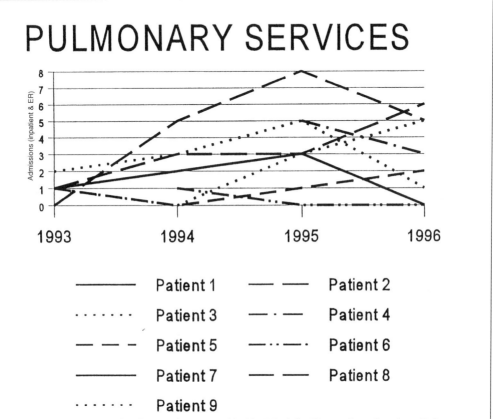

This graph represents the first patients enrolled in Meridia Home Care Services Pulmonary Services Monitoring program. This graph illustrates a general downtrend in 1996. Although this data shows a positive impact on re-hospitalization, some caution should be exhibited because the data represents only the first half of 1996. The data in this graph denotes yearly totals and does not reflect data points between years.

Courtesy of Meridia Home Care Services, Mayfield Village, Ohio.

Exhibit 18–C.2 Pulmonary Pilot Study: Program Screening Criteria

---

MERIDIA HOME HEALTH

PULMONARY MONITORING PROGRAM
SCREENING CRITERIA

- A chronic pulmonary disorder disables the patient to the point where he or she is unable to independently perform all ADLs and IADLs.
- The patient is a frequent user of the Emergency Department and/or has had more than 3 admissions in the last 12 months for an exacerbation of his or her chronic pulmonary disease.
- The patient is at high risk for the development of an exacerbation of pulmonary disorder:
  - advanced stages of disease
  - multiple diagnoses
  - frail elderly
  - noncompliant with medical regimen
  - poor support network—lack of reliable caregivers
  - malnourished/dehydrated

- Professional support in the home would enable the patient and family to provide the necessary care needed by the patient.
- The patient's home medical regimen includes the use of respiratory care modalities.
- Home professional services are required to monitor the patient's response to care and alert the physician of any needed modifications to the home care plan of treatment.
- The patient is agreeable to program admission and demonstrates compliance with the plan of treatment.

Courtesy of Meridia Home Care Services, Mayfield Village, Ohio.

Exhibit 18–C.3 Pulmonary Pilot Study: Inpatient Admission Analysis

---

Pulmonary Services Analysis
(Inpatient Admissions)
1990–1996

Patient #	Number of Admissions Since SOC	Total Days	Avg. # Days	Number of Admissions Prior to SOC	Total Days	Avg. # Days
1	0	0	0.00	8	74	9.25
2	2	6	3.00	11	49	4.45
3	0	0	0.00	4	26	6.50
4	2	14	7.00	6	43	7.16
5	2	20	10.00	1	11	11.00
6	0	0	0.00	1	4	4.00
7	0	0	0.00	3	33	11.00
8	4	27	6.75	12	118	10.72
9	0	0	0.00	11	81	7.36
10	1	4	4.00	4	25	6.25
11	0	0	0.00	12	148	12.33

Courtesy of Meridia Home Care Services, Mayfield Village, Ohio.

## CHAPTER 19

A Planning Model for the National Benevolent Association's Skilled Nursing Facility Costed Clinical Pathways: A Case Study

Judith J. Baker with Victor R. Barr and Karen S. Vroman

CHAPTER OUTLINE

INTRODUCTION

This case study profiles the actual process of planning an activity-based costing–oriented clinical pathway in a large and diverse nonprofit long-term care organization. The use of a task force (the data design and analysis team) would be expected in this size organization. The use of a multidisciplinary task force that is committed to the project is to be commended. The recognition of cost—in particular, activity-based costing—as an essential element in the process is to be further commended.

The National Benevolent Association (NBA) is the social and health services division of the Christian Church (Disciples of Christ) with 85 facilities in 25 states. NBA currently operates 4,898 housing units for seniors and 1,229 nursing facility beds. The organization was founded in 1887 in St. Louis, Missouri, where it now maintains its national administrative offices.

In recent years, long-term health care providers have struggled with the changing conditions that challenge the health care industry in general. Services have been developed and delivered without regard to their roles and places in the context of any semblance of a system. The result today is a seriously fragmented, practically unmanageable montage of programs and services. The current system is anything but systematic.

THE PROBLEM, THE PROJECT, AND THE PLANNING MODEL

Demands for increases in productivity, efficiency, and effectiveness are made on providers with little guidance or direction regarding the impact on historical clinical care standards and expectations. As an industry, long-term care providers are challenged to preserve their organizational integrity and pursue their missions in a fluid environment of evolving relationships and systems while assuming more of the risk involved in service delivery. Within such a changing paradigm, we are currently unable to truly assess the risk and make informed resource allocation decisions.

A virtual absence of efficient and effective care delivery systems that include outcome measurements, predictive care management, cost models, and ongoing quality improvement programs characterize the problem. (See Exhibit 19–l.)

This planning model for a skilled nursing facility's costed clinical pathway addresses the lack of integrated service delivery systems by developing an outcome-based, person-centered model of care management that is transportable among platforms. It enables clinical, administrative, and financial managers to develop cost-effective changes in care delivery that recognize and manage risk by identifying, measuring, validating, documenting, and tracking clinical and financial outcomes in a flexible and evolving learning process (Exhibit 19–2). The model presents a process for the structured development of clinical pathways and care protocols for skilled nursing patients. It emphasizes collaborative, multiorganizational effort that focuses on

---

Exhibit 19–1 The Problem

> **PROBLEM STATEMENT**
>
> We must preserve our ability to actualize our mission in a volatile and changing health care and reimbursement environment. This environment is characterized by evolving and transforming cost relationships, systems, and affiliations, where organizational security is based on achieving and maintaining financial viability.
>
> Within such a changing paradigm, we are currently unable to truly assess the considerable financial and programmatic risk to older adult programs and services, nor to make informed management decisions regarding allocation of resources.
>
> The absence of efficient and effective care delivery systems for the elderly that include outcome measurement systems, predictive care management, cost models, and ongoing quality improvement programs specifically characterizes and contributes to the problem.

Exhibit 19–2 The Project: Goal and Solution

> **GOAL AND SOLUTION**
>
> The goal of the proposed pilot program is to address this lack of integrated service delivery systems by developing a transferable, outcome-based, person-centered model of care management. This model will enable us to bring about cost-effective changes in the care delivery system that recognize and manage risk by identifying, measuring, validating, documenting, and tracking outcomes and costs in a flexible and evolving learning process.
>
> This model presents a process for the structured, sequential development of clinical pathways and care protocols for seniors. Our approach emphasizes collaborative effort that crosses organizational and profit-orientation boundaries, focusing rather on the synergistic effects of all participants' contributions to a person-centered, integrated team effort. The underlying philosophy of our model maintains that fit and function are more important to the continuum of care than are artificial boundaries among providers of that care.

Exhibit 19–3 Key Components for Success

KEY COMPONENTS FOR SUCCESS

- Multidisciplinary Approach
- Project Coordinator
- Administrative Team Support
- Staff Education
- Policies and Procedures for Use
- Format To Monitor Variances
- Information Support System
- Procedures To Assign Costs

---

the synergistic effect of all participants' contributions to a person-centered, integrated team effort. The underlying philosophy of the model maintains that fit and function are more important to successful outcomes throughout the continuum of care than are artificial boundaries among providers of that care.

KEY COMPONENTS FOR SUCCESS

Although each component of the costed clinical pathway model is necessary, experience has taught that anything less than full commitment in any of the following areas can quickly derail the entire project (Exhibit 19–3).

First there must be a multidisciplinary approach. One or two disciplines in an organization cannot carry off this project. Nor can one or two disciplines be omitted from the project without penalty. Cooperative interaction among all departments and all levels will eliminate or minimize intentional or accidental sabotage of the effort.

Second, a project coordinator is a must. One knowledgeable, respected person with real authority and responsibility for driving the multitude of issues and efforts is essential. This person becomes coach, taskmaster, visionary, mentor, and peacekeeper, often shifting roles many times a day.

Third, administrative team support is essential. Much of the ability to develop and translate

quantitative measures of qualitative events resides within this group. Systems for interpreting and monitoring data emanate from this area of the organization, making it imperative that this group collaborates responsibly and actively to ensure accurate and reliable management information.

Fourth, staff education is indispensable. Without understanding of the motives, methods, and expectations of this extensive effort, non-management staff cannot support and contribute to the success of the project. Without their support and contributions, the project will ultimately fail.

Fifth, policies and procedures for use are crucial. If it isn't written, it won't be done for long. And if it isn't written while it's being developed, it won't be written well. And if it isn't documented, it won't be reliable.

Sixth, a format to monitor variances is necessary. The ultimate proof of the project will be in management's ability to make adjustments that truly respond to the activities causing outcomes different from expected outcomes. The format to monitor variances must survive the time delay between system development and variance observation. It will be much more difficult to retrofit a format later than to thoughtfully and thoroughly plan that format as data capture and reporting systems are being developed and implemented.

Seventh, an information support system is incredibly important and incredibly difficult. Systems are being developed, but the necessary range of activities, data types, input sites, storage, retrieval, and reporting is beyond any currently available off-the-shelf system. Management expertise, user sophistication, access to information management professionals and budget all play roles in the type(s) of systems to be developed or purchased.

Eighth, a procedure to assign costs is vital. Assigning accurate costs to appropriate activities is crucial to this model. It is likely that concentrated education for key staff in the methods and applications of activity-based costing will need to be undertaken in early planning stages so that cost assignment is ingrained throughout the planning process.

ELEMENTS OF THE MODEL

The costed care path model requires six major elements (Exhibit 19–4).

First, improved, documented, and replicable patient outcomes are one of the major objectives of the costed care path project. The care path is the methodology by which the patient outcomes can be recognized and managed.

Second, the timeline(s) are an integral part of the pathway. A pathway consists of sequential steps. The documented passage of time—usually in units of twenty-four hours—is the method by which the pathway progresses.

Third, the collaboration of a multidisciplinary team is an absolute necessity. Note that multidisciplinary in this context is not limited to the various clinical disciplines; instead the concept also embraces costing, financial, and information services disciplines.

Fourth, a properly designed costed care path is comprehensive. It contains all aspects of care. A typical generic example contains assessment; teaching; consults; lab tests; other tests; medications; treatments and/or interventions; mobility and/or self-care; nutrition; lines, tubes, and monitors; and discharge planning.

Fifth, a case manager is required in the costed care path. Whatever the person's title, this individual is essential. A case manager's duties

should include daily planning, coordinating, and monitoring of care for the resident. A case manager's duties should ensure effective use of available resources and should oversee the meeting of outcomes within an appropriate length of stay.

Sixth, costing capability is an integral element of a costed care path model. The ease of costing should be a high priority in the model design.

MAJOR BENEFITS OF THE MODEL

The costed care path planning model has multiple benefits for the organization (Exhibit 19–5). The National Benevolent Association proposal identified the ten major benefits discussed below.

First, the ability to assign cost provides a powerful tool for management decision making. The ability to determine specific service delivery costs is the tool of the future for health care providers. The project can be justified from this standpoint alone.

Exhibit 19–4 Major Elements of Model

MAJOR ELEMENTS

- Patient Outcomes
- Timeline
- Collaborations (multidisciplinary)
- Comprehensive Aspects of Care
- Case Manager
- Costing Capability

Courtesy of National Benevolent Association, St. Louis, Missouri.

Exhibit 19–5 Benefits of Model

BENEFITS

- Ability to assign cost
- Standardize and organize care for routine situations
- Improve communication
- Better documentation
- Evaluation of current practice
- Improved customer and staff satisfaction
- Outline the "big picture"
- Integrates quality improvements, utilization management, and risk management activities
- Demonstrates quality care to accrediting bodies
- Enables better negotiation for managed care contracts

Courtesy of National Benevolent Association, St. Louis, Missouri.

Second, the ability to standardize and organize care for routine situations is the most common justification to undertake a care path project. It provides a guideline that decreases inconsistencies in care and allows clear continuing assessment of the resident's current condition.

Third, the implementation of care paths significantly improves communication among nursing staff. It increases communication among clinical, financial, and information system departments within the organization. It also enhances communication with the resident and family by informing them of care expectations and goals.

Fourth, by their very nature, care paths provide better documentation. The uniform requirements outline the optimal sequencing of interventions for particular diagnoses, procedures, or symptoms. The sequencing outline enables staff to document with more thoroughness and accuracy.

Fifth, the standardizing and organizing of care for routine situations and the better documentation allows a higher standard of evaluation for current practice.

Sixth, the incremental impact of all other benefits tends to result in improved customer and staff satisfaction. Customer satisfaction tends to improve substantially at first, then steadily over time. Staff satisfaction usually begins only after initial resistance to change is overcome and improved patient outcomes begin to be observed and related to the process.

Seventh, the costed care path outlines the overall positioning of the "big picture" of the facility. Strategic planning is empowered with this information as organizational confidence in its ability to direct its own destiny grows. The management reporting system informs planning and negotiating positions, enabling the organization to react swiftly and wisely to environmental and regulatory changes.

Eighth, the costed care model integrates quality improvement, utilization management, and risk management activities. Programmatic quality and appropriateness, managed so as to opti-

mize organizational risk, provide a planning platform that enhances both short-term operational and long-term strategic planning.

Ninth, the costed care path and its related variance analysis documentation provides a unique opportunity to demonstrate quality care to accrediting bodies. The level or standard of routine care is established by the pathway itself. The variances from the care paths, when documented, can be categorized. The patterns of variance can be reviewed. The facility can then demonstrate, from these categories and patterns, why and how the majority of the variances occurred. Thus, the quality of care—a qualitative attribute—can be quantified for accrediting bodies through costed clinical pathways.

Tenth, successful managed care contract negotiations require quantified information. The costed clinical pathway information provides the input that is necessary for a financially and clinically acceptable managed care contract. The confidence generated by this reliable, current information engenders similar confidence from the perspective of strategic position planning.

The National Benevolent Association proposal sets out an action plan as follows: "Identify resources and areas of collaboration needed to establish outcome-driven care." The phrase, *outcome-driven care,* says it all. A clinical pathway allows the measurement of outcomes.

CLINICAL PATHWAYS TO ACHIEVE COST-EFFECTIVE QUALITY

Outcomes are the primary secret weapon of clinical pathways. The action plan emphasizes this point. There are two basic types of outcomes—cost outcomes and clinical outcomes. Understanding the interdependent relationship of the two types of outcomes can truly galvanize the relationships among clinical, administrative, and financial managers (Exhibit 19–6).

Another way to view the two types of outcomes is Vic Barr's imagery. He says that they are two sides of the same coin. In other words, there are cost implications of clinical outcomes

Exhibit 19–6 Cost-Effective Quality

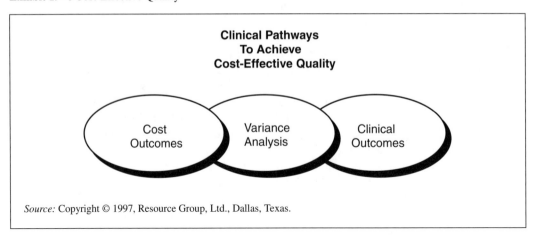

Clinical Pathways
To Achieve
Cost-Effective Quality

Cost Outcomes   Variance Analysis   Clinical Outcomes

Source: Copyright © 1997, Resource Group, Ltd., Dallas, Texas.

and there are outcome implications of cost controls. The management that thoroughly understands the extent of this interdependency has added a powerful element of wisdom to its decision-making prowess.

The measurement of clinical pathway outcomes leads to the measurement of the secondary secret weapon of clinical pathways—variance analysis. Analyzing unexpected outcomes will generally disclose certain patterns for a particular facility. Such analysis provides management decision makers with the answers to fluctuations in service or care delivery.

ACTIVITY-BASED COSTING AND CLINICAL PATHWAYS

ABC reflects resource consumption. Furthermore, resource consumption is identified at the clinical pathway level. In other words, we can specifically assign costs to the clinical pathway. We can then predict resource consumption by the facility when it is delivering the type of care represented by that particular clinical pathway.

ABC applications for clinical pathways include (1) assessments; (2) consults; (3) tests; (4) medications; (5) lines, tubes, and monitors; (6) treatments; (7) nutrition and elimination; (8) teaching; (9) mobility, self-care, and activity; (10) discharge outcomes; and (11) discharge

planning (Exhibit 19–7). The categories into which these components fall are discussed in detail in Chapter 20.

Activity analysis can center on the pathway components, which can be broken into primary, secondary, and support. The specifics of activity analysis in pathways is discussed in further detail in Chapter 20.

THE COSTED PATHWAY PROCESS

The process by which a costed pathway is achieved contains six steps: (1) identify the

Exhibit 19–7 Typical ABC Costing Components in Clinical Pathways

Typical Activity-Based Costing Components in Clinical Pathways

- Assessments
- Consults
- Tests
- Medications
- Lines/Tubes/Monitors
- Treatments
- Nutrition/Elimination
- Teaching
- Mobility/Self-Care/Activity
- Discharge Outcomes
- Discharge Planning

population, (2) assemble the team, (3) collect data, (4) build the pathway, (5) pilot the pathway, and (6) evaluate and revise (Exhibit 19–8).

First, identify the population. The pathways to be built must be selected from a field of many potential pathways. This selection is a basic first step. In order to select the pathways that will serve the highest and best good for the facility, it is necessary to identify the population that is being served by the facility. Thus, the first step in the process is to draw a profile of the patient population within the facility over the past three years. (We selected three years as an arbitrary time period. Three years is typically long enough to establish confidence in the profile and significant trends. Other time periods may be more appropriate in specific situations.)

Second, assemble the team. The multidisciplinary project team must be assembled. The composition of the team has been previously discussed, and the importance of this step cannot be emphasized enough. Of equal importance is an open and mutually respectful relationship among this team. This is not a place for bullies or prima donnas.

Third, collect data. A profile of various elements must be collected in order to make first-cut decisions about the proposal. The types of data to collect have been previously discussed. The important point to make within this context is this: It can't take too long to collect this data, and it can't cost too much to collect it, either. Remember, the collection of this information on

which profound management decisions will be made is being done by the persons on your staff most resistant to change of any sort. Data points are further discussed at a later point in this chapter.

Fourth, build the pathway. The expertise exists within the team to build the pathway, and generic samples are available in the literature. So build it. Don't get hung up on micromanaging the small stuff. That will be taken care of in the pilot. Just get it done. There will be plenty of opportunities to revise and refine. For the sake of the project at this point, good enough is good enough.

Fifth, pilot the pathway. The pilot is very important to the success of the project. Careful choice of the site for this pilot is essential. Three musts are crucial: There must be a need at the pilot site for the system, there must be facility leadership commitment to both ABC and clinical pathways, and there must be accessibility of all team members to the facility. The pilot should always include a test of the cost assignment procedures.

Sixth, evaluate and revise. The evaluation should be done within 60 to 90 days from the end of the pilot. Do not let the evaluation report turn into a political football. The team leader will have to shield the project from potential politics. Try for a neutral and objective evaluation. The purpose of evaluation should be purely to revise the pathway in order to prepare it for implementation, replication, and continuous improvement. Without this step, the organization will never know whether it has truly learned all it can learn from this extensive commitment of resources.

DESIGN ACTIVITY-BASED COSTING DATA FOR SUCCESS

The individuals involved in the data design and analysis team—the task force—must be accessible in order to provide their design and analysis expertise. For example, a capable and dedicated individual is appointed to the costed pathway design team. But she or he has to travel

---

Exhibit 19–8 The Costed Pathway Process

The Costed Pathway Process

- Identify the population
- Assemble the team
- Collect data
- Build the pathway
- Pilot the pathway
- Evaluate and revise

Courtesy of National Benevolent Association, St. Louis, Missouri.

70 percent of the time for the next year. Will this scenario work? No. The initial proposal must provide for replacement of those team members who cannot be accessible.

The data design and analysis team must strive for accuracy. That is, the concept must be translated into "computerese." The concept, at a macro level, must be converted into a workable detailed plan, at a micro level, for the actual system that will be in use. In other words, accuracy means this: The macroview team members must provide sufficient detail for the microview team members to correctly convert the concept into concrete detail. Note: It is nearly impossible for "concept people" to comprehend the minute level of detail needed for a computer to produce meaningful results. This step teems with frustration.

The data design and analysis team has their collective hands tied unless adequate hardware and software support is provided. The minimum requirements are: (1) Hardware support must have sufficient capability and reasonable speed. (2) Software support must be able to assign costs to activities and then to an array of cost objectives; allow tracing and allocation capabilities that are essential to activity-based costing, including the ability to assign activity drivers; and allow for ABC budgeting. (3) The system can (and probably will) stand alone. Thus, it must have import and/or export capability to and/or from other data sources. (4) Finally, the hardware and software must be affordable and must be implemented and debugged within a reasonable period of time. (We would project 120 days as a desirable time frame). The project can crash on these decision-making shoals. Our advice is this: Make a decision and go forward with it.

The data design and analysis team needs multidisciplinary knowledge. The team must have costing-specific, general-financial, clinical-specific (as to the particular pathway[s] being designed), clinical-administrative, and information-system–specific components. Early in the process the team needs to have consensus on mutual goals. The team also needs to have all roles clarified. Bottom line: There has to be a leader. Evaluation is recommended as an end point to the first pilot project, which informs the beginning of succeeding projects.

KEY INDICATORS

Key indicators are those pieces of information that the system will capture, store, retrieve, and report after implementation of the model. What makes this model work is that very specific outcomes and interventions are captured in the database in addition to the data that are normally collected. For an example of those historically recorded specific data points, see Exhibit 19–9. The planning team designs its best estimates of these indicators in the planning process and adjusts them as later learning and understanding refines the system's needs. It is very likely that much of this understanding won't be evident until the initial implementation and testing phase in spite of the best early planning efforts.

Exhibit 19–9 Data Points

Data Points
• Patient name
• ID number
• Medical record number
• Age
• Gender
• Admission date
• Admission source
• Discharge destination
• Readmission date
• Minimum data set (MDS) assessment date
• Clinical pathway designation
• Day path started
• Day path ended
• Variance points
• Costs

Source: Copyright © 1996, Resource Group, Ltd., Dallas, Texas.

Experience has taught that a highly efficient method of developing the initial set of key indicators is a modification of the traditional brainstorming session. Many (maybe hundreds) of individual data elements can be generated by a group of knowledgeable persons in a short period of time by asking, "What do we need to know about this pathway to enable wise management decisions regarding it?" This initial, unstructured list of items can then be quickly edited and sorted into a small number of categories by two or three persons. This categorized listing then becomes a working draft for the initial database.

OBSTACLES

Slow and cumbersome information management systems are significant obstacles to the process. If parallel systems are necessary in order to establish the costed care path process, then commit to acquiring a computer system specifically for this purpose.

A tendency often exists to use the persons who are the most familiar with the information being captured to enter those data into the system. This tendency often results in nursing staff entering the data. Usually, this is not the best use of clinical staff time. Although outstanding exceptions exist, clinical staff normally haven't been asked for refined computer or data-entry skills. A more productive approach is to seek out certain skills and characteristics. Without excluding any staff member, a search can be made for persons with computer data-entry skills, technical curiosity, and demonstrated tenacity in problem solving. Initial, large-scale data entry may be best accomplished by hiring temporary data-entry technicians.

Entering data is not all the battle. Once input, the data must be verified. Data verification must be performed by an individual who is conscientious and data oriented. This individual, in turn, should be supervised by someone who can and will listen to questions and make decisions about the data. Data analysis is essential to the

process. Once the data have been entered and verified, a designated individual should analyze the results. This individual must be committed to the enterprise. Furthermore, she or he must have the available time to do the job well.

SYSTEMS FOR TRACKING, ANALYZING, AND REPORTING

The data collection system should be integrated to collect statistics, demographics, financial information, and clinical information. Statistics might primarily consist of utilization statistics. Demographics might be comprised of such items as geographic location of residence, occupation, gender, and age. Financial information would consist of items such as primary and secondary payers, costs, and revenues. Clinical information would be gathered through the pathway forms.

The system for tracking, analyzing, and reporting should ideally be set up so that all clinical information can be gathered through input from the pathway form. Thus, no additional chart review would be required. When the initial pathway draft has been completed it should be reviewed and adjusted with this goal in mind.

A major method of analyzing is by variance monitoring. There are four major areas of variance monitoring: (1) patient or family, (2) community, (3) system, and (4) practitioner and caregiver. The care team has different degrees of control with these four areas. Those different degrees of control should be acknowledged in the variance tracking method adopted by the facility. Variances can be monitored with the aid of a variance tracking log, an example of which appears as Exhibit 19–10.

All systems for tracking, analyzing, and reporting should be computerized. If any portion of the process is not computerized, a bottleneck will occur at this spot. To repeat: No part of the pathway input process should be done by hand.

Exhibit 19–10 Variance Tracking Log

VARIANCE TRACKING LOG

Critical Path	Variance Item	Reason	Actions	Comments	Initials	Signature

Patient Stamp

Source: Copyright © 1997, Resource Group, Ltd., Dallas, Texas.

ANALYZING KEY COST AND CARE PRACTICE INDICATORS

The decision as to what to analyze will shape the project. In other words, what does the team want to see? What information is desired? And in what format? Common cost and care practice indicators are discussed below.

The acuity level is a good management tool. It cuts across cost and care. It is a good indicator at both the financial and the clinical level. When both cost and care are measured by acuity level, the potential for a management decision is much more powerful.

The care level is a basic indicator. It also cuts across cost and care. It is interesting to compare the care level indicator against the acuity level indicator.

Risk factor grouping is a sophisticated indicator if the facility has the capability to perform it. It is good planning to work the ability to track and analyze for risk factors into the initial project outline so the facility can take advantage of the opportunity when the capability is provided.

Payer type is a traditional indicator. It should always be included.

Contract type is a more current indicator. The initial project outline should allow for contract type tracking and analysis. Thus, the capability is built into the system. When managed care makes the contractual status an important indicator, the facility can readily utilize this indicator.

Rate or revenue per day is a traditional indicator. It should always be included.

The basic cost per day is another traditional indicator. However, much more opportunity for costing is opened up when activity-based costing is implemented. Cost per day can then be split into costing levels that reflect the true cost of service delivery.

In the past the custodial function of the old-fashioned nursing home made length of stay irrelevant to many managers. This should not be so. Length of stay at the various levels of care available within the facility is a basic indicator

that should be captured. Consider it essential in the initial process.

Certain other indicators may be chosen because the facility is part of a system or because it is participating in capitated contracts. One example of another factor for skilled nursing facilities is the identification of the attending physician—an indicator important to health systems. The system management generally will want this information. It is best to build it into the initial process.

PARALLEL AND INTERTWINED TRACKS FOR ADMINISTRATION AND CLINICAL MANAGEMENT

In its most comprehensive form, the costed clinical pathways planning model generates continuous evaluation and improvement efforts at all management levels for clinical and administrative leadership. These evaluation and improvement efforts focus on clinical, administrative, and financial practices and systems at three levels.

At the facility level, continuous evaluation and improvement efforts center on defining and improving current clinical practices and current costing, reporting, and monitoring systems.

At the peer, or community level, continuous evaluation and improvement efforts focus on discovering and understanding the current clinical practices as well as costing, reporting, and monitoring systems of other facilities that are serving the same geographic or market area.

At the industry level, continuous evaluation and improvement efforts are highlighted by a search for clinical benchmarks and industry best practices, and for costing, reporting, and monitoring benchmarks and industry best practices.

Being continuously aware, at all three levels, of developments and progress in clinical, administrative, and financial areas provides the management team a perspective and a bond that ensures responsive and highly efficient care management.

Exhibit 19–11 The Process

HOW

1. Sketch concept for key stakeholders.
2. Identify pilot team members.
3. Develop overall concept proposal and problem statement including: problem-purpose-process-design-tools-partici-pants-methodology-timelines-documen-tation-costs-benefits.
4. Establish roles and responsibilities of team members.
5. Develop and prioritize patient care areas to be addressed.
6. Develop clinical pathways for first patient care area.
7. Identify outcomes, measurements, and validation procedures.
8. Develop information and communications systems, procedural elements, flow, and application to implement clinical pathway pilot.
9. Develop training and education system for staff, physicians, and payers.
10. Implement, review, and adjust for best practices.
11. Repeat 6 through 10 for next resident care area.
12. Repeat 6 through 10 for remaining areas.
13. Evaluate program from outcomes perspective.
14. Report results of pilot to appropriate partners and others.

Courtesy of National Benevolent Association, St. Louis, Missouri.

SUMMARY: THE PROCESS

Exhibit 19–11 is a brief outline of the steps involved in developing costed clinical pathways and integrating them into the everyday life of a skilled nursing facility. The process is iterative to permit development and implementation of the pathway for one condition at a time or many pathways simultaneously. The choice depends on the resources available and the facility's sense of urgency. We present the basic process, leaving to the reader the permutations that may be necessary or desirable in a specific set of circumstances.

CONCLUSION

Leadership, teamwork, and vision are key (Exhibit 19–12). We have attempted to relate our own experience through this planning process. We do not want to leave the impression that the process is linear. In retrospect, we would have done some things in our original plan differently. The reader has the benefit of our struggles with the several detours and roadblocks we faced during the process. Much of the strongest emphasis in this chapter reflects the course corrections that we made. For readability, we have not highlighted these corrections, but rather have blended them with the areas we found we had planned correctly.

The path through pathway planning twists and turns. It causes travelers to detour and backtrack, speed up and slow down with enervating frequency. The road map provided herein will not eliminate these processes. It will, however, help an organization maintain focus on its purpose and vision. Strong, committed leadership, open communication, and motivated teamwork provide the fuel for the journey. The benefits are manifold.

Exhibit 19–12 Concluding Statement

"Leadership backing won't guarantee success but lack of it will guarantee failure."

V. Barr

BIBLIOGRAPHY

Brimson, J., and J. Antos. *Activity-Based Management for Service Industries, Government Entities, and Nonprofit Organizations.* New York: John Wiley & Sons, 1994.

Brimson, J. *Activity Accounting: An Activity-Based Costing Approach.* New York: John Wiley & Sons, 1991.

Dienemann, J., and T. Gessner. "Restructuring Nursing Care Delivery Systems." *Nursing Economics* 10, no. 4 (1992): 253–258.

Ignatavicius, D., and K. Housman. *Clinical Pathways for Collaborative Practice.* New York: W. B. Saunders Company, 1995.

Joint Commission on Accreditation of Healthcare Organizations. *Framework for Improving Performance: A Guide for Nurses.* New York: Joint Commission on Accreditation of Healthcare Organizations, 1994.

Definitions

Care Pathway: (1) Map that plots key events and interventions. (2) A patient management tool that supports continuous quality improvement (CQI), efficient resource utilization, and quality patient care. (3) A tool to build the set of interventions, procedures, and practices designed to achieve predetermined outcomes.

Clinical Path: A coordinated plan of treatment relating to a specific illness or condition to ensure quality, manage costs, and measure patient outcomes.

Multidisciplinary Care Plan: Documentation tool that encompasses the standard elements of care, expected clinical outcomes, and interventions to address variations.

Practice Guideline: A standardized specification for care that incorporates the best scientific evidence of effectiveness with expert opinion.

Variance: (1) A discrepancy between what actually happens and what is expected. (2) A test, assessment, or treatment that is a part of the path but is not done, or is not a part of the pathway but is done. (3) Deviations from the clinical pathway that potentially affect the expected outcome.

## CHAPTER 20

An Implementation Model for Columbia Overland Park Regional Medical Center's Skilled Nursing Facility Costed Clinical Pathways: A Case Study

Marta Hudson Ramsey and Judith J. Baker

PREFACE

This case study describes the implementation of a collaborative, or multidisciplinary, care path process. The Overland Park case study provides a detailed view of the process framework to which costs are attached in accordance with activity-based costing methodology. The hospital is a Columbia/HCA facility and includes a hospital-based skilled nursing facility. It is located in Overland Park, Kansas, within the Kansas City metropolitan area.

The contributor, Marta Hudson Ramsey, RN, MS, is currently assigned to Special Projects Administration at Columbia Overland Park Regional Medical Center. In 1994, she collaborated with the Overland Park Skilled Nursing Interdisciplinary Team to design and operationalize pathways in compliance with Health Care Financing Administration (HCFA) regulations for an interdisciplinary care plan.

BACKGROUND

A clinical pathway is a map that is comprised of interdisciplinary interventions and goals that are designed to navigate a health care consumer's course through a disease specific spell of illness or procedure. The pathway outlines the interventions that must be implemented in order to meet defined goals. The outcomes are derived from problems that are specific to a diagnosis or procedure. Why is a map necessary in this information age wrought by telecommunications and computer technology? The answer is simple. Consumers, regulators, providers, and payers demand financial and clinical data that fuels the health care industry.

Consumers demand outcome data in order to choose health care providers. Regulators demand outcome data to confer providers with licensure, certification, and accreditation, not to mention calming the fears of the consumer. In common terms, the Joint Commission on Accreditation of Healthcare Organizations (Joint Commission) and the HCFA enforce standards requiring that providers have an interdisciplinary plan of care for each consumer. Providers demand outcome data to satisfy internal customers (physicians, nurses, technicians, and therapists) and external customers (patients, payers, regulators). Finally, payers demand outcome data to fuel the engine of the health care industry. A pathway is basically a mechanism to generate and communicate data in a language that speaks to all constituencies.

In September 1995, the National Subacute Care Association Newsletter, *NSCA News,*[1] reported that the Medicare program expects to save $270 billion dollars in the next seven years. A portion of those cost savings would be achieved by shifting risk to the providers and by reducing inpatient hospital days by 34 percent by 1999. The average acute care length of stay (LOS) for patients under age 65 has already decreased by 3.8 percent (AHA 1994 study, cited in *NSCA News*[2]). The prospective payment system implemented in acute care in the 1980s in the form of diagnosis-related groups (DRGs) will be expanded to include skilled nursing and home health programs. Ultimately, payers will negotiate directly with providers to share risk by managing patients through the health care continuum for dollars per covered life. Hospitals will integrate services by forming affiliations with home health and long-term care providers. Integration of services will require interdisciplinary tools such as pathways to manage each covered life through the continuum of care.

Hospitals are pressed by payers to be a one-stop shop for services and to develop alternative methods of care delivery. To meet this challenge, hospitals have implemented skilled nursing programs, geropsychiatric programs, rehabilitation programs, and senior health centers. For example, the cost of patient care in a skilled nursing program is 20–60 percent below the cost of patient care in an acute care setting. Why are costs lower in a skilled nursing setting? Because the Medicare reimbursement system is based on the provider's costs whereby the provider is reimbursed for a daily per diem and ancillary services. For providers who implement new skilled nursing programs, Medicare waives routine cost limits for the first three cost report years. Existing skilled nursing programs have the option of submitting an application to Medicare, requesting an exceptions to routine cost limits. In addition, technological advances and expanded job descriptions of non-licensed health care workers have made it possible to care for patients in settings other than hospitals or separate, distinct units of hospitals. In the Medicare reimbursement system, the provider does not share risk with the payer.

Third-party payers, health maintenance organizations (HMOs), and managed care providers aggressively manage their members within the continuum of care that includes skilled nursing programs. These organizations reimburse providers via a contracted per diem rate regardless of the services provided to the patient. For example, an HMO may reimburse the provider $600 per day for services provided on acute care and $300 per day for services provided on the skilled nursing unit. Contrary to the Medicare reimbursement system for skilled nursing, the HMO shifts the risk to the provider who has to provide care for $300 per day. To manage costs, providers must have a system to determine the services that are necessary to care for each patient population. The system that was implemented by Columbia Overland Park Regional Medical Center is called Collaborative Care.

COLLABORATIVE CARE

At Columbia Overland Park Regional Medical Center, an advanced model of delivery care called Collaborative Care was implemented in the late 1980s to develop and operationalize pathways across the continuum of care. Jody Abbott, RN, MSN, COO; and Rita Haxton, RN,

MSN, Assistant VP Patient Care, resisted objections from corporate executives who did not support the development of pathways because they could not see how pathways improve care delivery in the future.

The collaborative care model is unit-based care that distributes resources to achieve specific patient goals within a specified time period. Care is organized by pathways that are designed by interdisciplinary continuous quality improvement (CQI) teams based on knowledge of a case type, average LOS, critical events, timing, anticipated goals, and utilization of resources. The goals in collaborative care are:

- to promote accomplishing preestablished patient goals
- to promote discharge within a preestablished LOS
- to efficiently appropriate resources
- to promote collaborative practice and continuity of care
- to create an environment for professional development and satisfaction of internal customers
- to guide interdisciplinary providers toward achievement of patient goals

Collaborative care is unique because no additional resources are used to start up the process. The staff registered nurse at the point of care is the coordinator 24 hours a day, seven days a week. There is no case manager. The interdisciplinary team members are recruited based on their clinical expertise in providing care. Initially, the pathways are physician specific. As the pathways develop, physician specific pathways are merged to case type specific pathways. Measurable goals and outcomes are identified prior to the implementation with a focus on quality, not decreasing costs.

Perhaps the most unique feature of the pathways is that they are operationalized in the documentation system as a permanent part of the medical record. Narrative charting by exception using the problem, intervention, and evaluation format documents variances from the pathway. Each interdisciplinary team member docu-

ments on the pathway as defined by policy and procedure. The CQI team reviews the pathway at regular intervals to continuously improve the process.

The Overland Park Regional Medical Center Patient Care Practice Model incorporates collaborative care (Figure 20–1). The nursing process is actually integrated into the pathway using nursing diagnoses. The model uses interdisciplinary CQI teams to design pathways. The CQI team members collaborate to provide patient care services efficiently, using pathways as tools. By using pathways, patient care services are provided efficiently and the quality of those services improves and costs decrease.

The team members who are involved in the CQI team represent those services that interact with the patient and family. For example, the Skilled Nursing Unit (SNU) Interdisciplinary Collaborative Care Path (CCP) Team includes the physician, nurse, respiratory therapist, physical therapist, occupational therapist, activity therapist, dietitian, social worker, clinical nurse specialist, and coordinator of clinical process improvement.

Because the team members themselves or their peers will actually provide patient care services, they have the expertise to design the pathway or plan of care. The team leader collaborates with the team to develop a mission statement and objectives that are submitted for approval by the CQI Quality Council. The staff members who assume the role of team leader have received extensive CQI training. The role of the CQI Quality Council is to coordinate all of the CQI teams in congruence with the mission and values of the organization, integrate regulatory standards, and measure organization performance in terms of quality and cost.

The information used by the team to design the pathway includes the disease specific or problem oriented pathway and variance identification data. Other tools include physician standing orders, the Resident Assessment Instrument (RAI), financial databases, medical record reviews, literature reviews, vendor information,

Figure 20–1 Patient Care Practice Model. Courtesy of Columbia Overland Park Regional Medical Center, Overland Park, Kansas.

and internal and external customer satisfaction data.

STEPS WHEN DEVELOPING A COLLABORATIVE CARE PATHWAY

The first step is to determine high volume, high risk, and/or problem prone diagnoses by the service area directors in the organization. When a new service or program is implemented, a CQI team is organized to design and improve the pathway. In January 1994, Columbia Overland Park Regional Medical Center implemented a new skilled nursing program. At the completion of the certification and licensure

process the SNU Interdisciplinary CCP Team was organized (Figure 20–2).

The mission of the team was to develop and operationalize pathways for SNU to meet HCFA standards. To accomplish this mission, the team chose a high volume patient population admitted for elective total hip replacement (THR). One orthopedic surgeon who demonstrated an aggressive approach to managing patients through the continuum of care collaborated with the team to design the initial physician specific CCP. Using the pathway allows the providers at the point of care to predict the progression of care from admission to discharge.

Figure 20–2 Overland Park Regional Medical Center Skilled Nursing Unit Organizational Chart. Courtesy of Columbia Overland Park Regional Medical Center, Overland Park, Kansas.

In the second step, team members begin documenting when they take certain steps during the caregiving process. Both standardized and nonstandardized patterns of care are identified during this process. Members of the team ask themselves, "Why do we wait until day four to implement this intervention?" "Could the intervention be implemented on day three?" "If we implemented the intervention on day three, would quality and efficiency be improved?" For example, the acute care LOS was dictated by

Medicare regulations, which require a three day acute care stay prior to admission to an SNU. An intervention to consult social services regarding SNU admission was added to day two of the acute care THR CCP. The team discovered that if they waited until day three to evaluate the patient for skilled nursing and communicate with the patient and family, admission to SNU could be delayed by one or two days.

Team members also discovered the process of care delivery in other disciplines. For example, in the SNU Interdisciplinary CCP, the team was challenged to provide a mechanism on the pathway whereby the physical or occupational therapist could communicate specific rehabilitation interventions to the nurses. On the pathway form, space was provided for the therapist to write directions (e.g., practice sliding board transfers).

As the team organizes the interventions and goals in the pathway format, regulatory standards are integrated into the pathway. The integration of regulatory standards operationalizes the standard for the direct caregiver. For example, the Joint Commission and state and federal standards require that all inpatients must be questioned about an advance directive. The advance directive entry on the first time segment of all pathways documents that the standard has been addressed. In addition, HCFA requires verification of patient rights and responsibilities, dietitian assessment, and therapeutic recreation assessment that also appear on the first segment of all SNU pathways.

In documenting the goals and interventions for the SNU THR CCP (see Exhibits 20–1 and 20–2), the team members had to predict at what activity of daily living (ADL) self-performance the patient would exhibit on each day. In addition, the physical and occupational therapists had to predict outcomes for a patient population who had different baseline function when they entered the continuum of care. In order to speak in the same language across the continuum, the team used the ADL Self-Performance scale from the Resident Assessment Instrument (RAI). The RAI is a federally mandated functional assessment for all long-term care facilities, including hospital-based skilled nursing units.

During the third step, the team organizes the information into a care path format by specifying the category and time increment for goals and interventions. A CQI process flowchart is used to map goals and interventions that must be accomplished to move from one step to the others. A timeline (Figure 20–3) is used along with the flowchart (Figure 20–4). The steps in

the flowchart include: start, process step, process step, decision, process step, and end.

By using this flowchart, the Interdisciplinary CQI Team formats goals and interventions or activities into seven different categories: (1) tests, (2) medications, (3) treatments, (4) diet, (5) activity, (6) teaching, and (7) discharge planning. The categories are based on Joint Commission and HCFA standards that require an interdisciplinary plan of care that incorporates the medical plan of care and includes teaching and discharge planning.

Disease specific pathways generally are formatted into time increments by day, while procedural pathways are formatted into time increments by hour or minute. The SNU THR CCP was formatted by day. Separate pathways build on one another to move the patient through the continuum of care (from pre-op, to acute care, to skilled care, to home health). The end of one pathway is used to develop the beginning of the next pathway. For example, the THR patient population was efficiently managed using an orthopedic pre-op teaching CCP and an acute care THR CCP. Naturally, the SNU THR began as an extension of the acute care CCP with the goal of decreasing the acute care length of stay by admitting the patient to the SNU. Each pathway is divided in two sections. The first section details the problems and goals for the specific case type or procedure (Exhibit 20–1). A generic set of problems (governed by regulatory agencies such as the Joint Commission) are used for all CCPs across the continuum, which include: anxiety related to hospitalization; knowledge deficit related to tests, procedures, and surgery; alteration in health maintenance related to disease process; and potential for injury related to hospitalization. Additional problems are added for each case type. The goals appear adjacent to the respective problem. For example in the SNU THR CCP one problem is "impaired skin integrity," and the goal is for the patient to "maintain intact skin margins." "NSG" appears at the beginning of the goal to indicate that nursing is the discipline to initial the box if the goal is met.

◄ — — — — — — — — — — — TIMELINE — — — — — — — — — — — ►

CATEGORIES	COLLABORATIVE CARE PATH						
	ADDRESSOGRAPH			COLLABORATIVE CARE PATH Case Type: Expected LOS: Developed by Key: M=Met, U=Unmet -----> Continued			
		Day/Hour/Visit					
		Admission	Day 1	Day 2	Day 3	Day 4	
	Consults						
	Tests						
	Medications						
	Treatments						
	Diet						
	Activity						
	Teaching						
	Discharge Planning						

Figure 20–3 Collaborative Paths Timeline and Categories. Courtesy of Columbia Overland Park Regional Medical Center, Overland Park, Kansas.

The second section details the interventions or activities that must be implemented to accomplish the goals (Exhibit 20–2). The interventions are organized into seven categories: (1) tests, (2) medications, (3) treatments, (4) diet, (5) activity, (6) teaching, and (7) discharge planning (see Figure 20–3). By structuring the interventions in a standardized format, the team documents the interventions for each case type or procedure and ensures regulatory compliance.

For documentation purposes, two boxes (one box for each 12-hour shift) appear beside each goal or intervention of the CCP. The staff nurse or therapist assigned to that patient during that shift documents that the goal or intervention

was met by initialing the box. If the goal or intervention was addressed only daily, one box would appear. When a goal or intervention is unmet a U is placed in the box and a variance note is written on the Variance ID (Exhibit 20–3). When a goal or intervention does not apply, a diagonal slash is drawn through the box. By using these documentation principles the CCP is individualized for each patient, and variances from the pathway are documented.

First are tests. In the SNU THR CCP, *lab as ordered* (see Exhibit 20–2), appears on day one to remind the staff nurse to review pertinent laboratory results. The arrows adjacent to the entry indicate for the staff nurse to review any pertinent laboratory results on subsequent days. The

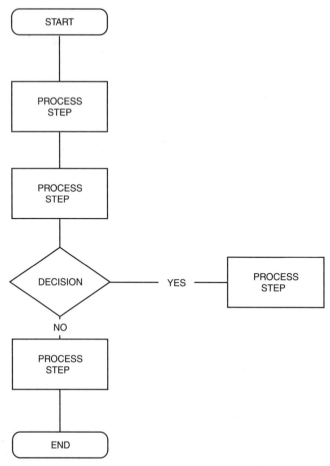

Figure 20–4 Collaborative Care Path Process Flowchart. Courtesy of Columbia Overland Park Regional Medical Center, Overland Park, Kansas.

dietitian's contribution to the CCP is evident by the intervention, *albumin if > 65 year old,* because patients of this case type frequently have low albumin that requires nutritional supplementation. The staff nurse will obtain an order for the albumin and the dietitian will use that information to recommend nutritional supplements.

Second is medications. *Verify home meds with patient and physician* is a standard intervention in the medication category because of Joint Commission standards. *PRN meds PO* notifies the staff nurse that the patient who is

now approximately three days post-op is now on oral pain medications. The staff nurse will document the time, description of symptoms, pain rating, intervention, and evaluation on the pain management flow sheet (Exhibit 20–4) in addition to initialing the intervention on the CCP. THR patients are anticoagulated following surgery as indicated by *anticoagulants as ordered.* In addition, *MOM or stronger lax if no BM,* was included in the SNU THR CCP because the immobility associated with THR causes constipation in most patients. All medications that are administered are documented on

Exhibit 20–1 Skilled Nursing Unit Total Hip Replacement Collaborative Care Path—Goal Section

COLLABORATIVE CARE PATH	ADDRESSOGRAPH	
Case Type: Total Hip Replacement		COLUMBIA OVERLAND PARK
Expected LOS: 6 days		REGIONAL MEDICAL CENTER
Developed by Skilled Nsg Unit		
Key: Initials = Met U = Unmet - - -> Continued		

	Day/Hour/Visit			
	POD # 3	SNU 1	POD # 4	SNU 2	POD # 5	SNU 3

Team Problem Identification	Intermediate Goals			
Potential for disturbance in self concept RT injury/illness	TR: Pt verbalizes self esteem rating _____ 0= no self esteem 10= highest level of self esteem	TR: Pt demonstrates leisure competency rating _____	TR: Pt participates in therapeutic milieu, i.e., dress, & attend TR groups TR: Pt verbalizes self esteem rating _____
	SS/NSG: Pt/family verbalizes concerns	- - ->	- - ->
	SS/NSG: Pt/family verbalizes understanding of Pt. rights		TR: Pt perceives therapy as beneficial
Potential for impairment of social &/or leisure skills to skilled care	TR: Pt./family verbalize interest in leisure activity	TR: Pt engages in social/ leisure activity c TRS: 1 on 1 or group setting	TR: Pt initiates or engages in leisure/social activity c TRS; 1 on 1 or group setting
Lack of knowledge R/T transfer to SNU	NSG: Verbalizes understanding of CCPs Goals and unit orientation		
Lack of knowledge R/T home care planning	NSG: Verbalizes discharge needs	- - ->	- - ->
	SS/NSG: Pt/family verbalize agreement with Advanced Directives/Living Will status		
	NSG: Verbalizes/demonstrates knowledge of total hip precautions	NSG: Demonstrates compliance with total hip precautions	- - ->
	SS: Pt/family will verbalize anticipated home care needs	- - ->	- - ->
Potential for impairment of skin integrity R/T surgery	NSG: Maintains intact skin margins	- - ->	- - ->
Alteration in bowel elimination R/T surgery	NSG: Patient demonstrates function	- - ->	
Potential for injury/infection R/T unfamiliar environment, surgery	NSG: Pt/family verbalizes under-standing of safety measures NSG: No symptoms of infection	NSG: No injury	- - ->
Alteration in comfort R/T incisional pain	NSG: Pain controlled with po meds	- - ->	- - ->
PT: Impaired mobility endurance & self care abilities R/T Surgery LE= Lower extremity	PT: Assessment with follow up therapy		PT: Progressive therapy: Level Bed mobility 2 Ambulation 1 Transfers 2 Exercise 2
	OT: Assessment with follow up therapy		OT: Progressive therapy Dressing 2 Bathing 1 Toileting 2
CODES/LEVELS 0 - Independent 1 - Supervised 2 - Limited Assist 3 - Extensive Assist 4 - Total Dependence			

SIGNATURES	SG	7-3	7-3	7-3
		3-11	3-11	3-11
		11-7	11-7	11-7
	PT			
	OT			
sthr(8/15/95)	SS			
BASELINE	TR			
	DS			

continues

Exhibit 20–1 continued

COLLABORATIVE CARE PATH	ADDRESSOGRAPH		
Case Type: Total Hip Replacement		COLUMBIA OVERLAND PARK	
Expected LOS: 6 days		REGIONAL MEDICAL CENTER	
Developed by Skilled Nsg Unit			
Key: Initials = Met U = Unmet - - -> Continued			

POD # 6 SNU 4	POD # 7 SNU 5	POD # 8 SNU 6	POD # 9 SNU 7
If dismissed see POD #8			Outcomes
TR: Pt verbalizes self esteem rating _____ 0= no self esteem 10= highest level of self esteem	TR: Pt demonstrates leisure competency rating _____	TR: Pt verbalizes self esteem rating _____	TR: Pt demonstrates leisure competency rating _____
SS/NSG: Pt/family verbalizes concerns	- - ->	- - ->	NSG/SS: Demonstrates coping mechanism
TR: Pt initates or implements social leisure activity independently	- - ->	- - ->	TR: Independent with initiating & implementing social &/or leisure
NSG: Verbalizes discharge needs			NSG: Verbalizes understanding of home care and follow up
NSG: Demonstrates compliance with total hip precautions	- - ->	- - ->	- - ->
	SS: Pt/family will verbalize understanding of an agreement with post hospital arrangements	- - ->	- - ->
NSG: Maintains intact skin margins	- - ->	- - ->	Maintains intact skin margins
NSG: Patient demonstrates function	- - ->	- - ->	NSG: Patient demonstrates function
NSG: No injury	- - ->	- - ->	NSG: No injury
NSG: No symptoms of infection	- - ->	- - ->	NSG: No infection
NSG: Pain controlled with po meds	- - ->	- - ->	NSG: Pain controlled with po meds
	PT: Progressive therapy: Level Bed mobility 0 Ambulation 1 Transfers 0 Exercise 1		PT: Progressive therapy: Level Bed mobility 0 Ambulation 0 Transfers 0 Exercise 0
	OT: Progressive therapy Dressing 0 Bathing 0 Toileting 0		OT: Progressive therapy Dressing Bathing Toileting
7-3	7-3	7-3	7-3
3-11	3-11	3-11	3-11
11-7	11-7	11-7	11-7

Courtesy of Columbia Overland Park Regional Medical Center, Overland Park, Kansas.

Exhibit 20–2 Skilled Nursing Unit Total Hip Replacement Collaborative Care Path—Intervention Section

COLLABORATIVE CARE PATH	ADDRESSOGRAPH
Case Type: **Total Hip Replacement**	COLUMBIA OVERLAND PARK
Expected LOS: **6 days**	REGIONAL MEDICAL CENTER
Developed by **Skilled Nursing Unit**	
Key: Nurses Initials = Met U = Unmet - - -> Continued	

			POD # 3	SNU 1	POD #4	SNU 2	POD # 5	SNU 3
C	CONSULTS							
O	TESTS	Lab as ordered			- - ->		- - ->	
L		• Albumin level if ^ 65 years old						
A	MEDICATIO	Verify home meds with patient and physician						
B		PRN meds PO			- - ->		- - ->	
O		Anticoagulant as ordered			- - ->		- - ->	
R		MOM or			- - ->		- - ->	
A		Stronger lax. if no BM						
T								
I	TREATMEN	VS Rt bid			- - ->		- - ->	
V		Neuro/Circ status routine & prn			- - ->		- - ->	
E		Ted hose both legs at all times			- - ->		- - ->	
C		Pulsatile stockings off when OOB			- - ->		Discontinue pulsatile stockings	
A		Primipor Dressing chg QOD & PRN						
R		Trapeze			- - ->		- - ->	
E								
P		IS independently			- - ->		- - ->	
A		NSG: Reg pillow at day - abductor @ HS			- - ->		- - ->	
T		NSG: Advance Directive in chart						
H		TR: Assessment			TR will offer daily-TR groups 1 on 1 interaction & leisure counseling Encouragement to attend TR groups		- - ->	
							PT therapy & reassessment	
							OT therapy & reassessment	
	DIET	Dietary Eval/Assessment			- - ->		- - ->	
		Diet as ordered			- - ->		- - ->	
		If NPO > 72 hours notify dietician			- - ->			
	ACTIVITY	Dining Rm for meals			- - ->		Amb. to dining room c walker	
		Amb. with walker to bathroom			- - ->		- - ->	
		Dressing with assist in street clothes following precautions			- - ->		Dressing c Adaptive Equip in street clothes	
		Bathing c assist for LE			- - ->		Bathing c Adaptive Equip as at home	
		Toileting c assist					- - ->	
	TEACHING	SS/NSG: Discuss Pt rights, obtain signed verification from Pt/family			Have family demonstrate drsg chg. Ted hose application			
		Review THR precautions						
		Drsg. chg/TED application						
		Review CCP & goals						
	DISCHARGE PLANNING	Assess home situation family support & discharge plans			Assess need - stool riser/reacher and order if needed			
		SS: Provide support/reassurance answer questions			- - ->			
		SS: Assess home situation and complete psychosocial assessment			- - ->			
	(8/15/95) STHR	SS: Discuss community resources with pt/family & assess needs			- - ->			

continues

Exhibit 20–2 continued

COLLABORATIVE CARE PATH   ADDRESSOGRAPH
Case Type: Total Hip Replacement   COLUMBIA OVERLAND PARK
Expected LOS: 6 days   REGIONAL MEDICAL CENTER
Developed by Skilled Nursing Unit
Key: Nurses Initials = Met   U = Unmet   - - -> Continued

POD #6 / SNU 4	POD #7 / SNU 5	POD #8 / SNU 6	POD #9 / SNU 7
Lab as ordered	- - ->	- - ->	
Verify home meds with patient and physician			
Anticoagulant as ordered	- - ->	- - ->	- - ->
MOM or	- - ->	- - ->	- - ->
Stronger lax. if no BM			
PRN meds PO	- - ->	- - ->	- - ->
VS Rt bid	- - ->	- - ->	- - ->
Neuro/Circ status	- - ->	- - ->	- - ->
routine & prn			
Ted hose both legs			
at all times	- - ->	- - ->	- - ->
NSG: Reassess appropriateness of			
Advance Directive			
Texas bandaid			
Chg QOD & prn	- - ->	- - ->	- - ->
Trapeze	- - ->	- - ->	- - ->
	- - ->	- - ->	- - ->
IS independently	- - ->	- - ->	- - ->
NSG: Reg pillow at day -	- - ->	- - ->	Tub & shower Indep
abductor @ HS			
TR will offer daily-TR groups	- - ->	- - ->	- - ->
1 on 1 interaction & leisure counseling			
Encouragement to attend TR groups			
	PT therapy & reassessment		PT therapy & reassessment
	OT therapy & reassessment		OT therapy & reassessment
Diet as ordered	- - ->	- - ->	- - ->
Amb. to dining room c walker	- - ->	- - ->	- - ->
Amb. in hall 200-250 ft	- - ->	Amb 250-300 ft	- - ->
Dressing c Adaptive Equip in	- - ->	- - ->	- - ->
street clothes			
Bathing c Adaptive Equip as at home	- - ->	- - ->	
Toileting - Independent	- - ->	- - ->	
			Dismissal Fact Sheet
			Ted Hose x 1 mo
			Total hip precautions reviewed
		PT/OT/TR: Finalize discharge plans	Give drsgs for home
			Call for f/u appt
SS: Provide support/reassurance and answer questions	SS: Arrange home & community services and transportation if needed	SS: Arrange home & community services and transportation if needed	SS: Finalize and confirm discharge plan
(8/15/95)			

Courtesy of Columbia Overland Park Regional Medical Center, Overland Park, Kansas.

Exhibit 20–3 Variance ID

Collaborative Care Path
A = Abnormal Assessment Findings/Descriptive
V = Variation

	Patient/Family	Caregiver/Clinician	Hospital	Community
1 - Event Not Applicable	3 - Patient Condition	7 - Physician Order	11 - Bed Availability	16 - Placement/ Home Care
2 - Unpredicted Event	4 - Patient/Family Decision	8 - Caregiver(s) Decision	12 - Information/Data Availability	Availability
	5 - Patient/Family Availability	9 - Caregiver(s) Response Time	13 - Supplies/Equip Availability	18 - Ambulance Delay
	6 - Patient/Family Other	10 - Caregiver Other	14 - Dept. Over- booked/Closed	19 - Community Other
			15 - Hospital Other	

I = Intervention/Action Taken
E = Evaluation of Plan of Care, Patient Response/Progress

DATE	TIME	CODE	DIAGNOSIS:	PROGRESS NOTES

ADDRESSOGRAPH

Courtesy of Columbia Overland Park Regional Medical Center, Overland Park, Kansas.

Exhibit 20–4 Skilled Nursing Unit Patient Care Flow Sheet

DAILY PHYSICAL ASSESSMENT PARAMETERS					0700-1500	1500-2300	2300-0700
HEART SOUNDS NORMAL *			INCISION CARE *				
LUNGS CLEAR BILATERALLY *			a. Site				
			b. Type of dressing D&I = Dry & Intact				
Abdomen Soft *			C = Changed R = Reinforced				
Bowel Sounds Present all Quads *			c. Incision intact & without inflamma-tion, purulent drainage				
			d. Incision cleansed				
LAST BM			PERIPHERAL I.V. CARE				
ABSENT DEPENDENT EDEMA			a. I.V. insertion* # of attempts (change q 72 hrs)				
FOLEY CATHETER CARE			b. Dressing change*				
a. Size inserted *			c. Size and type of needle				
b. DD = Dependent drainage			d. Sites without leaking, edema, redness, warmth, purulent drainage				
C = Clamped *			SITE: Right Hand				
c. Insertion site without inflammation, leaking, purulent drainage			Left Hand				
			Right Arm				
			Left Arm				

EQUIPMENT USED	R if replaced				CENTRAL LINE CARE			
Egg Crate		Knee Immobilizer			a. Site & type of catheter			
Blood Glucose Monitor		Abductor Pillow			b. Site without leaking, redness, warmth, purulent drainage			
Gomco / Air Shield		AFO			c. Dressing changed*			
Wall Suction		Back Brace						
Rental Bed		Type:___			OTHER INTERVENTIONS:			
Feeding Pump		Leg Brace			Isolation ___			
Traction / Trapeze		Type:___						
K-pad		Reacher___						
PCA Pump		Sock Aid ___						
Ted Hose		Long Handled Sponge ___						
Chux		Shoe Horn ___						
Pulsatile Stockings		Other: ___						
Sterile H$_2$0 / Saline		___						
IV Infusion Pump		___						

LEGEND

* = Specified times indicated	RSC = Right Subclavian
✓ = As described	LSC = Left Subclavian
AB = Abnormal / Deviates from description (refer to Patient Care Record)	GC = Groshong
	PICC = Peripherally Inserted Central Catheter

	0700-1500	1500-2300	2300-0700
TRACH CARE *			
a. Inner cannula care			
b. External care			
c. Dressing change			
d. Ties renewed			
SUCTIONED *			
ET = Endotracheal			
NT = Nasotracheal			
T = Tracheal			
O = Oral Y = Yankauer			
NG TUBE CARE			
a. Size inserted *			
b. Placement check q 8 hrs.			
c. To suction: H = High L = Low			
d. Suction liner change *			
e. Tubing change *			
FEEDING TUBE CARE / GASTROSTOMY			
a. Size inserted *			
b. Type of tube			
c. Dressing change *			
d. Residual / Position check q, 4°			
e. Tubing and Bag change			

NURSE ASSIGNED (SIGNATURE) TITLE	HOURS ASSIGNED
PLAN OF CARE REVIEWED BY RN	
	RN
	RN
	RN
	RN

ADDRESSOGRAPH

Date _____

continues

Exhibit 20–4 continued

TIME	L.O.C.	SKIN WARM/DRY	ADL SELF-PERFORMANCE RATING										RESPIRATORY			GU	NEURO		SAFETY CHECKS				POST PROCEDURE CHECKS				
			ACTIVITY	FEEDING	GROOMING	ORAL CARE	BATHING	DRESSING	TOILETING	R.O.M.	TRANSFER	O₂'s FLOW RATE MODE L/	TURNING/POSITIONING	SPUTUM	URINE COLOR	CPM	NEURO/CIRC MOVEMENT SENSORY INTACT	BED IN LOW POSITION LOCKED	RESTRAINT REMOVED q 2 HRS W SKIN ASSESSMENT NORMAL	SIDE RAILS UP X	CALL LIGHT IN REACH	TIME	TEMPERATURE	PULSE	RESPIRATION	BLOOD PRESSURE
07-08																											
08-09																											
09-10																											
10-11																											
11-12																											
12-13																											
13-14																											
14-15																											
15-16																											
16-17																											
17-18																											
18-19																											
19-20																											
20-21																											
21-22																											
22-23																											
23-24																											
24-01																											
01-02																											
02-03																											
03-04																											
04-05																											
05-06																											
06-07																											

LEGEND

ACTIVITY
BR = Bedrest
BSC = Bedside Commode
C = Chair
A = Ambulation
BRP = Bathroom Privileges
AB = Abnormal / Deviates
   from description (see
   Patient Care Record
✓ = As described

LOC
6 = Eyes Closed -
   Resp. Present
5 = Alert & Disoriented
4 = Alert & Oriented x 3
3 = Responds to Verbal
2 = Responds to Pain
1 = Unresponsive

RESTRAINTS
V = Vest
W = Wrist
A = Ankle
L = Leather

SPUTUM
Θ = Absent
B = Bloody
C = Clear
G = Green
Y = Yellow
W = White

URINE COLOR
Y = Yellow
B = Bloody
A = Amber
P = Blood Tinged
C = Clots

HYGIENE
TB = Teeth Brushed
D = Dentures
S = Swab
C = Complete
P = Partial
S = Shower
HCS = Handicap
   Shower

**ADL SELF -
PERFORMANCE**
0 = Independent
1 = Supervision
2 = Limited Assistance
3 = Extensive Assistance
4 = Total Dependence

continues

Exhibit 20–4 continued

Overland Park Regional Medical Center

PATIENT CARE FLOW SHEET

I.V. SITE:					I = INTAKE								O = OUTPUT						MISC.		
I.V. FLUID Number/Amt. ADDITIVES RATE LTC				IVPB AMOUNT	BLOOD PRODUCTS	NG IRRIGANT	ENTERAL FEEDINGS RATE	ORAL	% OF DIET EATEN	% OF SNACKS EATEN		URINE	POST VOID RESIDUAL	DRAIN/CBI	DRAIN	NG/EMESIS	STOOLS/STOMAL DRAINAGE	SPECIMEN TO LAB	PCA PUMP READING	
06-07																				
07-08																				
08-09																				
09-10																				
10-11																				
11-12																				
12-13																				
13-14																				
									8 HR INTAKE										8 HR OUTPUT	
14-15																				
15-16																				
16-17																				
17-18																				
18-19																				
19-20																				
20-21																				
21-22																				
									8 HR INTAKE										8 HR OUTPUT	
22-23																				
23-24																				
24-01																				
01-02																				
02-03																				
03-04																				
04-05																				
05-06																				
									8 HR INTAKE										8 HR OUTPUT	
24 HOUR TOTAL																				
LEGEND: LTC = Left to Count INC = Incontinent									24 HR GRAND TOTAL INTAKE			24 HR GRAND TOTAL OUTPUT								

ADDRESSOGRAPH

continues

Exhibit 20–4 continued

PAIN MANAGEMENT FLOW SHEET

Evaluate pain with each intervention for pain or once per shift at a minimum if patient has a patient controlled analgesia device.

Record PCA Pump readings on the miscellaneous section of flow sheet.

BEFORE INTERVENTION   AFTER INTERVENTION

TIME	DESCRIPTION / LOCATION OF PAIN	0–10 RATING	INTER-VENTION (SEE KEY)	INITIALS	TIME	0–10 RATING	INITIALS

Key of Interventions

Criteria for Rating 0 - 10

| | | | | | | | | | | |
|0|1|2|3|4|5|6|7|8|9|10|

No Pain — Mild — Moderate Pain — Severe — Worst Pain

po: PO med   B: Booster dose   R: Simple relaxation
IM: IM med   L: Loading dose   Progressive muscle
IV: IV med   H: Heat   Simple imagery
EPI: Epidural med   I: Ice   Music
PCA: PCA pump med   P: Positioning   Massage

Courtesy of Columbia Overland Park Regional Medical Center, Overland Park, Kansas.

a Medication Administration Record (MAR) and on the CCP.

Third is treatment. *VS Rt bid* is a generic entry to all pathways. Although the nurse documents that vital signs were taken on the CCP, the specific values are documented on the Graphic Flow Sheet (Exhibit 20–5). *Neuro/Circ status routine and prn, Ted hose both legs at all times, Pulsatile stockings off when OOB, Primipor dressing change QOD and PRN,* and so forth are all treatments specific to the THR case type. The treatments may be revised to address specific problems. For example, in recent months, an additional intervention, *Remove Ted hose q shift for one hour,* has been added to this section because patients were developing heel pressure ulcers. *PT therapy and reassessment* and *OT therapy and reassessment* indicate that on day three physical therapy (PT) and occupational therapy (OT) will reassess the patient's need for therapy. The details of PT and OT therapy sessions are documented in the therapist evaluations and progress notes.

Fourth is diet. *Dietary Eval/Assessment* appears in this category because of HCFA regulations that require that each patient have an assessment by a dietitian on day one. The dietitian initials the box when the assessment is complete. Specific details of the assessment are documented on the Food and Nutrition Services Evaluation form. *Diet as ordered* prompts the staff nurse to review the orders for a specific diet. The percentage of the diet consumed are documented on the OPRMC SNU Flow Sheet (see Exhibit 20–4). *If NPO > 72 hours notify dietitian* reminds the staff nurse of the Joint Commission standard that requires an assessment by a dietitian if a patient is NPO for > 72 hours, even though the occurrence would be unusual for the case type.

Fifth is activity. *Dining room for meals* and *dressing with assist in street clothes following precautions* are standard interventions on SNU CCPs because at this level of the continuum patients are encouraged to dress in street clothes and eat meals in the dining room. The philosophy is governed in part by HCFA regulations

and the need for patients to increase participation in activities of daily living in order to build strength and endurance in preparation for dismissal to home. *Bathing with assist for LE* notifies the staff nurse that certain restrictions apply to flexion of the hip to prevent dislocation. In this section, the interventions progress from *Amb with walker to bathroom* on day one to *amb to dining room with walker* on day three. Specific information about the patient's ADL self-performance would be found on the OPRMC SNU Patient Care Flow Sheet (see Exhibit 20–4) where the ADL self-performance scale from the RAI has been incorporated into the daily documentation system.

Sixth is teaching. *SS/NSG: Discuss pt rights obtain signed verification from patient/family* indicates that social services or nursing will review the patient rights and obtain a signature. Again, the entry is dictated by HCFA standards. *Review THR precautions, drsg chg/TED application* document the patient education that is completed by the staff nurse. *Review CCP/goals* provides a mechanism to meet both a HCFA and Joint Commission standard that the patient be involved in the plan of care.

Seventh is discharge planning. *Assess home situation, family support, and discharge plans etc.* provides the structure for social services to document that discharge planning begins on the day of admission. The details of the assessment are documented in the social services assessment.

In conclusion, the seven categories provide a standard structure for the activities or interventions that are required to achieve the goals for the patient. Both the goals and interventions are manipulated by the CQI team to improve quality and decrease cost. The challenge is to assign costs (resources expended) to each of the interventions or activities on the CCP. When the costs have been assigned to the interventions and activities, the pathway structure forms the framework for activity-based costing.

Finally, in the fourth step the team reviews the pathway with the health care providers for final approval before implementation. Input

Exhibit 20–5 Graphic Flow Sheet

DATE		
TIME		

TEMPERATURE (vertical label)

Temperature scale: 103° 102° 101° 100° 99° 98° 97° 96°

Time columns (repeated): 0800 1200 1600 2000 2400 0400

| Pulse | |
| Respiration | |

Blood Pressure	0800
	1200
	1600
	2000
	2400
	0400

| WEIGHT | |
| Type of Scale | |

Signature 0700 - 1500	
1500 - 2300	
2300 - 0700	

24 Hour Respiratory Assessment

Time / Resp	Time / Resp	Time / Resp	Time / Resp	Time / Resp	Time / Resp	Time / Resp	Time / Resp

ADDRESSOGRAPH

Courtesy of Columbia Overland Park Regional Medical Center, Overland Park, Kansas.

from the care providers is used to modify the final pathway. During the implementation, care providers must remember that the pathway is only an outline for the delivery of patient care. Therefore, the pathway cannot be followed exactly. Pathways for patients with coexistent diagnoses and/or severe functional limitations will require point of care modification and variance documentation (see Exhibit 20–3). Although the SNU THR CCP addresses goals and interventions for that case type, additional problem-oriented CCPs are supplemented to address additional problems, such as incontinence or psychotropic drug use (Exhibits 20–6 and 20–7).

The CQI teams convene on an ongoing basis to review variances from the CCP that include goals and interventions that are not met. Additionally, case types are identified as a new program is implemented. For example, the team has developed and implemented the following CCPs: Generic, Total Knee Replacement, Pneumonia, Chronic Obstructive Pulmonary Disease, Wound Care Stage III or IV, and Terminal Care. During the 1997 annual survey by the Kansas Department of Health and Environment, the surveyors identified a new high-volume patient population. As a result, the team implemented a previously developed CCP for the Removal of Infected Total Knee Replacement. Performance improvement data is also used by the team to improve performance by altering the CCP.

ABC METHODOLOGY: ASSIGNMENT OF COSTS TO INTERVENTIONS OR ACTIVITIES

When an activity or intervention is formatted into the pathway by the SNU Interdisciplinary CCP Team, the process does not end. The resources across all disciplines and departments must be associated with that activity. Each activity is classified into primary, secondary, or support categories. When a nurse administers an oral analgesic to the THR patient, that activity is classified as a primary activity because it is implemented at the point of care.

A secondary activity occurs when the nurse initials the intervention on the pathway and documents on the medication administration record indicating that the medication was administered. However, a support activity occurred prior to the administration of the medication at the point of care when the pharmacist dispensed the analgesic to the nurse. Manipulation of these activities directly affects both the cost and quality of the activity. The allocation of resources to implement the activity and the education of the staff to utilize the resource are key factors.

One of the best examples of the manipulation of activities occurred as the Pneumonia CQI Team analyzed data from chart audits that included the time between the patient's admission to the emergency department (ED) and the first dose of intravenous (IV) antibiotics. The team discovered that LOS increased proportionately with the wait time for the first dose of IV antibiotics. How did the Pneumonia CQI Team intervene? The team decided that the resources for administering the initial dose of IV antibiotics were located in the ED. The entry of the pathway in the ED was revised to communicate that IV antibiotic administration was planned for the first hour. The pulmonologist on the team communicated the data to the ED physicians who agreed to expedite ordering the IV antibiotic. When the team discovered that IV antibiotic administration was delayed due to wait times for the pharmacy to dispense the antibiotic, the pharmacist intervened and changed the process.

Now, when a patient is diagnosed in the ED with pneumonia, the physician writes the IV antibiotic order that is processed on a special requisition and delivered to the pharmacy (support activity). Once dispensed, the nurse administers the IV antibiotic to the patient in the ED (primary activity), and documents on the pathway that the intervention was a completed (secondary activity). By changing the process of resource allocation and using data to educate the staff, the Pneumonia CQI Team has been instrumental in reducing the LOS for the pneumonia

Exhibit 20-6 Skilled Nursing Unit Incontinence—Skin Care Collaborative Care Path

COLLABORATIVE CARE PATH
Case Type: Incontinence - Skin Care
DRG#
Expected LOS
Key: Initials = Met; U = Unmet - - -> continued

ADDRESSOGRAPH

COLUMBIA OVERLAND PARK
REGIONAL MEDICAL CENTER

Problem List and Goals	Day/Hour/Visit Day #	Day #	Day #	Day #
Potential for skin breakdown R/T incontinence	Verbalizes understanding of planned interventions			
	Demonstrates no evidence of skin breakdown			
	Braden Scale Score _____			
	Assess hx of incont./use of incon. products			
TREATMENTS	Toilet q 2 - 3 hours for bladder incontinence (up to commode or toilet if appropriate)			
	240cc q 2 hrs. po if not on restriction	- - ->	- - ->	- - ->
	Cleanse c Nursing Care Cleanser & apply Nursing Care Moisture Barrier p each episode	- - ->	- - ->	- - ->
	Assess Perineal Skin for:	Assess Perineal Skin for:	Assess Perineal Skin for:	Assess Perineal Skin for:
	Erythema + -	Erythema + -	Erythema + -	Erythema + -
	Rash + -	Rash + -	Rash + -	Rash + -
	Pruritis + -	Pruritis + -	Pruritis + -	Pruritis + -
	Pain + -	Pain + -	Pain + -	Pain + -
	If redness is present apply Extra Protective Barrier p each episode of incontinence in place of moisture barrier	If redness is present apply Extra Protective Barrier p each episode of incontinence in place of moisture barrier	If redness is present apply Extra Protective Barrier p each episode of incontinence in place of moisture barrier	If redness is present apply Extra Protective Barrier p each episode of incontinence in place of moisture barrier
	Incontinence products, ie. Attends, fecal incon. bags, etc.			
	Establish bowel program if indicated:			
	a. Use of suppository/meds	- - ->	- - ->	- - ->
	b. Digital stimulation used to induce reflex contraction of the colon, resulting in elimination	- - ->	- - ->	- - ->
	Record frequency of bowel movements	- - ->	- - ->	- - ->
DIET	Incorporate fiber and bulk, increased fluids	- - ->	- - ->	- - ->
ACTIVITY	Chair for meals	- - ->	- - ->	- - ->
TEACHING	Discussed planned interventions			
	Instruct pt/family in turning techniques	Reinforce teaching	- - ->	- - ->
	Give urinary incontinence pamphlet	Review urinary incont. pamphlet	- - ->	- - ->
	Dietary instruction as appropriate			

incon. (12/23/96)

Courtesy of Columbia Overland Park Regional Medical Center, Overland Park, Kansas.

Exhibit 20–7 Skilled Nursing Unit Psychotropic Drug Collaborative Care Path

ADDRESSOGRAPH	COLLABORATIVE CARE PATH Case Type: Psychotropic Drug Protocol Expected LOS: Developed by Skilled Nursing Unit Key: Nurse's Initials = Met U = Unmet - - -> Continued			COLUMBIA OVERLAND PARK REGIONAL MEDICAL CENTER
Day/Hour/Vl	1	2	3	4
Team Problem List	Intermediate Goals			
Alteration in psychosocial behavior R/T	Pt/family verbalize understanding of treatment plan	Pt demonstrates improvement in psychosocial behavior	- - ->	- - ->
1. Depression	Pt demonstrates inadequate response with alternative interventions			
2. Sleep pattern disturbance	No side effects of drug noted	- - ->	- - ->	- - ->
3. Anxiety				
COLLABORATIVE / ASSESSMENT	Assess response to alternative interventions: Music Backrubs Food or drink Family involvement Verbalization	- - ->	Evaluate response to medication q 3 days, focus on possibility of decreasing or discontinuing drug	- - ->
TREATMENTS	Monitor for side effects of psychotropic drugs	- - ->	- - ->	- - ->
CARE / MEDICATIONS	Psychotropic drugs as ordered	- - ->	- - ->	- - ->
PATH / TEACHING	Review side effects to report Check that drug cards were received while on the acute unit	Reinforce teaching on side effects to report	- - ->	- - ->

SNUDRUG 10/9/95

Courtesy of Columbia Overland Park Regional Medical Center, Overland Park, Kansas.

patient. Reducing the LOS decreases both the direct and indirect costs for the pneumonia patient.

DOCUMENTATION

When the pneumonia patient is dismissed from the ED and admitted to acute care, the staff nurse who is coordinating the patient's care initiates the acute care Pneumonia CCP. Both the goals and interventions for the pneumonia patient build on the ED pneumonia pathway. The pathway provides a mechanism for the acute care staff nurse to communicate with the ED staff nurse to ensure that resources are not duplicated or omitted.

Whereas the pathway documents compliance with the plan of care and progress toward goals, flow sheets are used to document normal assessment findings such as *lungs clear bilaterally, routine patient care IV site checks,* and the repetitive monitoring parameters of *intake and output*. A narrative entry on a variance note is required for abnormal assessment findings, *statim* (Stat) treatments and patient responses, and situations not listed on the pathway.

The variance notes are formatted in problem, intervention, and evaluation (PIE). Variance notes are categorized by patient and/or family, caregiver and/or clinician, hospital, and community, with subcategories for each. Categorizing the variances in the pathway or plan of care allows the CQI team to analyze data systematically. The data is used to continuously evaluate

and improve the pathway. The pathway guides the staff nurse who is coordinating the care of the pneumonia patient to evaluate the patient for skilled nursing and communicate that evaluation to the interdisciplinary team, including the physician. In summary, variances from the pathway are documented by the staff nurse and analyzed by the CQI team. The activities on the pathway are manipulated to decrease LOS and costs.

ANALYSIS OF VARIANCES

When a patient moves through the continuum of care to the skilled nursing unit, analysis of variances is expanded. State and federal regulations on the skilled nursing unit require weekly interdisciplinary team meetings (Exhibit 20–8). The day prior to the team meeting, the clinical nurse specialist selects those patients with variances for analysis in the interdisciplinary team meeting. The patient and family are invited to attend the interdisciplinary team meeting where one team member presents the patients' variances. The interdisciplinary team members, which include the medical director of the skilled nursing unit, collaborate with the patient and family to plan interventions that are specific to the variances and assign accountability for implementation of the interventions. By focusing on only the variances from the pathway and assigning accountability for interventions, variances are decreased or eliminated. Ultimately, quality improves and costs decrease.

Exhibit 20–8 Skilled Nursing Unit Interdisciplinary Team Meeting Record

OVERLAND PARK REGIONAL MEDICAL CENTER
SKILLED NURSING UNIT
INTERDISCIPLINARY TEAM MEETING RECORD
DATE _____

SNU DAY #_____MDS+DUE_____ESTIMATED LOS _____

DIAGNOSIS/PAST MED. HX. _____

_____

SKILLED SERVICE(S) _____

_____

PREVIOUS FUNCTIONAL/HOME STATUS _____

_____

CCP_____CCP SUPPLEMENTS _____

_____

VARIANCE	INTERVENTION(S)	ACCOUNTABILITY

RESTRAINTS	MEDICAL REASON	ALTERNATIVES	PATIENT/FAMILY INPUT/CONSENT
PHYSICAL RESTRAINT YES__ NO__			
CHEMICAL RESTRAINTS YES__ NO__			
PRESSURE ULCER YES__ NO__			

BLADDER	MEDICAL REASON	URINARY HX	ALTERNATIVES
FOLEY CATH YES__ NO__ Insertion Date_____		Check all applicable: RETENTION__ INCONTINENCE__ FREQUENCY__	

PLAN OF CARE REVIEWED WITH PATIENT/FAMILY: YES___ NO___IF NO, WHY_____

_____

continues

Exhibit 20–8 continued

PATIENT/FAMILY CONCERN	INTERVENTION(S)	ACCOUNTABILITY

GOAL _____

_____

_____

DISCHARGE PLAN/HOME HEALTH/DME NEEDS_____

_____

_____

NAME-INTERDISCIPLINARY TEAM MEMBER	DISCIPLINE

PATIENT/FAMILY/SIGNIFICANT OTHER NAME	RELATIONSHIP TO PATIENT

Courtesy of Columbia Overland Park Regional Medical Center, Overland Park, Kansas.

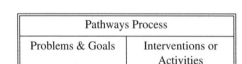

Figure 20–5 Pathways Process

COMMENTARY

The care path is a process. If the care path is utilized to structure an activity-based costing approach, then the ABC methodology is approached from a process view. In this case, the pathways process is set out in two major parts: (1) problems and goals and (2) interventions. The interventions can be broken out into activities (Figure 20–5). Note that any activity analysis that is conducted would be first dictated by the basic structure established through the care path itself.

Of particular note in this case study is the integration of information among various levels and types of service that is delivered. For example, the information flow about the patient moves from the initial contact in the emergency room to acute care and on to the skilled nursing unit. One of the purposes of a collaborative care path is to create seamless patient or resident

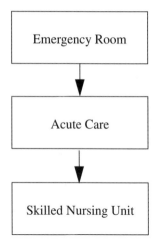

Figure 20–6 Information Flow

---

care. In this case, the information flow also seems to move in that direction (Figure 20–6).

Structural choices for ABC become simplified with the creation of care paths. Months of effort by many individuals on an interdisciplinary team are necessary in order to create the initial care paths. The effort accomplishes a dual purpose. It produces the clinical pathway on the one hand, and it also provides the process framework from which the costs can be attached in accordance with activity-based costing methodology.

NOTES

1. P. Madigan and S. Adams, *The Newsletter of National Subacute Care Association* 1, no. 2 (1995): 1–8.

2. Madigan and Adams, *The Newsletter.*

BIBLIOGRAPHY

Abbott, J. "Making the Commitment to Managed Care." *Nursing Management* 24, no. 8 (1993): 36–37.

Abbott, J. "How to Avoid Common Pitfalls in Implementing Case Management." *Hospital Case Management* (May 1993): 94–95.

Aiken, M. "Collaborative Care in the Acute Care Setting." *The Kansas Nurse* 68, no. 3 (1993): 10–11.

Beyers, M. "The Consequences of Change." *Nursing Management* 26, no. 5 (1995): 22.

Cohen, E.L. "Nursing Case Management: Does It Pay?" *Journal of Nursing Administration* 21, no. 4 (1991): 20–25.

Dienemann, J., and T. Gessner. "Restructuring Nursing Care Delivery Systems." *Nursing Economics* 10, no. 4 (1992): 253–258.

Fogel, L.A., and K. Gossman-Klim. "Getting Started with Subacute Care." *Healthcare Financial Management* (October 1995): 64–77.

Giuliano, K.K., and C.E. Poirier. "Nursing Case Management: Critical Pathways to Desirable Outcomes." *Nursing Management* 22, no. 3 (1991): 52–55.

Hicks, L., J.M. Stallmeyer, and J.R. Coleman. "Nursing Challenges in Managed Care." *Nursing Economics* 10, no. 4 (1992): 265–276.

Hronek, C. "Implementing Collaborative Care." *Main Dimensions* 4, no. 7 (1993): 1–4.

Kothmann, W.L. "Is Subacute Feasible?" *Healthcare Financial Management* (October 1995): 60–63.

Madigan, P., and S. Adams. *The Newsletter of National Subacute Care Association* 1, no. 2 (1995): 1–8.

McCabe, J.P. "Managing Financial Pressures with Subacute Care." *Healthcare Financial Management* (October 1995): 88–91.

Schaffer, C. "Moving Toward National Integration." *Continuing Care* (September 1995): 17–18.

Stahl, D.A. "Critical Pathways in Subacute Care." *Nursing Management* 26, no. 9 (1995): 16–18.

Stahl, D.A. "Phases of Managed Care: Where Does Subacute Care Fit?" *Nursing Management* 26, no. 5 (1995): 16–17.

Staff. "Congress Looking at Cutting Payments to Subacute Care Providers." *NSCA News* 1, no. 2 (September 1995): 1, 6.

Staff. "Study Claims Inpatient Days Could Drop by One-Third." *NSCA News* 1, no. 2 (September 1995): 5.

## CHAPTER 21

Community-Based Care—Carving out the Costs in a New York State School-Based Health Center: A Case Study

Patricia Hinton Walker, Judith J. Baker, Patricia Chiverton,
Nancy M. Bowllan, Nancy H. Chevalier, and Lorraine Lawrence

CHAPTER OUTLINE

PREFACE

This case study introduces a community-based care example. In this case it is a grant-funded, school-based health center, providing both primary care and mental health care. This project is of particular interest because very little has been done to date about isolating the costs of community-based care. When this project was funded, one of the expectations of the New York State (NYS) grant was that the center would begin to determine the costs of care in order to eventually assume the risk of providing care under a capitated rate. The activity-based costing potential takes on additional importance due to these future capitation expectations.

Another area of interest in this case is the calculation of activity-based costs related to undercapacity. The school-based health program had just completed its first year of operation, and management devised their calculation of the program undercapacity burden during the course of the ABC project.

INTRODUCTION

Changes in the health care delivery system due to health reform and market forces have placed increased emphasis on prevention, outcomes (cost and quality), population-based care, and access to care for underserved populations. New models of health care delivery that are designed to improve the health status of communities are receiving increased interest, and one of these models is the school-based health center (SBHC). School-based health centers are a community-level health intervention strategy that targets specific student populations such as children and adolescents. The goal of this relatively new model of care is to reduce health risks, identify problems, and provide primary health care, all of which is consistent with the broad health goals articulated in *Healthy People 2000*.[1]

School-based health centers provide excellent opportunities for primary prevention (nutrition counseling, surveillance, and health promotion) to alter risk-taking behaviors. Secondary prevention interventions for early detection of sexually transmitted disease, teen pregnancy, and screening for disease are also part of these centers.[2] In the past decade, school-based care has expanded rapidly from 31 school-based care sites in 1984 to 327 in 1991. By 1992, 415 school-based and 95 school-linked centers were identified.[3] This expansion has increased access to health care services and has the potential to reduce risk in elementary schools, junior high schools, and high schools. With increasing risks for the adolescent population, SBHCs can be an investment in our future because they have the potential to reduce risk and address costly health problems that have long-term negative impact on the health and well-being of individuals, families, and communities. There is a need, however, to identify the unique role and cost implications of school-based care in a changing health care environment. Schools are rapidly becoming primary care practice sites, staffed by advance practice nurses.[4] Nurse practitioners in many states staff these SBHC sites. In some states, nurse practitioners have prescriptive privileges and also receive third-party reimbursement for services. Charges and reimbursement, however, do not tell us the nature and type of services that are delivered, nor is charge data necessarily indicative of actual costs. There is clearly a need to demonstrate the effectiveness of new models of community-based care such as school-based health centers; however, the most significant challenge is to determine costs of care.

BACKGROUND AND DEVELOPMENT OF COALITIONS

As health care costs continued to rise significantly in the 1980s, one of the ways that businesses and employers tried to control costs was through the development of coalitions. Coalitions may develop for many different reasons. The major reason usually is that one organization does not have all the required resources, skills, knowledge, and expertise to produce a particular product.[5] Such is the case of an SBHC affiliated with the University of Rochester School of Nursing Community Nursing Center, which is the site used for measuring costs of community-based care in this chapter. The development of both business and volunteer (community agency) coalitions were necessary to the success and funding of this school-based care site. These coalitions and partnerships are described below.

The Community Nursing Center (CNC) in the University of Rochester School of Nursing was created to implement faculty practice of advance practice nurses (nurse practitioners and psychiatric-mental health practitioners) in community-based settings. Over the last seven years (from 1990 to 1997), the CNC has developed a number of partnerships and/or business coalitions for the purpose of delivering new models of community-based care. A variety of services were and are provided by advanced practice nurses in urban and rural settings, including practices in rural community hospitals, a rural hospital consortium, group homes for troubled teens, primary care offices, county health departments, and a rural county jail.[6] Because of the CNC faculty's commitment to true community partnerships for practice, the CNC submitted a grant to New York State in 1994 to obtain funding for a school-based health center.

A major requirement for proposals and subsequent success in obtaining funding from the New York State Department of Health was the development of a coalition among businesses, providers, and community agencies such as the county health department, which traditionally provided selected school health services; the city school system; a hospital (for 24-hour care and hospitalizations); physician providers for referral and consultation with advanced practice nurses; and the local school where the school-based health center would actually be housed. Of course, the school partnerships included participation of parents, teachers, students, and administrators.

The particular SBHC used in the chapter as a site for the implementation of activity-based costing was developed by the CNC of the University of Rochester School of Nursing in concert with the Rochester City School System, the Monroe County Health Department, the University of Rochester School of Medicine, and Strong Memorial Hospital in Rochester, New York. Ongoing advisory committees, memorandum of agreement, and contracts provide the links among the businesses, providers, and community agencies involved in this project (Figure 21–1). This SBHC was initially funded by a New York State Department of Health grant and continues to be funded at the time of this writing; however, the practices are still being developed, so the SBHC site is not func-

tioning at full capacity. At this time, the continued costs related to the development of projects such as these with business and coalitions are somewhat buried in the nonappointment time of the on-site providers and indirect costs. However, the authors have taken these costs into consideration, and they have been included in the undercapacity burden calculations that will be explained later in this chapter.

CHALLENGE OF DEFINING COSTS

With the shift from hospital to community-based care, the identification of true costs of care in community-based practices has been a challenge. This is particularly true of new models of care that involve preventive care as well as primary care in nontraditional sites such as school-based health centers. There is no history in the literature of attempts to assign costs or describe specific activities of the providers in

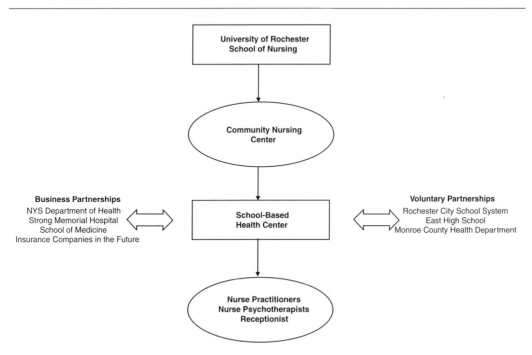

Figure 21–1 Organization Chart Reflection of Community Partnerships/Coalitions. *Source:* Copyright © Patricia Hinton Walker, Ph.D., F.A.A.N.

school-based health center practices—particularly those that provide mental health services as well as primary care services. Because the current reimbursement structure is essentially built on medical care related to illness, there is very little data on well populations, such as adolescents. Also, frequently, adolescents seek care in settings outside the traditional pediatrician's practice because of confidentiality issues, and there has been little data generated about the health seeking behaviors of adolescents and the patterns of interventions needed by this population.

The motivation for this application of activity-based costing and this chapter came from the need to estimate costs of care in a future capitated system of care for Medicaid populations in New York State. One of the expectations related to the NYS grant was that providers would begin to determine the costs of care in order to eventually assume the risk of providing care for the population under a capitated rate. The potential of this plan increased the need and value of determining actual costs of care by using activity-based costing methodology in order to develop future contracts for care for this adolescent population in a SBHC.

DESIGN OF THE STUDY

A pilot study was designed by the project director of the grant (Patricia Hinton Walker, PhD, RN, FAAN) and the grant consultant (Judith J. Baker, PhD, CPA) to assist CNC administrators and faculty in determining actual costs of this model of community-based care. Activity-based costing methodology was used in this setting to determine the on-site and indirect costs of providing care in this SBHC setting. The SBHC was used as the pilot project; however, this methodology and the process of determining costs can also be used in the future to identify the provider activities, types of services, and costs of care for other community-based sites offering interdisciplinary care with the advanced practice nurses on the front end of care.

The nine steps of this activity-based costing study were:

1. preliminary review of the billing and encounter records for types and patterns of care
2. estimation of resources consumed by the practitioners and receptionist in SBHC care
3. creation of activity categories and activity mapping
4. design of the data collection forms and procedures
5. administration of the time study
6. costing the activities
7. identification and application of activity drivers
8. consideration of the costs of building community partnerships in a new practice
9. calculation of and reporting the results

For the purposes of this pilot study, we adapted the three components of the model for activity-based costing. Instead of using the term primary costs, we used the term client-focused costs, because one of the types of service was primary care, and we did not want to confuse the two similar terms. Consequently, the three components as depicted in Figure 21–2 are (1) client-focused costs—face-to-face activities with the client (student) by the provider and receptionist in the health care encounter; (2) secondary costs—activities that support the direct care, such as charting, recording, and preparation time for the provider and data entry, scheduling, and client-oriented telephone time for the receptionist; and (3) administrative costs—activities such as billing, collections, financial and data management, and costs related to administration.

Preliminary review of the billing and encounter records related to 30 patients (totaling 267 encounters) allowed identification of patterns of care; estimations of time of encounters along with the different types of services provided (primary care and mental health care); and resources consumed during the provision of care according to the activity-based care model.

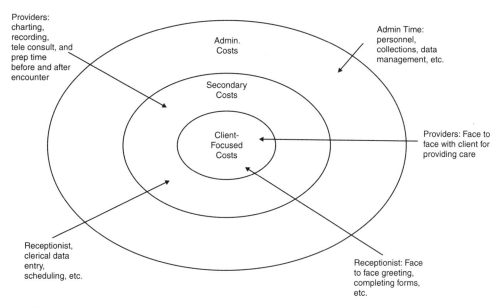

Figure 21–2 Model for Activity-Based Costing Methodology. *Source:* Copyright © 1996, Patricia Hinton Walker, Ph.D., and Judith J. Baker, Ph.D.

Within each type of service, different levels of care were identified, including initial visits, brief visits for lab tests, follow-up visits, and extended mental health counseling visits. The mean encounter time for primary care visits based on estimations from the billing and encounter forms was 20.8 minutes. The mean encounter time for mental health visits was estimated at 33.7 minutes based on review of the billing records and encounter forms (see Exhibit 21–1). Estimates of resources used were then considered. For the purposes of this preliminary analysis, the primary source of costs that were related to client-focused costs were the mean salary and benefits of the practitioners. Primary care was costed out separately from mental health services. Additionally, it was estimated that 70 percent of the receptionist's time was client-focused care, and administrative time (means of salaries and benefits) were limited by NYS grant to no more than 10 percent. Based on the mean salary of practitioners and fringe benefits (without consideration of the costs of supplies, other secretarial services, and the cost

of billing services), the cost per primary care services for this preliminary group was $8,359.20 with a potential estimated cost of $60.57 per encounter. Based on similar estimates of resources used for mental health services using mean salary of practitioners and fringe benefits, the total cost for mental health services was $6,851.35, with a potential estimated cost per encounter of $53.10. This preliminary analysis helped provide the framework for the design of the activity-based costing pilot study used to carve out the costs of community-based care in the school-based health center.

CREATING ACTIVITY CATEGORIES

The next step for the consultant and the project director of the grant was to create the activity categories and map the activities of care. Included in the activity mapping were duties and functions of the receptionist/clerk such as enrollment of students, data entry, and clerical functions related to visits charts and billing; activities of the practitioners related to

Exhibit 21–1 Total Cost per Encounter*

Levels of Care	# Min Encounter	# Min Encounter	Mean Cost/ Man-Hour	Client- Focused Cost	Second/ Support Costs	Admin % Distributed	Total Costs
Primary Care							
Initial Visit	30.0	15	23.28	174.60	1992.77	25.7	2167.37
Lab Visit	5.0	70	23.28	135.02	1543.46	19.9	1678.49
Pre Visit	13.0	30	23.28	151.32	1656.89	22.3	1808.21
Brief follow-up	20.5	17	23.28	135.02	1534.15	19.8	1669.18
Intermediate	35.5	6	23.28	83.81	952.15	12.3	1035.96
Subtotal		138		679.78	7679.43		8359.20
Psych Care							
Initial Visit	45.0	46	28.37	978.77	1940.51	42.6	2919.27
Psy/Sol	15.0	6	28.37	42.56	87.95	1.9	130.50
Brief Visit	20.5	21	28.37	204.26	405.69	8.9	609.96
In Therapy	35.5	40	28.37	672.37	1336.23	29.3	2008.60
Ext Therapy	52.5	16	28.37	397.18	785.85	17.3	1183.03
Subtotal		129		2295.13	4556.22		6851.36

*Note: All financial data (dollars) reflected in the document and in spreadsheet exhibits are not actual figures, but have been altered for confidentiality reasons.

Source: Copyright © 1996, Patricia Hinton Walker, Ph.D., and Judith J. Baker, Ph.D.

building and maintaining community partnerships, school advisory committee functions, and marketing; and activities related to the types of services provided (primary care and mental health).

Examples of the type of care provided include "primary care, preventive services including human immunodeficiency virus (HIV) testing, pregnancy testing, anticipatory guidance, symptom management and treatment of common recurring problems of the adolescent"[7] in addition to sports physicals, annual physicals, and employment examinations. Psychiatric-mental health services include "psychosocial assessment, mental status assessment and individual, group and family counseling when appropriate and feasible."[8]

To better understand and map the activities within the services provided and the duties of

the receptionist, a workshop/orientation to activity-based costing was held with all the practitioners and staff within the school-based health center. The outcome of this workshop would be the development of the data collection instruments that would be used to collect data for the time studies. These time study instruments would allow the consultant and project director to determine the costs of the three components of activity-based costing mentioned previously—client-focused costs, secondary costs, and administrative costs. At this workshop, the consultant and project director facilitated the discussion of the specific activities of the primary care practitioners, the mental health practitioners, the receptionist, and of the administrative function of the SBHC.

The workshop was held informally with activities written on a flip chart as the practitioners and receptionist walked through the daily activities that were involved in providing both primary care and mental health services. The practitioners were asked to identify detailed activities that were performed immediately before the face-to-face encounter, during the encounter, and immediately after the face-to-face encounter as part of the routine encounter. This information, gathered in the workshop, was then collapsed somewhat, categorized, and developed into an instrument to be used in time study. The outcome would be the before-during-after-appointment data collection instruments used for primary care and mental health encounters (see Exhibit 21–2 for the primary care form).

Because the consultant and project director recognized that case management activities are a significant component of any community-based practice, the forms were designed to identify and cost out this particular function as a service component in the future. This component of care, however, would be collected on the subsequent to appointment form (see Exhibit 21–3), which was designed to track and measure supplemental activities related to the encounter but not necessarily accomplished on the same day as the encounter.

After the activities related to primary care and a mental health encounter were identified and categorized, the consultant and project director facilitated a discussion of the supplemental activities related to the encounter, such as telephone calls to the primary care physician, the family, the teachers, and other activities related to specific encounters that occurred when the practitioners were not scheduled for an appointment or walk-in with a student in the SBHC. Also, follow-up care and other documentation related to a specific encounter was relevant. The outcome of this discussion was the development of the subsequent to appointment for data collection related to the encounter (Exhibit 21–3).

Next, the practitioners were led through the activities that occurred during the day that were not related to a specific encounter, but were part of the usual work day and were required to keep the SBHC functioning smoothly. Activities included in this discussion were administrative and staff meetings, routine meetings with the physician consultants, marketing and enrollment tasks, on-site collaboration with the county health department staff, and advisory committee meetings or other meetings with school personnel. Personal time such as lunch, restroom time, and personal telephone time were also included in this category of time. The outcome of this discussion is reflected in the form designed for nonappointment related activities (Exhibit 21–4).

A summary form was developed that facilitated accounting of the total minutes of activities for the day (Exhibit 21–5). Staff were instructed that the numbers of minutes and hours on all of the other forms were to equal the total number of minutes on the summary form.

As mentioned previously, four sets of forms were developed for the primary care practitioner and the mental health practitioner that included appointment-related activities (Before-During-After Appointment), supplemental activities (Subsequent to Appointment), and nonappointment activities (Nonappointment Related Activities). The primary care practitioner forms have been previously presented as Exhibits 21–2, 21–3, 21–4, and 21–5.

The mental health practitioner forms are set forth as follows: Exhibit 21–6 is for the mental health appointment related activities; Exhibit 21–7 is for the supplemental activities; Exhibit 21–8 is for the nonappointment activities; and Exhibit 21–9 is the time summary for the mental health practitioner.

The receptionist was also interviewed during the workshop and her activities (including face-to-face time with patients) were also identified, collapsed, and categorized. Subsequently data collection instruments were designed for her based on this input. In addition to the set of four forms previously described, an additional form for enrollment activities was designed for the receptionist to use. The receptionist forms are set forth as Exhibits 21–10, 21–11, 21–12, 21–13, and 21–14.

The interrelationship of the various data collection instrument sets is detailed in Exhibit 21–15.

ADMINISTERING THE TIME STUDY

After the data collection forms were developed based on the workshop with the practitioners and receptionist, these forms were printed on different colors of paper to assist staff, the consultant, and project director to review and enter the data correctly without confusion. The first step was to test the instruments for two days, then review any questions or confusion about where to place certain activities with the on-site administrator. The practitioners and receptionist tested the data collection instruments and then decisions were made regarding where certain information would be placed on the forms during the time study. Most of the questions and decisions pertained to the use of the supplemental to appointment form and the nonappointment related forms.

A self-reported time study method was selected. For a determined period of time (3 weeks or 15 days), all personnel in the SBHC would complete all the forms and the summary form for each day. Staff were encouraged to complete the form as soon as possible after the experience occurred and before the amount of time spent would be forgotten or distorted by memory. The completion of these forms was particularly difficult for the staff because of the busy work environment and practice. Additionally, it is a relatively uncontrolled environment with students walking in for care without an appointment as well as having scheduled appointments.

COSTING THE ACTIVITIES

After the data was collected, it was entered into Microsoft Access for each practitioner and for each activity. Subsequently, the data was placed into an Excel spreadsheet and the means of the activities before, during, and after the encounter were calculated. These means are reflected on Exhibit 21–16.

The mean minutes for the category during the encounter, which equaled client-focused costs, was 39.61 minutes for practitioner A (the nurse psychotherapist). The mean times in minutes for practitioner A for immediately before and after the encounter, which equaled secondary costs, were 5.31 minutes and 10.24 minutes, respectively. Subsequent appointment mean time in minutes, which also contribute to secondary costs, was 16.57 minutes. The mean time for nonappointment related activities, which equaled part of the administrative costs, was 173.67 minutes. Because the SBHC practice is still developing and building, an undercapacity burden calculation was used later in the costing process to more appropriately calculate the actual contribution to the costs of nonappointment related time to the cost of encounters. Based only on salary and fringe benefit costs of the practitioner, the total costs were $98.54. (This figure does not reflect other administrative costs that are derived from indirect costs and from costs brought forth from the receptionist's time that contribute to the cost of an encounter and the total costs of care.)

The mean minutes for the category during the encounter, which equaled client-focused costs for practitioners B and C (pediatric nurse practitioners responsible for primary care), were 15.97 minutes and 15.87 minutes, respectively. (These means are also reflected on the spreadsheet presented as Exhibit 21–16.) The mean times in minutes for practitioners B and C for immediately before and after the visit, which equaled secondary costs, are 1.03 and 3.40 minutes (before) and 8.40 and 7.32 minutes (after). Subsequent appointment mean times in minutes, which also contribute to secondary costs, were 5.40 and 6.64 minutes, respectively. The mean times for nonappointment related activities, which are part of the administrative costs, were 165.17 and 173.33 minutes. As mentioned previously, because the SBHC practice is still developing and building, an undercapacity burden calculation was used later in the costing

Exhibit 21–2 Primary Care Data Collection Instrument: Before-During-After Appointment

APPOINTMENT SUPPLEMENTAL SHEET—PRIMARY CARE   Page No._____

Your Name_____ Today's Date_____

Student Name_____ ID# _____

Enrolled? __Yes __No   Initial Appointment? __Yes __No

No. Minutes

BEFORE

Assemble medical supplies   _____

Set up test equipment/material   _____

Review chart from last visit (if applicable)   _____

DURING

Acute treatment_____   _____

Counseling_____   _____

Interview/Assessment/Anticipatory Guidance   _____

Diagnosis/problem identification OR follow-up prior diagnosis/problem   _____

Physical examination   _____

STD complaints -TX   _____

Pregnancy test   _____

HIV test   _____

Vaccination   _____

Other_____   _____

AFTER

Disassemble test equipment   _____

Clean up room, equipment   _____

Charting   _____

Scheduling of next appointment   _____

Consult w/psych-mental health practitioner as needed   _____

Total Minutes (carry forward to Summary Sheet)   _____

Source: Copyright © 1997, Judith J. Baker, Ph.D. and Patricia Hinton Walker, Ph.D.

Exhibit 21–3 Primary Care Data Collection Instrument: Subsequent to Appointment

---

SUBSEQUENT PRIMARY CARE APPOINTMENT ACTIVITIES

Your Name_____Today's Date_____

(carry right-hand time totals forward to Summary Sheet)

Today's Total Time
(in minutes)

WRITTEN COMMUNICATION W/EXTERNAL PRIMARY CARE PHYSICIAN

Student Name_____   _____

Student Name_____   _____

Student Name_____   _____

Student Name_____   _____

Student Name_____   _____

Student Name_____   _____

Student Name_____   _____   _____

TELEPHONE W/PRIMARY CARE PHYSICIAN/PARENT/ETC. AS NEEDED

Student Name_____   _____

Student Name_____   _____

Student Name_____   _____

Student Name_____   _____

Student Name_____   _____

Student Name_____   _____

Student Name_____   _____   _____

REFERRAL TO EXTERNAL RESOURCES AS NEEDED

Student Name_____   _____

Student Name_____   _____

Student Name_____   _____

Student Name_____   _____

Student Name_____   _____

Student Name_____   _____

Student Name_____   _____   _____

INTERFACE W/HEALTH DEPARTMENT AS NEEDED

Student Name_____   _____

Student Name_____   _____

Student Name_____   _____

Student Name_____   _____

Student Name_____   _____

Student Name_____   _____

Student Name_____   _____   _____

Exhibit 21–4 Primary Care Data Collection Instrument: Nonappointment Related

---

NONAPPOINTMENT ACTIVITIES

Your Name_____ Today's Date _____

Today's Total Time
(in minutes)

ENROLLMENT PROCESS (describe duties performed on lines below)

_____   _____

_____   _____

_____   _____

_____   _____

MARKETING PROCESS (describe duties performed on lines below)

_____   _____

_____   _____

_____   _____

_____   _____

ADMINISTRATIVE PROCESS (describe duties performed on lines below)

_____   _____

_____   _____

_____   _____

_____   _____

CLERICAL PROCESS (describe duties performed on lines below)

_____   _____

_____   _____

_____   _____

_____   _____

OTHER (describe duties performed on lines below)

_____   _____

_____   _____

_____   _____

_____   _____

PERSONAL (describe on lines below)

_____   _____

_____   _____

Total Minutes (carry forward to Summary Sheet)   _____

Source: Copyright © 1997, Judith J. Baker, Ph.D. and Patricia Hinton Walker, Ph.D.

Exhibit 21–5 Primary Care Data Collection Instrument: Summary

---

DAILY PRIMARY CARE TIME SUMMARY

Your Name_____ Today's Date_____

Begin Time_____End Time_____ = Total Time* _____

APPOINTMENT SUMMARY: Today's Total Time
                                                                        (in minutes)

Appointment: (name)_____   (suppl sheet #)_____   =   _____

Appointment: (name)_____   (suppl sheet #)_____   =   _____

Appointment: (name)_____   (suppl sheet #)_____   =   _____

Appointment: (name)_____   (suppl sheet #)_____   =   _____

Appointment: (name)_____   (suppl sheet #)_____   =   _____

Appointment: (name)_____   (suppl sheet #)_____   =   _____

Appointment: (name)_____   (suppl sheet #)_____   =   _____

Appointment: (name)_____   (suppl sheet #)_____   =   _____

SUMMARY OF SUBSEQUENT APPOINTMENT ACTIVITIES
(From SA summary sheet # _____: insert total minutes by line item below)

Written communication w/external primary care physician   =   _____

Telephone w/primary care physician/parent/etc. as needed   =   _____

Referral to external resources as needed   =   _____

Interface w/health department as needed   =   _____

Other   =   _____

SUMMARY OF NONAPPOINTMENT ACTIVITIES

(From NA Summary Sheet # _____ : insert total minutes)   =   _____

                          Total Minutes   _____
(*Note: Total Minutes should equal Total Time at top of this sheet)

Source: Copyright © 1997, Judith J. Baker, Ph.D. and Patricia Hinton Walker, Ph.D.

Exhibit 21–6 Mental Health Data Collection Instrument: Before-During-After Appointment

---

APPOINTMENT SUPPLEMENTAL SHEET—PSYCH/MH

Page No. _____

Your Name_____Today's Date_____

Student Name_____ID# _____

Enrolled? __Yes __No/ Initial Appointment? __Yes __No/ Scheduled? __Yes __No

Crisis? __Yes __No   Immediate Internal Referral? __Yes __No

No. Minutes

BEFORE

Assemble materials   _____

Set up equipment (as needed)   _____

Review chart from last visit (if applicable)   _____

Consult w/primary care practitioner as needed   _____

Locate and assist student to appointment as needed   _____

DURING

Interview/Psychosocial assessment   _____

Establish goals   _____

Contract with student   _____

Identify other resources for liaison   _____

Establish plan of care   _____

Set up plan of care   _____

Other _____   _____

AFTER

Disassemble equipment/materials etc.   _____

Clean up room, equipment   _____

Charting   _____

Scheduling of next appointment   _____

Consult w/primary care practitioner as needed   _____

Total Minutes (carry forward to Summary Sheet)   _____

Source: Copyright © 1997, Judith J. Baker, Ph.D. and Patricia Hinton Walker, Ph.D.

Exhibit 21–7 Mental Health Data Collection Instrument: Subsequent to Appointment

SUBSEQUENT PSYCH/MH APPOINTMENT ACTIVITIES

Your Name_____Today's Date_____

(carry right-hand time totals forward to Summary Sheet)   Today's Total Time (in minutes)

WRITTEN COMMUNICATION W/EXTERNAL PRIMARY CARE PHYSICIAN

Student Name_____   _____

Student Name_____   _____

Student Name_____   _____

Student Name_____   _____

Student Name_____   _____

Student Name_____   _____

Student Name_____   _____   _____

COMMUNICATION WITH EXTERNAL RESOURCES AS NEEDED

Student Name_____   _____

Student Name_____   _____

Student Name_____   _____

Student Name_____   _____

Student Name_____   _____

Student Name_____   _____

Student Name_____   _____   _____

REFERRAL TO EXTERNAL RESOURCES AS NEEDED

Student Name_____   _____

Student Name_____   _____

Student Name_____   _____

Student Name_____   _____

Student Name_____   _____

Student Name_____   _____

Student Name_____   _____   _____

INTERFACE W/HEALTH DEPARTMENT AS NEEDED

Student Name_____   _____

Student Name_____   _____

Student Name_____   _____

Student Name_____   _____

Student Name_____   _____

Student Name_____   _____

Student Name_____   _____   _____

Exhibit 21–8 Mental Health Data Collection Instrument: Nonappointment Related

---

NONAPPOINTMENT ACTIVITIES

Your Name_____Today's Date_____

Today's Total Time
(in minutes)

ENROLLMENT PROCESS (describe duties performed on lines below)

_____   _____

_____   _____

_____   _____

_____   _____

_____   _____

MARKETING PROCESS (describe duties performed on lines below)

_____   _____

_____   _____

_____   _____

_____   _____

_____   _____

ADMINISTRATIVE PROCESS (describe duties performed on lines below)

_____   _____

_____   _____

_____   _____

_____   _____

_____   _____

CLERICAL PROCESS (describe duties performed on lines below)

_____   _____

_____   _____

_____   _____

_____   _____

_____   _____

OTHER (describe duties performed on lines below)

_____   _____

_____   _____

_____   _____

_____   _____

_____   _____

PERSONAL (describe on lines below)

_____   _____

_____   _____

Total Minutes (carry forward to Summary Sheet)   _____

Source: Copyright © 1997, Judith J. Baker, Ph.D. and Patricia Hinton Walker, Ph.D.

Exhibit 21–9 Mental Health Data Collection Instrument: Summary

---

DAILY PSYCH/MH TIME SUMMARY

Your Name_____Today's Date_____

Begin Time_____ End Time_____ = Total Time* _____

Today's Total Time
(in minutes)

APPOINTMENT SUMMARY:

Appointment: (name)_____   (suppl sheet #)_____   =   _____

Appointment: (name)_____   (suppl sheet #)_____   =   _____

Appointment: (name)_____   (suppl sheet #)_____   =   _____

Appointment: (name)_____   (suppl sheet #)_____   =   _____

Appointment: (name)_____   (suppl sheet #)_____   =   _____

Appointment: (name)_____   (suppl sheet #)_____   =   _____

Appointment: (name)_____   (suppl sheet #)_____   =   _____

Appointment: (name)_____   (suppl sheet #)_____   =   _____

SUMMARY OF SUBSEQUENT APPOINTMENT ACTIVITIES
(From SA summary sheet # _____: insert total minutes by line item below)

Written communication w/external primary care physician

Communication w/external resources as needed   =   _____

Referral to external resources as needed   =   _____

Interface w/health department as needed   =   _____

Other   =   _____

SUMMARY OF NONAPPOINTMENT ACTIVITIES
(From NA Summary Sheet # _____ : insert total minutes)   =   _____

       Total Minutes   =   _____

(*Note: Total Minutes should equal Total Time at top of this sheet)

Source: Copyright © 1997, Judith J. Baker, Ph.D. and Patricia Hinton Walker, Ph.D.

Exhibit 21–10 Receptionist Data Collection Instrument: Preparation for Appointment

---

PREPARATION FOR APPOINTMENT—CLERICAL/ADMIN. ACTIVITIES

Your Name_____Today's Date _____

(carry right-hand time totals forward to Summary Sheet)   Today's Total
                                                                 Time (in minutes)

ASSEMBLING FILES/CHARTS IN PREPARATION FOR APPOINTMENT

Student Name_____   _____

Student Name_____   _____

Student Name_____   _____

Student Name_____   _____

Student Name_____   _____

Student Name_____   _____

Student Name_____   _____   _____

GREETING STUDENT UPON ARRIVAL FOR APPOINTMENT

Student Name_____   _____

Student Name_____   _____

Student Name_____   _____

Student Name_____   _____

Student Name_____   _____

Student Name_____   _____

Student Name_____   _____   _____

OTHER (Specify)_____

Student Name_____   _____

Student Name_____   _____

Student Name_____   _____

Student Name_____   _____

Student Name_____   _____

Student Name_____   _____   _____

OTHER (Specify)_____

Student Name_____   _____

Student Name_____   _____

Student Name_____   _____

Student Name_____   _____

Student Name_____   _____

Student Name_____   _____   _____

Exhibit 21–11 Receptionist Data Collection Instrument: Subsequent to Appointment

---

SUBSEQUENT CLERICAL/ADMINISTRATIVE APPOINTMENT ACTIVITIES

Your Name_____Today's Date_____

(carry right-hand time totals forward to Summary Sheet)   Today's Total
                                                                Time
                                                            (in minutes)

WRITTEN COMMUNICATION W/EXTERNAL PRIMARY CARE PHYSICIAN

Student Name_____   _____

Student Name_____   _____

Student Name_____   _____

Student Name_____   _____

Student Name_____   _____

Student Name_____   _____

Student Name_____   _____   _____

SCHEDULING NEXT APPOINTMENT

Student Name_____   _____

Student Name_____   _____

Student Name_____   _____

Student Name_____   _____

Student Name_____   _____

Student Name_____   _____

Student Name_____   _____   _____

OTHER SUBSEQUENT TO APPOINTMENT (Specify)

Student Name_____   _____

Student Name_____   _____

Student Name_____   _____

Student Name_____   _____

Student Name_____   _____

Student Name_____   _____

Student Name_____   _____   _____

OTHER SUBSEQUENT TO APPOINTMENT (Specify)

Student Name_____   _____

Student Name_____   _____

Student Name_____   _____

Student Name_____   _____

Student Name_____   _____

Student Name_____   _____   _____

Source: Copyright © 1997, Judith J. Baker, Ph.D. and Patricia Hinton Walker, Ph.D.

Exhibit 21–12 Receptionist Data Collection Instrument: Nonappointment Related

---

NONAPPOINTMENT/ENROLLMENT ACTIVITIES

Your Name_____Today's Date_____

Today's Total Time
(in minutes)

MARKETING PROCESS (describe duties performed on lines below)

_____   _____
_____   _____
_____   _____
_____   _____
_____   _____

DATA ENTRY (describe duties performed on lines below)

_____   _____
_____   _____
_____   _____
_____   _____
_____   _____

ADMINISTRATIVE PROCESS (describe duties performed on lines below)

_____   _____
_____   _____
_____   _____
_____   _____
_____   _____

CLERICAL PROCESS (describe duties performed on lines below)

_____   _____
_____   _____
_____   _____
_____   _____
_____   _____

OTHER (describe duties performed on lines below)

_____   _____
_____   _____
_____   _____
_____   _____
_____   _____

PERSONAL (describe on lines below)

_____   _____
_____   _____

Total Minutes (carry forward to Summary Sheet)   _____

Source: Copyright © 1997, Judith J. Baker, Ph.D. and Patricia Hinton Walker, Ph.D.

Exhibit 21–13 Receptionist Data Collection Instrument: Enrollment Activities

---

ENROLLMENT ACTIVITIES (NONAPPOINTMENT RELATED)

Your Name_____Today's Date _____

(carry right-hand time totals forward to Summary Sheet)   Today's Total
                                                                 Time (in minutes)

STEP A: _____

Student Name_____   _____

Student Name_____   _____

Student Name_____   _____

Student Name_____   _____

Student Name_____   _____

Student Name_____   _____

Student Name_____   _____   _____

STEP B: _____

Student Name_____   _____

Student Name_____   _____

Student Name_____   _____

Student Name_____   _____

Student Name_____   _____

Student Name_____   _____

Student Name_____   _____   _____

STEP C: _____

Student Name_____   _____

Student Name_____   _____

Student Name_____   _____

Student Name_____   _____

Student Name_____   _____

Student Name_____   _____

Student Name_____   _____   _____

OTHER: _____

Student Name_____   _____

Student Name_____   _____

Student Name_____   _____

Student Name_____   _____

Student Name_____   _____

Student Name_____   _____   _____

Student Name

Source: Copyright © 1997, Judith J. Baker, Ph.D. and Patricia Hinton Walker, Ph.D.

Exhibit 21–14 Receptionist Data Collection Instrument: Summary

---

DAILY CLERICAL/ADMINISTRATIVE TIME SUMMARY

Your Name_____ Today's Date_____

Begin Time_____ End Time_____ = Total Time* _____

	Today's Total Time (in minutes)

SUMMARY OF PREPARATION FOR APPOINTMENT ACTIVITIES
(From PFA Summary Sheet # __: insert total minutes by line item below)

Assembling files/charts in preparation for appointment   =   _____

Greeting student upon arrival   =   _____

Other_____   =   _____

Other_____   =   _____

SUMMARY OF SUBSEQUENT APPOINTMENT ACTIVITIES
(From SA summary sheet #__: insert total minutes by line item below)

Written communication w/external primary care physician   =   _____

Scheduling next appointment   =   _____

Other_____   =   _____

SUMMARY OF ENROLLMENT ACTIVITIES
(From EA Summary Sheet # __: insert total minutes)   =   _____

SUMMARY OF NONAPPOINTMENT/ENROLLMENT ACTIVITIES
(From NEA Summary Sheet # __: insert total minutes)   =   _____

                          Total Minutes   _____

(*Note: Total Minutes should equal Total Time at top of this sheet)

Source: Copyright © 1997, Judith J. Baker, Ph.D. and Patricia Hinton Walker, Ph.D.

Exhibit 21–15 Interrelationship of Three Data Collection Instrument Sets

PRIMARY CARE TIME SHEETS

1. Daily Primary Care Time Summary   = 1 sheet per day

2. Appointment Supplemental Sheet—Primary Care   = 1 sheet per appointment

3. Subsequent Primary Care Appointment Activities = 1 sheet per day
                                                     (addtl sheets if needed)

4. Nonappointment Activities   = 1 sheet per day

PSYCH/MH TIME SHEETS

1. Daily Psych/MH Time Summary   = 1 sheet per day

2. Appointment Supplemental Sheet—Psych/MN   = 1 sheet per appointment

3. Subsequent Psych/MH Appointment Activities   = 1 sheet per day
                                                     (addtl sheets if needed)

4. Nonappointment Activities   = 1 sheet per day

CLERICAL/ADMINISTRATIVE TIME SHEETS

1. Daily Clerical/Administrative Time Summary   = 1 sheet per day

2. Preparation for Appointment—Clerical/Admin   = 1 sheet per day
                                                     (addtl sheets if needed)

3. Subsequent Clerical/Admin Appointment Activities = 1 sheet per day
                                                     (addtl sheets if needed)

4. Nonappointment/Enrollment Activities   = 1 sheet per day
                                                     (addtl sheets if needed)

5. Enrollment Activities   = 1 sheet per day
                                                     (addtl sheets if needed)

Source: Copyright © 1997, Judith J. Baker, Ph.D. and Patricia Hinton Walker, Ph.D.

process to more appropriately calculate the actual contribution to the costs of nonappointment related time to the cost of encounters. Based only on salary and fringe benefit costs of the practitioners, the total costs were $90.31 and $67.92 respectively for primary care practitioners B and C. (Again, this figure does not reflect other administrative costs that are derived from indirect costs and from costs brought forth from the receptionist's time that contribute to the cost of an encounter and the total costs of care.)

The mean minutes for the category during the encounter, which equaled client-focused costs, was 00.00 minutes for clerical A, the receptionist. These data are also reflected on Exhibit 21–16. The mean times in minutes for clerical A for immediately before and after the encounter, which equaled secondary costs, were 2.10 (before) and 2.71 (after). The mean time for subsequent to appointment activities was 9.13 minutes (which contributed to secondary costs). The mean time for nonappointment related activities, which equaled part of the administrative costs, was 197.05 minutes. Again, because the SBHC practice is still developing and building, an undercapacity burden calculation was used later in the costing process to more appropriately calculate the actual contribution to the costs of nonappointment related time to the cost of encounters. Based only on salary and fringe benefit costs of the receptionist, the mean clerical costs were $41.24. (As mentioned previously, this figure does not reflect other administrative costs that are derived from indirect costs and are reflected in the total costs of care.)

These mean minutes and calculations of dollars related to client-focused and secondary costs of care serve as the basis for many of the subsequent calculations and spreadsheet exhibits. These calculations are not actual figures but have been modified appropriately for confidentiality reasons. Calculation of the dollars in each of the fields in Exhibit 21–16 was accomplished as follows: Actual salaries were obtained for all personnel; fringe benefit percentages were obtained; salaries were "loaded" with the fringe benefits. The gross salary-plus-fringes figure then was converted to a gross hourly rate for use in the calculations.

ACTIVITY DRIVERS USED TO ASSIGN COSTS

After the time study was completed, the mean times were calculated, and the dollars related to practitioner and receptionist costs were assigned, the next step is to determine the activity drivers that would be used to assign costs to the different types of services provided in the school-based health center. At this time, the activity drivers need to be determined as well as questions need to be answered regarding the application of specific activity drivers to the indirect costs of running the SBHC. Activity drivers for this activity-based costing project were the number of full-time-equivalent employees (FTEs), enrollment of students, number of encounters, number of patients seen, and number of square feet in the SBHC.

The activity drivers for this example were obtained from the budget, and from one year's experience in the practice as reflected in the patient records and in the billing reports. In this study, because the practice is still developing and all enrollees were seen at least once on the SBHC for an initial assessment, the number of enrollees and the number of patients are the same. For the purposes of this project, the number of encounters were calculated separately for primary care and mental health components of the practice, based on one year's experience in the practice from the billing data. Also, the number of square feet was not required because the space was provided by the school system for the SBHC and there were no indirect costs related to utilities, rental of space, and so forth. The activity drivers and the values assigned are presented in Exhibit 21–17.

These numbers were then applied to indirect costs in order to assign costs respectively to the primary care service and to the mental health

Exhibit 21–16 Activity and Salary Summary

ACTIVITY:		Primary		Secondary						Support	
		During		Before +		After +		Subsequent to Appt.		Nonapptmt	
		Minutes	Dollars	Minutes	Dollars	Minutes	Dollars	Minutes	Dollars	Minutes	Dollars
Practitioner A	Totals	2020.00	$1,146.23	186.00	$105.54	502.00	$284.86	1011.00	$584.48	2487.00	$1,411.22
	Means	39.61	$22.48	5.31	$2.93	10.24	$5.81	16.57	$9.41	173.67	$98.54
Practitioner B	Totals	1821.00	$995.76	224.00	$122.48	924.00	$505.26	439.00	$240.05	1982.00	$1,083.80
	Means	15.97	$8.74	1.03	$0.56	8.40	$4.60	5.40	$2.98	165.17	$90.31
Practitioner C	Totals	603.00	$236.27	68.00	$26.64	278.00	$108.92	73.00	$28.60	520.00	$203.75
	Means	15.87	$6.30	3.40	$1.48	7.32	$2.87	6.64	$2.60	173.33	$67.92
Clerical A	Totals	0.00	$0.00	1135.00	$237.55	747.00	$156.35	822.00	$172.04	4398.00	$920.51
	Means	0.00	$0.00	2.10	$0.44	2.71	$0.56	9.13	$1.91	197.05	$41.24

Source: Copyright © 1997, Judith J. Baker, Ph.D. and Patricia Hinton Walker, Ph.D.

Exhibit 21–17 Activity Drivers

ACTIVITY DRIVERS					
FTE	Enrollment	Encounters	# Patients	# Sq. Ft.	Undercapacity
Total PC FTE = 1.60	# Enrollees = 402	# PC = 963.6	# PC = 301.2	1000	Burden MH = 61.86%
# FTE PC = 1.00		% PC = 74.98%	% PC = 74.93%		Burden PC = 69.40%
% PC = 62.50%		# MH = 321.6	# MH = 100.8		Avg. Cap. Burden = 73.15%
# FTE MH = 0.60		% MH = 25.02%	% MH = 25.07%		
% MH = 37.50%		Total = 1285.2	Total = 402		

Source: Copyright © 1997, Judith J. Baker, Ph.D. and Patricia Hinton Walker, Ph.D.

service components of the practice (Exhibit 21–18).

Examples and rationale for the use of activity drivers are as follows:

- Direct administration costs specifically related to salaries of the project director and other administrators would be allocated based on the activity driver of FTE because the amount of time and use of time for the administrator in the SBHC is usually related to time spent with the personnel.
- The allocation of the costs related to the mental health consultant and the medical consultant would be based on the activity driver of enrollment because this is usually determined by the number of enrollees and/or patients that are seen in the school-based health center.
- The allocation of costs related to a community health worker, who was hired to assist in the implementation of the marketing plan, would be based on the activity driver of number of patients in the SBHC.
- The allocation of other costs such as hazardous waste, lab fees, medications, and clinical supplies were specifically related to the primary care service component of the practice. Therefore, these were allocated only to primary care costs based on encounters; however, other costs such as marketing, office supplies, billing, equipment, and so forth were allocated-based using activity drivers based on the number of encounters for the primary care service component (see Exhibit 21–18).
- Some of the costs such as medications, hazardous waste, clinical supplies, and so forth did not apply to the mental health service component; consequently these were not allocated to mental health services. However, other items such as office supplies, telecommunication costs, and travel costs were allocated based on FTE or encounter as activity drivers (see Exhibit 21–18).

- Lastly, the receptionist's time for secondary and administrative costs needed to be allocated to the costs of both primary care and mental health services. The activity driver that was used to allocate the receptionist's time to the services was based on the number of encounters for both primary care and for mental health (see Exhibit 21–18).

THE TRUE COST OF BUILDING COMMUNITY PARTNERSHIPS AND DEVELOPING A NEW PRACTICE

The school-based health center used as the example for this chapter had only been in business for one full year when this activity-based costing study was done. Consequently, the practice was not in full service and SBHC staff time was still being used to develop policies, procedures, and build community partnerships with business and volunteer members of the community coalition mentioned earlier in this chapter. Therefore, the number of patients and the number of encounters are lower than would be anticipated for the number of FTEs assigned by the grant to this practice. The inflated costs of care are reflected in the nonappointment related activities for all of the staff in the SBHC and in some of the indirect costs. Also, some of the activity drivers are unusually low for the volume expected in this practice in the future.

To accommodate and be more accurate in the estimations of costs of primary care services and mental health services in this growing practice, an underburden capacity was calculated and taken into consideration. As the SBHC practice positions itself in a managed care market, it is critical to determine as much as possible the real costs of encounters instead of a cost that reflects the practice in the process of development. Otherwise, the value of new models of community-based care such as the SBHC would be disproportionately out of line with other primary care and mental health services to basically well populations. The approach to

Exhibit 21–18 Indirect Costs with Application of Activity Drivers

Linked to onsite costs sheet...do not change

ACTIVITY	FTE	Enrollment	Encounters		# Patients		# Sq. Ft.
Total PC FTE =	1.60	# Enrollees = 402	# PC =	963.6	# PC =	301.2	1000
# FTE PC =	1.00		% PC =	74.98%	% PC =	74.93%	
% PC =	62.50%		# MH =	321.6	# MH =	100.8	
# FTE MH =	0.60		% MH =	25.02%	% MH =	25.07%	
% MH =	37.50%		Total =	1285.2	Total =	402	

	Cost Factors	Activity Driver Used	PC Allocations	Allocation Per PC Encounter	MH Allocations	Allocation Per MH Encounter
Direct Admin Costs						
Project Director	$12,399.60	FTE	$7,749.75	$8.04	$4,649.85	$14.46
Co-Project Director	$12,399.60	FTE	$7,749.75	$8.04	$4,649.85	$14.46
Mental Health Consultant	$6,019.20	ENR			$6,019.20	$14.97
Medical Consultant	$6,199.20	ENR	$6,199.20	$15.42		
Community Health Worker	$12,523.20	PTS/ENC	$9,383.05	$9.74	$3,140.15	$9.76
Other Direct Costs						
Hazardous Waste	$1,248.00	ENC	$1,248.00	$1.30		
Lab Fees	$2,400.00	ENC	$2,400.00	$2.49		

Mail Courier	$840.00	ENC	$525.00	$0.54	$315.00	$0.98
Marketing	$1,200.00	ENC	$899.10	$0.93	$300.90	$0.94
Meds	$3,000.00	ENC	$3,000.00	$3.11		
Clinical Supplies	$3,600.00	ENC	$3,600.00	$3.74		
Office Supplies	$1,200.00	ENC	$750.00	$0.78	$450.00	$1.40
Telecomm	$2,400.00	ENC	$1,500.00	$1.56	$900.00	$2.80
Travel/Conference	$1,200.00	ENC	$750.00	$0.78	$450.00	$1.40
Indirect Costs						
CNC Secretary Salary	$4,783.20	ENC	$2,989.50	$3.10	$1,793.70	$5.58
School Health Consultant	$7,215.60	ENC	$4,509.75	$4.68	$2,705.85	$8.41
Billing Fee	$4,316.40	ENC	$3,236.29	$3.36	$1,080.11	$3.36
Equipment	$1200.00	ENC	$750.00	$0.78	$450.00	$1.40
Totals	**$84,144.00**		**$57,239.40**	**$68.39**	**$26,904.60**	**$79.92**
			68.03%		*31.97%*	

Source: Copyright © 1996, Patricia Hinton Walker, Ph.D. and Judith J. Baker, Ph.D.

calculating undercapacity burden for this practice is presented in Exhibit 21–19.

The givens presented in this spreadsheet were determined from analysis of one year's experience in the practice. Because this is a school-based health center, the number of weeks the practice is open is largely based on the time that the school is in session. Based on data collected by administration of number of weeks open when students were seen in the clinic from September to June of the 1995–96 academic year, the SBHC was seeing students regularly 36 weeks of the year. As anticipated, the staff normally worked eight hours per day even though the actual SBHC was not open eight hours per day because actual school hours are less than eight hours. Because the NYS grant mandated availability of practitioners for care during the summer in order to provide continuity of care as primary care providers, the first year was experimental based on the level of activity in the SBHC. After two to three weeks of determining the number of students served by appointment in the summer, staff and administration set summer hours at four hours per day for the 12 weeks of summer. Consequently, the total number of hours available for practice (based on respective FTEs) was 1,008 hours for mental health service and 1,680 for primary care. Using the mean total minutes for before, during, and after the encounter from the time study, it was estimated that the total encounters possible for one year could be 3,991.69, serving a total of 1,248.43 patients. Specifically this would break down to a maximum number of mental health encounters that could be as high as 843.16 during one year. Concurrently, the maximum number of primary care encounters for one year could be as high as 3,148.52. Consequently, the practice was considered to be functioning at only 31.79 percent of its capacity for mental health, and at only 25.50 percent capacity for primary care. These calculations were then applied to the final determine of costs of care per encounter for this new practice.

REPORTING THE RESULTS

Based on the consideration of all of the above calculations, one goal of this project was to determine the total costs of primary care services and mental health services within the SBHC. However, in the context of managed care, it is more important to determine the average cost per encounter (primary care and mental health) to predict the costs of care for this population or others like it in the future. The summary calculations for this level of analysis are presented in Exhibit 21–20.

The calculations include consideration of the undercapacity burden computations. These calculations result in the costs presented in Exhibit 21–21. The mean cost of a mental health encounter was determined to be $162.80, while the mean cost of a primary care encounter was determined to be $119.30.

At the same time this activity-based costing study was being designed and implemented, data were being collected and analyzed related to risks of the population along with diagnoses and treatments provided. The purpose of collecting data related to the risk assessment of a specific adolescent population such as the students served in this clinic was to attempt to determine the relationship between selected risks and costs. Analysis of the risk data as related to cost data using the encounter as the unit of analysis has revealed that there is a predictive relationship between risk and costs. Subsequently a predictive model was developed that allows projections of the number of encounters and the estimated costs of population-based care in a school-based health center. This study needs to be replicated to determine the reliability of the data, but the intent is to replicate this process in other school-based health centers and other community-based practices in order to more fully predict the costs of care in new and innovative models of community-based care.

Another immediate and practical application of the cost data obtained through this activity-based costing study is more effective management of resources. These data will assist the

Exhibit 21–19 Undercapacity Burden Calculations

Givens:

# practice weeks/school year =	36
# work hours/school year day =	8
# practice weeks/summer =	12
# work hours/summer day =	4

	Prac Hrs per schl yr	Prac Hrs per summer	From Act. Drvr FTE	Total hrs avail/year	From Act. Drvr Mean sans NA	Encounters Capacity/Under Capacity Burden		Patients Capacity Under Capacity Burden	
Mental Health	1440	240	0.60	1008	71.73	Max # Enc.	843.16	Max Pts. Poss.	264.27
						Act. # Enc.	321.60	Act. # Pts.	101
						Below Cap. %	38.14%	Below Cap. %	38.14%
						Under Cap. Burden	61.86%	Under Cap. Burden	61.86%
Primary Care	1440	240	1.00	1680	32.02	Max # Enc.	3148.52	Max Pts. Poss.	984.16
						Act. # Enc.	963.60	Act. # Pts.	301.20
						Below Cap. %	30.60%	Below Cap. %	30.60%
						Under Cap. Burden	69.40%	Under Cap. Burden	69.40%
Totals	2688			103.75		Total Enc. Poss. =	3991.69	Total Pts. Poss. =	1248.43

Source: Copyright © 1996, Patricia Hinton Walker, Ph.D. and Judith J. Baker, Ph.D.

Exhibit 21–20 Summary of Cost with Undercapacity Burden

| | | Primary | | | | Secondary | | | | Support | |
| | | During | | Before + | | After + | | Subsequent to Appt. | | Nonapptmt | |
		Minutes	Dollars	Minutes	Dollars	Minutes	Dollars	Minutes	Dollars	Minutes	Dollars
Mental Health	Means	39.61	$22.48	5.31	$2.93	10.24	$5.81	16.57	$9.41	173.67	$98.54
Recep/Clerk	Means/Enc	0.00	$0.00	0.53	$0.11	0.68	$0.14	2.29	$0.48	49.41	$10.34
	Totals	39.61	$22.48	5.84	$3.04	10.92	$5.95	18.86	$9.89	223.08	$103.89
Under Cap. Burden										137.99	$67.35
	Allocation									85.09	$41.53
PC	Avg means	15.92	$7.52	2.22	$1.02	7.86	$3.73	6.02	$2.79	169.25	$79.12
Recep/Clerk	Means/Enc	0.00	$0.00	1.57	$0.33	2.03	$0.42	6.84	$1.43	147.64	$30.90
	Totals	15.92	$7.52	3.79	$1.35	9.89	$4.15	12.86	$4.22	316.89	$110.02
Under Cap. Burden										219.91	$76.35
	Allocation									96.98	$33.67

Source: Copyright © 1996, Patricia Hinton Walker, Ph.D. and Judith J. Baker, Ph.D.

Exhibit 21–21 Total Cost per Encounter

Mean Minutes per MH Enc 71.73	Mean Onsite Cost per MH Enc	Onsite Admin Allocation	Indirect Allocations	Total Cost per MH Enc
75.23	$41.35	$41.53	$79.92	$162.80
Mean Minutes per PC Enc 32.02	**Mean Onsite Cost per PC Enc**	**Onsite Admin Allocation**	**Indirect Allocations**	**Total Cost per PC Enc**
42.46	$17.24	$33.67	$68.39	$119.30

Source: Copyright © 1996, Patricia Hinton Walker, Ph.D. and Judith J. Baker, Ph.D.

project directors and other administrators in the University of Rochester School System to project the number and type of FTEs needed, based on number of enrollees and risk in this SBHC and future SBHC initiatives. The under-capacity burden process will also assist administrators in developing more accurate projections of care and the number of FTEs needed when developing other new practice sites in community-based settings. Also, this activity-based costing study has implications for identification of the activities and costing out of services provided by other nonphysician providers such as physician assistants, nurse practitioners, and nurse midwives. There is a growing interest in the contributions and cost-effectiveness of care that is provided by these nonphysician providers because in many cases they are the "key to increasing access to care for underserved populations, particularly in these emerging models of community-based care such as school-based health centers, free-standing birth centers, neighborhood community health centers, and rural outreach clinics."[9] Determining the cost-effectiveness of many of these nonphysician providers is of interest as managed care companies realize that these are new models of purchasers of care such as church wellness clinics, neighborhood centers serving homeless populations, and rural health clinics manned by nurse practitioners.

NOTES

1. U.S. Department of Health and Human Services, *Healthy People 2000: National Health Promotion and Disease Prevention Objectives* (Washington, DC: U.S. Government Printing Office, 1990).
2. L.S. Majer et al., "Adolescent Reproductive Health: Roles for School Personnel in Prevention and Early Intervention," *Journal of School Health* 62, no. 7: 294–297; S. Hagedorn, "Student Views of the School Nurse's Role in a Secondary School Condom Availability Program," *Journal of School Health* 63, no. 8 (1993): 358–360; "The Role of the School Nurse in Providing Sex Education," *Nursing Times* 90, no. 23 (1994): 36–38; C.

Passarelli, "School Nursing: Trends for the Future," *Journal of School Health* 64, no. 4 (1994): 141–149; G.M. Koenning et al., "Health Services Delivery to Students with Special Health Care Needs in Texas Public Schools," *Journal of School Health*, 65, no. 4 (1995): 119–123.

3. L.H. Edwards, "The School Nurse's Role in School-Based Clinics," *Journal of School Health* 57, no. 4 (1987): 157–159.

4. Majer et al., "Adolescent Reproductive Health"; Hagedorn, "Student Views of the School Nurse's Role"; "The Role of the School Nurse in Providing Sex Education"; Passarelli, "School Nursing: Trends for the Future"; Koenning et al., "Health Services Delivery to Students with Special Health Care Needs"; Edwards, "The School Nurse's Role in School-Based Clinics"; P.L. Schneider and R.M. Grimes, "Potential Bias in Teacher Referrals to the School Nurse," *Journal of School Health*, 63, no. 10 (1993): 426–428.

5. A.D. Kaluzny et al., "Partners for the Dance: Forming Strategic Alliances in Health Care," in *Strategic Alliances: A World Wide Phenomenon Comes to Health Care*, ed. G.B. Walton (Ann Arbor, MI: Health Administration Press, 1995).

6. P.H. Walker, "Dollars and ene in Health Reform: Interdisciplinary Practice and Community Nursing Centers," *Nursing Administration Quarterly* 19, no. 1 (1994): 1–11.

7. P.H. Walker and P.A. Chiverton, "Case Study No. 2: The University of Rochester Experience," *Nursing Management* 28, no. 3 (1997): 30.

8. Walker and Chiverton, "Case Study No. 2."

9. P.H. Walker and P.A. Stone, "Exploring Cost and Quality: Community-Based Versus Traditional Hospital Delivery Systems," *Journal of Health Care Finance* 23, no. 1 (1996): 23–24.

## CHAPTER 22

ABC System Upgrade Implementation

Judith J. Baker

CHAPTER OUTLINE

Introduction
ABC and Existing Information Systems
The ABC Upgrade Implementation
Conclusion

INTRODUCTION

This book has already made the case for activity-based costing systems. We have already discussed the fact that traditional cost systems do not systematically identify and appropriately cost indirect costs. Traditional cost systems do not readily convert to health care, in large part because hospitals typically exhibit high proportions of indirect costs.[1] Alternative cost accounting methods (in particular activity-based costing) are more useful for specific treatment of indirect costs. How does the alternative cost accounting method operate? Within the existing system or parallel to it? What should management expect?

ABC AND EXISTING INFORMATION SYSTEMS

Once management has decided to implement ABC, a decision must be made about information systems. Will the existing information system accommodate ABC? Is there a module that can be added to the general ledger system? Or,

should information be exported to a stand-alone activity-based costing system? What about the varied demands of new programs, expanded ambulatory services, or multiple service sites?

Management can do some basic homework by investigating its costing requirements in a strategic manner. For example, it might estimate a profitability matrix such as that illustrated in Figure 22–1 to determine the initial requirements for specific types of cost information to be demanded from the system. (Note that this matrix derives from an example presented in an earlier chapter.[2])

In addition to investigating its planning requirements, management should ask some basic questions about system capability. These questions can be posed about the existing system(s) and also about proposed additions or replacements to the system. Ask the following questions about the system under discussion:

- What types of direct costing methods are available?
- Will the system allocate indirect cost? How? Specifically, can you control multiple allocations of indirect cost?
- Will the system separate direct costs into fixed and variable costs? Specifically, can you set how many different cost assignment categories will be used?
- Will the system separate overhead into fixed and variable costs? Specifically, can

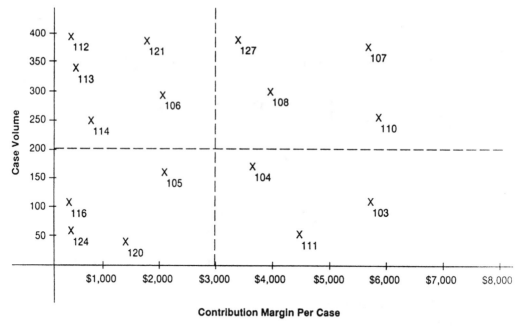

Note: Numbers relate to DRG categories.

Figure 22–1 Sample DRG Volume—Profitability Matrix. *Source:* Reprinted from S. Udpa, Activity-Based Costing for Hospitals, *Health Care Management Review*, Vol. 21, No. 3, p. 85, © 1996, Aspen Publishers, Inc.

you set how many different allocation bases will be used?

- Will the system perform variance analysis?
- Will the system break out labor? Supplies? Semivariable costs?
- Will the system cross over cost center barriers? Or will the system accumulate costs only by cost center?
- Will the cost system pick up chargeable supplies? How about nonchargeable supplies?
- Will the cost system handle standard costs? How flexible are the standard-setting features?
- Does the system have flexible report-writer capability?
- Can the system report on a patient-specific per-day basis? If so, can the system receive medical history and demographic information from other sources within the organization?

Management decision making should be influenced by flexibility and capability as well as cost and time frame to implement.

THE ABC UPGRADE IMPLEMENTATION

A major decision revolves around multiple cost systems. The general propensity to have multiple cost systems has been discussed by Kaplan.[3] He believes that diverse uses of cost information may well require more than one cost system. He therefore proposes three cost system use categories. The first merely values inventory and meets the requirements of outside reporting. It is the simplest from a costing standpoint. The second system allows the control of cost at a responsibility center level, thus providing swift feedback to operational personnel. The third and highest level system is a product cost system that can support strategic management decisions.

Later Kaplan[4] expanded on his position concerning multiple cost systems. His expanded view was that present technology is not yet capable of what he terms cost system design. Instead, it can be called cost system evolution. His four-stage cost system evolution and its effect on his three uses of cost information (as discussed above) are summarized as: stage one—poor data quality (inadequate to meet any of the three needs); stage two—focus on external reporting (tailored to meet financial reporting needs, inaccurate product costs [strategic support], limited feedback [operational control]); stage three—innovation—managerial relevance (operational control information with emphasis on operating performance direct measures); stage four—integrated cost systems (expanded activity-based cost systems to support financial reporting as well as product cost management [strategic support]). The operational control system provides feedback and input interface on budgeting and current operations.

We agree with Kaplan's proposition that multiple cost systems are necessary due to diverse uses of cost information. We further agree that present technology is not yet capable of meeting all cost needs in one system—especially for health care purposes. In many cases, another system that runs parallel to the existing system will answer health care cost accounting needs. We propose a cost system, running parallel to the existing system, that will increase its ABC precision as additional information is added to it. We call the increasingly sophisticated parallel system an *ABC upgrade implementation*. It has a rolling implementation capability.

We expand on Kaplan's four stages by perceiving each stage as a range of capability, moving from low through moderate to high capability within the assigned stage. Thus, in Kaplan's four-stage cost system design his stage three is defined as innovation—managerial relevance, and includes the development of an activity-based cost system (product costs for strategic support) and the development of an operational performance measurement system (operational control). We propose an initial parallel cost system that will begin at the low end of stage three and will move upward through the moderate range and on into the high range of stage three as its components are upgraded; thus, an ABC upgrade implementation.

The benefits of this approach answer the challenge: Without disturbing the existing system (which functions primarily for financial reporting purposes), create and implement an ABC-oriented system that can meet the cost-benefit test, can initially be put into place in a reasonable time frame, and whose ABC capability can be sequentially improved upon in a rolling implementation subsequent to initial installation.

To illustrate a low-range ABC initial implementation approach we turn to an emergency department example. Note that the authors of this example did not contemplate the ABC System Upgrade Implementation when their article was published. Their proposal focused on the argument that ABC estimates of cost are better than no ABC at all, and they concentrated on how to accomplish these estimates. We have assigned a three-tier range of capability (low, moderate, high) to stages two, three, and four. We now use the authors' estimation concept to identify a low-range initial implementation approach. We explore how the ABC estimation concept works. We also recognize the potential to apply our rolling implementation concept to a starting point that incorporates ABC estimation. We can then upgrade the system over time. This example, authored by Holmes and Schroeder,[5] illustrated ABC *estimation* of unit costs for emergency department (ED) services. As an ABC *estimation* it does not meet Kaplan's stage three definition, but is rather within his lower stage two (inaccurate product costs for strategic support, due to estimation of costs and limited feedback for operational control, due to estimation of costs). This example provides the potential for an ABC system to be developed beyond the estimation stage as illustrated. (Using our proposal, if it developed out of the estimation stage, it could develop to a low-range stage three.) We shall see this potential as we work through the example.

Holmes and Schroeder argue that full costs for individual services provided—called "fully loaded" costs by some managers—have little bearing on profitability or management in health care today.[6] The prevalence of substantial contractual allowances negates the use of full costs for charge setting. And many of the indirect costs present in full cost amounts have been arbitrarily allocated to the individual services. Instead, a case is made for the relevance of incremental costs—the cost of an additional unit of service, or the avoidable cost if one unit less is provided. Holmes and Schroeder propose that better management decisions will result by accepting what they call feasible imperfect information (e.g., containing some estimates) on incremental activity-based costs rather than using traditional full cost data.[7]

Their proposition is supported by Christiansen and Sharp,[8] who look at the problem from the standpoint of responsibility accounting. They advocate reporting on the basis of a manager's controllable costs (e.g., subject to his or her decision) rather than incorporating the manager's noncontrollable costs (e.g., outside his or her decision-making powers). Their argument additionally supports the philosophy of the incremental activity-based costs presented in this example.

The incremental activity-based cost estimates are discovered in a series of six steps.

1. Identifying all relevant costs.
2. Sorting costs in support of ED functions, discarding those that are not relevant or not affected by volume or availability of services.
3. Clustering into groups for counting and costing (such as ambulatory patient groups [APG] or physicians' current procedural terminology [CPT] groups) those services that create similar demands for ED functions.
4. Identifying and counting the activities or cost drivers for each service group. (Such activities or drivers are the characteristics of the service that trigger the performance of an ED function.)
5. Estimating the costliness of each ED function, permitting quantification of the relationship between costs and the triggering characteristics.
6. Aggregating the functional costliness (individual activity costs) for all ED functions of a service to determine the incremental cost of one unit.

Upon completion of the six steps, a rough unit incremental cost has been calculated.[9] Tables illustrating calculations and accompanying comments appear below.

Step one—identifying all relevant costs: In this example costs are categorized into three types—direct, departmental, and external. Direct costs can be captured directly (in ABC terminology, they are traced). To summarize, the authors' approach is this: Start with the basic cost center treatment that is traditional to Medicare cost reporting. That is, departmental costs have been charged directly to the department whereas external costs have been allocated to the department from other departments or cost centers. Direct costs that can be identified and traced are isolated, labeled as direct, and subtracted from the departmental costs. We now have three types of cost: (1) direct or traced; (2) the remaining departmental cost that originated in the department, designated as indirect departmental cost; and (3) the external costs that have been allocated and that originate from other cost centers.

Table 22–1 illustrates external costs that are charged to the ED by the traditional cost accounting system. As explained in the preceding paragraph, all these costs have been allocated to the department from other cost centers.

Table 22–2 illustrates departmental costs—those that have been charged directly to the department. Their total is labeled gross costs on Table 22–2. As explained above, the direct costs that can be identified and traced are isolated. They are labeled direct on Table 22–2.

Table 22–1 External Costs Charged to the Emergency Department by the Traditional Cost Accounting System*

External costs June 1995

Cost center	Amount	Relevance	% Variable	Driver	DRG[†] 193 (Biliary tract)	DRG 209 (Major joint/limb)
Pharmaceuticals	$2,544	1	70%	Wtd procs	$312	$534
Clinical pathology	$1,648	1	60%	RVUs	$271	$415
Anatomical pathology	$433	1	10%	DRG-wts	$7	$12
Blood bank	$654	1	90%	BUs	$133	$233
Diagnostic radiology	$3,781	1	30%	Radfilms	$123	$246
Electrocardiography	$476	1	80%	EKGs	$73	$73
Pulmonary	$537	1	40%	RTs	$72	$0
Central sterile	$2,358	1	90%	DRG-wts	$335	$564
Anesthesiology	$3,561	1	70%	ORmins	$580	$1,035
Operating room	$6,443	1	45%	ORmins	$675	$1,203
Recovery room	$2,766	1	55%	ORmins	$354	$631
Depreciation	$43,577	0				
Corporate office	$12,433	0				
Clinical spt division	$1,542	1	5%	DRG-wts	$12	$20
Special staff	$2,677	0				
Nursing	$4,877	1	70%	NAcuity	$636	$773
Preventive med	$3,778	0				
Immunizations	$745	1	80%	Shots	$ 0	$ 0
Total	$143,039				$3,670	$5,886

*Some rows have been omitted from the display, as have all columns for other types of services to the right of those shown. The abbreviated cost drivers in the fifth column are described in Table 22–4.

[†]Diagnosis-related group.

Source: Reprinted from R. Holmes and R. Schroeder, ABC Estimation of Unit Costs for Emergency Department Services, *Journal of Ambulatory Care Management*, Vol. 19, No. 2, p. 25, © 1996, Aspen Publishers, Inc.

The remaining costs are designated as indirect departmental costs, and they are labeled indirect on Table 22–2. The direct costs identified in Table 22–2 are now set out in Table 22–3.

Step two—sorting costs: This is an incremental cost analysis; thus, inappropriate costs must be sorted out and disregarded (indicated by 0 in the relevance columns of Tables 22–1 and 22–2). Sunk costs expended in the past and fixed costs that do not vary with the production of a service and could not be avoided in the absence of the service meet the inappropriate criteria. (Sunk costs have been invested in assets for which

there is little—if any—alternative or continued value except salvage.) For example, see depreciation and corporate office (or home office) on Table 22–1; both are coded 0. Also, some costs are viewed as relevant for only a portion of their total. When that is the case, the relevant percentage is entered in the percent variable column. (Standard cost pools were accepted in the case of this example.)

Step three—clustering and counting of services: A classification system must be chosen to sort the ED services. CPT codes (Current Procedural Terminology, fourth edition) would be a

Table 22–2 Costs Recorded Specifically against the Emergency Department Cost Center

| | Indirect cost of services traced to the ED | | | | | | June 1995 | |
| | Gross | | | | % | | DRG* | DRG |
Cost Type	$	− Direct $	= Indirect $	Relevance	Variable	Cost driver	193	209
Number services							8	16
Clinician labor	$62,355	$31,250	$31,105	1	90%	Protocol-C	$4,923	$9,300
Nursing labor	$61,056		$61,056	1	95%	Protocol-N	$7,975	$12,722
Paraprofessional	$8,576		$8,576	1	100%	Protocol-T	$892	$1,903
Admin/clerk	$3,615		$3,615	1	60%	Protocol-A	$317	$605
Supplies	$201,356	$163,246	$38,110	1	90%	DRG-wts	$5,414	$9,118
Equipment	$22,334		$22,334	0		DRG-wts	$0	$0
Contracts	$15,015		$15,015	1	95%	Protocol-C	$2,509	$4,738

*Diagnosis-related group.

Source: Reprinted from R. Holmes and R. Schroeder, ABC Estimation of Unit Costs for Emergency Department Services, *Journal of Ambulatory Care Management*, Vol. 19, No. 2, p. 25, 1996, © Aspen Publishers, Inc.

common choice. APGs might also be a choice. In the case of this example, DRGs (diagnosis-related groups) have been chosen. Two particular DRGs (193 and 209) are utilized in this example.

Step four—identifying activity measures or cost drivers: The cost driver statistics are set out in Table 22–4. As other examples in this book have demonstrated, cost drivers may be measured, may reflect protocols or clinical pathways, or may reflect published norms. Choices are impacted by the degree of accuracy that is desired.

Step five—estimating the costliness of the factors: This step is a spreadsheet calculation procedure. If a factor increases by one unit, how

Table 22–3 Direct Traceable Costs Recorded against Each Type of Service*

| | Direct costs of each type of service | | June 1995 | |
Cost type	Department total	DRG[†] 193	DRG 209
Clinician labor	$31,250	$2,300	$7,200
Nursing labor			
Paraprofessional			
Admin/clerk			
Supplies	$163,246	$49,988	$93,254
Equipment			
Contracts			

*Blank rows have no direct costs recorded in the ED.

[†]Diagnosis-related group.

Source: Reprinted from R. Holmes and R. Schroeder, ABC Estimation of Unit Costs for Emergency Department Services, *Journal of Ambulatory Care Management*, Vol. 19, No. 2, p. 26, 1996, © Aspen Publishers, Inc.

Table 22–4 Cost Drivers and Allocation Bases Used To Assign Costs To Services

	Cost driver statistics per procedure		June 1995	
Cost driver	Brief description	Total basis	DRG* 193	DRG 209
BUs	Expected units of blood	141.5	4	3.5
DRG-wts	DRG weights from Medicare	96.3	1.9	1.6
EKGs	Standard electrocardiographs	84	2	1
NAcuity	Nursing acuity hours	2190	51	31
ORmins	OR minutes	11063	322	287
Protocol-A	Protocol minutes/admin or clerk	1148	21	20
Protocol-C	Protocol minutes/clinician	81.88	1.8	1.7
Protocol-N	Protocol minutes/nurse	34796	598.0	477.0
Protocol-T	Protocol minutes/technician	3461	45	48
RTs	Standard respiratory therapies	24	1	0
RVUs	Laboratory tests in relative value	991	34	26
Radfilms	Radiology films	369	5	5
Shots	Standard immunizations (tetanus)	7	0	0
Wtd procs	Pharmaceuticals in weighted amount	20	7	6

*Diagnosis-related group.

Source: Reprinted from R. Holmes and R. Schroeder, ABC Estimation of Unit Costs for Emergency Department Services, *Journal of Ambulatory Care Management*, Vol. 19, No. 2, p 26, 1996, © Aspen Publishers, Inc.

much does the cost change? Spreadsheet formulas were utilized to arrive at the DRG cost columns in Tables 22–1 and 22–3.

Step six—aggregating the functional costliness of a unit of service: This final step collects all costs and reports them as aggregates. (See Table 22–5.) Table 22–5 first presents the aggregate costs for each of the two DRGs, in total and broken into the three types of cost (external, indirect, and direct); and then presents the incremental cost units for each of the two DRGs, again in total and broken into the three types of cost. Two statistical tables are also presented as illustrations of the type of data to be collected for performance measures. Table 22–6 sets out the quantity of services provided by each ED clinician and Table 22–7 sets out the laboratory testing ordered by each clinician for the two DRGs.

This estimated system can be adjusted to accommodate actual ABC costs when they are acquired. The authors use patient scheduling as an example of how this process would work.

They suppose that ABC study information (e.g., fresh information acquired through proper ABC methodology) is determined for patient scheduling. To integrate this new information into the system, they remove all ABC-determined patient scheduling costs from all three cost types of the model (direct, indirect departmental, and external). Without these costs, the model calculates and subtotals incremental cost exclusive of patient scheduling. To achieve full incremental cost, the new ABC patient scheduling unit cost is added back to calculate full incremental cost incorporating the new information. Other factors will change and improve as fuller implementation is adopted.

CONCLUSION

In summary, this example provides the potential for an ABC system to be developed beyond the estimation stage as illustrated. As better data are made available, this method can be applied to achieve more accuracy in unit costs.

Table 22–5 Total Incremental Costs and Incremental Unit Costs for Each Service

Emergency department summary June 1995

Product list (by DRG* or APG†)	DRG 193	DRG 209
Brief description of service:	biliary tract	major joint/limb
Quantity provided during the period:	8	16
Aggregate costs for type of service		
External costs	$3,669.96	$5,886.12
Indirect costs	$22,029.83	$38,385.77
Direct costs	$52,288.00	$100,454.00
Total:	$77,987.79	$144,725.89
Incremental unit costs		
External costs	$458.74	$367.88
Indirect costs	$2,753.73	$2,399.11
Direct costs	$6,536.00	$6,278.38
Total:	$9,748.47	$9,045.37

*Diagnosis-related group.

†Ambulatory patient group.

Source: Reprinted from R. Holmes and R. Schroeder, ABC Estimation of Unit Costs for Emergency Department Services, *Journal of Ambulatory Care Management*, Vol. 19, No. 2, p. 28, 1996, © Aspen Publishers, Inc.

Table 22–6 Quantity of Services Provided by Each Clinician*

Physician case workload	June 1995		
		DRG†	DRG
Product	Total	193	209
Quantity for all providers:	60	8	16
Abrams Dr. William		2	7
Jones Dr. Sherry		6	9
Smith Dr. John L.		0	0
Thomas Dr. Enid		0	0
Cases unaccounted by provider		0	0

*This portion of the spreadsheet is optional. However, if any clinician profiling is to be calculated, this table must also be present.

†Diagnosis-related group.

Source: Reprinted from R. Holmes and R. Schroeder, ABC Estimation of Unit Costs for Emergency Department Services, *Journal of Ambulatory Care Management*, Vol. 19, No. 2, p. 28, 1996, © Aspen Publishers, Inc.

To repeat: We propose an ABC system upgrade implementation. We identify costing system stages and assign a three-tier range of capability to each stage. We recommend implementation with subsequent upgrades of the costing system through a sequence of planned ABC improvements. The benefits of this approach (1) can meet the challenge—without disturbing the existing system, (2) can create and implement an ABC-oriented system that can meet the cost-benefit test, (3) can initially be put into place in a reasonable time frame, and (4) can be sequentially improved upon in a rolling implementation subsequent to initial installation.

Table 22–7 Laboratory Testing Ordered by Each Clinician for Each Type of Service*

Physician laboratory testing		June 1995	
	Total basis	DRG[†] 193	DRG 209
Aggregate	991	274	414
Abrams Dr. William		65	161
Jones Dr. Sherry		209	253
Smith Dr. John L.		0	0
Thomas Dr. Enid		0	0
Unaccounted		0	0
Per case average:		34	26
Comparison to mean			
Abrams Dr. William	−0.8811	32.5	23
Jones Dr. Sherry	1.05819	34.83	28.11
Smith Dr. John L.	0.97701	0	0
Thomas Dr. Enid	1.11538	0	0
Unaccounted	1.25	0	0

*This table illustrates clinician use of one resource—laboratory testing. Additional tables could be created for other resources, such as pharmaceuticals, supplies, radiography, and so forth.

[†]Diagnosis-related group.

Source: Reprinted from R. Holmes and R. Schroeder, ABC Estimation of Unit Costs for Emergency Department Services, *Journal of Ambulatory Care Management*, Vol. 19, No. 2, p. 29, 1996, © Aspen Publishers, Inc.

NOTES

1. J.J. Baker, "Provider Characteristics and Managed Care/ Competition Environmental Factors Associated with Hospital Use of Costing Systems" (Ph.D. diss., Fielding Institute, Santa Barbara, CA, 1995).

2. S. Udpa, "Activity-Based Costing for Hospitals," *Health Care Management Review* 21, no. 3 (1996): 83–96.

3. R.S. Kaplan, "One Cost System Isn't Enough," *Harvard Business Review* (January–February 1988): 61–66.

4. R.S. Kaplan, "The Four-Stage Model of Cost Systems Design," *Management Accounting* (February 1990): 22–26.

5. R. Holmes and R. Schroeder, "ABC Estimation of Unit Costs for Emergency Department Services," *Journal of Ambulatory Care Management* 19, no. 2 (1996): 22–31.

6. See S.A. Finkler, *Essentials of Cost Accounting for Health Care Organizations* (Gaithersburg, MD: Aspen Publishers, Inc., 1994); and Holmes and Schroeder, "ABC Estimation," 22.

7. Holmes and Schroeder, "ABC Estimation," 23.

8. L.F. Christensen and D. Sharp, "How ABC Can Add Value to Decision Making," *Cost Management* (May 1993): 39.

9. Holmes and Schroeder, "ABC Estimation," 23.

## CHAPTER 23

Choosing a System and Implementing an ABC Pilot Program: A Case Study

Richard G. Melecki

CHAPTER OUTLINE

PREFACE

This case study concerns choosing a cost accounting system. It is a realistic look at the nuts and bolts of the decision, authored by someone who has been there. Central Hospital deals with assorted stakeholders on the steering committee as the issue is explored. The software criteria and setup are detailed. Finally, the choices about initial cost information and use of the results are set out along with an epilogue. The white paper used to explain activity-based costing to stakeholders is a part of this case study.

The chief financial officer's (CFO's) decision to call the project a "procedure-based" costing system pilot instead of an "activity-based" costing system is of particular interest. The CFO had already focused on clinical procedures as her primary targets for cost management and had been setting the stage for this pilot for the previous two years. She believed that "proce-

dures-based" would be readily understood and better accepted by the clinical personnel, even though the terminology was a departure from traditional labels for ABC. Thus, activity-based costing methodology was presented under a designation of procedures-based costing for the Central Hospital costing pilot.

GETTING STARTED IN ACTIVITY-BASED COSTING: A CASE STUDY

Central Hospital is a community general hospital located in the midwestern United States. The hospital is licensed for 300 beds but only maintains 150 inpatient beds and averages an inpatient census of 114. Most of these patients are admitted through its emergency department, which sees about 28,000 visits per year. Because the hospital is the only major medical facility in a rural area crossed by three major superhighways, Central's emergency department sees a high volume of trauma cases caused by automobile accidents. In fact, the hospital is certified as a type-three trauma center.

At least 36 percent of Central's patient cases are covered by Medicare. Another 20 percent—mostly nursing home patients—have Medicaid coverage. Its major nongovernment payer (10 percent) is a for-profit Blue Cross/Blue Shield affiliate located in a large city 70 miles to the south. Most of the small manufacturing businesses in the area insure their employees under that program's HMO plan. Fortunately, virtually all of Central's admitting physicians are on the HMO panel. Other payment sources include a local preferred provider organization (PPO) (4 percent), workers' compensation (4 percent), a self-insured national corporation (9 percent), and self-pay (17 percent).

Over the past two years, Central has gradually been shifting its services toward outpatients. It recently renovated a wing of the hospital to accommodate outpatient traffic and has a total of nine outpatient clinics operating five days per week. This has been a very profitable shift for the hospital, which had about an 8 percent operating surplus last year.

There are major financial challenges on the horizon, however. Blue Cross recently announced that it would be negotiating more capitated coverage for inpatients over the next 18 months. More important, it is moving to implement APGs (ambulatory patient groups) next year. This will put significant pressure on Central's outpatient revenues. The last piece of bad news is that Medicare has chosen the state's capital city as one of its selected sites for full-risk capitation. If this program works, Central believes that most of its patient population, both inpatient and outpatient, will be under some form of capitated reimbursement in the near future.

Fortunately, Central has a proactive CFO. When Mary Johnson joined the hospital two years ago, she began a gradual shift toward a relative value unit (RVU)-based cost accounting system. This allowed the hospital to begin to focus on clinical procedures as the primary targets for cost management. However, Mary is painfully aware that relative value units are at best averages. With full-risk capitation on the near horizon, she knows that she must have the most accurate cost information possible to negotiate favorable rates for Central. As a result, she recently sought and received permission from the CEO to implement an activity-based costing pilot program.

The unique ability of activity-based costing to assign cost to specific cost objects makes accurate reporting of product, service line, and provider performance relatively easy. However, departments, that are typically the focus of traditional cost accounting, are not normally cost objects in an ABC system. At the same time, most procedures tend to be performed in specific departments or cost centers so it is easy to trace costs to procedure-based areas. In addition, Mary had already focused on clinical procedures as her primary targets for cost management. After taking the ease of reporting and management focus over the prior two years into account, procedures became the proposed reporting unit of choice for this activity-based costing pilot program.

Mary also suggests that the pilot program be called a procedures-based costing pilot. She feels that procedures-based would be readily understood and better accepted by the clinical personnel. The procedures-based terminology is a departure from traditional labels for activity-based costing, but it accurately reflects the unit of work that generates most clinical costs: the procedure. The decision is therefore made to call Central Hospital's activity-based costing pilot a procedures-based costing pilot program.

The president of the medical staff gives his blessing to the project on the condition that the data not be used "to beat up physicians." In fact, many of the physicians in the community are already having to accept capitated payment rates for their office services. Accurate cost data will be just as useful to them in their practices as it is to the hospital.

Mary has a white paper about activity-based costing—called procedures-based costing—prepared for the steering committee. The white paper ensures that all steering committee members have a certain basic level of knowledge about the subject before the project proceeds. (The white paper appears later in this chapter.)

Mary has established the following four goals for the procedures-based costing pilot program:

1. To provide detailed cost information for three of Central's high-volume diagnosis-related groups (DRGs):
   - DRG 125, circulatory disorders except acute myocardial infarction
   - DRG 127, heart failure and shock
   - DRG 89, simple pneumonia, age greater than 17 with comorbidity and complications (CC)
2. To identify the profit margin for DRGs 127 and 143 by payer as a first step in establishing a cardiac service line with full profit and loss responsibility.
3. To provide accurate cost information by provider for each of the DRGs in scope. This cost information must show how each admitting physician for these DRGs compares to his peers on a case-mix adjusted basis.
4. To provide accurate cost information to support the variable budgeting process now being instituted at Central Hospital.

Mary would prefer to have a high degree of statistical confidence in the cost data generated by the procedures-based costing system. She realizes, however, that this level of accuracy comes over time as the cost database is developed and refined. For this pilot, she is primarily concerned that the cost information make sense to the major stakeholders—administration, physicians, and hospital department heads.

Each of these major stakeholder groups (administration, physicians, and hospital department heads) is represented on the project's steering committee. Mary Johnson and the president of the medical staff share executive sponsorship for the project. Together they have agreed to appoint Dr. Mike Czlinski, the hospital's pathologist, as the leader of the project team. The project team itself is composed of the head nurse of the ICU, a former industrial engineer with an MBA; the director of laboratory services; a senior physician from the emergency department; the director of dietary services; the associate director of information services; the manager of human resources operations; the

director of medical records; the hospital's controller; and an external consultant with experience in health care activity-based costing.

Central Hospital's information systems are reasonably up to date. Central runs most of its applications on an IBM AS400. This central computer is networked to all major departments, including the laboratory and the human resources department. Three years ago Central purchased an integrated patient information package from a well-known national vendor. The package included a cost accounting module that the hospital never implemented. Other major software packages include an integrated human resources information system (includes payroll, benefits, time, and attendance modules), a materials management package, and, of course, a financial accounting and reporting package.

Central's chart of accounts is typical of most hospitals—there are literally dozens of accounts. To implement the procedures-based costing system, the project team simplifies this account structure by grouping related accounts into a limited number of cost centers. Most of these cost centers will have both fixed and variable costs. The three tiers of cost centers are listed below.

Tier one cost centers include cumulative effect on prior years of change in an accounting principle; unrestricted gifts and bequests; income gains/losses on investments; extraordinary gains and/or losses; gains and/or losses on disposal of plant equipment; unassigned depreciation; insurance, excluding medical malpractice and employee benefit insurance; medical malpractice; interest expenses; tax expenses, excluding FICA and payroll taxes; cash discounts, rebates, and refunds; and purchased services, general.

Tier two cost centers include services to other entities, dietary services, plant operations, plant maintenance services, housekeeping services, laundry and linen services, social services, fiscal services, administrative services, nursing administration, medical records, information systems services, and medical education.

Tier three cost centers include the emergency department; med/surg one north; med/surg two north; med/surg three north; med/surg one south; med/surg two south; ICU; CCU; short-term observation unit one; short-term observation unit two; OB/GYN/pediatrics; recovery room; laboratory; pathology; diagnostic radiology; therapeutic radiology; OB/GYN clinic; ear, nose, and throat clinic; psychiatric outpatient clinic; pediatric outpatient clinic; chest pain outpatient clinic; pain management clinic; dermatology clinic; occupational rehabilitation clinic; and urology clinic.

The expense categories for tier two and tier three cost centers are set out in Exhibit 23–1. This exhibit also breaks out the listed expenses between direct and indirect costs (vertically) and between variable and fixed costs (horizontally).

IMPLEMENTING THE ABC PILOT PROGRAM

When Central Hospital purchased its patient information software from a national vendor three years ago, a cost accounting module had

---

Exhibit 23–1 Expense Categories for Tiers 2 and 3 Cost Centers

Expense Category	Variable Costs?	Fixed Costs?
Direct Costs		
Labor	Yes	Yes
• Salaries		
• Taxes		
Benefits	Yes	Yes
• Vacation/Sick Time/Holidays		
• FICA		
• Other Benefits		
Materials	Yes	No
Supplies	Yes	No
• Forms & Stationery		
• Office Supplies		
• Medical Supplies		
• Syringes and Needles		
• Intravenous Solutions		
• Drugs		
• Dietary Foods & Beverages		
Other Expenses	Yes	Yes
• Dues & Subscriptions		
• Books & Journals		
• Purchased Services		
Indirect Costs		
Other Expenses	Yes	Yes
• Capital Depreciation Overhead		
• Other Allocated Overhead		

Courtesy of Ryerson Management Associates, Inc., Akron, Ohio.

come as part of the software bundle. The first inclination of the project team is to simply use this software because it is fully integrated with other aspects of patient accounting.

Several of the team members, however, are concerned that this cost accounting module is not as flexible as it needs to be and that they will not be doing true procedure-based costing. In addition, the reports generated do not fully meet the objectives of the project. As a result, several members of the team undertake a search for a third-party vendor package that will more fully meet their needs. The entire project team agrees that the final package would meet all of the following criteria:

- It must assign costs to procedures and then to a variety of cost objects.
- It must integrate with other key data sources, including patient accounting and payroll.
- It must provide allocation strategies consistent with procedure-based costing, including step-down cost allocation and the assignment of activity drivers.
- It must support variable budgeting.
- It must be able to generate detailed reports consistent with the project's goals.
- It must be supported by a reputable vendor.
- It must permit multiple-scenario simulation to support strategic planning.
- It must be up and running within 6 to 12 weeks from the date it is finally selected by the project team.

The search committee develops a request for proposal (RFP) outlining these criteria in detail. Four vendors respond with proposals. One vendor is ruled out because of price. The rest are permitted to conduct an on-site demonstration and are subjected to rigorous questioning by the team members. After some debate, the project team agrees on a package that is supported by a midsize consulting organization, also based in the Midwest. Installation begins almost immediately using a two-person team supplied by the vendor.

An important part of setting up the software package is the development of a data dictionary. This involves selecting and configuring the various data fields used in procedure-based costing. Some of the fields set up by the vendor team are the cost center name, procedure name, procedure number, resource driver name, activity driver name, position names, capital equipment, inventoried materials, case type name, case type number, clinical service name, provider name, provider number, and payer name. Once the field names are set up, the vendor team develops rules for allocating costs. Part of this step includes determining activity drivers. This is especially difficult, because not everyone on the project team understands the concept of an activity driver. Finally, the leader of the vendor team explains that an activity driver is used in much the same way as a relative value unit. It is used to "weight" the allocation of resources to a particular procedure or activity. The difference, however, is that relative value units are averages developed either by Medicare or by a private vendor from studying a given procedure across multiple providers. Activity drivers need to be developed from a study of actual clinical procedures at Central Hospital.

After some discussion, the project team adopts a suggestion of the director of medical records. For the pilot, use the diagnostic ICD-9 code for each patient to establish a weighting factor based on the presence of comorbidities and other complicating factors. The simplest case in a family of principal diagnoses will have a weight of one, while more complex cases will be weighted according to their relative severity. As an example, the director of medical records outlines how this scheme would work with some of the more common principal diagnoses for DRG 127 (Exhibit 23–2).

The vendor team then programs a series of cost allocation rules into the package. Among these rules is one that says in effect: For a given procedure, multiply the total variable costs (both direct and indirect) by the patient's (ICD-9) diagnostic weighting level.

Exhibit 23–2 DRG 127: Heart Failure and Shock*

ICD-9 Code	Principal Diagnosis	Relative Weight
402.11	Hypertensive, heart disease, with congestive heart failure, benign	1.0
402.01	Hypertensive, heart disease, with congestive heart failure, malignant	1.5
404.11	Hypertensive, heart and renal disease, with congestive heart failure, benign	2.0
404.03	Hypertensive, heart and renal disease, with congestive heart failure, malignant	2.5

*NOTE: For each weighting factor, multiply by 1.25 if patient age is greater than 70. For each weighting factor, multiply by 1.5 if patient is diabetic or if other significant comorbidities are present.

Courtesy of Ryerson Management Associates, Inc., Akron, Ohio.

The vendor team also assists in establishing the resource drivers for each procedure. Virtually all of the procedures use full-time equivalents (FTEs) as a resource driver. Most tier two indirect costs are allocated to the labor hours that are involved in conducting each procedure. The vendor team also studies each procedure and establishes engineered standards for direct labor to support the variable labor budget.

Once they have configured the software package to meet Central's needs, the vendor team imports data from the hospital's patient, human resource, and materials management information systems. This allows them to run an initial set of reports. The reports of greatest interest to the project team are profitability, case type; profitability, case type by procedure; profitability, by payer; profitability, procedure by payer; profitability, by provider; profitability, procedure by provider; procedure cost analysis, summary by expense class type; procedure cost analysis, and detail by expense class type. For example, part of the physician profitability report appeared as set out in Exhibit 23–3.

As the team examines this report, it becomes clear there are some problems with the data. For instance, Physician #107 has more than three discharges this year. This inconsistency, plus others identified in other parts of the report, suggest incorrect data from the patient accounting system. After the considerable review and correction of input data, the project team begins to have a high level of confidence in reports such as the one found in Exhibit 23–4.

Once the project team feels that they have solid data to work from, Dr. Czlinski schedules a presentation to the steering committee. The project team has already made the following three recommendations about how to use the cost data:

1. The data should be published to the medical staff at large but without specific provider names. Individual providers, however, should be sent their own performance data separately and be allowed to compare themselves to their peers.

2. For case types where significant cost and clinical practice variation becomes evident, a problem-solving, continuous improvement approach should be used to correct the situation. The focus should remain on fixing the problem, not on fixing the blame.

3. The performance of individual hospital departments should be secondary to the performance of the overall clinical process. This will require cross-departmental

Exhibit 23–3 Sample Profitability by Physician Report

MDC NC7PLDET					mm/dd/yy		Page 1	

Central Hospital
Physician Profitability Report
Period Ending mm/dd/yy Year-to-Date

Physician Number: ALL   Inpatient/Outpatient: Both
Case Type Number: ALL   Normal/Outlier: Both

	Total	Per Case	%
Gross Revenue	38,035,710	881	100
Net Revenue	23,169,403	537	60.9
Gross Margin	9,441,490	219	24.8
Fixed Costs	13,727,913	318	36.1
Net Income	1,650,475	38	4.3

Physician	Discharge	Revenue		Costs			Net Income
		Gross	Net	Variable	Fixed	Total	
#103	459	108,456	79,507	22,764	29,521	52,284	27,223
Per Case		236.29	173.22	49.59	64.32	113.91	59.31
#105	75	19,534	13,835	3,064	5,198	8,262	5,574
Per Case		260.45	184.47	40.85	69.30	110.15	74.32
#107	3	184	148	56	37	93	55
Per Case		61.33	49.33	18.61	12.38	30.99	18.34
#108	76	105,145	49,686	23,550	34,956	58,505	−8,819
Per Case		1,383.49	653.76	309.86	459.95	769.81	−116
#112	112	167,059	117,815	42,086	52,460	94,546	23,269
Per Case		1,491.60	1,051.92	375.76	468.39	844.16	207.76

Courtesy of Ryerson Management Associates, Inc., Akron, Ohio.

cooperation. Only departments that refuse to cooperate should face appropriate sanctions by management.

Despite the fact that there were still some "bugs" to work out of the procedure-based costing system, the steering committee was highly impressed with the results of the pilot. Mary Johnson, the CFO, received permission to proceed with a full-scale implementation. Over the coming months, Central would be expanding the number of case types included for procedure-based costing.

One year after the full implementation of the procedure-based costing system at Central Hospital, virtually all of the administration and many on the medical staff view the initiative as a success. The hospital now has detailed cost data on some 20 DRGs for which it has developed treatment protocols. Also, each admitting physician on staff gets a quarterly private report of his or her cost performance relative to other physicians in his or her specialty.

When this reporting system was implemented, a number of physicians on staff objected strenuously. However, through a series of one-on-one meetings with these doctors, Mary Johnson and Dr. Czlinski were able to persuade most that the cost of care is simply the quality of care dressed up in dollar signs.

Exhibit 23–4 Performance Report—Physician by Procedure Cost Detail

Central Hospital
Performance Report: Physician by Procedure Cost Details
Period Ended: Year-to-Date

Physician: 115 Galen, C.S.
Case Type: 127 Heart Failure & Shock
Cost Method: Actual
Number of Cases Physician: 15 Peer Group: 37

Cost Center Procedure	Procedures for Case			Actual Cost per Proc	Cost for Case		
	Phys. Avg.	Peer Grp Avg.	Var.		Phys	Peer Grp	Var.
Med/Surg 2 North							
0001 Rm & Bd	2.20	2.85	.66	306.54	674.39	875.83	201.44
TOTAL COST CENTER	2.20	2.85	.66		674.39	875.83	201.44
Med/Surg 3 North							
0001 Rm & Bd	4.46	2.42	−2.04	293.76	1312.3	713.42	−598.71
TOTAL COST CENTER	4.46	2.42	−2.04		1312.3	713.42	−598.71
Med/Surg 1 South							
Rm & Bd	2.13	2.00	−.13	427.76	912.55	855.52	−57.03
TOTAL COST CENTER	2.13	2.00	−.13		912.55	855.52	−57.03
ICU							
Rm & Bd	1.40	1.42	.03	628.64	880.10	898.06	17.96
TOTAL COST CENTER	1.40	1.42	.03		880.10	898.06	17.96
Pharmacy							
0002 Inj Antibiotic	1.93	2.57	.64	17.54	33.91	45.10	11.19
0003 IV Admin	.46	.42	−.04	74.16	34.61	31.78	−2.83
0005 TPN	.73	.85	.12	66.19	48.54	56.73	8.19
0006 Unit Dose	5.80	6.14	.34	10.55	61.19	64.81	3.62
8888 All Other	7.80	8.28	.49	12.48	97.34	103.41	6.07
TOTAL COST CENTER	16.72	18.26	1.55		275.59	301.83	26.24
Diagnostic Radiology							
0032 Chest P & L	1.80	1.85	.06	86.79	156.22	161.18	4.96
0108 ABD-KUB	.06	.13	.07	85.49	5.70		−5.70
0161 Chst AP	1.20	1.57	.37	64.04	76.85	100.63	23.78
8888 All Other	.33	.28	−.05	58.13	19.38	16.61	−2.77
TOTAL COST CENTER	3.39	3.83	.46		258.15	278.42	20.27

Courtesy of Ryerson Management Associates, Inc., Akron, Ohio.

Except for a few "bitter-enders," most of the physicians now look forward to their monthly costing report.

Mary believes that even in its first year the new procedure-based costing system has more than paid for itself. Central's goal for the coming fiscal year will be to have 35 out of 40 top DRGs monitored under the new system. And for the first time ever, the leadership at Central Hospital feels ready to face the challenge of managed care. At the same time, Utilization Review received direction to start working actively with physicians and staff to make changes in problem areas. And, finally, Central's CEO identified a new management team whose job it would be to plan for managed care negotiations. The team would include both financial and clinical specialists and would be chaired by Mary Johnson.

STEERING COMMITTEE WHITE PAPER

There are basically two types of accounting: financial accounting and managerial accounting. Financial accounting is primarily concerned with reporting the health care organization's financial performance to external constituencies at the community, state, and national levels. In the case of for-profit health care organizations, these external constituencies might include shareholders as well.

Managerial accounting is primarily designed to support decision making within the organization itself. These decisions may include which products and services will be profitable, which departments are making efficient uses of their resources, and which providers are achieving the best outcomes for the least amount of resource.

Cost accounting is used in both financial reporting and in internal decision making. It is primarily a form of managerial accounting. Before management can decide on the potential profitability of a new service line, it must know how much it will cost to produce the services. This cost knowledge is especially important during negotiations with payers. If a commercial payer proposes to cut its daily payment for a particular case type, management must be prepared with detailed cost information in order to respond appropriately.

Cost accounting information is equally important in managing organizational performance. To determine whether a department is operating within budget, management must understand in dollar terms how that department is using labor and material resources. At the same time, payers and other funding sources often require information about the cost of products (such as DRGs) and clinical procedures. Cost accounting is the primary way those costs are identified and reported. As such, it also fulfills some of the goals of financial accounting.

In managerial accounting terms, cost is simply the dollar value of resources (such as people, supplies, building space, capital equipment, and so forth) that is expended during the process of delivering medical care. Accountants classify costs as variable vs. fixed costs and as direct vs. indirect costs. Variable costs increase or decrease in proportion with changes in volume. If, for example, a health care organization increases the number of nurses in the emergency department during times of peak traffic, the cost of nursing labor for this department would be considered a variable cost. Fixed costs remain at generally the same level even if volume increases or decreases. In the short run, the cost to provide heat and lighting for an emergency department will probably not increase, no matter how many patients arrive for treatment.

Costs that can be traced directly to discrete actions in the provision of medical care are categorized as direct costs. But there are many costs in a health care organization that are necessary but that cannot be traced directly to patient treatment. For example, most hospitals use a computer to help manage patient information. But this computer is used for many patients, not just for one. It is an indirect cost, because its cost must be spread over the entire patient population. In the same way, all hospitals have some form of administration. The CEO, the director of nursing, and other key administrators support patient care, but the cost of their salaries must be also be considered as indirect costs that are spread over many patients. Exhibit 23–5 illustrates how some costs might be classified.

How to fairly allocate indirect costs—either fixed or variable—is one of the most difficult problems in cost accounting. There are three primary methods: (1) ratio of cost to charges,

Exhibit 23–5 Types of Cost

The following table illustrates how some costs might be classified.

	Variable Costs	Fixed Costs
Direct Costs	• Staff Nurse Salaries • Staff Nurse Benefits • Direct Supplies	• Rent for Facility • Contractual Payments to the ER Physician Group
Indirect Costs	• Nursing Supervision Salaries and Benefits • Information Systems Temps To Handle Increased Workload • Clinical Education Expenses	• Executive Salaries • Building Depreciation • Non-liability Insurance

Courtesy of Ryerson Management Associates, Inc., Akron, Ohio.

(2) relative value units, and (3) activity-based, or procedure-based, costing.

The ratio of cost to charges (RCC) method is still probably the most widely used cost accounting method in health care today. The approach is simple: Total revenues are divided by total indirect costs. There are three fundamental assumptions behind this basic costing method. First, RCC assumes that direct costs of delivering health care at least equal revenues generated. Second, the method assumes that all indirect costs are essentially the same. Third, RCC assumes that all indirect costs can be allocated across functions in equal proportions. The RCC method has worked well under traditional fee-for-service reimbursement schemes because the method encourages managers to seek more highly reimbursed lines of service. But the method provides only very general cost information. More important, many managed care reimbursement strategies constrain the provider's ability to seek higher revenues. For most managed care negotiations, cost information developed through the RCC method is inadequate.

Cost accounting using the relative value unit method is an improvement over the traditional RCC approach. Relative value units are standardized measures of resource consumption. In contrast to the RCC costing method, which focused on revenue as a measure of work performed, relative value units are assigned to actual clinical procedures.

For example, two clinical procedures, procedure A and procedure B, could be assigned a specified number of relative value units. Procedure A, the "baseline" procedure, might be assigned one RVU. Procedure B, which takes twice as long to complete and uses twice the manpower, would be assigned two RVUs. Other procedures would be assigned a number of RVUs depending on whether they are easier or more difficult than procedure A. RVUs are then used to allocate indirect costs to specific departments. First, all the clinical procedures conducted by a department are identified, along with their associated relative value units. The RVUs are then multiplied by the number of procedures that department conducted and totaled to get the overall RVU count for the department. This process is illustrated in Exhibit 23–6.

All total relative value units are then totaled for all departments and indirect costs are allocated proportionally. Thus, if a health care institution had to allocate $1,000,000 in indirect cost to six departments using RVUs, the distribution of costs might look something like the RVU cost allocation illustrated in Exhibit 23–7.

Exhibit 23–6 Total RVUs by Department

Procedures Conducted	Procedure RVUs	Number of Procedures Conducted	Total RVUs
Procedure A	1	100	100
Procedure B	2	35	70
Procedure C	.25	250	62.5
Procedure D	3.5	50	175
Total			407.5

Courtesy of Ryerson Management Associates, Inc., Akron, Ohio.

Using relative value units to allocate indirect costs is an improvement over the RCC method in a number of ways. First, the RVU approach uses clinical procedures as the basis for allocating costs. This relates cost to the way health care services are actually delivered. It also recognizes that the indirect costs are not consumed equally by all clinical activities. As such, the RVU costing method provides a more accurate picture of the way in which resources are consumed in an organization.

The RVU costing method is not without its drawbacks, however. There is no standard way of determining relative value units. A number of organizations market standardized RVU tables; however, many of these systems vary among vendors. Also, a number of these RVU schemes are determined largely on the basis of labor required to complete a procedure. Although labor is a significant part of most health care budgets, the cost of materials is also important for most providers.

Procedure-based costing is a managerial accounting methodology that measures the cost of producing goods and services based on the way those goods and services are actually produced. Many traditional cost accounting methods attempt to determine the cost of producing goods and services. The approach used by procedure-based costing is unique. Based on an analysis of the organization's work processes, procedure-based costing measures the cost performance of specific "cost objects" such as finished products, identifiable services, customers, markets and market segments, and suppliers and vendors.

Exhibit 23–7 RVU Cost Allocation

Department	Total RVUs	% of Total	Indirect Cost Allocation
Department 1	407.5	17%	$ 170,000
Department 2	223	10%	$ 100,000
Department 3	547	23%	$ 230,000
Department 4	199	9%	$ 90,000
Department 5	357.5	15%	$ 150,000
Department 6	603	26%	$ 260,000
Total	2337	100%	$1,000,000

Courtesy of Ryerson Management Associates, Inc., Akron, Ohio.

At the heart of any cost accounting methodology is its strategy for distributing or allocating indirect costs, both fixed and variable. Many traditional costing methods use a method called a step-down approach to allocating costs. The approach to stepping down costs is a relatively simple one. It begins with the concept of cost centers. Cost centers are logically related accounts (from the organization's chart of accounts) that are grouped together in order to collect and simplify cost information.

For example, a health care provider may decide to group all administrative services into a single cost center. The general ledger accounts that are assigned to this cost center might be executive office nonpersonnel expenses, governing board nonpersonnel expenses, auxiliary group nonpersonnel expenses, chaplaincy services nonpersonnel expenses, public relations nonpersonnel expenses, purchasing nonpersonnel expenses, communications nonpersonnel expenses, information services nonpersonnel expenses, printing and duplicating nonpersonnel expenses, receiving and storing nonpersonnel expenses, employee medical services nonpersonnel expenses, and administrative services personnel-related expenses.

Administrative services personnel-related expenses include salaries and wages, employee benefits, and taxes payable.

Employee benefits include vacation, holiday, sick pay, and other nonworked compensation; social security taxes; federal and state unemployment taxes; group health and life insurance; retirement plan expenses; workers' compensation insurance; and group disability insurance.

Taxes payable includes income tax expense, federal income tax currently payable, provision for deferred federal income tax, state income tax expense currently payable, and provision for deferred state income tax.

In a step-down cost allocation approach, costs from specific cost centers are allocated or added to those of other cost centers. This is done hierarchically. That is, certain cost centers allocate their costs to others but do not receive allocated costs in return. Some cost centers both

receive and allocate costs. And some cost centers *only* receive allocated costs. They do not distribute their costs to other cost centers. Thus, the typical step-down approach uses a multilevel cost allocation structure, with at least two and sometimes more tiers of cost centers, as illustrated in Figure 23–1.

First-tier cost centers represent resources (and expenses) applicable to the entire organization. First-tier cost centers might include facilities and properties, insurance other than professional liability, nonpayroll taxes, licenses, other professional fees (e.g., legal services, auditing services, and so forth), and charity services.

Second-tier cost centers frequently represent services that are used indirectly in the production of the organization's marketable products and services. Examples of second-tier cost centers might include fiscal services, plant operation and maintenance, administrative services, housekeeping, laundry and linen services, medical education, medical records, medical library services, and cafeteria.

Third-tier cost centers are typically involved directly in the production of the organization's marketable/reimbursable products and services. These might include nursing services, emergency and ambulance services, central sterile reprocessing, laboratory services, electrodiagnosis, radiology—diagnostic, radiology—therapeutic, pharmacy, rehabilitation services, and dietary services

Costs are distributed down this hierarchy according to clearly defined allocation factors. For example, an organization might consider the facilities and properties a first-tier cost center. The logical way to allocate the cost of building depreciation to second-tier cost centers would be on the basis of the square feet of building space that they occupy. Thus, if the administrative services was a second-tier cost center, it would be allocated a certain number of building depreciation dollars based on the total amount of office space its associated departments occupied in company buildings.

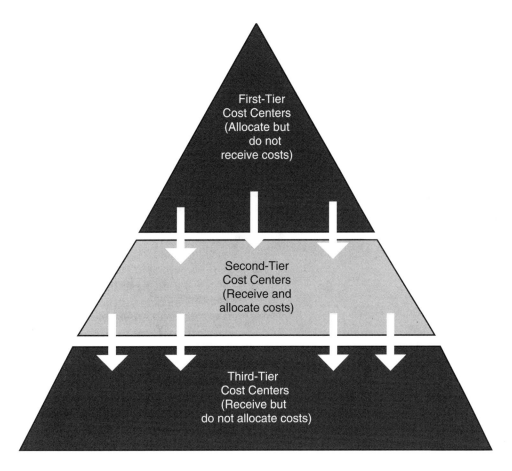

Figure 23–1 Step-Down Cost Allocation. Courtesy of Ryerson Management Associates, Inc., Akron, Ohio.

Other logical allocation factors might include volume, direct labor hours, cycle time (time from start to finish), CPU time, and number of transactions.

Procedure-based costing uses this step-down cost allocation approach as well. However, what makes procedure-based costing unique is the approach that is used to assign these allocated costs to various cost objects. To understand how this is done, it is necessary to review how work processes operate.

A work process is simply a related group of activities that convert some input into an output. An activity, in turn, is a measurable unit of work

that is a part of the overall conversion process. Manufacturing provides the most understandable example of how a process operates. Consider, for example, the process used to produce an automobile. Early in the twentieth century, Henry Ford pioneered the process of converting raw materials into finished cars. Unrefined ore was processed into auto parts, which were then assembled into complete automobiles. In simple terms, the manufacturing process might be diagrammed as illustrated in Figure 23–2.

Each major step in Figure 23–2 involves the transformation of one thing into another. Ore is transformed into metal, metal is stamped and

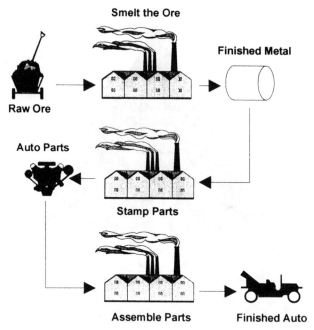

Figure 23–2 A Manufacturing Process. Courtesy of Ryerson Management Associates, Inc., Akron, Ohio.

transformed into auto parts, and so on. A process, then, is a series of linked work activities that transform some input into an output (Figure 23–3).

Of course, a health care organization is not an auto manufacturing plant. However, some principles of manufacturing processes also apply to health care. Patients (an input) are transformed from unstable to stable or from unhealthy to healthy through a series of activities that can be represented as a work process. Consider, for example, a simplified version of the process that is associated with treating heart attack patients (Figure 23–4).

Through a series of work activities—or in health care terms, procedures—performed in settings such as surgery and the cardiac care unit, the patient is transformed from someone who is critically ill to someone who has the potential for a healthy and productive life.

Activity-based costing uses a two-stage approach (Figure 23–5) to assign overhead cost to activities and then through those activities to the products and other things associated with those activities. In the first stage, indirect costs, both fixed and variable, are assigned to activities in the process by using a resource driver. Resource drivers are very much like the alloca-

Figure 23–3 Linked Transformations Form a Process. Courtesy of Ryerson Management Associates, Inc., Akron, Ohio.

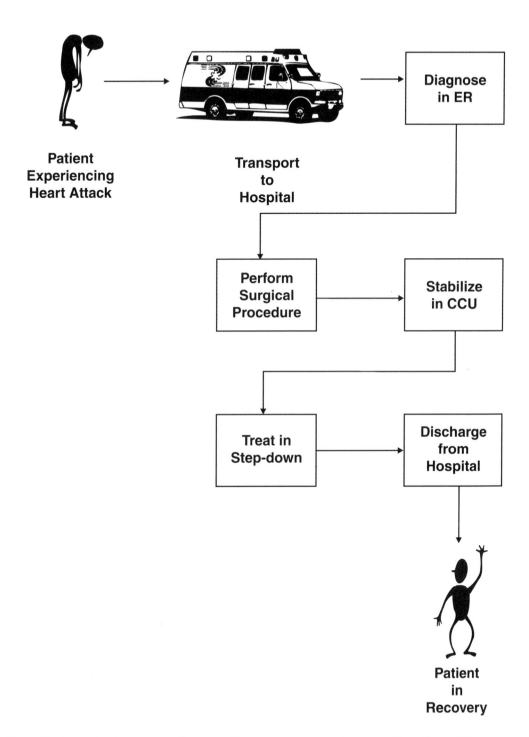

Figure 23–4 A Health Care Process. Courtesy of Ryerson Management Associates, Inc., Akron, Ohio.

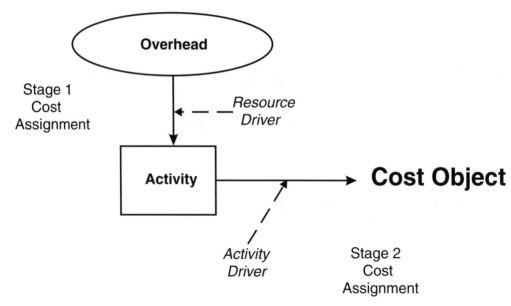

Figure 23–5 Two-Stage Cost Assignment. Courtesy of Ryerson Management Associates, Inc., Akron, Ohio.

tion factors used to step down indirect costs between tiers. Health care resource drivers might include FTEs, square footage, discharge volume, number of visits, nursing acuity levels, College of American Pathologists (CAP) standards, and engineered standards.

During the second stage of procedure-based costing, the total costs that are assigned to the activity are further assigned to one or more cost objects. In simple terms, a cost object is anything that can be directly associated with an activity. Examples of health care cost objects are illustrated in Figure 23–6 and include service line, provider, case type, payer, and population or population segment. (Individual organizations may well focus on numerous cost objects other than these examples.)

Not all of these cost objects, however, consume activity resources to the same degree. For example, consider a situation in which a patient case type such as a heart attack is the cost object. Two patients of this same case type might undergo a diagnostic procedure such as a chest X-ray; however, because one patient is

alert and aware of his surrounding, he is able to work with the radiology technician to complete the X-ray quickly and efficiently. Another patient, who is confused and disoriented at the time of the diagnostic procedure, may not be as cooperative. Both patients undergo the same procedure. One patient, however, requires considerably more time and effort than another.

To account for this difference in resource consumption, procedure-based costing uses an activity driver in stage two to weight the allocation of costs to each cost object. Some possible activity drivers in health care include presence of patient comorbidities, specialized sterile requirements, the number of times a provider conducts a surgical procedure per year, specialized laundry processing requirements, specialized meal requirements, and requirements for patient isolation. In the example of the two patients given above, the patient who is disoriented would require more effort and would therefore be assigned a higher percentage of the cost resources in the activity "conduct stereo chest X-ray."

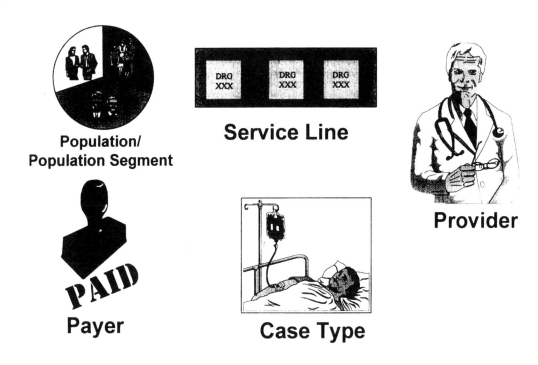

Figure 23–6 Health Care Cost Objects. Courtesy of Ryerson Management Associates, Inc., Akron, Ohio.

In a procedure-based costing approach, the patient—or case type—can be used as a cost object. That is, after the indirect costs of the tier one and tier two cost centers are allocated to the activities required to treat a heart attack patient, the total cost of these activities is assigned to that patient type. These activity costs can also be assigned to other cost objects such as the provider, the payer, a service line, and so on.

In simple terms, then, the entire procedure-based cost assignment process looks like the diagram presented in Figure 23–7. Note that in certain situations it may be advisable to assign some second-tier costs directly to a cost object.

Of course, this simplified picture does not take into account the fact that there are multiple levels of activity in any process. In the health care process depicted in Figure 23–7, diagnose in ER is shown as an activity. But treatment in the emergency room may involve many other identifiable activities such as medical examinations, lab tests, and so on. In other words, all activities can be decomposed or broken down into smaller amounts of work. In a health care process, it is usually a good idea to decompose activities to the level where they may be given a discrete CPT code.

And so, procedure-based costing allows assignment of indirect cost to specific cost objects based on the way work is actually done. In effect, each cost object is assigned a bill of activities. For the process "diagnose and treat in ER" this bill of activities might look something like Exhibit 23–8. Specific, codable activities are frequently identified in prescribed testing panels and in care pathways or other clinical guidelines.

Thus far, the focus has been on allocating indirect costs. Direct costs, both fixed and variable, are also a significant part of the cost for

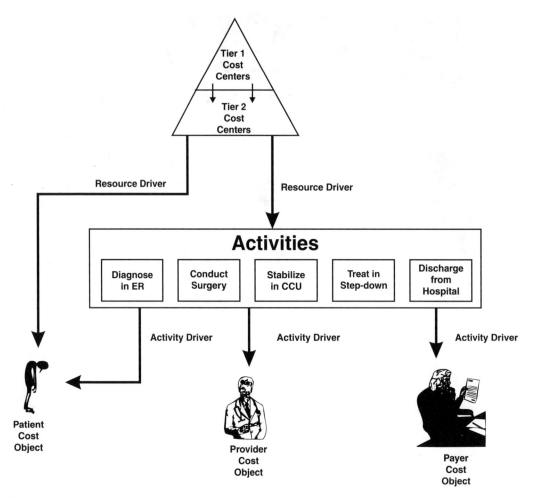

Figure 23–7 Activity-Based Cost Assignments. Courtesy of Ryerson Management Associates, Inc., Akron, Ohio.

delivering health care services. Most direct costs are variable: They increase or decrease with changes in volume. The use of expendable materials used to conduct lab tests, such as reagents or culture mediums, increases when more lab tests are performed. The same is true for direct labor such as technician time. Assuming that a lab is as productive as possible, a higher volume of tests generally requires a higher staffing level.

Direct costs, like indirect costs, are allocated to procedures in activity-based costing. Besides any assigned indirect costs, each procedure will have a bill of labor and a bill of materials. A complete cost profile for a clinical procedure might look like the example of an EKG Cost Profile presented in Exhibit 23–9.

The purpose of managerial accounting is to provide data to support management decisions. The data that is generated by an activity-based

Exhibit 23–8 Bill of Activities

1.0	Cost Object: 55-Year-Old Female Experiencing Heart Attack (DRG 121/ ICD-9 Code 786.5)
1.1	Diagnose and Treat in ER
1.1.1	Conduct Medical Examination
1.1.2	Conduct 2-View Portable Chest X-ray
1.1.3	Conduct Myoglobin Test
1.1.4	Conduct Tryponin Test
1.1.5	Conduct ABG Test
1.1.6	Conduct CBC Test
1.1.7	Conduct PT and PTT Test
1.1.8	Conduct Sedimentation Rate Test
1.1.9	Administer Aspirin
1.1.10	Administer Heparin

costing profile such as the one in Exhibit 23–9 is useful for both day-to-day operational management and for strategic decision making. From an operations standpoint, what makes procedure-based costing so powerful is that it is based on the way health care is actually delivered. Procedure-based costing focuses not only on procedures but also on the reasons procedures consume different levels of resources— the activity drivers. From a strategic perspective, activity-based, or procedure-based costing is capable of aggregating the cost of doing business to the cost objects that matter to executives: providers, payers, case types, and service lines.

The three major uses of procedure-based costing data are to: (1) improve clinical activities, (2) assist in strategic planning, and (3) monitor and manage organizational performance (performance management).

Improving clinical activities is a key element. There is a strong relationship between cost and quality. In a manufacturing environment, poor quality leads not only to customer dissatisfaction but also to scrap and rework. The same principle applies in health care setting. Failures in a clinical process may lead to things such as incorrect diagnoses, repeat surgeries, hospital-based infections, laboratory and radiology rework, and unexpected medical complications. Frequently, these outcomes show up as both increased cost and increased length of stay.

Consider the graph for a particular case type that was developed using activity-based cost information (Figure 23–8). The graph illustrates charges per admission—case mix adjusted, on the vertical axis, and average length of stay— case mix adjusted, on the horizontal axis.

The charge per admission is generated by a software-driven activity-based costing system. The average length of stay is determined from

Exhibit 23–9 EKG Cost Profile

CPT Code	Procedure Name	Variable Costs				Fixed Costs	Total Cost
		Direct Labor Cost			Direct Material Cost		
		Variable Cost	Assigned Indirect Cost	Total Labor Cost			
93000	12-lead EKG w/interp & report	$46	$15	$61	$4.00	$20.00	$85.00

Courtesy of Ryerson Management Associates, Inc., Akron, Ohio.

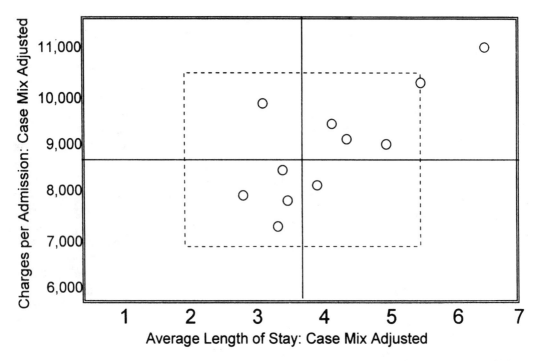

Figure 23–8 Activity-Based Clinical Data. Courtesy of Ryerson Management Associates, Inc., Akron, Ohio.

utilization data. The square in the center (broken lines) represents the range of expected cost and length of stay for this type of case. Each of the circles represents the actual annual performance of individual physicians, adjusted for certain case-mix factors such as the presence of comorbidities.

As the graph shows, the standard of practice on this type of case falls well within the expected cost and length of stay. However, one physician falls outside the expected levels. Why? The next step would involve reviewing cost data for individual procedures performed by this provider as well as patient medical records and other clinical information. After quality assurance or utilization review has formed one or more hypotheses regarding the root causes of this unexpected variation, they will be in position to work with this physician to improve his or her clinical treatment of this case type.

The fact that a single provider falls outside the standard of practice for this case type suggests that individual practice patterns may be the cause. The data, however, could also tell a different story. If more physician data points fell outside the center box, this health care institution may indeed have a broken clinical process. The variation in cost and length of stay may be driven by many failures in dealing with this type of patient. The solution may require a true clinical process improvement project involving every function, from the emergency department to housekeeping, which provides care and service to these patients.

Figure 23–8 was developed from activity-based cost data for a single DRG or case type. Suppose this case type was part of a service line? For example, a cardiac service line might be defined as in Exhibit 23–10.

In order to identify the cost for the service line, the cost of each procedure would first be summed by DRG. Then the cost of each DRG in the service line would also be summed to get the total costs for that set of services. Assuming that the procedures-based costing system was

Exhibit 23–10 Cardiac Service Line

Cardiac Pacemaker Services
    DRG 115, Permanent Cardiac Pacemaker with Acute Myocardial Infarction, Heart Failure, and Shock
    DRG 116, Other Permanent Cardiac Pacemaker Implant
    DRG 117, Cardiac Pacemaker Revision Except Device Replacement
    DRG 118, Cardiac Pacemaker Device Replacement
Cardiac Disorders
    DRG 121, Circulatory Disorders with Acute Myocardial Infarction and Cardiovascular Complication, Discharged Alive
    DRG 122, Circulatory Disorders with Acute Myocardial Infarction without Cardiovascular Complication, Discharged Alive
    DRG 123, Circulatory Disorders with Acute Myocardial Infarction, Expired
    DRG 124, Circulatory Disorders Except Acute Myocardial Infarction with Cardiac Catheterization and Complex Diagnosis
    DRG 125, Circulatory Disorders Except Acute Myocardial Infarction with Cardiac Catheterization and Complex Diagnosis
    DRG 126, Acute and Subacute Endocarditis
    DRG 127, Heart Failure and Shock
Chest Pain
    DRG 140, Angina Pectoris
    DRG 143, Chest Pain

capable of identifying the revenues associated with each DRG (preferably by payer), it would be possible to determine the profitability of each case type individually and of the service line as a whole.

Being able to relate the cost of doing business to the reimbursement received from each payer also has another important use: supporting executives in negotiating managed-care contracts. To be able to attain favorable rates for any of the numerous types of managed-care payment arrangements, health care organizations must be able to have detailed cost information. If the payer offers a rate that is lower than the actual cost of providing service, it is better not to enter into that payment arrangement. Of course, it is ideal if these cost data reflect the level of accuracy achieved with procedures-based costing.

Finally, procedures-based cost information can be used in the selection of a health care organization's panel of providers. For example, a physician group practice may need to know the extent to which each physician contributes to—or detracts from—the profitability of the practice. By associating the cost of each procedure with the physicians who perform those procedures, it is possible to get an accurate profile for each provider in the group.

Procedure-based cost information can also be used by executives to monitor and manage performance at multiple levels, such as total organization/strategic performance against goals, or at the service line level, the product/service level, the department level, or the individual (provider) level. Many cost accounting systems allow assessment of the organization against strategic cost goals. The level of accuracy provided by a procedure-based cost system makes it ideal for this purpose.

The unique ability of procedure-based costing to assign cost to specific cost objects makes accurate reporting of product, service line, and provider performance relatively easy. Departments, which are typically the focus of traditional cost accounting are not normally cost objects in a procedure-based costing system. At the same time, most procedures tend to be performed in specific departments or cost centers, so it is easy to trace costs to those areas. Procedures are thus the reporting unit of choice for this activity-based costing pilot program.

CONCLUSION

In a cost-plus era where health care financial managers could afford to work from averages and estimates, simple cost accounting methods such as ratio of cost to charges provided adequate information for good decision making. But in times of constrained revenues and increasing financial risk, health care financial managers need powerful tools. Their cost accounting systems must be proven, accurate, and reliable. Procedure-based accounting is just such a tool. Proven in multiple industries over the last ten years, procedure-based costing can provide health care decision makers with their most accurate information to date.

NOTE

1. T. West et al., "Contrasting RCCD, RVU, and ABC for Managed Care Decisions," *Healthcare Financial Management* (August 1996): 54–61.

## CHAPTER 24

The Future for ABC/ABM in Health Care

Judith J. Baker with Beau Keyte

CHAPTER OUTLINE

ABC in Integrated Systems: Supporting
  Redesigned Care Delivery
Redesigning Financial Performance
  Measures
Implementation
Obstacles
Opportunities
Conclusion

The future for ABC/ABM in health care hinges on two issues. The first concerns using ABC/ABM to support the new strategies and tactics of delivering care, including adaptation to management information systems. The second concerns implementation. Both are key to the future. Beau Keyte has contributed his view of progressive health care delivery, management information support, and their relationship to the future of ABC/ABM.

ABC IN INTEGRATED SYSTEMS: SUPPORTING REDESIGNED CARE DELIVERY

There is a frenzy of merger and acquisition activity in health care aimed at gaining market share and contracting leverage. This acquisition strategy, however, is rarely coordinated with an operations strategy designed to make fundamen-

tal changes in the way health care is delivered. Most integrated delivery systems (IDSs) consist of a variety of organizations that still have the same activities and processes as they had prior to the merger. Figure 24–1 shows the progression of an episode of care within a delivery system with selected clinical and administrative activities. Redundant activities, such as patient registration and assessment, are not coordinated throughout the organization, thus creating unnecessary costs and patient dissatisfaction.

In addition to the redundant activities, the care path for a patient is not predictable. Figure 24–2 demonstrates the various care paths that a patient can experience for a single service line. Caregivers may send patients to any of several proceeding interventions with very little justification, planning, or communication. The combination of duplicate activities and multiple patient paths results in ineffective services, dysfunctional experiences, and unhappy patients.

Operational strategies to coordinate a care continuum are also held hostage by existing financial performance systems and measures. Although a system may attempt to standardize the financial information system throughout all organizations, some care partners, such as physicians, may not be part of the IDS and not have access to the financial system. In addition, each organization utilizing the agreed-upon system incorporates different standards and assumptions

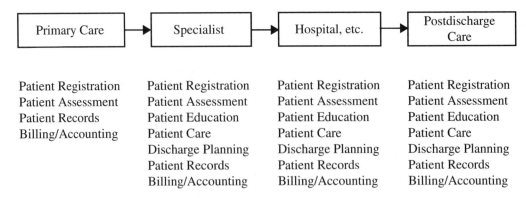

Figure 24–1 Progression of an Episode of Care within a Delivery System. *Source:* Copyright © 1996, Branson, Inc. Further reproduction is strictly prohibited.

within their standard costs. A system with 20 different organizations will experience 20 different ways to develop costs and allocate overhead. Does anyone know or agree on the true cost of the interventions involved in a service line?

Creating fundamental changes in care delivery usually involves redesigning and redirecting care among the various providers. This effort will challenge not only the cost structure but also the revenue of organizations, regardless of the type of contracts they have for their patients. For instance, if care is shifted from the hospital to home care, the hospital loses the cost or revenue and home care wins the cost or revenue. Consolidating patient intake responsibilities (history, physical, and patient education) would change the cost or revenue of anyone currently involved in these activities.

An integrated delivery system in Virginia designed a care continuum for joint replacements that is focused on surviving the advent of managed care and capitated populations. They developed an operations strategy and a model for end-to-end patient care that transformed the service line depicted in Figure 24–2 to the continuum depicted in Figure 24–3.

Features of this model include:

- one production path for patient and patient information regardless of the provider involved

- patient intake performed at the physician office and shared with all downstream providers
- progressive (as opposed to redundant) patient education and therapy throughout the continuum
- dedicated postacute care providers for each patient path

This delivery system employed a straightforward but rigorous approach to achieve this continuum that involved:

- identification of core services and features to meet the orthopedic market needs
- rationalization of these services against internal (the system) and external (the competition) strengths and weaknesses
- identification of continuum partners inside and outside the boundary of the IDS organizations
- redesign of the organizations and functions supporting the continuum to improve clinical, economic, and service outcomes

Activity-based costing is the economic outcome that has been used to create an apples-to-apples cost comparison within the continuum. The redesign project created baseline activity direct costs by measuring internal processes without regard to the budgeted cost of each function. The various cost drivers were identi-

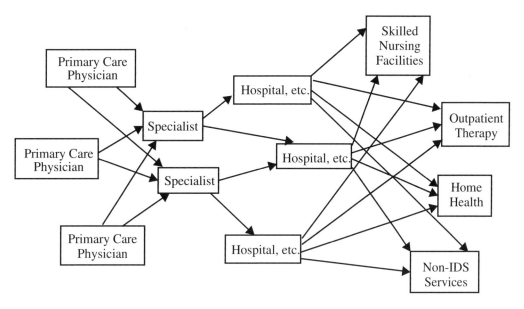

Figure 24–2 Possible Care Paths for a Single Service Line. *Source:* Copyright © 1996, Branson, Inc. Further reproduction is strictly prohibited.

fied and classified as value-added or nonvalue-added. A sample of the nonvalue-added drivers are shown in Table 24–1. Each of these cost opportunities span several individual department or organization budgets.

The redesign vision minimized nonvalue-added activities, which projected a 25 percent reduction in costs for the procedure. "Drilling down" through the ABC analysis allowed each provider to establish the specific implementation cost goals that rolled up to the system's 25 percent target.

The delivery system avoided dealing with the different financial reporting systems in the development of baseline continuum costs. As a result, the implementation effort has no automatic link between the goals and the financial reporting systems. To create this link, a spreadsheet was developed that mapped each activity cost improvement to the appropriate line item in the general ledger chart of accounts. An example of this reconciliation is seen in Table 24–2, which documents where the savings will be coming from by eliminating the first cost driver

in Table 24–1. As the improvements are made, the implementation teams will know where to look in their budgets to document the savings.

In integrated information systems, form follows function. The health care industry is rushing to develop large, complex integrated information systems to capture and manage information. There are two potential weaknesses in this strategy: (1) Information systems (IS) are supposed to support the operational needs of an organization. If the operational redesign of care delivery has not occurred, the IS design and its effectiveness is in jeopardy. (2) Organizations relying on a multimillion dollar, three- to five-year IS development effort to make them effective are missing out on a fundamental opportunity: How can you create a simple, flexible means of sharing data to assist you in winning market share from your competitors tomorrow?

The delivery system in Virginia is using standardized e-mail and on-line faxing capabilities to transmit information such as patient intake, pre-op orders, and case management data to all the partners in the episode of care. The main-

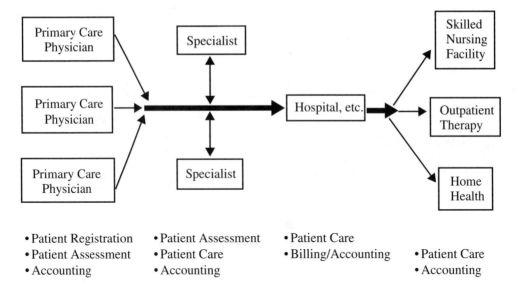

Coordinated Discharge Planning, Patient Education, and Patient Records

Figure 24–3 Care Continuum. *Source:* Copyright © 1996, Branson, Inc. Further reproduction is strictly prohibited.

frame solution that connects all the providers is still in development. The flexible and minimal

Table 24–1 Nonvalue-Added Cost Drivers

Orthopedic Service Line Activity Cost Reduction Opportunities

Activity	Cost Driver	Annual Potential
Physical Therapy	Untimely communication of PT needs in continuum	$ 140,700
Post-op Care	Late discharges due to excessive documentation	$ 89,250
Pre-op Intake	Tracking down MD orders and lab results	$ 24,500
Blood Bank	Unnecessary blood draws and tests	$ 31,500
PACU	Late discharges due to X-ray, PACU delays	$ 42,000

Source: Copyright © 1997, Branson, Inc. Further reproduction is strictly prohibited.

IS solution eliminates much of the paperwork and most of the phone calls while improving the cost-effectiveness and patient satisfaction of coordinated care. A basic desktop database could also be used to bootstrap a new operations strategy. This would serve as a minimal information system while the new continuums are being implemented. Once the operational strategy implementation is well under way, the mainframe computer solution can be designed and implemented to reflect the actual needs of the operations.

REDESIGNING FINANCIAL PERFORMANCE MEASURES

Organizational change will not occur as long as financial incentives exist that support the status quo. As care continuums are considered, the providers must understand that their financial performance will probably change.

For example, coordinating care differently impacts financial performance. Financial per-

Table 24–2 Reconciliation of Activity Cost to General Ledger

Activity Cost to General Ledger Reconciliation

Redesign Activity: Coordinated physical therapy through a dedicated PT Team

Org./Dept.	Budget Item	Budget Savings
MD Office	overtime labor	6,000
Hospital		
Physiatry	temporary labor	28,000
2nd Floor	direct labor	5,000
	labor benefits	3,700
PT/Rehab	direct labor	28,000
	labor benefits	7,000
	dept. supplies	1,000
	clinical supplies	2,200
Home Care		
	temporary labor	30,300
	lab services	12,000
	mileage	2,500
	clinical supplies	5,000
Total		$130,700

Source: Copyright © 1997, Branson, Inc. Further reproduction is strictly prohibited.

formance ratios are also impacted by coordinated care. Shifting care to a nonacute setting will reduce lengths of stay by eliminating the low-cost recuperative days and by keeping the high-cost operative days of the patient's acute stay. As a result, a hospital will keep most of the costs and lose per-diem revenue, driving up the equivalent cost per inpatient day or admission. The high fixed costs of the hospital can quickly drive down the operating margin in a redesigned continuum.

A key organizational paradigm impeding fundamental changes in care delivery is that care administrators usually have bonuses tied to the performance of specific organizations. Any changes to the financial performance could put these bonuses, and their careers, in jeopardy. And of all the delivery system players, the hospital probably has the most to lose as care is continually shifted away from acute care settings. New performance measures, in addition to new care processes, are needed to achieve the mission that is aimed at improved care for reduced costs.

Performance measures should be developed that entice the partners to work together for the good of the continuum. Sometimes this means forgiving those providers who will see their revenue and operating margins suffer within the continuum, and not excessively rewarding the partners who see improved performance at the expense of others. In other instances, it may be more effective to reestablish performance goals based on the projections of the new continuum design.

Activity-based costing is an economic outcome that can be used at an activity level or a system level. The Virginia delivery system has specific activity cost goals for each department and partner involved in the orthopedic continum. Each of these components roll up to an overall activity cost for the continuum. A managed care company recently approached them for a "bundled" contract involving all services within the continuum. The activity-based costs were used in the development of the contract pricing in addition to partner discussions concerning revenue sharing. ABC took all the guesswork out of the system's different costing algorithms and created a strategic advantage for bundled contracts and capitated populations.

Health care integration has a long way to go to achieve the fundamental changes that are necessary to demonstrate better care at lower costs. Current acquisition strategies and integrated information systems developments may not be coordinated with an operations strategy that is focused on providing better care. Activity-based costing can support a delivery system's operations strategy by taking the guesswork out of service line costs throughout a continuum of care. This makes it an attractive attribute to support the marketing of bundled services and capitated populations. However, functional integration of care will not be successful without redefining traditional financial performance measures.

ABC has been demonstrated as a powerful tool in quantifying unnecessary costs among providers. Linking ABC with an existing financial reporting system may be difficult due to the wide variety of costing algorithms in a delivery system. Reconciliation with the general ledger, however, can still take place through a stand-alone system, including a moderately sophisticated spreadsheet.

Beau has presented the case for an IDS parallel system. ABC provides a clear picture of resource use across service lines and across entities. Thus, it works in tandem with IDS management needs for cost information. Practical uses of an IDS parallel system include measurement links in early integration stages when total information systems for the IDS are not yet in place. Use of ABC at this juncture can reveal what information is most desirable and highlight difficulties due to differences within the IDS.[1]

IMPLEMENTATION

The future for activity-based costing and activity-based management in health care indicates an increasing trend of implementation efforts. As more and more organizations implement ABC, more information about the system will be disseminated. At present, most health care facilities that are planning for ABC or attempting implementation find themselves casting about for information.

Strategic planning for structural issues is crucial to ABC implementation efforts. Management decision makers must address what is required from the system. A cost-benefit analysis must be performed on desired precision versus cost of measurement. In the past, substantial capital investment and labor have been invested in cost information systems that did not yield even the most basic costing information. Coordinating management expectations and desires with strategic planning and cost-benefit analysis will allow your organization to avoid this trap.

The second critical element for implementation is support. The system must have sufficient labor, sufficient funds, and an adequate time frame to implement. Top-level support for the project is essential. The ABC project needs a champion at the top decision-making level.

OBSTACLES

Lack of consensus on strategic planning for system structural issues is a fundamental obstacle to a successful ABC/ABM project. A number of factors can impact this issue, but we find the most common to be this: The executives do not spend enough time to understand the project or the issues. They do not do their homework. A succinct executive summary and strong leadership is a must for this type of project.

The system is not that complex, but it is perceived as complex, primarily because there are variations on the basic system that create confusion. It is essential to sort the issues into macro and micro levels. Then use the appropriate executive or staff levels for brainstorming and problem solving at the appropriate level. A white paper that communicates the basic structure of ABC is a recommended tool. The white paper should graphically depict the inputs and the outputs, give the organization's rationale for system structure decisions and recap cost-benefit decisions.

The implementation task can appear overwhelming, especially if standard-setting at initial implementation is involved. The best approach to overcoming this obstacle is project management. Communicate levels of available staff, timelines, and expected implementation by project segment. This approach defuses the size issue and provides performance measure guidelines as an additional benefit.

OPPORTUNITIES

An enormous opportunity exists for continuous improvement initiatives in conjunction with activity-based costing and activity-based management. Continuous improvement initiatives operate through the identification of process, which is a strength of ABC/ABM. Continuous improvement initiatives operate on a cycle; so can ABC/ABM. Performance measures are an integral part of ABC/ABM and of continuous improvement initiatives. And value-added versus nonvalue-added issues are always a part of the cycle of reducing costs through continuous improvement, while identification of nonvalue-added activities is an essential part of ABC/ABM. When the two concepts work together, synergy is achieved.

Survival in health care today hinges on good decision making. There is great opportunity for ABC/ABM to support this decision-making function with accurate costing and performance information. The competitive environment has spawned frequent offers to become part of integrated delivery systems. The ABC/ABM multidisciplinary cost and performance approach allows forecasting of IDS stakeholder positions prior to committing to the IDS. Bitter experience by past IDS participants will attest to the advantages that this forecasting ability offers.

There are multiple opportunities for ABC/ABM in managed care. In fact, managed care requirements are a primary reason why ABC/ABM health care implementation is rapidly increasing. Decision makers have the opportunity to quantify both cost and performance outcomes for payers. The multidisciplinary strengths of ABC/ABM particularly fit the cost and performance information requirements of managed-care payers. For example, the organization can quantify outcomes to fit payer-specific requirements. There is substantial opportunity to use the ABC/ABM-generated cost and performance information as a powerful negotiating tool with managed-care payers. Proposed carve-outs for the next contract period, for example, can be supported with when, where, why, how much contract-specific information. Finally, we find an increase in managed-care payers who are requesting bundled service delivery-capitation rates. The multidisciplinary strengths of ABC/ABM turn this complex request into an opportunity.

CONCLUSION

Activity-based costing is the chameleon of cost accounting. Users see it as providing for their needs. Those needs are wide and varied, yet ABC is flexible enough to accommodate them. That same flexibility creates an illusion of complexity. The various solutions to accommodate diverse users make the outcomes appear to be different, yet they are not. The underlying structure remains.

The enduring strength of ABC/ABM is its adaptability. Study the framework and you will see the underlying structure of the system. Make it your own.

NOTE

1. J.J. Baker, "Activity-Based Costing for Integrated Delivery Systems," *Journal of Health Care Finance* 22, no. 2 (1995): 58.

Glossary

Activity: (1) Work performed within an organization. (2) An aggregation of actions performed within an organization that is useful for purposes of activity-based costing.

Activity Attributes: Characteristics of individual activities. Attributes include cost drivers, cycle time, capacity, and performance measures. For example, a measure of the elapsed time that is required to complete an activity is an attribute.

Activity Category: The division within a classification of activities.

Activity Cost Assignment: The process in which the cost of activities are attached to cost objects using activity drivers.

Activity Driver: A measure of the frequency and intensity of the demands placed on activities by cost objects. An activity driver is used to assign costs to cost objects. It represents a line item on the bill of activities for a product or customer. Sometimes an activity driver is used as an indicator of the output of an activity, such as the number of purchase orders prepared by the purchasing activity.

Activity Driver Analysis: The identification and evaluation of the activity drivers used to trace the cost of activities to cost objects. Activity driver analysis may also involve selecting activity drivers with a potential for cost reduction.

Activity Level: A description of how an activity is used by a cost object or other activity. Some activity levels describe the cost object that uses the activity and the nature of this use. These levels include activities that are traceable to the product, to the customer/patient/payer, to a market, or to a project.

Activity Map: A graphic illustration of the interrelationship between function, business processes, and activities. Also known as a *Process Map.*

Activity-Based Budgeting: A budgeting approach that focuses on the costs of activities that are necessary to produce and sell services or products.

Activity-Based Costing: A methodology that measures the cost and performance of activities, resources, and cost objects. Resources are assigned to activities, then activities are assigned to cost objects based on their use. Activity-based costing recognizes the causal relationships of cost drivers to activities.

Activity-Based Management: A discipline that focuses on the management of activities as the route to improving the value received by the customer and the profit achieved by providing this value. This discipline includes cost driver analysis, activity analysis, and performance measurement. Activity-based management draws on activity-based costing as its major source of information.

Allocation: (1) An apportionment or distribution. (2) A process of assigning cost to an activity or cost object when a direct measure does not exist, or when the cost-benefit of measurement cannot be justified.

Ambulatory Practice Groups (APGs): Each APG represents a categoy of patients. This category contains patients whose resource consumptions, on statistical average, are equivalent.

Avoidable Cost: A cost associated with an activity that would not be incurred if the activity was not required. The telephone cost associated with vendor support, for example, could be avoided if the activity were not performed.

Benchmarking or Best Practices: A methodology that identifies an activity as the benchmark by which a similar activity will be judged; is used to assist in identifying a process or technique that can increase the effectiveness or efficiency of an activity. The source may be internal (taken from another part of the company) or external (taken from a competitor). Another term used is *competitive benchmarking*.

Bill of Activities: A listing of the activities required (and optionally, the associated costs of the resources consumed) by a product or other cost object.

Bottom-Up Approach: Focusing on the significant activities within the process and attaching costs to those activities. Recognized as a process approach.

Budget: (1) A projected amount of cost or revenue for an activity or organizational unit covering a specific period of time. (2) Any plan for the coordination and control of resources and expenditures.

Business Process Improvement: A type of performance measure based on process analysis that often incorporates such steps as minimizing unused capacity and encouraging best practices.

Care Path/Pathway: (1) A map that plots key events and interventions. (2) A patient management tool that supports continuous quality improvement (CQI), efficient resource utilization, and quality patient care. (3) A tool to build the set of interventions, procedures, and practices designed to achieve predetermined outcomes.

Change Readiness: The degree to which an organization is open to change.

Client-Focused Costs: Costs assigned to client-focused activities (also known as *primary activities*).

Clinical Path/Pathway: A coordinated plan of treatment relating to a specific illness or condition to ensure quality, manage costs, and measure patient outcomes.

Collaborative Care Model: An advanced model of managed care designed to develop and operationalize pathways across the continuum of care. The model is interdisciplinary.

Continuous Improvement Program: A program to eliminate waste, reduce response time, simplify the design of both products/services and processes, and improve quality.

Continuous Improvement Standards: A standard cost that is successively reduced over a series of succeeding time periods. Also known as *moving cost reduction standard cost*.

Continuous Quality Improvement (CQI): Allows a never-ending search for higher levels of performance within the organization.

Cost Assignment: The tracing or allocation of resources to activities or cost objects.

Cost Center: The basic unit of responsibility in an organization for which costs are accumulated.

Cost Driver: Any factor that causes a change in the cost of an activity.

Cost Driver Analysis: The examination, quantification, and explanation of the effects of cost drivers.

Cost Management: A set of actions that managers take to satisfy patients/payers/customers as those managers continuously reduce and control costs.

Cost Object: Any customer/patient, product/service, contract, project, or other work unit for which a separate cost measurement is desired.

Cost Pools: Key resources. Costs are accumulated into groups representing key resources in an effort to determine the relative significance of each resource.

Cost Pool Rate: The marginal cost of performing one more activity.

Current Procedural Terminology (CPT) Codes: Physicians' Current Procedural Terminology, or CPT, codes is a listing of descriptive terms and identifying codes for reporting medical services and procedures performed by physicians.

Customized Standards: Standards specific to a particular organization; generally a blend of more than one type of methodology and generally exhibiting wide variability.

Diagnosis Related Groups (DRGs): DRGs are part of the prospective payment reimbursement methodology. Each DRG represents a category of patients. This category contains patients whose resource consumptions, on statistical average, are equivalent.

Diagnostic Cost: Example of a cost grouping composed of the resources necessary to perform laboratory and radiology tests in-house.

Direct Cost: A cost that is traced directly to an activity or a cost object. For example, the drugs issued to a particular patient are direct costs to that patient's episode of care.

Engineered Labor Standards: Standards that describe the amount of work that a normal employee should be able to do on a particular task in order to produce work results of acceptable quality. These standards are developed from a careful study of the job and from observation using statistically valid work sampling techniques.

Financial Performance Measures: Those measures of performance that focus on financial outcomes. For example, return on equity (ROE) is a financial performance measure. Patient satisfaction, on the other hand, is a nonfinancial performance measure.

Flexible Budget: A budget that is created using budgeted revenue or budgeted cost amounts and that is adjusted to the actual or expected level of output achieved during the budget period.

Fixed Cost: A cost element of an activity that does not vary with changes in the volume of cost drivers or activity drivers. The depreciation of a machine, for example, may be direct to a particular activity, but it is fixed with respect to changes in the number of units of the activity driver. The designation of a cost element as fixed or variable may vary depending on the time frame of the decision in question and the extent to which the volume of production, activity drivers, or cost drivers changes.

Forcing: Allocating the costs of a sustaining activity to a cost object even though that cost object may not clearly consume or causally relate to that activity.

Front Office Cost: Example of a cost grouping composed of the resources necessary for attending to front office activities such as scheduling appointments and checking patients in and out.

Fully Loaded Costs: Full costs for individual services provided.

Function: A group of activities having a common objective within an organization.

Indirect Cost: The cost that is allocated—as opposed to being traced—to an activity or a cost object. For example, the costs of supervision or heat may be allocated to an activity on the basis of direct labor hours.

Integrated Delivery System (IDS): A financially integrated and centrally managed network of health care providers offering a comprehensive continuum of health care services to a defined community within a geographic region.

International Classification of Diseases, Ninth Revision (ICD-9): A statistical classification system that arranges diseases and injuries into groups according to established criteria.

Major Diagnostic Categories (MDCs): The umbrella classification system for Diagnosis Related Groups (DRGs).

Nonvalue-Added Activity: An activity that is considered not to contribute to customer/patient value or to the organization's needs. Reflects a belief that the activity can be redesigned, reduced, or eliminated without reducing the quantity, responsiveness, or quality of the output required by the customer or the organization.

Opportunity Cost: The economic value of a benefit that is sacrificed when an alternative course of action is selected.

Outcome Measurement: A type of performance measurement that focuses on measures of outcomes. The outcomes may be financial, nonfinancial, or a combination of both.

Pareto Analysis: An analytical tool employing the Pareto principle, also known as the 80/20 rule. The Pareto principle states that 80 percent of an organization's problems, for example, are caused by 20 percent of the possible causes.

Performance Measures: Indicators of the work performed and the results achieved in an activity, process, or organizational unit. Performance measures may be financial or nonfinancial.

Physician Profiling: The presentation of selected performance data points as an overall measure of comparative physician performance.

Price Variance: That portion of the overall variance caused by a difference between the actual and expected price of an input. Calculated as the difference between the actual and budgeted unit price or hourly rate multiplied by the actual quantity of goods or labor consumed per unit of output and by the actual output level. Also known as the *rate variance.*

Primary Activity: For purposes of health care ABC, a primary activity is one that is face-to-face with the patient. Sometimes termed *patient-focused.*

Process: A series of activities that are linked to perform a specific objective. For example, the paying of a bill or claim involves several linked activities.

Process Map: See *Activity Map.*

Product Line: A grouping of similar products. Also known as a *service line.*

Profit Center: A segment of the business (e.g., a project, program, or business unit) that is accountable for both revenues and expenses.

Prospective Payment System (PPS): In health care, a payment system that pays for the service in advance of service delivery.

Quantity Variance: The portion of the overall variance that is caused by a difference between the budgeted and actual needed quantity of input. Calculated as the difference between the actual quantity of inputs used per unit of output, multiplied by the actual output level and the budgeted unit price. Also known as the *use variance* or *efficiency variance.*

Ratio of Cost to Charges (RCC) Costing Method: The RCC costing method estimates the cost of procedures through charges.

Relative Value Units (RVU) Costing Method: The RVU costing method measures the relative value of resources consumed by each procedure.

Resource: An economic element that is applied or used in the performance of activities. Salaries and materials, for example, are resources used in the performance of activities.

Resource Consumption: The relative or proportional use of resources available to an organization.

Resource Cost Assignment: The process by which cost is attached to activities. The process requires the assignment of cost from general ledger accounts to activities using resource drivers.

Resource Driver: A measure of the quantity of resources consumed by an activity. An example of a resource driver is the percentage of total square feet occupied by an activity. This factor is used to allocate a portion of the cost of operating the facilities to the activity.

Resource-Based Income Statement: An income statement approach that takes into account costs at both the variable (marginal) level and the fixed (capacity) level.

Responsibility Accounting: An accounting method that focuses on identifying persons or organizational units that are accountable for the performance of revenue or expense plans.

Secondary Activity: For purposes of health care ABC, a secondary activity supports the primary activity to complete a patient encounter or an episode of care. Charting (necessary to complete the patient encounter but not necessarily face-to-face with patient) is a good example of a secondary activity.

Secondary Costs: Costs assigned to secondary activities.

Service Line: A grouping of similar products. Also known as a *product line*.

Standard Cost: The per-unit cost for a good level of performance or best level of performance.

Standard Input: The set quantity of inputs for one unit of input at a good level of performance or best level of performance. An example of the set or allowed quantity of inputs is hours of labor.

Static Budget: A budget that is based on a single level of output and is not adjusted once it has been finalized.

Sunk Costs: Costs that have been invested in assets for which there is little (if any) alternative or continued value except salvage. Using sunk costs as a basis for evaluating alternatives may lead to incorrect decisions. Examples are the invested cost in a scrapped part or the cost of an obsolete machine.

Support Activity: A support activity supports the activities involved in the patient encounter or the episode of care. Administrative duties are an example of a typical support activity.

Sustaining Activity: An activity that benefits an organization at some level (e.g., the company as a whole or a division, plant, or department) but not any specific cost object. An example is support of community programs.

Target Cost: A cost that is calculated by subtracting a desired profit margin from an estimated (or a market-based) price to arrive at a desired production, engineering, or marketing cost.

Target Costing: A method used in analyzing product and process design that involves estimating a target cost and designing the product/service to meet that cost.

Technology Costs: A category of cost associated with the development, acquisition, implementation, and maintenance of technology assets. An example is the cost of software development.

Time Study: A time study employs continuous timed observations of a single person during a typical workday.

Top-Down Approach: Choosing a financial data structure and beginning with this point when choosing how to assign the various categories of costs. Recognized as a financial approach.

Traceability: The ability to assign a cost directly to an activity or a cost object in an economically feasible way by means of a causal relationship.

Tracing: The assignment of cost to an activity or a cost object using an observable measure of the consumption of resources by an activity. Tracing is generally preferred to allocation if the data exist or can be obtained at a reasonable cost.

Value Analysis: A cost-reduction and process-improvement tool that utilizes information collected about business processes and examines various attributes of the processes (e.g., diversity, capacity, and complexity) to identify a candidate for improvement efforts.

Value-Added Activity: An activity that is judged to contribute to customer/patient value or satisfies an organizational need. Reflects a belief that the activity cannot be eliminated without reducing the quantity, responsiveness, or quality of output required by a customer or organization.

Variable Cost: A cost element of an activity that varies with changes in volume of cost drivers and activity drivers. The cost of material handling to an activity, for example, varies according to the number of material deliveries and pickups to and from that activity.

Volume Variance: The portion of the overall variance that is caused by a difference between the expected workload and the actual workload. Calculated as the difference between the predetermined expected workload level expressed as total budgeted cost and the amount that would have been budgeted if the actual workload had been known in advance.

Work Process: A related group of activities that convert some input into an output.

Work Sampling: Work sampling uses discrete and instantaneous observations of routine activities performed by a variety of staff personnel. A large number of random observations are made and used to determine the number and type of activities.

Index

About the Contributors

An accountant by training, a communicator by choice, **Victor R. Barr, BS,** for 15 years provided leadership in finance and accounting as well as budgeting and operations for as many as 33 service units in 25 states from the National Benevolent Association's corporate office in St. Louis, Missouri. In these capacities, he counseled retirement communities throughout the National Benevolent Association system of social and health services in start-up, operational, strategic, and crisis recovery planning. Prior to finding his true calling in the not-for-profit world, he worked in industry and government environments. A firm advocate of the power of teams and continuous learning in organizations, Mr. Barr is currently putting all this experience together as executive director of St. Andrew's At-Home Services, a nonprofit home services organization serving the elderly in the St. Louis area.

Clark B. Bitzer, BSci, is Cost Analyst for the Lake Hospital System in Painesville, Ohio. He is responsible for the highly successful implementation of an ABC system that supports the cost and quality initiative for Lake Hospital System. He is a veteran of over 30 years experience with General Electric's Lighting Business Group where he was Manager of Financial Analysis and Distribution Cost. Mr. Bitzer earned a BS in Business Administration from Ohio State University and is a graduate of GE's Financial Management and Advanced Marketing Management programs. He served two years active duty in the US Navy as a supply officer.

Georgia F. Boyd, BS, is Cost Accountant for Valley View Hospital in Glenwood Springs, Colorado, where she continues to implement and develop procedure costs for product line profitability. Ms. Boyd earned a BS in Accounting from Metropolitan State College of Denver. Prior to changing her cost accounting focus toward health care, she was a cost accountant in the hardware and software industry in Denver.

John J. Brocketti, MBA, is Vice-President of Finance for Meridia Health System in Cleveland, Ohio. With seventeen years experience in health care finance, he has held positions as hospital Chief Financial Officer, and Vice President of Finance, and Vice President of Operations. He received an undergraduate degree in accounting from John Carroll University and a Master of Business Administration from Cleveland State University, Cleveland, Ohio.

Patricia Chiverton EdD, RN, is Associate Dean of Clinical Affairs at the University of Rochester Medical Center, Rochester, New York. She has extensive experience as a psychiatric clinician, administrator, and researcher and has been instrumental in the development of a community based psychiatric nursing case management program. Dr. Chiverton is also the CEO of the Community Nursing Center at the University of Rochester School of Nursing.

John F. Congelli, BBA, is the Vice President of Finance for Genesee Memorial Hospital in Batavia, New York. He has held this position for six years. Prior to being promoted to the position of Vice President, he held the position of Assistant Controller and Controller positions for four and six years respectively. Mr. Congelli has a BBA degree in Accounting from Niagara University and is an Advanced Member of the Healthcare Financial Management Association. Prior to working for Genesee Memorial Hospital, John worked for Ernst & Whinney, now known as Ernst & Young, on their Management and Consulting staff.

Mec B. Cothron, DPh, is Director of Pharmacy at Columbia Hendersonville Hospital, Hendersonville, Tennessee. She has held the position for seventeen years. As Director of Pharmacy she has been successful in formulary management, Joint Commission surveys, and development of innovative clinical programs for optimal utilization of medications. She earned a BS in Pharmacy from the University of Tennessee in Memphis. Prior to working for Columbia, she was the coordinator of the First Division meetings for Directors of Pharmacy in Tennessee and served as their representative on the Pharmacy Advisory Committee for Health Trust, Inc.

Michael A. Fitzpatrick, MD, FAAFP, is Chief Financial Officer of PrimeCare, a family practice Professional Service Corporation located in Elizabethtown, Kentucky. He also remains in private practice. Dr. Fitzpatrick attended medical school at the University of Kentucky and completed his Family Practice residency at the Chippenham Hospital/Chesterfield Family Practice residency program in Richmond, Virginia. In addition to his professional duties, he is an Associate Clinical Professor at the University of Kentucky and at the University of Louisville. He lives on a farm outside Elizabethtown with his wife and two children.

Victoria G. Hines, MHA, is Associate Dean for Administration and Finance and Clinical Nursing Instructor at the University of Rochester School of Nursing, where she is actively pursuing cost effective new models of health care delivery. She earned a Master of Health Administration at the Medical College of Virginia, Virginia Commonwealth University. Prior to joining the School of Nursing, she was Director of Ambulatory Care and Program Administrator for Surgery at Strong Memorial Hospital, The University of Rochester Medical Center.

Charles A. Keil, AAS, is currently Cost Accountant for Genesee Memorial Hospital, Batavia, New York, where he continues to implement and develop procedure costs for product line profitability. He has earned an AAS in Accounting from Genesee Community College with additional courses at State University of New York at Buffalo and at Rochester Institute of Technology. Prior to changing to health care, he worked 28 years in the finance department of a construction equipment manufacturer in all areas of the department including Controller and Treasurer.

Beau Keyte, BSE, MBA, (University of Michigan) is President of Branson, Inc., an innovator in care continuum redesign. He earned a BSE and an MBA from the University of Michigan. Mr. Keyte's firm assists health care organizations in creating integrated delivery systems that build on existing market advantages. Branson focuses on designing competitive service lines as care continuums while addressing both strategic and operational requirements in a financially sound manner. Clients develop the internal skills necessary to support their strategic visions and organizations.

Cynthia McClard, DPh, MS, is President of Clinical Management Consultants, Brentwood, Tennessee. Her firm focuses on developing innovative strategies for cost containment. Dr. McClard obtained a BS in Pharmacy and an MS in Hospital Pharmacy Administration from the University of Tennessee in Memphis. She is a member of the American Society of Health-System Pharmacists, American Society of Consultant Pharmacists, and the Association for Pharmacoeconomics and Outcomes Research.

Richard G. Melecki, MA, MPA, is a Principal in Ryerson Management Associates, Inc. (RMA), Akron, Ohio. Mr. Melecki is a health care reengineering specialist and a Certified Quality Engineer with a strong background in process analysis and statistical problem solving. He holds a master's degree in Business and Public Administration with a dual concentration in Quantitative Analysis and Information System Design from Kent State University. He has over 11 years of experience with progressive management engineering and continuous quality improvement activities at community hospitals, large teaching hospitals, and HMOs. Prior to joining RMA, he served as an executive with a Big 6 consulting firm, managing reengineering engagement for health care providers, for Blue Cross/Blue Shield of Maryland, and for a series of Fortune 500 firms.

Christine A. Pierce, MSN, RN, CS, is Vice President for Home Care Services, Meridia Health System, Cleveland, Ohio, and a Certified Adult Nurse Practitioner. Specializing in home care for the past ten years, she has managed home infusion, medical equipment, perinatal, and home hemodialysis business lines as well as Medicare certified home health. Ms. Pierce has served as Chair of a National Health Policy Committee, as Chair-Elect to the Intravenous Nurses Certification Corporation, and is a member of the Clinical Faculty at Frances Payne Bolton School of Nursing, Case Western Reserve University, Cleveland, Ohio.

Marta Hudson Ramsey, RN, MS, is currently assigned to Special Projects Administration at Columbia Overland Park Regional Medical Center in Overland Park, Kansas. Ms. Ramsey received a bachelor's degree at Fort Hays State University and a master's degree at Kansas University. In 1994, she collaborated with the Skilled Nursing Interdisciplinary Team to design and operationalize pathways in compliance with HCFA regulations for an interdisciplinary care plan. In 1996, Ms. Ramsey presented papers on the pathways at the National Case Mix Conference and at HCFA's Annual Resident Assessment Instrument Conference.

Ted J. Stuart, Jr., MD, MBA, a family physician, practices full time in Glendale, Arizona. He is board certified by the American Board of Family Practice. He received his MBA degree from Arizona State University and his MD from Baylor Medical School. Activity-based costing and process analysis help him to compete in the managed care arena in the Phoenix metropolitan area. He was recently published in the Physician Executive. He is a past president of the Arizona Academy of Family Physicians.

Karen S. Vroman, RN, BSN, MEd, AAHA, registered nurse and licensed nursing home administrator, is Associate Vice President of Health Care and Older Adult Services for the National Benevolent Association's (NBA's) Department of Program Planning and Evaluation. Ms. Vroman also serves on NBA's national Management Team and oversees NBA's care centers that are participating in the accreditation process. Before joining NBA, she taught nursing education at the university level for fourteen years. Ms. Vroman serves as an evaluator for the Continuing Care Accreditation Commission (CCAC) and is a preceptor for the School of Public Health, St. Louis University, St. Louis, Missouri.

Patricia Hinton Walker, PhD, FAAN, is dean and professor at the University of Colorado Health Sciences Center, School of Nursing, Denver, Colorado. Previously, she served as the Kate Hanna Harvey Visiting Professor in Community Health at the Frances Payne Bolton School of Nursing at Case Western Reserve University and was associate dean at both Emory University and the University of Rochester. Dr. Walker's research interests include cost and quality outcomes of care, interdisciplinary practice and advanced practice nursing, and development of practice-based care.

Timothy D. West, PhD, CPA, is Assistant Professor of Accounting at Iowa State University, Ames, Iowa. He teaches primarily managerial/cost accounting, and his research has emphasized the application of activity-based costing in both health care and manufacturing. Professor West recently published health care related articles in *Management Accounting, Healthcare Financial Management,* the *Journal of Health Care Finance,* and the *Journal of the American Medical Association (JAMA).* He received the Institute of Management Accountants' Lybrand Silver Medal in 1996, and the HMFA's Best Article Award in 1997 for his research related to activity-based costing in health care.

MERIDIA STAFF:

Cindyleigh Mocilnikar, RN, is the Manager of Specialty Programs at Meridia Home Health, Mayfield Village, Ohio. She has over 20 years of nursing experience. Ms. Mocilnikar has held a variety of nursing positions, including direct care, education, staff development and managerial in acute care and home care. In her current position she is responsible for the development and operationalization of specialized pulmonary, behavioral health, and cardiac care teams within a large home care agency. Ms. Mocilnikar was appointed as a Clinical Instructor of

Nursing at the Frances Payne Bolton School of Nursing at Case Western Reserve University.

Jan Steinel, RN, RRT, BSN, registered nurse and registered respiratory therapist, serves as the team leader for a pulmonary disease management program at Meridia Home Health in Cleveland, Ohio. He received his respiratory therapy training at St. Petersburg Junior College and his nursing training at Bowling Green State University. His area of specialization is the management of individuals in the advanced stages of chronic pulmonary disease.

SBHC STAFF:

Nancy M. Bowllan, RN, MN, CS, is the Program Coordinator and Mental Health Counselor for the East High School-Based Health Center funded by the New York State Department of Health grant to the Community Nursing Center, University of Rochester. She has 17 years experience as a psychiatric nurse, completing her undergraduate work at Alfred University and obtaining her master's in Psychiatric Mental Health Nursing at the University of Rochester. Ms. Bowllan is certified by the ANA as a Clinical Specialist in Child and Adolescent Psychiatric Nursing and has for the past 13 years held dual appointments in administration and mental health service provision in an array of clinical settings, both hospital and community based.

Lorraine Lawrence, MSN, is the Pediatric Nurse Practitioner for the East High Health Center in Rochester, New York, where she provides medical and preventative services to adolescents within an inner-city high school. Ms. Lawrence earned her MSN in Nursing from the University of Rochester and has five years experience in OB/GYN and adolescent health care.

About the Author

Judith J. Baker, PhD, CPA, is Executive Director of Resource Group, Ltd., a Dallas-based health care consulting firm. She earned her Bachelor of Science degree in Business Administration at the University of Missouri, Columbia and her Master of Liberal Studies with a concentration in Business Management at the University of Oklahoma, Norman. She earned her Master of Arts and her Doctorate in Human and Organizational Systems with a concentration in costing systems at the Fielding Institute, Santa Barbara, California.

Judith has thirty years of experience in health care. She has worked with health care systems, costing, and reimbursement throughout her career. As an HCFA subcontractor she assists in validation of costs for new programs and for rate setting and consults on cost report design. She has been a consultant on numerous health care systems and costing problems. She has written over 40 articles, manuals, and books and has developed a seminar entitled "Activity-Based Costing to Survive Capitation," which is presented nationwide.

She is an adjunct faculty member at the University of Texas at Houston Health Science Center School of Nursing and at the Case Western Reserve University Frances Payne Bolton School of Nursing.

She serves as co-editor of the *Journal of Healthcare Finance,* published by Aspen Publishers, Inc.